MW01528319

Chinese Architecture: Art and Artifacts

英汉对照

为什么研究中国建筑

梁思成 著　林洙 编

外语教学与研究出版社
FOREIGN LANGUAGE TEACHING AND RESEARCH PRESS
北京 BEIJING

图书在版编目（CIP）数据

为什么研究中国建筑 ＝ Chinese Architecture: Art and Artifacts ：英汉对照 / 梁思成著 ；林洙编. — 北京 ：外语教学与研究出版社，2011.2（2020.3 重印）
ISBN 978-7-5135-0614-4

Ⅰ. ①为… Ⅱ. ①梁… ②林… Ⅲ. ①建筑艺术－中国－文集－英、汉 Ⅳ. ①TU-862

中国版本图书馆 CIP 数据核字（2011）第 018938 号

出 版 人　徐建忠
系列策划　吴　浩
责任编辑　任小玫
责任校对　张昊媛
装帧设计　视觉共振设计工作室
出版发行　外语教学与研究出版社
社　　址　北京市西三环北路 19 号（100089）
网　　址　http://www.fltrp.com
印　　刷　天津市光明印务有限公司
开　　本　650×980　1/16
印　　张　25
版　　次　2011 年 4 月第 1 版　2020 年 3 月第 6 次印刷
书　　号　ISBN 978-7-5135-0614-4
定　　价　66.00 元

购书咨询：（010）88819926　电子邮箱：club@fltrp.com
外研书店：https://waiyants.tmall.com
凡印刷、装订质量问题，请联系我社印制部
联系电话：（010）61207896　电子邮箱：zhijian@fltrp.com
凡侵权、盗版书籍线索，请联系我社法律事务部
举报电话：（010）88817519　电子邮箱：banquan@fltrp.com
物料号：206140001

除非我们不知尊重这古国灿烂文化，如果有复兴国家民族的决心，对我国历代文物，加以认真整理及保护时，我们便不能忽略中国建筑的研究。

——梁思成

“博雅双语名家名作”出版说明

1840年鸦片战争以降，在深重的民族危机面前，中华民族精英“放眼看世界”，向世界寻求古老中国走向现代、走向世界的灵丹妙药，涌现出一大批中国主题的经典著述。我们今天阅读这些中文著述的时候，仍然深为字里行间所蕴藏的缜密的考据、深刻的学理、世界的视野和济世的情怀所感动，但往往会忽略：这些著述最初是用英文写就，我们耳熟能详的中文文本是原初英文文本的译本，这些英文作品在海外学术界和文化界同样享有崇高的声誉。

比如，林语堂的 *My Country and My People*（《吾国与吾民》）以幽默风趣的笔调和睿智流畅的语言，将中国人的道德精神、生活情趣和中国社会文化的方方面面娓娓道来，在美国引起巨大反响——林语堂也以其中国主题系列作品赢得世界文坛的尊重，并获得诺贝尔文学奖的提名。再比如，梁思成在抗战的烽火中写就的英文版《图像中国建筑史》文稿（*A Pictorial History of Chinese Architecture*），经其挚友费慰梅女士（Wilma C. Fairbank）等人多年的奔走和努力，于1984年由麻省理工学院出版社（MIT Press）出版，并获得美国出版联合会颁发的“专业暨学术书籍金奖”。又比如，1939年，费孝通在伦敦政治经济学院的博士论文以 *Peasant Life in China—A Field Study of Country Life in the Yangtze Valley* 为名在英国劳特利奇书局（Routledge）出版，后以《江村经济》作为中译本书名——《江村经济》使得靠桑蚕为生的“开弦弓村”获得了世界性的声誉，成为国际社会学界研究中国农村的首选之地。

此外，一些中国主题的经典人文社科作品经海外汉学家和中国学者的如椽译笔，在英语世界也深受读者喜爱。比如，艾恺（Guy S. Alitto）将他1980年用中文访问梁漱溟的《这个世界会好吗——梁漱溟晚年口述》一书译成英文（*Has Man a Future? —Dialogues with the Last Confucian*），备受海内外读者关注；此类作品还有徐中约英译的梁启超著作《清代学术概论》（*Intellectual Trends in the Ch'ing Period*）、狄百瑞（W. T. de Bary）英译的黄宗羲著作《明夷待访录》（*Waiting for the Dawn: A Plan for the Prince*），等等。

有鉴于此，外研社人文社科出版分社推出"博雅双语名家名作"系列。

博雅，乃是该系列的出版立意。博雅教育（Liberal Education）早在古希腊时代就得以提倡，旨在培养具有广博知识和优雅气质的人，提高人文素质，培养健康人格，中国儒家六艺"礼、乐、射、御、书、数"亦有此功用。

双语，乃是该系列的出版形式。英汉双语对照的形式，既同时满足了英语学习者和汉语学习者通过阅读中国主题博雅读物提高英语和汉语能力的需求，又以中英双语思维、构架和写作的形式予后世学人以启迪——维特根斯坦有云："语言的边界，乃是世界的边界"，诚哉斯言。

名家，乃是该系列的作者群体。涵盖文学、史学、哲学、政治学、经济学、考古学、人类学、建筑学等领域，皆海内外名家一时之选。

名作，乃是该系列的入选标准。系列中的各部作品都是经过时间的积淀、市场的检验和读者的鉴别而呈现的经典，正如卡尔维诺对"经典"的定义：经典并非你正在读的书，而是你正在重读的书。

胡适在《新思潮的意义》（1919年12月1日，《新青年》第7卷第1号）一文中提出了"研究问题、输入学理、整理国故、再造文明"的范式。秉着"记载人类文明、沟通世界文化"的出版理念，我们推出"博雅双语名家名作"系列，既希望能够在中国人创作的和以中国为主题的博雅英文文献领域"整理国故"，亦希望在和平发展、改革开放的新时代为"再造文明"、为"向世界说明中国"略尽绵薄之力。

外语教学与研究出版社·人文社科出版分社

前言

2011年是梁思成先生（1901–1972）诞辰110周年纪念，因此外语教学与研究出版社准备将先生的古建筑英文文稿整理，以平装本和限量珍藏本两种形式出版。先生的英文文稿大多完稿于1946年以前，是在古建调研工作的空隙中完成的。他在忙于撰写调研报告的同时，为什么还要坚持用英文写中国古建筑的介绍文章呢？

他始终认为，中国古建筑史上各民族不同文化的交流濡染是极有趣的现象，也是丰富和发展本民族文化必不可少的要素。比如，印度的塔（“窣堵坡”，stupa）流传到我国，经汉民族文化的濡染演化而成为各种形式的塔，成为中国建筑文化中一个独特的标志，而窣堵坡却变成了中国式塔的塔刹。

先生在美国研习时曾对西方古建筑下过苦功夫，因而他也热衷于把中国的古建筑介绍给外国读者。这次集录的英文文稿，绝大多数是他在20世纪三四十年代发表在美国一些刊物上的。特别指出的是，《蓟县独乐寺观音阁山门考》因篇幅较长，原准备出一个小册子，但未实现，这次一并发表，虽非完全英汉对照，却呈文稿本真原貌。书中图版及照片大部分是由先生当年亲自绘制和拍摄的。外研社人文社科分社社长吴浩和编辑任小玫、张昊媛为本书的出版，花费了很多心血。我再次感谢外研社的朋友们，他们完成了先生未竟的遗愿。谢谢！

林洙 · 2010年6月15日

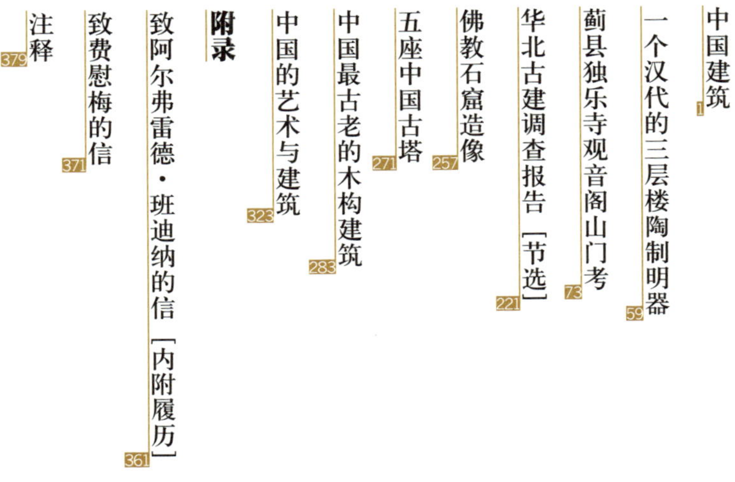

附录

Appendix

CHINESE

[年份不详]

中国建筑

ARCHITECTURE

I. GENERAL CHARACTERISTICS

Ⓐ Early Origin

Among the family of architecture of the world, Chinese architecture may be considered an independent branch by itself. Its history is as long as the history of Chinese civilization.

From every source of information—literary, graphical and exemplary—there can be gathered convincing evidences testifying to the fact that the Chinese people have always employed an indigenous system of construction and a conception of planning which have retained their principal characteristics from the earliest times till the present day. Over the vast area from Xinjiang to the Northeast, from Inner Mongolia to the South Sea coast, the same system of construction and planning is prevalent. Beyond China, in Korea and Japan in the east and Vietnam in the south, the same system of construction and similar plan arrangements are much used. And these have all along been the countries whose people have established very intimate contacts with the Chinese for thousands of years. The ability of this system to perpetuate itself for over four thousand years over such a vast area and still remain a living architecture, and to retain its principal characteristics in spite of repeated and continuous foreign influences, hostile or friendly, economical, cultural or military, is a phenomenon comparable only to the continuity of the civilization of which it forms an integral part.

1. Neolithic Remains

Excavation in 1954 at the village of Banpo, near Xi'an, led to the discovery of a number of pits in the loess stratum. They were identified as remains of human habitations of the Neolithic period. Along the periphery of one of the larger pits of an oblong plan, of which only a portion now remains and estimated to have a major axis of about 20 meters long, is a low earthen wall in which are a row of holes containing charred studs of logs, evidently the lower ends of posts of a house that was later destroyed by fire. It is the remains of the earliest houses known in China today. Of course, it would be too far-fetched to assume that any of the characteristics of the architecture that later developed in China may be traced in these primitive sites.

壹 概览

❶ 早期溯源

中国建筑在世界建筑群体中，可谓自成一体。中国建筑的历史与中国文明史相生相伴、源远流长。

从收集到的一些遗存文字、图案和标本等实物中可以找到充分的证据证明，国人一向采用的本土营造体系和设计构思，其主要特征从古至今未曾改变。在广袤的大地上，从新疆到东北，从内蒙古到南海沿岸，同样的营造和设计体系被广泛采用。甚至在周边国家，如东边的朝鲜和日本，以及南边的越南，也常常采用中国的营造体系和类似的平面布局。数千年来，这些国家一直和中国保持着密切的往来。四千多年来，尽管中国接连不断地受到外界的影响，无论是敌视的或是友善的，还是在经济、文化或军事方面，但在如此广袤的土地上，中国的建筑体系依然能够持久留存，栩栩如生，从而构成了绵延不断的中华文明的一部分。

1. 新石器时代的遗存　1954 年在西安附近半坡村考古挖掘时，发现了黄土地层的数个地坑，经确认是新石器时代人类聚居的穴居地遗址。[1] 其中的一个四方平面只有部分得以保存，据估算其主轴长约 20 米。当中的一个较大坑穴的外围是一堵低矮的土墙，上有一排洞眼，洞眼内为烧焦的木楔残物，显然是木骨泥墙房屋的柱础毁于火灾的痕迹。这是迄今所知中国最早的房屋遗址。当然，如果认为以后中国建筑发展的任何特征都可以追溯到这一原始遗址，那也未免太牵强附会了。

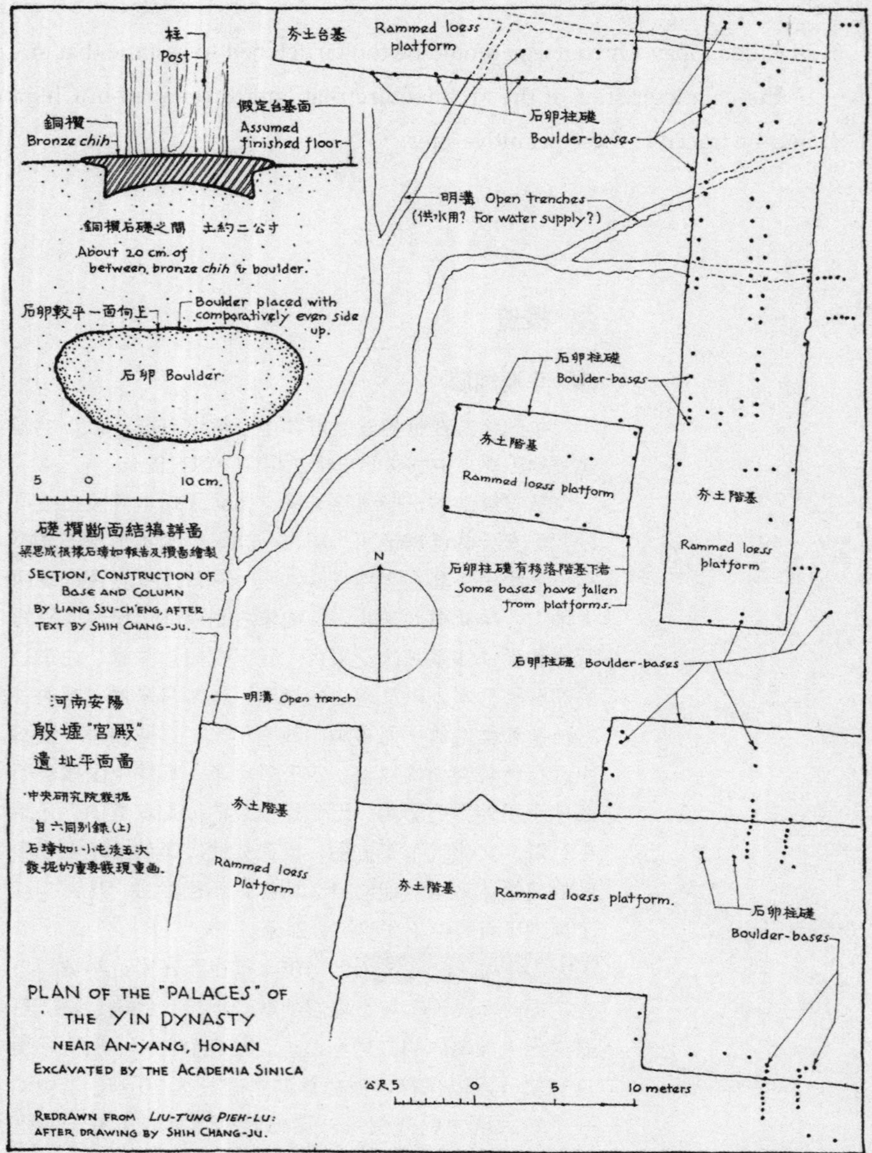

柱
Post
銅櫍
Bronze chih
假定台基面
Assumed finished floor
銅櫍石礎之間 土約二公寸
About 20 cm. of between bronze chih & boulder.
石卵較平一面向上
Boulder placed with comparatively even side up.
石卵 Boulder
5 0 10 cm.
礎櫍斷面結構詳圖
梁思成根據石璋如報告及櫍圖繪製
SECTION, CONSTRUCTION OF BASE AND COLUMN
BY LIANG SSU-CH'ENG, AFTER TEXT BY SHIH CHANG-JU.
河南安陽
殷墟"宮殿"
遺址平面圖
中央研究院發掘
自六同別錄(上)
石璋如:小屯後五次
發掘的重要發現重画.
夯土台基
Rammed loess platform
石卵柱礎
Boulder-bases
明溝 Open trenches
(供水用? For water supply?)
石卵柱礎
Boulder-bases
夯土階基
Rammed loess platform
夯土階基
Rammed loess platform
石卵柱礎有移落階基下者
Some bases have fallen from platforms.
N
石卵柱礎 Boulder-bases
明溝 Open trench
夯土階基
Rammed loess Platform
夯土階基
Rammed loess platform.
石卵柱礎
Boulder-bases
PLAN OF THE "PALACES" OF THE YIN DYNASTY
NEAR AN-YANG, HONAN
EXCAVATED BY THE ACADEMIA SINICA
公尺5 0 5 10 meters
REDRAWN FROM LIU-T'UNG PIEH-LU: AFTER DRAWING BY SHIH CHANG-JU.

1

2. Earliest Site Suggestive of Later Chinese Characteristics

Near Anyang, Henan Province, at the site of the palaces and necropolis of the Yin emperors, circa 1400 BC–1120 BC, archaeologists found the earliest remains of buildings that suggest the possible embodiment of the basic characteristics which later evolved and matured into architecture unique to China and her neighboring countries. At the site is large rammed-earth platforms, on top of which are placed at regular intervals undressed boulders, each covered by a bronze disc. On top of these discs are found charred logs—the lower ends of wooden posts that once supported the superstructures which were burnt down at the sack of the capital circa 1120 BC. The arrangement of these bases of columns testifies to the existence of a structural system that had by this time already taken a very definite form. (Figure 1)

Ⓑ Basic Characteristics

The basic characteristics of Chinese architecture may be considered from two aspects—the structural system and the plan arrangement. The structure of the individual building, as it is found today as well as more than three thousand years ago, consists of, in general parti, a raised platform or stylobate which forms the base for a structure with a timber skeleton of posts and lintels which in turn supports the roof, generally pitched and with overhanging eaves.

2. 具有中国建筑特征的最早遗址 在河南安阳附近所发现的公元前约 1400 年到公元前 1120 年殷商王宫和陵墓遗址中，考古学家找到了后来演变和发展成为中国及周边国家建筑独有的基本特征的可能例证。遗址中大型夯土台基的顶端，间隔均匀铺陈着原料石块，石块上均覆盖着青铜圆板，上置柱础，即曾经用以支撑上部结构的木柱下端。大约在公元前 1120 年，都城被攻陷，上部结构被焚。从这些柱础的排列看来，此时的结构体系已明显成型。（图 1）

❷ 基本特点

中国建筑的基本特点可从结构体系和平面布局两方面来考量。现今发现三千多年前的单体建筑，其结构通常包括一个垒抬提升的台基或柱座，以作为整座建筑的基础。建筑有着木结构的立柱和横梁，用以支撑屋顶；屋顶则通常带坡度，有飞檐。

2

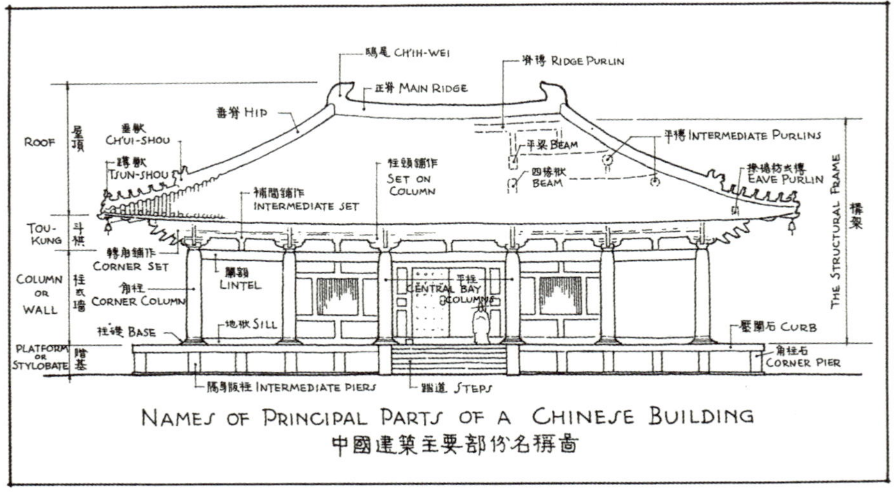

NAMES OF PRINCIPAL PARTS OF A CHINESE BUILDING
中國建築主要部份名稱圖

This osseous construction lends complete freedom in walling and fenestration and renders a house, by merely adjusting the proportion between walls and openings, practical and comfortable in any climate varying from that of the tropical south to that of sub-artic Manchuria. (Figure 2) It is this extremely high degree of flexibility and adaptability that enables this architecture to follow the Chinese people to wherever place they chose to settle down and live without encountering any difficulty in sheltering its occupants from the elements, however diverse they may be. Perhaps nothing analogous is found in the architecture elsewhere until the invention of the reinforced concrete and the steel framing system in the nineteenth century.

这一框架结构在屋墙上开窗通风极为方便，只需调节好墙体和门洞、窗口之间的比例，即可使房屋不管是处于炎热的南方还是在寒冷的东北都既实用又舒适。（图 2）正是由于这一建筑结构极高的灵活性和适应性，中国人无论走到哪里，在哪里居住，无论他们生活方式如何不同，都不会受到恶劣天气的困扰。在 19 世纪钢筋混凝土及钢结构出现之前，恐怕很难在其他地方找出类似的建筑。

In plan, a "house" in the Chinese sense of the word is generally composed of a number of such individual buildings which are then connected to each other by auxiliary buildings—verandas, loggias, portals, etc.—so disposed of to form one or a series of courtyards or patios. Such courtyards are generally paved and often planted with trees and flowers, forming very pleasant "outdoor living rooms." As a rule, the buildings around a courtyard are generally symmetrically arranged along a principal axis. But for gardens, or when required by the topography, informal arrangements become the rule.

1. The Structure of the Individual Building

It is necessary to analyze the Chinese frame construction in order to have a better understanding of Chinese architecture. The basic unit of the skeleton is a frame composed of two posts supporting a beam, on top of which, in turn, are one or two or even three successive tiers of beams standing on studs. As the tiers pile up, the lengths of the beams above diminish, and, on the uppermost and shortest beam stands a king post, the top of which forms the apex of a triangle thus formed. This is what one will see in a transversal section drawing of a building. Such a unit is called a liangjia or "beam-frame." A pair of such liangjia placed side by side at certain distances, and connected to each other by lintels or tie-beams reaching from the top of the post of one liangjia to that of the adjacent liangjia, define a space called jian or bay.

在平面布局术语中，汉语的“房屋”一词，通常是指数座单体建筑，通过游廊、凉廊、门廊等附属建筑，将彼此连接起来，形成一个或一系列院落。这些庭院一般都经过铺设，莳花种树，形成赏心悦目的“露天客厅”。院落四周的建筑，通常沿中轴线对称排列。对于园圃，可因顺地形地势不拘一格，予以适当变通。

1. 单体建筑结构 如想更好地了解中国建筑，就有必要分析中国的框架结构。其基本框架单位是由两根柱子支撑着一根横梁的结构。横梁之上，相继依次排列着单层或两三层用直立柱支撑的横木。层层垒高的同时，横木长度向上依次缩短，最上层也就是最短的横木上架设中柱，其上端由此构成三角形稳定结构的顶点。这就是建筑剖面图中所显示的形式。这样的一个单位称为一副“梁架”。梁架组对间隔排列，由从一个梁架立柱顶端延伸到相邻梁架的横梁或系梁连接组成的空间，称作“间”或“格”。

A building, usually oblong in shape, is constructed by a repetition of these jian and liangjia. On the ends of the successive tiers of beams are placed purlins on which, in turn, are placed rafters. The rafters are covered with sheathing and tiles to complete the roof. The spaces between every two posts can be filled with walls, windows, doors or light movable partitions, or as for a garden pavilion, left entirely open on all sides.

2. The Dougong

One particular feature in this structural frame deserves special attention. It is the dougong, employed generally in buildings of a monumental character. In order to counteract the shearing stress at the joints of vertical and horizontal members, particularly at the points where the beam is supported by the post, the architect of perhaps more than two thousand years ago invented the method of putting trapezoidal blocks and bow-shaped "arms" in tiers as corbels, and thus created a transitory element known as dougong. The term means simply block (dou) and "arm" (gong). The tiers of "arms," when extending into the interior of the building, receive the ends of the principal beams, while the other half of the "arms," extending outward, receive the overhanging eaves of the roof. The dougong was originally conceived as a structural element, but its decorative potentiality was soon discovered and exploited to the utmost degree. (Figure 3)

建筑通常呈矩形，由若干“间”和“梁架”组成。横木各层末端架设桁条，其上架椽。椽上覆盖木板，木板上铺置瓦片，构成屋顶。每两根立柱间为墙体、门窗或轻型活动隔扇，为花园亭台时四面则完全敞开。

2. 斗拱 这种框架结构的一个显著特点值得格外关注，这就是通常在大型建筑中采用的斗拱。为了平衡垂直和水平部件连接处的剪应力，尤其在立柱支撑横梁的部位，大约两千多年前的建筑师就想出了一个办法，将梯形的“斗”和弓形的“拱”作为枕梁托置于梁之间，因而创造出了斗拱这一过渡构件。这一名称包含了“斗”和“拱”两层意思。一层层的“拱”的一端延伸至建筑内部，以承托主梁末端；“拱”的另一端则向外延伸，以承托屋顶飞檐。最初，斗拱只被视为一个结构部件，但其装饰潜能很快被发现，并被发挥到极致。（图3）

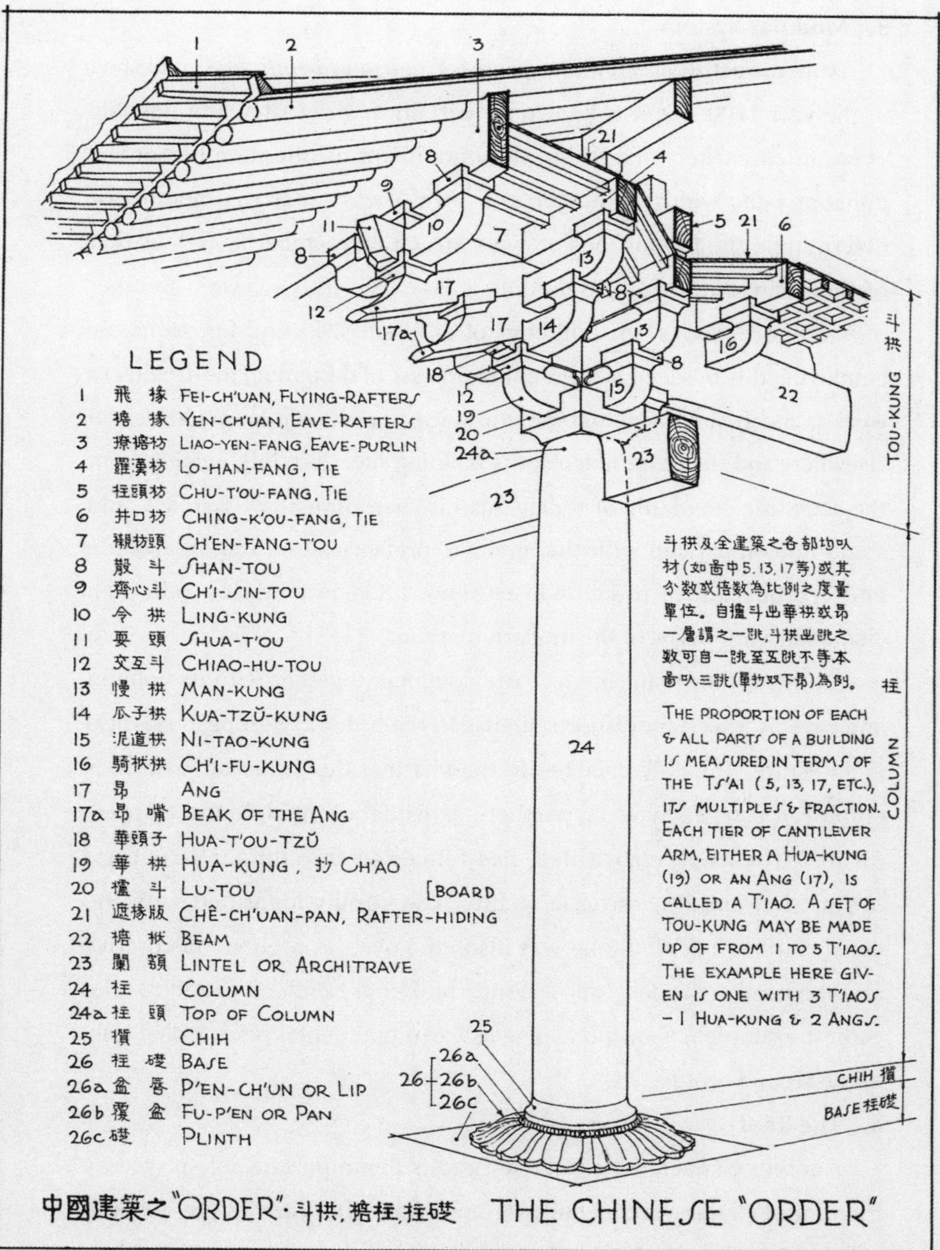

1
2
3
21
4
5
21
6
8
9
11
10
7
8
13
8
17
12
17
14
13
16
17a
8
18
15
22
12
19
20
24a
23
23
24
斗拱
TOU-KUNG
柱
COLUMN
斗拱及全建築之各部均以材(如圖中5.13.17等)或其分數或倍數為比例之度量單位。自櫨斗出華拱或昂一層謂之一跳，斗拱出跳之數可自一跳至五跳不等本圖以三跳(單抄双下昂)為例。
THE PROPORTION OF EACH & ALL PARTS OF A BUILDING IS MEASURED IN TERMS OF THE TS'AI (5, 13, 17, ETC.), ITS MULTIPLES & FRACTION. EACH TIER OF CANTILEVER ARM, EITHER A HUA-KUNG (19) OR AN ANG (17), IS CALLED A T'IAO. A SET OF TOU-KUNG MAY BE MADE UP OF FROM 1 TO 5 T'IAOS. THE EXAMPLE HERE GIVEN IS ONE WITH 3 T'IAOS – 1 HUA-KUNG & 2 ANGS.
25
26 26a 26b 26c
CHIH 櫍
BASE 柱礎
LEGEND
1 飛椽 FEI-CH'UAN, FLYING-RAFTERS
2 檐椽 YEN-CH'UAN, EAVE-RAFTERS
3 撩檐枋 LIAO-YEN-FANG, EAVE-PURLIN
4 羅漢枋 LO-HAN-FANG, TIE
5 柱頭枋 CHU-T'OU-FANG, TIE
6 井口枋 CHING-K'OU-FANG, TIE
7 襯枋頭 CH'EN-FANG-T'OU
8 散斗 SHAN-TOU
9 齊心斗 CH'I-SIN-TOU
10 令拱 LING-KUNG
11 耍頭 SHUA-T'OU
12 交互斗 CHIAO-HU-TOU
13 慢拱 MAN-KUNG
14 瓜子拱 KUA-TZŬ-KUNG
15 泥道拱 NI-TAO-KUNG
16 騎栿拱 CH'I-FU-KUNG
17 昂 ANG
17a 昂嘴 BEAK OF THE ANG
18 華頭子 HUA-T'OU-TZŬ
19 華拱 HUA-KUNG, 抄 CH'AO
20 櫨斗 LU-TOU
21 遮椽版 CHÊ-CH'UAN-PAN, RAFTER-HIDING BOARD
22 檐栿 BEAM
23 闌額 LINTEL OR ARCHITRAVE
24 柱 COLUMN
24a 柱頭 TOP OF COLUMN
25 櫍 CHIH
26 柱礎 BASE
26a 盆唇 P'EN-CH'UN OR LIP
26b 覆盆 FU-P'EN OR PAN
26c 礎 PLINTH
中國建築之"ORDER"·斗拱，檐柱，柱礎 THE CHINESE "ORDER"

3. Modular System

From a treatise on architecture, the *Ying-tsao-fa-shih*, first published in the year 1100 AD, it is known for certain that not later, and possibly even much earlier, than then, the dimension of one member of the dougong—the width of the gong or "arm"—was set as the module for determining the proportions of every structural member as well as that of the entire building. The module is classified into a certain number of "sizes" or "classes" for buildings of different sizes and functions. By employing this modular system in the process of designing, the architect's work is much simplified and structural members could be prefabricated elsewhere and then assembled at the building site. Certainly, judging from the scientific standards of today, this rather rudimentary system could stand no comparison with the modular, prefabrication, standardization and typification of today. Nevertheless, it may justly be called an elementary prototype of the modern method.

From another point of view, the dougong, together with its column and eave, is in certain respects similar to the order in European classical architecture. The difference lies in the fact that the European order was employed essentially as an aesthetic consideration while the Chinese "order," if it may be so called, has remained throughout structural in function and its aesthetic quality is integrally identified with the construction. The dougong was also employed as a purely decorative architectural treatment on masonry buildings, such as pagodas. The earliest example is found on some ashlar monumental piers, called qüe, of the second century AD.

4. The Roof

Another characteristic to be noticed is the important role played by the roof in Chinese architecture. From poems of as early as the eleventh century BC, there were already verses eulogizing the beauty of the roof. Wings of birds were used as metaphor for describing the out-stretching eaves. The typical Chinese roof is pitched and the surface is formed by a slightly "sagged" plane. This effect is acquired by adjusting the lengths and elevation of each tier of beam of the liangjia. The ridges where two roof-planes meet are usually accentuated by raised moldings and decorated with ornaments of mythological animal motifs. Perhaps by the time not later than the eleventh century AD, colored glazed tiles, usually of yellow or green, were used on roofs. The glistening colors make the roof a glorious crowning feature of the building.

3. 模数制　从最初刊行于公元1100年的建筑专著《营造法式》中可以确切得知，当时甚至是更早些时候，就把斗拱的拱的宽度确定为决定每个结构部件乃至整个建筑比例的度量单位。这一度量单位根据建筑的不同尺寸和功能分为一定数量的“尺寸”或“级别”。这一模数体系在设计中的应用使建筑师的工作大为简化。一些建筑构件可以在别处预制，然后在建筑工地组装。当然，从今天的科学标准来看，这一相当原始的建筑程式无法与今天的模件、预制、标准化和典型化相提并论。尽管如此，将其称之为现代化建筑程式的基本原型还是当之无愧的。

从另一个角度看，斗拱结构，加之立柱和屋檐，在某些方面类似于欧洲古典建筑中的“柱式”。不同之处在于，欧洲的“柱式”的应用本质上出于审美的考虑，而中国的“柱式”——如果可以这么表达的话——则自始至终承担着结构功能，而其审美特性与建筑整体是融为一体的。斗拱在砖石建筑中也只是起着装饰性的作用，比如砖石砌筑的宝塔。斗拱的这一功能，已从公元2世纪遗留下来的、被称为“阙”的石碑基中找到了最早的例证。[2]

4. 屋顶　另一个值得注意的特点是屋顶在中国建筑中扮演的重要角色。早在公元前11世纪的诗歌中，就有了称颂屋顶之美的诗文，用飞禽的双翼来比喻向外延展的屋檐。[3] 典型的中国式屋顶，是由稍微倾斜的斜坡平面层层组成的。这种效果是通过调整“梁架”每一层梁的长度和高度而形成的。屋顶坡面两两相交的屋脊，通常通过加高的线脚予以强化，并用神兽饰物点缀。或许在不晚于公元11世纪之时，明黄色或碧绿色的琉璃彩瓦就已经常用于屋顶。熠熠生辉的色彩，使得建筑物的屋顶如同灿烂的冠冕一般辉煌。

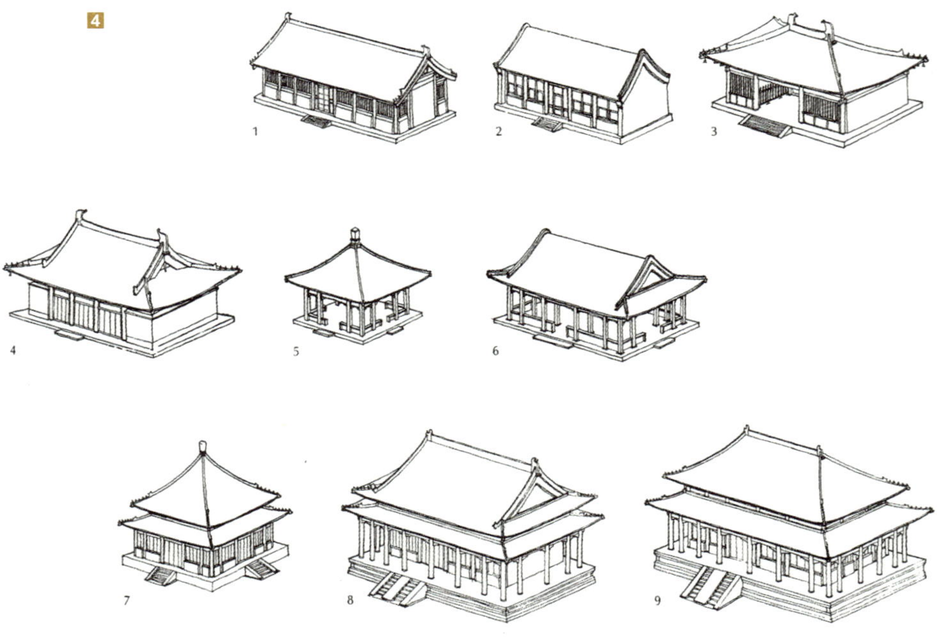

The architects of ancient China paid much attention to the depth of the overhang of the eave. Generally it is designed so that the entire south wall will be completely under the shadow of the eave during the latter part of June to assure maximum coolness in the summer and, while in the winter months, the sunlight may reach far into the back part of the room. (Figure 4)

中国古代的建筑师非常重视飞檐的进深。设计时通常要使6月的下半个月期间整面南墙都处于檐影遮蔽之下，以保证夏季最大限度的凉爽。而在冬季的岁月里，关于采光条件，又能做到让阳光可以一直照射到房屋后部。（图4）

5. Color

The decorative potentiality of paint, a material at first employed essentially for the protection of timber, was discovered by the architect and made the maximum use of since about a thousand years ago. From the *Ying-tsao-fa-shih*, one can see that by the Song Dynasty (960–1279 AD), the decorative use of paint had already formulated into a definite system, which was, in general principle, followed till today. The posts, doors and windows and the walls of monumental building are usually painted red, while the lintels and dougong above are decorated with patterns painted principally in a combination of blue and green, relieved with specks of red and gold. Thus the parts exposed to direct sunlight are warm while the shadowed portions are cold in tone of colors, thereby accentuating the effects of contrast between light and shade. The same distribution of colors is also carried into the interior of the building. Indeed, in the handling of colors, the architects of ancient China have displayed, perhaps, more audacity than their colleagues in other countries.

5. 色彩 最早基于保护木材的目的而使用的油漆材料，其装饰效果直到大约一千年前才被建筑师发现并应用到极致。根据《营造法式》的记载，我们可以得知，及至宋朝（公元960—1279年），油漆的装饰性使用已成固定程式，其总体原则沿用至今。重大建筑的柱体、门窗和墙体通常为朱红色，而上方门楣和斗拱装饰有以蓝绿色为主色、以朱红色和金黄色为点缀辅色的图案。这样一来，直接向阳的部分为暖色调，而阴影部分为冷色调，加强了光与影的对比效果。同样的色彩分布也适用于建筑内部。的确，在色彩的处理上，中国古代的建筑师比其他国家的建筑同仁或许要大胆破格得多。

Of course, such lavish play of color is generally employed on buildings of monumental character. The same color scheme, but more restrained and subdued, are also used on residential buildings in North China. But in the south, where the climate is warm, especially in the average dwelling houses, white walls and natural or dark brown timber is generally the rule. Such quiet combination of colors is perhaps more apt to induce a feeling of coolness.

6. Versatility in Planning

The skeleton system of construction lends great versatility in plan arrangements. This system, besides the freedom it gives to fenestration, also permits the free arrangement of interior partitions to fulfill different requirements. Through the manipulation of columniation, almost any desired shape of plan can be acquired. The skeleton system also possesses a high degree of adaptability to the ups and downs of tricky topography. This asset the Chinese architect did not fail to utilize to the highest degree.

Needless to say that the above mentioned are not all the characteristics of Chinese architecture. But they are the basic and most outstanding ones that give Chinese architecture its own character.

当然，浓艳重彩的装饰，主要是用于某些标志性的重大建筑。同样的色彩装饰也见于华北民居，但色调更加拘谨柔和。而在气候温暖的南方，尤其在普通民居中，则较常采用白色的墙体和自然色或深棕色的木材。这种素色搭配可能更易于产生清凉之感。

6．布局的多样化 中国建筑的骨架结构体系带来了平面布局的多样化。这一体系，除了给开门辟窗提供自由空间外，还可根据不同需求对内部间隔进行自由安排。通过调整柱间距，几乎可以形成任何想要的平面布局。这种结构体系也具有高度的适应性，可适用于各种高低不平的复杂地势。关于这一点，中国的建筑师将其发挥到了极致。

毫无疑问，以上所述并非中国建筑的全部特点，但却是中国建筑基本的同时也是最突出的特征。

II. A BRIEF REVIEW OF THE HISTORICAL DEVELOPMENT OF CHINESE ARCHITECTURE

Before proceeding into a discussion of the types and certain representative examples of Chinese architecture, perhaps it is necessary to trace, however briefly, the development of Chinese architecture through the past three or four thousand years. Taking into consideration the social, economical, political and technological developments as they were reflected in architecture, the developments of Chinese architecture may be tentatively divided into the following six principal stages.

A The First Stage: Before 220 AD

From the very early days of primitive society to the downfall of the first great Chinese empire—the Han Dynasty—in the year 220 AD, is the stage marking the dawn of Chinese architecture to its age of early maturity. The natural cave was a natural solution to the primitive man's domicile problem. The site of the famous Peking Man at Zhoukoudian near Peking revealed to us the fact that the primitive man living in North China five hundred thousand years ago had not yet made any attempt to construct for himself a shelter.

贰 中国建筑发展历程概述

在讨论中国建筑的具体类型和代表性实例之前，或许有必要简要回顾一下中国建筑在过去三四千年之间的发展情况。考虑到建筑所反映的社会、经济、政治和技术发展历程，可试将中国建筑的发展历程分为以下六个主要阶段。

❶ 第一阶段：公元 220 年以前

时间起始点为原始社会早期，至公元 220 年中国伟大的封建王朝汉朝衰败，这一阶段标志着中国建筑从起步发展到早期成熟阶段。天然洞穴是原始人类解决居住问题的自然途径。著名的京郊周口店“北京猿人”遗址，向我们证明了 50 万年前生活在华北地区的原始人还未曾有过为自己建造房屋的任何尝试。

The remains of the earliest constructed dwelling are those found at the village of Banpo, as mentioned above. But the first indications of the basic characteristics of Chinese architecture are not to be seen until the Yin Dynasty, circa fifteenth century BC to eleventh century BC, at Anyang, the site of the Yin capital.

From about 1000 BC to 220 BC is a period in which several hundred semi-independent principalities were gradually unified into a centrally administered empire, as a result of which the Qin Dynasty was founded. A certain number of tombs and a few gigantic earthen terraces are the only remnants we have of this period. But from a few decorative patterns engraved on bronze vessels, depicting dwelling houses of the time, it can be seen that the characteristics mentioned above had by this time definitely taken shape. From literary sources, we learned that the palaces and tombs of the emperor who for the first time unified China—Qin Shihuangdi—were indeed extremely extensive in scale, rich and elaborate in architectural treatment and luxurious in furnishing.

Principles for laying out the capital city of a ruling king or emperor were specified as early as the eleventh century BC.

From 206 BC to 220 AD is the period of the famous Han Dynasty, the great dynasty that, on the basis of the short-lived Qin Dynasty, consolidated China into a great empire. By this time, China had already entered into a stage of fully matured feudalism. As a result of the political and economical unification and the redistribution of land after several centuries of incessant wars, together with the introduction of ferro implements, productivity reached an unprecedented high. The prosperity of the period was reflected vividly in its architecture, which was given the opportunity of making a big stride forward in its development. According to literary records, the palaces of the Han emperors were so vast that they had "a thousand doors and ten thousand windows." There were "warm pavilions" for the winter and "cool palaces" for the summer. The beams and columns were decorated with gold and precious stones. The dougong were elaborately painted and the rafters exquisitely carved. The walls were covered either with mural paintings of mythological beings and ethereal clouds or with rich brocade hangings. During the later half of the dynasty, when land and wealth became more and more concentrated, nobilities, high officials and even rich merchants, fattened by unscrupulous exploitation, also built for themselves luxurious mansions and gardens. Meanwhile the housing of the urban poor became a problem. History recorded a decree mandated by an emperor ordering the erection of "two hundred regions of houses in Chang'an to house the poor."

最早的人为建造的住所遗址，为上文提到的西安半坡村。但中国建筑早期的基本特点，直到大约在公元前 15 世纪至公元前 11 世纪时期的殷朝才开始显现，遗址位于都城所在地安阳。

大约在公元前 1000 年至公元前 220 年的这段时期，数百个半独立的诸侯王国逐渐统一成一个中央集权的帝国，于是秦朝建立了。这一时期除几处陵墓遗址和为数不多的巨型土台之外，并无其他遗迹史料可循。但是从青铜器上所刻的几处描绘当时居住房舍的装饰性图案可以看出，此时上文所述特点业已成型。文献表明，历史上第一位统一中国的皇帝秦始皇的宫室与陵墓规模极其宏大，建筑富丽堂皇，装饰极为豪华。

君主或帝王的都城布局原则，早在公元前 11 世纪时就有规定。

公元前 206 年至公元 220 年，为著名的两汉王朝。在短命的秦王朝基础上，汉朝将中国建成为一个强大的帝国。此时，中国已经进入封建主义完全成熟的阶段。历经数世纪之久的战事之后，政治和经济上重新统一，土地重新分配，铁器开始推广，生产力达到了空前的高度。这一时期的繁荣景象，从其建筑中得到了生动的体现，建筑也得以向前迈进了一大步。据文字记载，汉朝皇帝的宫殿宏伟壮丽，有"千门万牖"的说法。这些宫廷建筑冬有"暖亭"，夏有"凉宫"。横梁立柱，金雕玉刻；斗拱彩绘繁复，椽子精工雕琢。墙上绘有神灵和祥云壁画或饰以绫罗绸缎。后汉即东汉时期，土地和财富更加集中，贵族、高官甚至富商大贾大肆搜刮掳掠，也为自己建造豪华的宅第和苑囿。与此同时，广大城市贫民的住房却成为一个问题。据历史记载，曾有皇帝下诏，命令在长安城里划出两百个"闾里""街巷"的面积建房造屋，以供下户贫民居住。[4]

It was the belief of that time that the gods and immortals had the preference to dwell in high towers. So, in order to induce the condescension of these heavenly beings, very high towers were also erected in the imperial parks.

Trade contacts with West Asia during this period also brought from the West cultural elements which are reflected also in architecture. The arch appeared for the first time in this period. Some archaeologists and architectural historians brought forth the contention that it is an importation from the West. But no agreement has been reached on the controversy. History also records for the first time the using of human figures as architectural embellishments. Notable among these are the twelve bronze figures in front of the palace of Qin Shihuangdi. The winged-lion, probably of Assyrian origin, appeared in sculpture and the grape, then a new comer to China, became a favorite decorative motif.

Buddhism was also introduced into China at this time. At the end of the second or the beginning of the third century AD, the Buddhist pagoda, developed from the indigenous high towers for the gods and immortals, was recorded in history to have made its appearance.

All these new elements from the West had greatly enriched the architecture of China.

Ⓑ The Second Stage: Buddhist Influence, 3rd to 6th Century

From the beginning of the third century to the end of the sixth century AD was a period in Chinese history in which the situation of division lasted longest and war was almost incessant. It was also a period in which Chinese culture, including architecture, was greatly influenced by, and absorbed most from, Indian and Central Asian culture. In such a period of political unrest and economic insecurity, the newly imported religion of Buddhism found a favorable soil for nurture.

The social situation was duly mirrored in architecture. Miniature capitals for petty "emperors" were built and destroyed as the "dynasties" were established and vanquished. The Han people (the national majority of China today), whose rulers being driven to the south of the Yangzi River, saw six dynastic changes in three centuries. Only the Northern Wei Dynasty in the north, founded by the Toba tribe, enjoyed a comparatively long regime of one and a half centuries. Buddhist temples and pagodas were built almost everywhere. It may be assumed that, prior to this time, the only monumental buildings in the cities were the palaces of the emperors and mansions of the nobilities. But with the sporadic construction of Buddhist temples and pagodas, there appeared in the cities, besides the palaces and mansions, rich and monumental temple buildings and ensembles accessible to the public and, therefore, of a more or less popular nature. These undoubtedly greatly altered the general appearance and silhouette of the Chinese cities.

当时据信，长生不老的神仙喜居高塔。因此，为了赢得天神的青睐，皇家园林中也修建了很多高塔。

与西亚贸易的接触，给中国带来西方的文化元素，同样在中国建筑中有所反映。拱门在这一时期首次出现。一些考古学家和建筑史学家对拱门的建造是否由西方引入争论不休，但迄今尚无定论。此外，建筑装饰中人形也首次出现，其中较为著名的是秦始皇宫殿前的 12 个铜人。雕塑中还出现了带翼的狮子，可能是来自亚述文化；而当时刚传入中国的葡萄，也成了热门的装饰性主题图案。

佛教也在此时传入中国。在公元 2 世纪末或 3 世纪初，从为神灵修建的本土高塔发展而来的佛塔，如记载所示，已在历史上出现了。

所有这些来自西方的新元素，都极大丰富了中国的建筑。

❷ 第二阶段：佛教的影响（公元 3 世纪至 6 世纪）

从公元 3 世纪初到 6 世纪末，是中国历史上纷争历时最久、战争频繁不断的时期，同时也是包括建筑在内的中国文化吸收印度和中亚文化最多、受其影响最大的时期。这样一个政局动荡、经济萧条的情况，就为新近传入的佛教的滋生和发展，创造了良好条件。

当时的社会状况也相应在建筑中有所反映。那时候，群雄割据、交相秉政、称霸一方的“帝王”，都各自兴建了规模不大的国都，随后朝纲衰落凌替，都城也烟消云泯。汉族（当今中国人口最多的民族）的统治者被驱逐到长江以南，在三个世纪中经历了六次王朝更迭。只有由拓跋部在北方建立的北魏王朝，持续了相对较长的一个半世纪。佛教寺庙和宝塔几乎遍及各地。据推测，此前城市中最雄伟的建筑就是帝王宫殿及贵族宅邸。但随着佛教寺庙和佛塔的零星建造，城市中除了宫殿官邸之外，还出现了华丽而巨大的庙宇建筑和建筑组群，准许民众入内，因而也就多少带有亲民的大众化性质。这无疑极大改变了中国城市的整体景观和风貌。

History cited the donation by an empress to a Buddhist temple, a pagoda measuring "one thousand feet in height," only to be destroyed in a war a few years after its completion.

The principal remains of this period are a number of rock-cut or cave temples and a few masonry pagodas. Some of the cave temples, such as those at Yungang near Datong, at Maiji Shan near Tianshui and at Tianlong Shan near Taiyüan are given architectural treatments of a high degree of perfection.

The oldest Buddhist pagoda standing in China today is one from this period. The pagoda of Songyue Si in the Song Mountains, Henan Province, built in the year 520 AD, measuring about 40 meters high and sparsely embellished with a few motifs of Indian origin, heralded the appearance of a new architectural type in China.

From these remains of the period, is seen that Chinese architecture in this stage was how much influenced by that of India, Western Asia, and even, Greece. Buddhism brought forth to the Chinese architects new problems and laid down new requirements. These new requirements and problems must be fulfilled and solved with new conceptions. The architects of the period successfully accomplished their task by ingeniously adapting and developing their traditional architecture and created new types and ensembles to meet the new demands. Western influences are also seen in decorative motifs, some of which have, in due course of time, so climatized that they became inseparable and indiscernible elements in Chinese art and architecture.

C The Third Stage: the Glorious Tang Dynasty, 7th to 9th Century

By the end of the sixth century, China was once more unified. The recovery of production after a long period of wars, the political reunification and the development of foreign trade all became powerful impetus to architectural activities.

The Sui Dynasty, a mere "prelude" to the Great Tang Dynasty, planned and started building an imperial capital—Chang'an, Xi'an of today—

in magnitude unprecedented in history. With a definite attempt to build a city with zoning according to functions, the imperial palaces, the area for government offices, residential super-blocks (called fang) and trading squares were all arranged with precise order in the rectangular, walled city. All these areas and blocks were divided and inter-connected by a checker-board system of boulevards, arterial streets and minor streets. (Figure 5)

据历史记载，某皇后曾为佛教寺庙捐赠一座佛塔，“高千尺”，但建成数年之后即毁于战乱。

这一时期的主要遗存建筑物，包括一些石窟或洞窟以及凤毛麟角的砖石宝塔。其中一些石窟，如大同附近的云冈石窟、天水附近的麦积山石窟以及太原附近的天龙山石窟，建筑处理都达到了较高的水准。

中国保存至今最古老的佛塔就出自这一时期。河南省嵩山嵩岳寺塔，建于公元 520 年，高约 40 米，雕饰有一些印度图案，标志着一种新的建筑形式在中国的出现。

从这一时期遗存的建筑可以看出，中国建筑在此时期很大程度上受到了印度、西亚甚至希腊的诸多影响。佛教为中国建筑师带来了新的问题，并提出了新的要求。要满足新要求，解决新问题，就必须采用新的理念。当时的建筑师成功地做到了这一点：他们巧妙地修改、发展了传统建筑，对形式和整体进行了创新，以适应当时新的要求。西方的影响也可从装饰图案中看出，其中的一些随着时间的推移变得非常本土化了，甚至已演变发展成为中国艺术和建筑中不可分割的部分。

❸ 第三阶段：盛唐时期（公元 7 世纪至 9 世纪）

到公元 6 世纪末，中国再度统一。连年战乱之后生产的恢复、政治上的重新统一以及对外贸易的发展，都对建筑业的繁荣起到了强有力的推动作用。

为大唐揭开历史序幕的隋朝建立后，开始大兴土木，在汉长安城（即今日西安）旧址的基础上建造新都。其规模之宏大，可称史无前例。新都的建设明确根据建筑的性质进行分区规划；宫殿、官府和坊市都在城墙围蔽的四方城垣里归整排列。所有这些区域都由畦分棋布的纵横干道和大街小巷分隔和连接。（图 5）

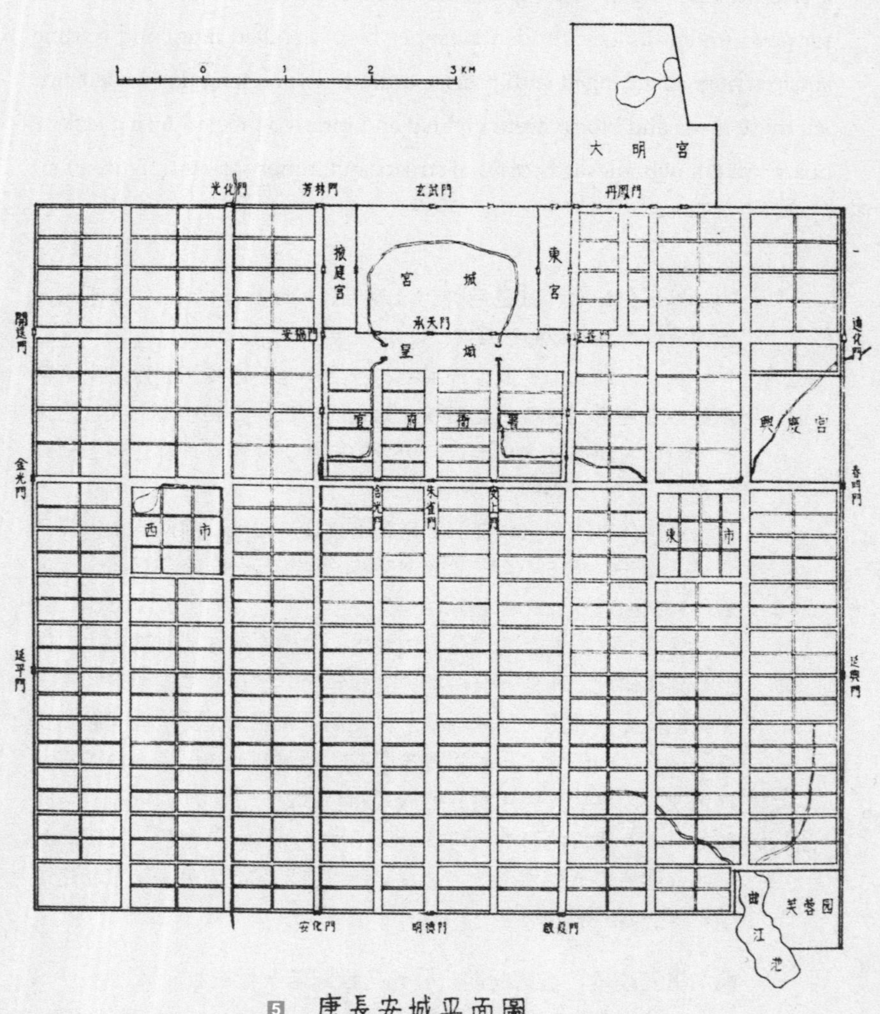
1 0 1 2 3 KM
大明宮
光化門
芳林門
玄武門
丹鳳門
掖庭宮
宮城
東宮
承天門
安福門
延喜門
皇城
開遠門
通化門
官府衙署
興慶宮
金光門
春明門
含光門
朱雀門
安上門
西市
東市
延平門
延興門
安化門
明德門
啟夏門
曲江池
芙蓉園

5 唐長安城平面圖

In the city of Chang'an during the Tang Dynasty, there were traders in large numbers from various Western Asian countries. There were also Buddhist missionaries from India and artists from Khotan, Afghanistan, etc. Painting, sculpture, music, dancing were all enriched by the absorption of Western influences. In architecture, either technologically or artistically, an unprecedented high tide was reached.

The oldest specimen of the timber skeleton structures existing in China date from the Tang Dynasty. Here we see that the carpenter's art had reached a high degree of mastery. The structural members are logically and organically integrated. The architectural treatment shows a high degree of refinement and sensitiveness. The only two examples are the principal halls of the Nanchan Si and of Fokuang Si, both situated in the Wutai Mountains in the Province of Shanxi.

The pagoda, which in the previous stage of development was mostly built with wood, was, by this time, gradually substituted by masonry structures. New types of pagodas were innovated from time to time. The facades of some pagodas were given architectural treatments representing the forms of timber construction—the column, the lintel, the dougong and the eave. This conception is identical with the way the classic orders were employed on the facades of European architecture.

唐朝的长安城内，来自西亚诸国的商贩为数颇多，还有来自印度的佛教徒和来自和阗、阿富汗等地的艺术家。绘画、雕刻、音乐、舞蹈均因受西方影响而得以大大丰富。建筑方面，不管是技术或是艺术方面，均进入了前所未有的全盛时期。

中国现存最早的木结构建筑典范就出自唐代，从中可见木匠工艺的精湛程度。结构部件合理而有机地耦合在一起，建筑处理手法也展现了高度的精湛入微的水平。仅存的两个实例是均位于山西省五台山的南禅寺和佛光寺的主殿。

此前佛塔多用木造，此时首次逐渐以砖石结构取而代之，形式上不断推陈出新。部分佛塔的立面进行了木结构式的处理——采用了立柱、横梁、斗拱和屋檐。这一概念与欧洲建筑立面采用的古典柱式相同。

The plan of the pagoda in this period is generally squared in shape. The superstructure is hollow, like a covered smoke stack. The floor is of wood. The treatment of the mass form may be classified into two main categories according to the division of floor heights and the application of eaves. One we may call the "multi-storied" pagoda, which is a super-position of a number of single-storied pavilions. Another we may call the "multi-eaved" pagoda, which takes the form of a lofty main story topped by tiers of eaves almost one right on top of another. In general effect, the pagodas of this period are rather austere, some very robust and even severe.

The wide spread use of masonry indicates the advances made in both the technique of making and using of brick. The arch was used on almost all openings of brick pagodas. One arched structure of supreme importance in the history of bridge architecture is the open-spandrel bridge at Zhao Xian, Hebei Province. Built during the Sui Dynasty (588–618 AD), with a principal arch spanning nearly 38 meters, it boasts to be the earliest open-spandrel bridge known in the world. (Figure 6)

Ⓓ The Fourth Stage: Large Ensembles Standardization and Refinement, 10th to 14th Century

From the beginning of the tenth century to the middle of the fourteenth century, there were a series of wars among the Han people themselves and also between the Han people and various branches of the Tungus and Mongols from the north. The quick succession of the Five Dynasties and Ten States were eventually, in the year 960 AD, unified by the Song Dynasty, only to be, in turn, incessantly oppressed first by the Khitans and later by the Nüchens from the northeast. Finally, in 1280, the Mongols conquered the entire land and China became a part of the great Mongol Empire, called the Yuan Dynasty in Chinese history.

Except for the mere half-a-century after the founding of the Song Dynasty, there were hardly any interlude of peace. Corrupt government officials and high concentration of land piled up wealth for the ruling class, who became great patrons in architecture and *objet d'art* in general. Meanwhile peasants were driven into rebellion and "vacuums" were created to invite invasion.

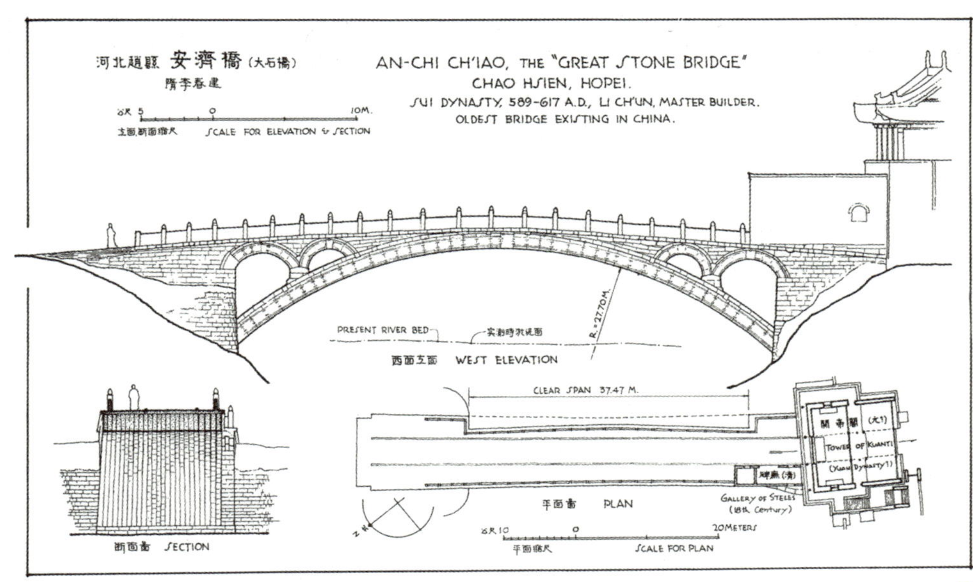

6

这一时期佛塔的平面布局基本呈方形。上部结构中空，类似加盖的烟囱；地面则为木制的。根据地面高度的分隔和屋檐的应用，可以将佛塔形式分为两大类。一种即所谓“多层”佛塔，即楼阁式塔，由多个单层亭阁重叠起来。另一种称作“多重檐”佛塔，即密檐式塔，形式上类似于较高的主楼层上屋檐层层错位堆叠的处理手法。总体效果上，该时期的佛塔相当朴实无华，有的则显得庄严甚而肃穆。

大规模使用砖石标志着砖石制作和运用技术上的进步。几乎所有砖塔的入口都采用拱门。在桥梁建筑史上非常重要的一座拱形建筑是河北省赵县的安济桥。它建造于隋朝（公元588—618年），主拱跨度几乎达38米，为世界上目前所知最早的空腹拱桥（又称敞肩拱桥）。（图 6）

❹ 第四阶段：大型建筑群标准化和精细化（公元 10 世纪至 14 世纪）

从公元 10 世纪初到 14 世纪中叶，汉族内部及汉族与北方的通古斯族和蒙古族之间爆发了一系列战争。五代十国迅速更替之后，宋朝终于在公元 960 年统一中原，但仍然不断地受到东北的契丹以及后来女真族的侵扰。最终于公元 1280 年，蒙古征服全部疆土，中国成为大蒙古帝国的一部分，这在中国历史上称为元朝。

这一时期除了宋朝建国初期的半个世纪以外，鲜有和平的缓歇。朝廷官员的腐败和土地的高度集中化，为统治阶级积累了大量财富，他们由此得以出资促进建筑和艺术发展。与此同时，农民被迫起义造反；由此形成的“真空地带”，招致了外来侵略。

The principal developments of this stage are the great increase in the sizes of architectural ensembles and the advances made in architectural refinements. The imperial palaces of the Song rulers were cited in history to have consisted of more than three thousand jians. In order to economize on materials and labor and to speed up the processes in designing and construction in such vast scale, the method of typification and standardization was sought. Thus, centuries of heritage in the art and technique of building was summarized, systematized, and compiled into the famous treatise on architecture, the *Ying-tsao-fa-shih*. As mentioned above, a modular system was definitely set, with which the dimensions and proportions of the building was computed and structural as well as decorative members could be prefabricated elsewhere and be shipped to and assembled at the building site. Ever since, standardization and typification with the modular system has become the common practice in Chinese architecture. Specific dimensions and proportions may vary from time to time and in different localities, but the principle is the same. The compilation and publication of the *Ying-tsao-fa-shih* must thus be considered an event of great historical significance in the development of Chinese architecture.

这一时期的主要发展在于建筑群规模扩大以及手法日趋华丽精细。史书记载，宋朝的皇宫超过三千来间。为节约材料和劳力，并且加快大规模建筑物的设计速度和建造进程，出现了对典型化和标准化的追求。因此，数世纪以来的建筑艺术和建造技术得以总结、系统化并编成著名的建筑文献《营造法式》一书。如前所言，模数制已确定下来，并据此规制计算建筑的尺寸和比例。结构性部件和装饰性部件可以在别处预先制作，尔后运至建筑现场进行组装。自此以后，应用模数制的标准化和典型化在中国建筑中成为惯例。[5]具体的尺寸和比例因时因地制宜，但原则始终如一。《营造法式》的编撰出版因而成为中国建筑发展史上的一个重要事件。

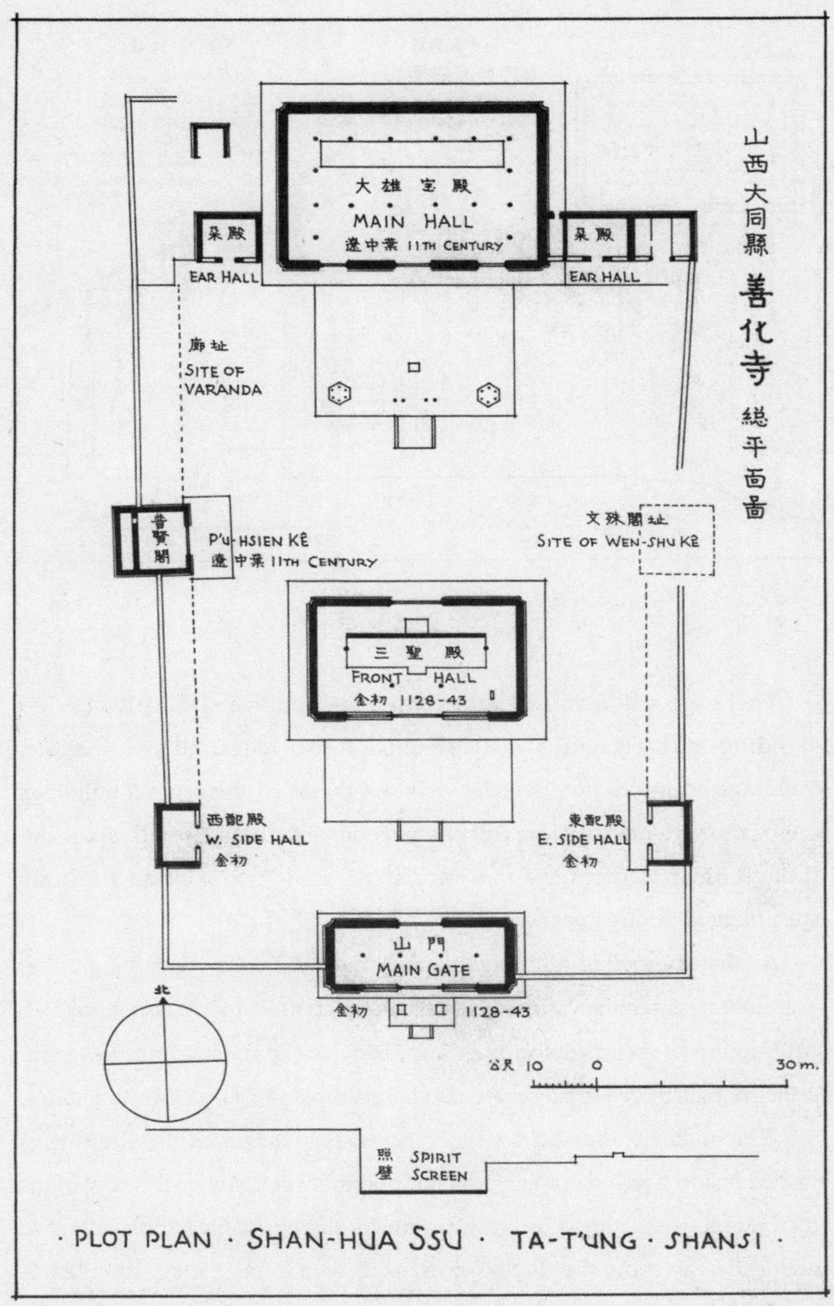
山西大同縣 善化寺 総平面圖
大雄宝殿
MAIN HALL
遼中葉 11TH CENTURY
朶殿
EAR HALL
朶殿
EAR HALL
廊址
SITE OF VARANDA
普賢閣
P'U-HSIEN KÊ
遼中葉 11TH CENTURY
文殊閣址
SITE OF WEN-SHU KÊ
三聖殿
FRONT HALL
金初 1128-43
西配殿
W. SIDE HALL
金初
東配殿
E. SIDE HALL
金初
山門
MAIN GATE
金初 1128-43
北
公尺 10 0 30 m.
照壁
SPIRIT SCREEN
· PLOT PLAN · SHAN-HUA SSU · TA-T'UNG · SHANSI ·

8

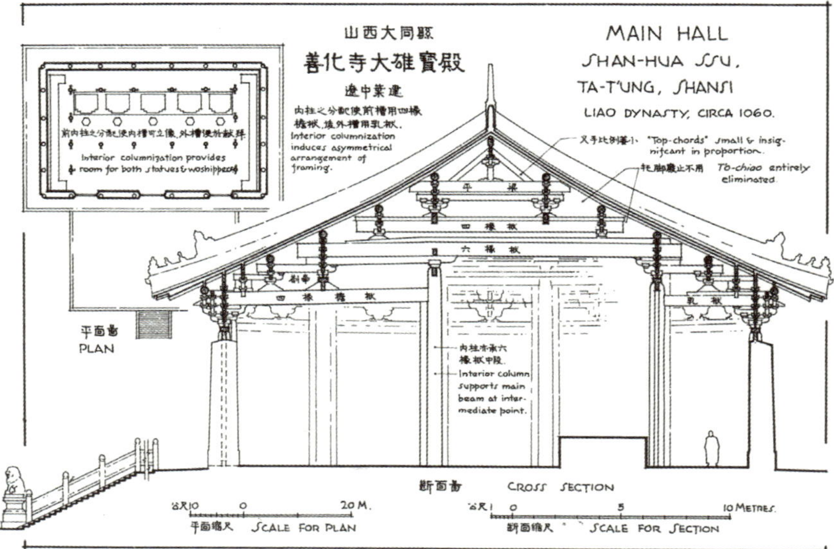

There are still a considerable number of edifices from this period standing today. (Figures 7, 8) Except a few bridges, all are religious buildings—temples and pagodas. Among these, all the temple buildings are of timber construction; but the pagodas left to us from this period, though most of them are masonry structures, also include a unique specimen of wooden pagoda. (Figures 9, 10)

As the number of buildings that survived till today became greater, examples representing varieties in use, construction and form also increased. Among the timber skeleton buildings, besides the most commonly seen principal hall, there are preserved also libraries, side-halls, gateway buildings, etc. The buildings are also seen in various story-heights, from the single-storied hall to a pagoda of five principal and four mezzanine stories. Various roof forms—the wudian or hip-roof, the xieshan or gabled-roof with eave under the gable and the double-eaved roof—are found. These roof forms, although known to have been created perhaps even as early as the Han Dynasty, and depicted in paintings and sculpture in the cave temples, but with the exception of the wudian, no actual specimen survived from the former periods. The dougong became smaller, in comparison with the former stage of development, in proportion. But still, in the northern provinces, and during the early part of this stage of development, the more robust proportion of the former stage was retained for a considerable length of time. Thus, local characteristics can be more noticeably detected.

In plan arrangement, there are a few ensembles partly, or to a certain degree completely, preserved. A principal building is often flanked by a smaller building on each side, all arranged in a row and facing the same direction. Buildings on either side of the courtyard are given more importance. Instead of the veranda or gallery of uniform height, it is accentuated by placing in its middle a building of more prominence. With this treatment, a cross-wise axis is definitely introduced.

现存的这一时期的宏伟建筑，数目较大。除寥若晨星的几座桥梁之外，全部为寺庙和佛塔等宗教建筑。（图 7，8）其中，所有寺庙均为木结构。至于此阶段所有留存的佛塔，则大多为砖石结构，只有一座独特的木构架八角塔（即山西应县佛宫寺释迦塔，俗称应县木塔）除外。（图 9，10）

随着遗留实物数量的增多，用途、建造和形式方面各种类型的个案也随之增加。在木骨架建筑中，除最常见的主殿外，还保留有藏经楼、配殿、山门等。建筑层高不定，从单层的殿堂到主层五层和夹层四层的佛塔都有。不同的屋顶形式，如庑殿、歇山、重檐等，均可找到实例。这些屋顶形式虽然可能早在汉代就已建造出来，并在石窟的壁画和雕刻中也都有所呈现，但是除了庑殿之外，并无更早的实物得以留存下来。较先前阶段，斗拱的比例变小。但在北方诸省中，这一阶段的早期，在较长一段时间内仍保持了前一阶段的较大比例的斗拱。因此，地方特征表现较为显著。

在平面布局上，屈指可数的几个建筑群得到了部分的或某种程度上全面的保存。主建筑两侧经常排列有较小的建筑，按同一方向连成轴线。庭院两侧的建筑也得到了重视。长廊或走廊也并非高度取齐，而是在庭院正中设置更为突出的建筑。如此一来，形成了鲜明的十字交叉轴线布局。

9 山西應縣佛宮寺遼釋迦木塔

中國營造學社測繪　民國廿三年九月實測　廿四年六月製圖

10

11

12

13

It is quite natural that the number of masonry pagodas that survived till today should be much greater than that of wooden buildings. With the single exception of the wooden pagoda mentioned above, all the pagodas from this period that are still standing are masonry structures.

Pagodas of this period assume a greater variety of forms. Instead of the square plan, which was almost the absolute rule in the former stage of development, the octagon became the favorite plan shape of this period and thereafter. (Figures 11, 12)

相比于木建筑而言，留存至今的砖石佛塔数量自然更多。除上文提及的应县木塔这一例外，这一时期所有保留下来的佛塔均为砖石结构。

这一时期的佛塔形式多样。布局方面，除了此前阶段几乎作为绝对法则的方形，八边形成为了此时和之后最受欢迎的平面布局。[6]（图 11，12）

The "multi-storied" and the "multi-eaved" are still the two principal types in the treatment of the mass and silhouette of the pagoda. But the octagonal plan has given them an effect of slenderness and richer play of light. In general, the pagoda of this period became more refined and elegant. Some of them are more restrained, attaining their aesthetic effect by well studied proportion and are sparingly ornamented. But there are also a considerable number of them that are given architectural embellishments in imitation of the timber construction, giving the pagoda a richness unseen in masonry structures in former periods. (Figure 13)

Ⓔ The Fifth Stage: Age of Peking European Influence, 1368–1949

From the latter half of the fourteenth century to the first decade of the present century, there were only two dynasties and they both succeeded in maintaining their regimes for a comparatively long duration. The Ming Dynasty drove away the Mongols and reestablished a regime of Han rulers. It was an age of national revival. The Yuan capital Dadu was sacked and a new capital was built in Nanjing. But only thirty years later, the capital was moved to Peking, utilizing the greater part of the destroyed Dadu. The Qing Dynasty, established by the Manchus, inherited Peking almost intact. For more than five centuries, Peking was twice enlarged and survived without going through any large scale destruction. The city, with its palaces and parks, stands as the most important monument of this period.

Every newly founded dynasty brought along with it a redistribution of land and a rise in production and consequently greater building activity. The first hundred years or so of both these dynasties were periods of comparative peace and prosperity. All kinds of handicraft were brought to ever higher perfection. All these factors found expression in the architecture of the time. Both the Ming and Qing Dynasties left to posterity innumerable buildings, some still standing today in perfect state of preservation. Unlike the earlier periods, dwelling houses of the ordinary people have also been preserved.

Needless to say, the Imperial Palaces of Peking, first laid out and built in the early part of the fifteenth century and renovated, some even completely rebuilt, in later ages, as a group, stand one of the most magnificent ensemble created by any architect of any time. (Figures 14, 15)

"多层"和"多檐"仍然是佛塔体量和轮廓处理方面主要的两个类型。八角形的平面布局产生了纤细修长、光影重重的效果。整体而言，这一时期的佛塔更加精致典雅。有一些较为保守，比例恰切，装饰简约，从而达到了审美效果。但也有相当数量的佛塔模仿木结构建筑的装饰风格，这样就使砖石佛塔相较此前更加富丽华美。(图 13)

❺ 第五阶段：北京—欧式影响风行的时代（公元 1368 至 1949 年）

从 14 世纪下半叶到 20 世纪头十年，经历了两个朝代，且均持续了相对较长的时间。明朝赶走了蒙古人，重新建立了汉族统治，可算是民族复兴。元大都遭到劫掠，新的都城在南京兴建。但仅 30 年之后，明朝又迁都北京，在元大都的大部分废墟旧址上兴建新都。清朝是由满人建立的，大体沿袭了前朝北京的格局。在五个多世纪里，北京城两度扩建，免遭大肆破坏而得以保存。北京城及其宫殿苑囿，是这一阶段最重要的历史遗迹。

14

新建各朝之初，土地重新分配，生产力得到提升，并由此促进了建筑业的发展。这两个朝代开初的一百年左右，均是相对和平、繁荣的时期。各种手工业空前蓬勃发展。所有这些因素，在当时的建筑中都得以展现。明清两代留下来不胜枚举的建筑，有些至今仍得到完好保存。和前期不同，这一时期的一些民居也被保存下来。

毋庸置疑，开始设计并营造于 15 世纪早期、其后又整修甚至重建的故宫建筑群，是任何时期、任何建筑师能建造出的最宏伟壮丽的建筑作品之一。(图 14，15)

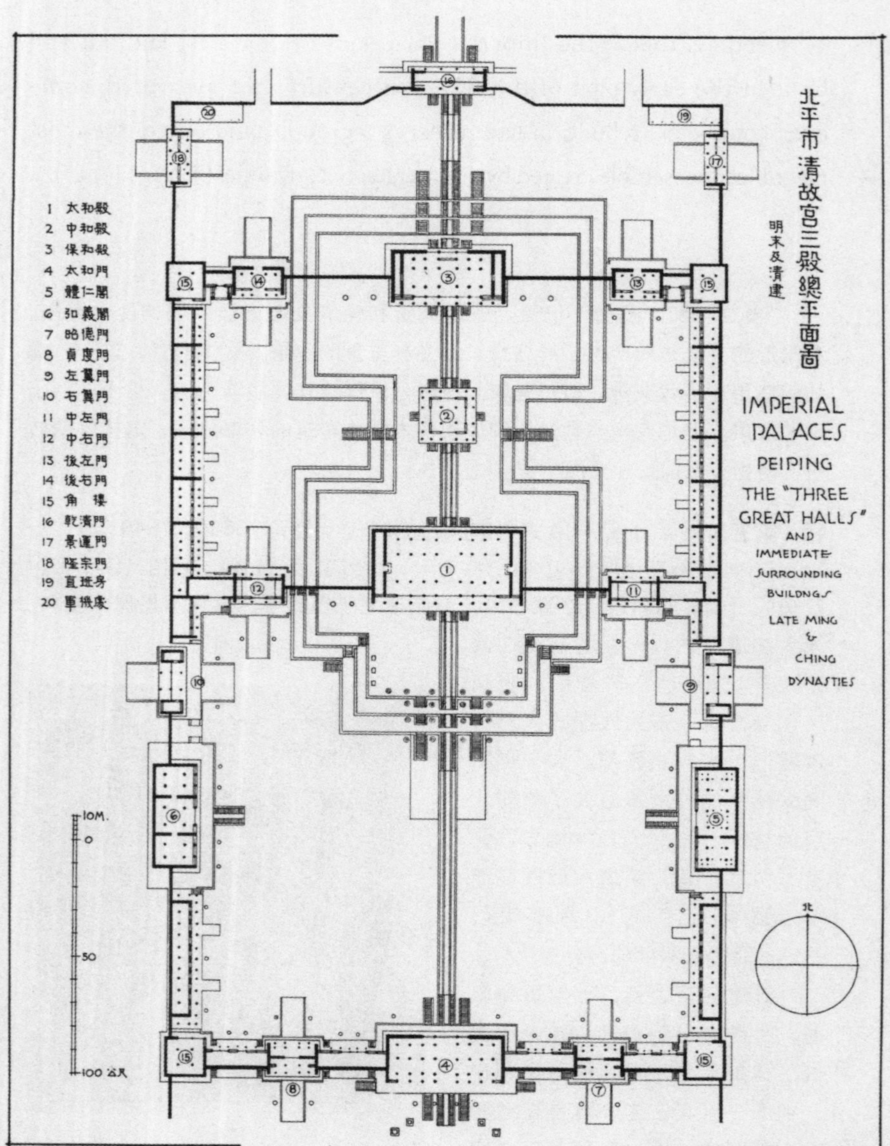

北平市清故宮三殿總平面圖
明末及清建
IMPERIAL PALACES
PEIPING
THE "THREE GREAT HALLS"
AND IMMEDIATE SURROUNDING BUILDNGS
LATE MING & CHING DYNASTIES
1 太和殿
2 中和殿
3 保和殿
4 太和門
5 體仁閣
6 弘義閣
7 昭德門
8 貞度門
9 左翼門
10 右翼門
11 中左門
12 中右門
13 後左門
14 後右門
15 角 樓
16 乾清門
17 景運門
18 隆宗門
19 直班房
20 軍機處
10M.
0
50
100 公尺
北

15

16

18

17

19

Mansions of nobilities and high officials as well as dwellings of the common people, some built four or five centuries ago, still stand in good condition. Compared to remains of earlier periods, religious buildings are found to be of less importance. Parks and gardens several hundred years old still give pleasure to the mass of people in their time of leisure. (Figures 16, 17) Even tombs of emperors, pompous ensembles, magnificently laid out and originally surrounded by groves of evergreens, have become favorite weekend resorts. (Figures 18, 19)

许多达官贵族的宅邸，乃至普通民居，四五百年后依然保存得相当完好。宗教建筑，与早期遗存的建筑相比，则相形式微。具有数百年历史的各种园林景区，仍是公众休闲游乐的好去处。（图 16，17）不少皇帝陵墓，修建得十分华丽壮观，气势恢宏，周围绿树成荫，蕴含有“万年长青”之寓意；也已成为最受欢迎的周末游览胜地。（图 18，19）

20

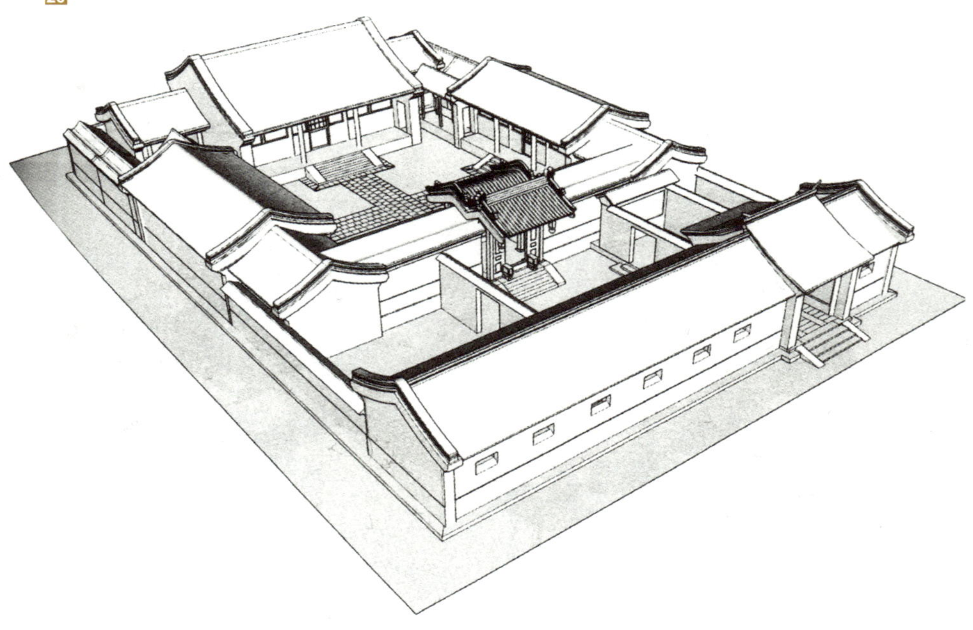

From the architecture of this period, we see most clearly the marked class imprint of the social system. From the palaces and mansions to the houses of the ordinary well-to-do, besides the spacious, comfortable quarters for the "masters and mistresses," without exceptions there are "servants' quarters," a miniature slum attached to every house. Nevertheless, they are still much better than the real slums of the masses of city poors. (Figures 20, 21)

From the plans, especially those of ensembles built in strict accordance with the official regulations, there is found the traditional preference for symmetrical arrangements. But one conspicuous characteristic is that when two or more groups of quadrangular courtyards are put adjacent to each other, there is an almost complete lack of correlation between the major axes of the groups which are parallel to each other. In places away from Peking, especially in the dwellings of the working people, great liberty is taken so as to arrange the houses to meet the demands of work and living.

Certain changes in construction details influenced to a considerable extent the general proportions of the buildings. The beam is brought into more direct contact with the column. To counteract the shearing stress, the width of the beam is increased to a dimension wider than the diameter of the column and placed directly on top of it. Even when the dougong is used, it is used merely as a "cushion," although still functioning as a weight bearing unit, but primarily for decorative purposes. On account of this, the size of the dougong, in proportion to the height of the building, is very much reduced, and the overhang of the eave becomes less far. Thus the buildings of this stage of development, especially those of the Qing Dynasty, present an appearance so restrained that it looks almost rigid when in comparison with the earlier buildings.

21

我们可从这一时期保存下来的建筑中清楚地看出，在当时的社会体制下，阶级划分的明显痕迹。从宫殿宅邸到小康民居，除供老爷和夫人使用的宽敞舒适的上房、正房外，无一例外都附有简陋的（倒座或鹿顶）平房供仆役使用。不过，这些仆役居室的条件仍远远优于广大城市贫民的栖身之所。（图 20，21）

在平面布局上，尤其是严格遵循官方规制的建筑组群，可以看出对对称布局这一形法传统的偏好。但还有一个显著的特点，即两组或多组四合院毗连时，这些庭院的主轴彼此平行，但其间几乎没有任何关联。在北京以外的地方，尤其是劳动人民的聚居地区，房屋布局视劳作和居住的需要而定，非常自由随意。

建筑细节上的某些改变，在很大程度上影响了建筑的整体比例。横梁更直接地与立柱相连。为了抵冲剪应力，横梁的宽度扩展得比柱径还要宽，并直接置于柱顶。即便是斗拱派上用场，也只是作为建筑中的一个“枕垫”；尽管仍然起着承重作用，但主要是装饰性的用途了。因此，斗拱的尺寸就建筑高度的比例而言大幅减小了，屋檐的外悬出檐部分也大幅缩水。这样一来，这一阶段尤其是清朝的建筑，和以往的相比，造型上较为拘谨，甚至几乎显得刻板了。

The nineteenth century was an epoch of profound changes in the history of China. Capitalism and imperialism brought the West to China, and along with it, Western architecture. New methods of construction, new architectural styles, new ways of using buildings, etc., etc., in short, an entirely new conception of architecture was introduced. In some coastal cities, where the imperialists acquired "concessions," even the city of the nineteenth-century Europe was reproduced.

The Qing Dynasty was overthrown in 1911 and a republic was founded. For a quarter of a century, China was torn by successive wars between the "warlords" and then eight years' war against the Japanese invaders. It was also in these years that Marxism-Leninism was introduced into China and eventually led to the formation of the Chinese Communist Party and finally the founding of the People's Republic in 1949.

The architecture of the first half of the twentieth century in China mirrored most faithfully the height of semi-feudalistic and semi-colonial state of Chinese society. In the countries and in the smaller towns, the traditional Chinese building is still the people's choice. But in the larger cities, especially in the so-called "treaty ports," the "foreign-style house" is the mode. Eclecticism, including the so-called "Chinese style" was the vogue for three decades or so, followed by a high tide of "contemporary architecture."

It was in such a state that the architects of China found themselves when China was liberated in 1949.

F The Sixth Stage of People's China, People's Architecture

In 1949, the Chinese people liberated themselves from the bondage of more than two thousand years of feudalism and a century of imperialism and founded the People's Republic of China. Architecture immediately became the common affair of the entire populace. As soon as the period of economic recovery, from 1949 to 1952, is over, with the generous help of the Soviet Union and the people's democratic countries, the reconstruction work under the First Five-Year Plan was launched forward. Numerous new industrial towns have been planned and started building. Certainly many more will be planned and built in the future. Reconstruction plans for many of the old cities are also gradually taking shape.

19 世纪是中国发生深刻变化的历史时期。资本主义和帝国主义使西学东渐，也带来了西洋建筑，包括新的建筑方法、新的建筑风格、新的建筑功用等等。简而言之，引入了全新的建筑理念。一些中国沿海城市，在帝国主义者得到“特许”的“租界”中，甚至复制了不少 19 世纪欧洲的城市建筑。

1911 年，清朝政府被推翻，民国建立了。此后的四分之一个世纪，中国饱受“军阀”混战之苦，后又经历了八年抗日战争。也正是在这一时期，马列主义被带进了中国，中国共产党成立了，并最终于 1949 年建立起了中华人民共和国。

20 世纪上半叶的中国建筑如实地反映了中国半殖民地半封建社会鼎盛时期的风貌。在田间乡下和小城小镇，传统中国建筑仍然是人们的选择。但在较大的城市，尤其是在所谓的“通商口岸”，“洋房”甚为时髦。大约三十来年间，包括所谓“中式风格”在内的折中主义建筑蔚然成风，随后则是“当代建筑”的盛行时期。

1949 年中国解放时，建筑师们正是处于这样一种历史背景之中。

❻ 第六阶段：人民的中国，人民的建筑

1949 年，中国人民从两千年多的封建主义和一个世纪的帝国主义束缚中解放出来，建立了中华人民共和国。建筑很快成为全体民众的共同事业。1949 年到 1952 年的经济恢复时期刚一结束，在苏联和人民民主国家的慷慨相助下，随即开始了第一个“五年计划”，开展重建工作。无数新兴的工业城市开始进行规划兴建，当然，还有更多的要在未来进行规划和建造。很多古城的重建计划正在逐渐形成。

The Chinese people are at present endeavoring with all their efforts to have their four-thousand-year-old agricultural country basically industrialized in the short span of three Five-Year Plans. For the realization of this historical task, architects and engineers of China are offering every ounce of their strength.

Many old cities have changed considerably. New cities are planned and old cities, replanned. Workers' homes and dormitories are built in unprecedented numbers and with great speed, but they still lag behind the need of the people. Plans for residential buildings and certain public and office buildings have been worked towards the direction of standardization since 1953. A considerable number of hotels were built to accommodate the increasing number of visitors to various cities.

Public buildings of diverse nature, from government offices to department stores, etc., constitute none too small a part of the architects' work. The great number of educational buildings, from nurseries to institutions of high education, testifies the great attention the People's Government is paying to the education of the next generation. Hospitals and sanitariums are also built for the health of the great mass of workers, while the number of theaters, palaces of culture, clubs, exhibition galleries, gymnasium, etc., is also considerable.

Needless to say, the one field in building activities that ranks in supreme prominence is that of industry. It is in this field that the Chinese architects found themselves face to face with entirely new problems. The state of industrial development under the reactionary regimes offered hardly any opportunity for the architects to practice in industrial architecture. But with the help of architects from the Soviet Union and other people's democratic countries, Chinese architects not only have learned, but are now able and competent designers in this particular field. The problems facing the Chinese architects are complex and difficult. To plan and build to answer the demands of socialism and of the great masses of working people is no simple task, but, under the leadership of the Chinese Communist Party, with the guiding principles of Marxism-Leninism, and, with the inexhaustible strength and wisdom of the working people, the Chinese architects are filled with self-confidence that they will create an architecture that is socialist in nature and endowed with national characters.

Having made a brief review of the stages of historical development of Chinese architecture, we shall now proceed with the examination of some of the representative specimens.

中国人民目前正在竭尽全力，力争在短短的三个“五年计划”的时间之内，将这个拥有四千年历史的农业大国基本实现工业化。为了实现这一历史任务，中国的建筑师和工程师正在贡献自己的全部力量。

很多古城已经大为改观。新城市正在规划，旧城市则在重新规划。以前所未有的数量和速度修建了不少工人住宅和宿舍，但依旧不能满足人民的需求。1953 年以来，民用住宅、公共建筑和办公建筑正朝着标准化的方向进行规划。大批酒店已经建成，以满足各个城市不断增长的游客的需求。

种类不同的公共建筑，从政府办公室到百货公司等，在建筑师的工作中也占据着不小的分量。兴建的从幼儿园到大学的大量教育建筑，体现了人民政府对下一代教育的重视。医院和疗养院为广大劳动人民而建造，而剧院、文化宫、俱乐部、展览馆以及体育馆等的数量也很可观。

无需多言，建筑活动中最重要的就是工业建筑。正是在这一领域，中国的建筑师发现自己遇到了全新的问题。反动政府统治之时，工业发展完全没有为建筑师修建工业建筑创造任何机会。但是，有了苏联和其他人民民主国家同行的帮助，中国建筑师不仅学会了方法，还成为了这一特殊领域能干的设计师。中国建筑师遇到的问题是复杂和困难的。设计和建造符合社会主义和广大劳动人民需要的建筑，绝非易事。但是，有了中国共产党的领导，有了马列主义的指导原则，有了劳动人民无穷无尽的力量和智慧，中国的建筑师们满怀信心，一定能够兴建兼具社会主义与民族特色的建筑大业。

简要回顾了中国建筑发展的历程之后，我们可再来审视一些具有代表性的实例。

III. CITY PLANNING

Ⓐ Principles for Planning a Capital

As mentioned above, the principles for laying out the capital city of a ruling king or emperor were specified as early as the eleventh century BC. In the *Zhouli* or *Book of Rites*, in the chapter "Kaogong Ji" which narrates the work of crafts, is mentioned that the capital of a king should be "nine li[7] square with nine boulevards running longitudinally and nine boulevards running latitudinally. The longitudinal boulevards should be the width of nine carriages. The palaces should be located in front and the market places, at the rear; the ancestral temple to the left and the temple of the god of lands to the right."

In this simple statement, the basic principles are precisely put down. It is a faithful testimony of the social and political systems of the early days of feudalism. The lord was supreme. His palaces must be put in the center-front. The two temples to the left and right were to stand as permanent proclamations to his noble lineage of decent and indisputable right of sovereignty. The market places, which were the only places for the common people, logically, were located in the least important quarter.

It is interesting to note that this principle was not strictly adhered to in earlier days, such as the Chang'an of the Han Dynasty. It was not until the time when the teachings of Confucius were proclaimed by the feudal rulers as state teachings and the *Zhouli* included into the Thirteen Classics that the planning of an emperor's capital was given such ritual considerations.

Ⓑ The Sui and Tang Capital Chang'an

The Chang'an of the Sui and Tang Dynasties was the first and largest city in the history of China that was planned and built, with certain modifications, on the principle specified in the *Zhouli*. Though completely destroyed at the end of the Tang Dynasty (beginning of the tenth century), exact and minute descriptions by an early Song author and recent researches enable us to have a fairly accurate plan of the city as it existed before destruction. It was a rectangular city completely surrounded by walls on all sides, with three gates on each side. Streets were laid out like a chessboard, with the principal streets in line with the gates. The central part of the northern portion of the city was the Palace City within which were the palaces of the emperor.

叁 城市规划

❶ 都城规划原则

如前所言，公元前 11 世纪就已经明确提出了帝王所在都城的规划原则。《周礼·考工记》，即专门描述工艺之术的章节中，讲到了都城应“方九里，（旁三门，）国中九经九纬，经涂九轨，左祖右社，面朝后市”[8]。

这一简单的语句精确地阐述了基本的规划原则，并如实反映了封建社会初期的社会关系及政治体系。封建领主有着至高无上的权力，因此其宫殿必须位于正前方正中央的位置。[9] 左右两庙象征着王室世系相传的高贵血统及毋庸置疑的统治权威。与平民百姓唯一有关的“市”，自然占据最不重要的位置。

有意思的是，早期规划帝王之都时这些原则并未得以严格的遵循，比如汉朝的长安城就是这样。直到孔子的儒家学说被封建统治者确立为官方学说并且将《周礼》列入“十三经”之后，对国都建设的规划，才开始有了礼制性的考量。

❷ 隋唐都城长安

隋朝和唐朝的都城长安，是中国历史上第一座同时也是最大的一座根据《周礼》的礼制营造原则规划建成的都城，当然也作了些变通。虽然唐朝末年（10 世纪初）都城被毁，但是根据宋初某位作家精确而细致的描述和最新的研究发现，我们能够相当准确地了解到长安城被毁前的规划设计。该城为长方形，四周完全被城墙包围，各面开三座城门。街道格局如同棋盘般区划整齐，主道贯穿城门。城北中央是宫城，即皇帝的宫殿所在地。

To the south of this was the Imperial City, where the ministries of the government were located. Surrounding the Imperial City on three sides was the fang, each also surrounded by walls with a gate on each side and with crossroads within. To the left and right and slightly in front of the Imperial City were two spacious market squares. At the southeastern corner of the city was a "green area" with attractive natural sceneries. It was a favorite resort for the rich and poor alike and had inspired many poets who immortalized the place through their verses.

All the common people lived in the walled fang or blocks, the gates of which would be locked as soon as the "evening drum" was beaten. Hence all residents must be home before that time. Only officials above a certain rank were permitted to open their gates facing the principal streets and had the right of way night and day. The basic conception of the city of Chang'an is a congregation of small cities surrounded by wall to form a big city. The small cities—fang—were separated and connected to each other by major and minor arterial streets. Such arrangements and restrictions mirrored the policy of discouragement of commerce, for no shop was permitted to open onto the principal streets. The street scene of the Chang'an during the Tang Dynasty must have been rather austere. However, official restrictions could not bind social and economical progress forever. By the tenth century, the walls of the fang were broken through and shops were built facing the streets. The street scene in the Chinese city took up an entirely new and different appearance.

C Peking, Capital of the Ming and Qing Dynasties

On the site where Peking, the capital of the People's Republic of China, stands today, a town or settlement have been in existence as far back as the Yin Dynasty (1765 BC–1122 BC). After having sacked the capital of the Jin Dynasty, Yanjing, which had grown up through nearly thirty centuries of development, Kublai Khan of the Mongols ordered the building of a new capital just to the northeast of it, called Dadu, the "Great Capital" and known as Khanbaliq in *Marco Polo's Travels*. It was planned according to the principle set in the *Zhouli*—the palace in the front, the market place at the rear, the ancestral temple to the left and the temple of the god of lands to the right. But Dadu suffered the same fate as that of Yanjing when the Mongols were driven out by the Han people who established the Ming Dynasty in 1368.

宫城之南是皇城，即行政官署所在地。皇城的三面外围均为坊，各坊四面又有围墙，城墙上各有一门，内有出入通路。皇城左侧、右侧及略偏南边，为两个面积宽敞的集市区。[10] 长安城的东南角是有着秀美景色的“绿色园林区”，不但为贫富世人共爱，而且激发了不少文人骚客的诗兴，从而使此地不朽于世。

所有的平民都居住在坊内，坊门在“暮鼓”敲响之时便会锁上。因此，所有居民必须在此之前赶回家中。只有朝廷百司一定级别以上的官员才能将府门开向主街道，并享有不分昼夜均可通行的特权。长安城的基本建设理念，是由畦分棋布的、内向性封闭的小城围合聚拢而成一个大城的格局。小城即指“坊”，由大小主干道相隔相连。这种排列规整的布局及其限制作用，禁止在大街上开设商铺，体现了当时的禁商政策。唐朝那时的长安街道，一定非常俭朴无华。然而，官方的限制不能永久地阻挡社会和经济的进步。到公元 10 世纪时，各坊城墙被打破，店面朝街而开。当时中国的城市街景，呈现出一副截然不同的全新面貌。

❸ 明清都城北京

中华人民共和国现在的首都北京城，始建于殷商时期（公元前 1765 —公元前 1122 年）。在蒙古可汗忽必烈攻占劫掠金朝的首都燕京（已有几近三千年历史）后，他下令在燕京的东北方向建立了一座新的都城，称为“大都”，取“伟大的都城”之义，而在《马可・波罗游记》中被称为“可汗大都”。该城依据《周礼》的原则规划，即“左祖右社，面朝后市”。而当汉人于 1368 年将蒙古人逐出中原并建立明朝之后，大都也遭遇了和燕京类似的被洗劫的命运。

Shortly afterwards, the ruined capital was reconstructed and renamed Beijing, the North Capital, known to Westerners as Peking. It has been, except for two short intervals, the capital of China ever since. The Peking up till the liberation in 1949, as the capital of an absolute monarchy, took its final shape in the year 1553, after three successive large-scale alterations. The reconstruction in 1553 added an "outer city" to the original square city, thus lengthened the principal axis of the city to eight kilometers. The composition of the entire city was basically symmetrical. The street system was laid out with that of the Mongol city as basis. The chessboard main streets divide the city into large "super-blocks," within which most of the minor streets run in the east-west direction. This "fish-bone" pattern of street system defines clearly the different functions of the major and minor streets on the one hand and enabled all the houses to have a southern exposure on the other. The planner had shown great ingenuity in the creation of such a system.

The string of natural lakes in the heart of the city did not embarrass the planner. The effect of symmetry in the street system was by no means destroyed. On the contrary, he made the best use of the irregular lines of the lakes to help soften the possible effect of harshness due to excessive emphasis on symmetry and succeeded in adding a touch of unexpected joy of playfulness to the majestic city. When a casual visitor who comes to Peking for the first time, after passing through streets lined with buildings on both sides and comes suddenly to the head of a bridge, he is brought, most unexpectedly, face to face with a vast stretch of water surface, lined with such informal shorelines, and, on the slopes of the island-hill, such wooded shades of evergreens. He will be standing on or strolling over the marble bridge with exquisitely carved balustrades and enjoying the scenery composed of fairyland-like pavilions and loggias. It makes one wonder whether he is in the middle of a city of over three million inhabitants.

One of the unseen achievements of ancient Peking must not be overlooked, that is the sewage system first laid down six centuries ago.

There was originally in Peking an ancient sewage system totaling more than three hundred kilometers in length, slowly built up through the centuries. Portions of it have already collapsed during the past few decades, but there are still more than two hundred kilometers of it in usable condition. After the liberation, the People's Government drained and repaired the still usable portion of the entire system and it is now an integral and important part of the new sewage system.

不久之后，这座被毁的都城得以重建，并被重新命名为“北京”，即“北方的京城”，西方人称之为 Peking。除了两个短暂的时期以外，自此北京一直是中国的首都。[11] 直至 1949 年解放之前，北京一直是君主专制政权的都城。历经三次大规模整修之后，它最终定型于 1553 年——这一年的重建工作主要是在原来方城的基础上增加了“外城”，从而将城市的中轴线延长至八公里。整座城市的构造基本呈对称状。街道设计以大都为基础，格网状的主干道将城市分为大的坊区，区内多数支干道为东西向。这种鱼骨状的街道体系一方面清晰地体现了主干道和支干道的不同功能，同时也使得所有房屋都能坐北朝南。这种体系的创建，体现了设计者的匠心独具。

城中心的天然湖区（即“海子”），也没能难倒设计师。这些海子更没有破坏街道体系的对称效果。恰恰相反，设计师充分利用了它们的不规则形状，来弱化因过分强调对称而有可能导致的刻板印象，成功地为这座庄严的城市增添了意外的愉悦之感。初次造访北京城的游客穿过两侧建筑林立的街道时，突然走到了一个桥头，与他不期而遇的，是一片河岸蜿蜒的广阔水域，以及水域当中小岛斜坡上成片的绿荫。他会驻足或漫步在有着精雕细刻的汉白玉栏杆的小桥上，欣赏着如梦如幻仙境般的亭台楼阁，间或怀疑自己是否真的置身于聚居着三百多万市井居民的凡尘闹市当中。

古都北京还有一项无形的、不容忽视的成就，那就是最先在 600 年前建成的排水系统。数世纪来逐渐建成的老北京城的排水系统总长为三百多公里，近几十年来部分已经坍塌，但仍有两百多公里的管道在继续发挥作用。解放后，人民政府排干沟渠中的废水并修缮了依旧可用部分，如今它已成为新排水系统中不可或缺的重要组成部分。

It must be pointed out here that the entire city of Peking was planned with the emperor's palace—the Forbidden City—as the dominant feature occupying a vast area in the center of the city, surrounded by a massive wall and a moat. It solved excellently the problem of guarding the safety of the emperor, but today it stands an insoluble problem in a modern city as an obstacle to traffic.

这里必须说明的一点是，整个北京城的规划基于一点，即以皇宫紫禁城为中心，它在城中央占据了很大面积，其外围是宏伟的城墙和护城河。这一设计曾成功解决了护卫皇帝安全的问题，但如今却成为现代城市中堵塞交通的难题。

Ⓓ Smaller Cities and Towns

For thousands of years, a city, regardless of its size, was seldom built without a wall. Whenever the topography permits, the city was laid out either square or rectangular, with chessboard-like road systems. But in the mountainous regions, cities were always planned and built in conformity to the terrain.

❹ 小城镇

中国数千年来，凡是城市，不论大小如何几乎都筑墙而建。只要地形允许，城市格局非方则长，街道格网状分布。但是在山区，城市通常则要根据地形地势规划建造。

IV. ARCHITECTURE OF DOMESTIC AND PUBLIC BUILDINGS

Ⓐ The Emperor's Palaces, Peking

The Emperor's Palaces, an enormous ensemble surrounded by a massive wall, called the Purple Forbidden City, are the nucleus around which the entire city of Peking was planned. The Forbidden City has within its enclosure numerous ensembles with a total of several hundred buildings, including halls of audience, offices for government administration, secretariats, living quarters for the emperor and his enormous family, living quarters for the army of courtiers and court ladies, kitchens, stables and other service quarters for the entire court. There are also in the precinct the emperor's private Buddhist chapel, libraries, art galleries and gardens. All these buildings for different purposes are arranged in numerous ensembles, each consisted of several courtyards. Almost every building is roofed with yellow glazed tiles. The walls are all painted red and the shaded portions under the eaves of the buildings are decorated with painted patterns in blue, green and gold. Halls and pavilions of importance, as a rule, are elevated on top of white marble terraces which are arranged into one or three tiers according to the importance of the building. Each ensemble in the Forbidden City is composed with one axis, and, as mentioned before, little attention is paid to the axes of adjacent ensembles.

肆 民用建筑与公共建筑

❶ 紫禁城——北京城的皇宫

巍峨高墙之内的皇家宫殿群，被称为“紫禁城”，也是整个北京城规划的核心。城内有数百座建筑，包括征召臣工觐见的大殿、奏事议政处、内廷机要用房、皇帝本人及皇室的寝宫、侍臣宫女的住所、御膳房、牲口厩以及宫廷里其他杂役的居住区域。城内还设有皇帝的专用佛堂、书房、雅玩收藏室以及御花园。这些功能不一的建筑都自成一体，每个建筑群由几个庭院构成。几乎所有建筑的屋顶都铺着黄色的琉璃瓦；城墙都刷成朱红色，檐下部分则以金黄、翠绿及碧蓝色的图案装饰。凡是重要的大殿和楼阁，通常都要建在汉白玉台阶之上。至于台阶的数目，通常是一层或三层，根据建筑的重要性而定。紫禁城中，各宫殿群均由一条中轴线贯通；但是正如此前提及，不太注意相邻宫殿群的轴线之间的关联关系。

1. Two Groups of Three Big Halls

On the principal axis of the Forbidden City are rhythmically placed in a string a double "triads" of monumental buildings, popularly known as the "Front Three Big Halls" and the "Rear Three Big Halls." Each of the "triad" consists of one rectangular hall in the front, a square hall in the middle and another, but smaller, rectangular hall at the rear. The rear "triad" is a repetition of the front "triad" in a reduced size. Both these "triads" each as a group, is raised on a marble terrace of three tiers and surrounded by galleries, pavilions, etc. and preceded in the forefront by a monumental gateway.

The Taihe Dian or Hall of Supreme Harmony is the principal hall of audience in the palaces and focal point of the whole Forbidden City. With its six rows of twelve columns each, forming a hypostyle hall eleven bays in length and five in depth, double-eaved and hip-roofed, it is the largest single building of its kind in China. The present structure dates back no farther than 1697, being the substitute for the one destroyed by a fire in 1679. The seventy-two columns arranged in monotonous regularity, seemingly showing not much ingenuity, are yet a most impressive sight. The structure stands on a low marble platform, which in turn is elevated by three tiers of balustraded terraces, profusely decorated with the most exquisite carvings.

Compared to buildings of earlier dates, as will be seen from some examples to be cited later in this discussion, the dougong of this gigantic hall is very small in proportion. It has lost its original function as a structural unit and degenerated into mere decorations. From a distance, the presence of dougong is hardly noticeable. The walls, columns, doors and windows are painted red, the dougong and the architraves in blue and green and accentuated with gold. The whole structure is crowned by a roof of glazed yellow tiles, glistening like gold in the bright sunshine against the blue sky of North China. Elevated on the white marble terraces that seem to vibrate with their exuberant carvings, the great hall is an apparition of grandeur, dignity and gorgeousness that, once seen, is never forgotten.

Behind the Taihe Dian is the Zhonghe Dian, the Hall of Middle Harmony. It is a square, small pavilion-like structure with a pyramidal roof. Further back is the Baohe Dian, the Hall of Retained Harmony, a structure slightly smaller than the Taihe Dian that concludes the Front Triad with an appropriate rhythmic accent.

Both Triads are places for the most solemn ceremonies: the Front Triad is for audiences of the greatest importance and the Rear Triad was used exclusively for imperial nuptial ceremonies. Thus the buildings were rarely used. Their function is almost purely symbolic.

1. 前后“三大殿” 沿紫禁城的中轴线上，有节奏地间隔分布着两组建筑群，即通常说的“前三大殿”和“后三大殿”，各由前面的长方形宫殿、中间的正方形宫殿及后面稍小的长方形宫殿构成。后三大殿是前三大殿的缩小复制版。这两组宫殿群都位于三层汉白玉高台之上，并由廊台亭榭环绕，前方则是气势恢弘的入口通道。

太和殿是宫殿群乃至整个紫禁城中朝觐的主殿。殿内 6 排柱子，每排 12 根，其殿面阔 11 间，进深 5 间，重檐庑殿顶，它是中国现存古建筑中规模最大的殿宇。这座宫殿在 1679 年的火灾中被焚毁，现存的宫殿修建年代不迟于 1697 年。殿内 72 根柱子排列整齐，乍看并无创意，整体上却蔚为壮观。整个建筑位于低矮的汉白玉基座之上，基座之下是三层精雕细琢的汉白玉栏杆。

与文后将提到的早期建筑相比，在雄伟的太和殿中，斗拱的尺寸极小。它已经失去原先的构造功能，而沦为纯粹的装饰品，从远处看几乎毫不起眼。殿墙、柱子、门窗被刷成朱红色，斗拱和额枋刷成碧蓝色和翠绿色，间以鲜艳的金黄色。[12] 整个建筑的屋顶铺饰着黄琉璃瓦，在北方艳阳蓝天的映衬下闪烁着熠熠金光。高踞在雕刻逼真生动的汉白玉基座之上的这座大殿，如此宏伟壮观、庄严华丽，真叫人过目难忘。

太和殿之后是中和殿。这是一座方形的亭状建筑，屋顶为攒尖形。再后方是保和殿，只比太和殿略小。这三者生动而有韵律地构成了前一组的三大殿。

前后三大殿是普天之下最庄重的礼仪之地：最重要的朝会在前三大殿举行，后三大殿则在操办皇家婚礼时方才启用。因而，它们鲜有机会使用，功能几乎只是象征性的。

2. Other Groups in the Forbidden City

To the left and right, or east and west, of the two Triads of ceremonial halls are numerous smaller ensembles within the confines of the Forbidden City. Consisted of several courtyards and surrounded by high walls, each of such an ensemble is a separate unit by itself. Such walled ensembles are "apartments" for the everyday living of members of the imperial family. To each person—an empress dowager, an empress, a concubine, a prince or a princess—or, rarely, to two or three persons is assigned such an "apartment." Such arrangements reflect most vividly the demand imposed by the rules in court life for the highest degree of exclusiveness or isolation, not only with the outside world of common people, but even from each other of the family. The impression one gets today from these luxurious "apartments" is that they were once upon a time nothing but beautiful, gilded "cells" for the life-term imprisonment of those unfortunate blue-blooded "inmates."

Ⓑ Dwelling of the People

The palaces in Peking are by no means the norm exemplifying the dwelling houses of the great mass of people. In a classed society, needless to say, the best part of the working people's labor is robbed and enjoyed by the ruling-exploiting class. So, aside from the imperial palaces, outstanding buildings in the towns and countries were usually those of the landlords, officials and well-to-do. As a rule, these dwellings are also composed of courtyards and surrounded by walls. But in different localities, under different natural conditions and social requirements as well as possibilities in technical and material supplies, great variation is found. But in the countries, especially in South China, the "orthodox" plan arrangement of courtyards and symmetry is not so strictly followed. Irregularity in planning is found everywhere. The construction also shows tendencies towards lightness.

In Peking, the average dwelling house is planned with one or several courtyards, with buildings on three or four sides. The construction is usually in strict accordance with the standards set by the Ministry of Construction in the eighteenth century. The buildings forming the quadrangle are detached from each other and so are usually arranged that they do not obstruct each other's view or sunshine. Thus the courtyards also function as very pleasant "outdoor living rooms."

2. 紫禁城里的其他建筑群 在前后三大殿的东西两侧，分别是紫禁城里众多的小型宫殿群。每组宫殿都自成一体，各由几个庭院构成，并被高墙环绕。这些高墙之内的宫殿是皇室成员的寝宫。皇太后、皇后、嫔妃、皇子或公主都独居一间，偶尔也有两三位皇室成员共用一处的情况。这种布局安排，生动地反映了宫廷生活准则中对最高级别的特权亦或说隔离的需要，不仅体现了皇家同外界隔绝，还体现了皇亲之间的相互孤立。如今，人们从这些奢华的寝宫看出，它们历史上只是漂亮豪华的、终身禁锢着不幸有着皇家血统之人的“金丝鸟笼”。

❷ 百姓居所

北京城内普通大众的居所与宫殿却差之千里。在阶级社会里，劳动人民的成果无疑被统治阶级、剥削阶级掠夺和享用了。因此，除帝王宫殿之外，城里乡间耀眼的建筑通常也是那些地主、官僚及富豪的宅第。通常，这些建筑也由数个庭院构成，并被高墙环绕。但由于位于不同的地点，自然条件、社会要求及工艺和材料的限制，建筑格局上有很大的差异。但在农村，尤其是南方，正统的庭院和对称规划格局并没有得到严格遵守。不规则的构造到处可见，而营造也倾向于简洁轻巧的风格。

北京城里的普通民居包含一个或几个院落，周围三面或四面建有房屋。营造通常都严格依据了 18 世纪内务府内工部（后改称营造司）的规定。构成四合院的各房屋互不相连，所以通常互不遮挡视线或采光。因此，院子也担当起了宜人的“露天客厅”的作用。

In the towns and countries, less attention is paid to the formal arrangement of the buildings and to the size and shape of the courtyards. In North China, where the rainy season is short, buildings in the same ensemble are, as a rule, detached from each other like those in Peking. But in the rainy south, very often the buildings on all three or four sides of the courtyard are joined up into a continuous whole, or, when detached, connected with each other by verandas. An old residence in Shanghai is typical of this kind of arrangement.

In the North China plain, dwellings are usually only one story in height. But in certain places in the south and southwestern provinces, houses of two or three stories are quite common. The mansion of a former official in Yungding, Fujian Province is an ensemble composed of buildings of different story heights. In the Province of Yunnan, as in the typical residence of Kunming, the two story height is the norm. In the latter case, the plan of the house is usually arranged into a very compact square, leaving a small courtyard in the center, while the exterior is treated with rather forbidding walls relieved with a few small windows.

It is in the farm houses in South China that one finds the highest degree of flexibility in planning. One excellent example is the former home of Comrade Mao Zedong in Xiangtan, Hunan Province. The house is located at the foot of a gentle hill, facing a pond in front. The living quarters is in the form of an asymmetrical "U," part of it two stories in height and tile-roofed, while one leg of the "U" is lower and thatch-roofed. Adjacent to the other leg is a service yard in which are located the flour mill, cow barn, pig style, etc. It is to be noticed that here the enclosed courtyard idea is completely discarded. There is neither the quadrangle nor the forbidding walls. The house is comfortably in harmony with nature and presents an appearance of cozy picturesqueness. Farm houses of this character are quite common in the regions south of the Yangzi River.

Ⓒ Cave Dwellings

In the loess districts in North China, especially at places where the terrain is worn by nature into steep ravines, cave dwelling is quite common. The caves are usually dug horizontally into the wall or cliff of the loess like a tunnel. The interior is vaulted with brick masonry and the open end is closed by a wall with a door and a window. Cave dwellings have the advantage of being warm in the winter and cool in the summer. A "house" or family may consist of several such caves, but they are usually placed parallel to each other without interior communications.

至于小城小市和乡间郊野的建筑，更加不注重房屋合乎规格的布局及庭院的大小与形状。华北地区的雨季较短，同一组群的房屋，和北京城里的一样，通常也是互不相连的。但在雨季较长的江南地区，院子里四周的或三面的房屋是连为一体的，或者即使隔开也由走廊相连。上海的老房子就是这种格局的典型。

华北平原的民居通常是单层的。但在华南或西南诸省，却常见两三层的房子。福建省永定某位官员的府邸是由数座层高不同的房屋构成的客家土楼。至于云南典型的民居，以昆明为例，则以两层楼最为常见。其构造整体为紧凑的正方形，中间是天井，而外围则是仅有几扇小窗的高墙。

中国南方的农家院设计体现了建筑规划中最大程度的灵活性。一个典型例子便是毛泽东同志在湖南湘潭的故居。它位于起伏和缓的小山脚下，并面朝池塘。居住房屋呈非对称的马鞍型，一侧为两层的瓦顶楼，而另一侧则为低矮的茅草屋。楼房旁边是个农家场院，里面有磨房、牛栏、猪圈等。值得注意的是，庭院围合的思想在这里完全没有体现出来，既不用四合院的形式，又没有森严的高墙环绕。整个房屋与自然非常和谐，展现出温馨生动的场景。这种类型的农家院在江南非常普遍。

❸ 窑洞

在华北的黄土高原地区，尤其是地表被侵蚀成险壑的沟谷之处，窑洞便很常见。窑洞通常水平打入黄土崖壁中，有如隧道。内部用砖石砌成拱顶，出入口的那堵墙有门有窗。窑洞有冬暖夏凉的好处。一家可由几个这样的窑洞构成，但通常窑洞并排，之间并不打通相连。

V. RELIGIOUS ARCHITECTURE

Cave Temples

The earliest remains of Buddhist architecture existing in China today are the cave temples. Unquestionably the conception was imported from India, having its prototypes in Karli, Ajanta and elsewhere in India. Although rock-cut tombs were already hewn during the Han Dynasty, possibly shortly after the beginning of the Christian era, and some of them given architectural treatment, nevertheless they were used exclusively for the dead. Although cave dwellings, like those just mentioned above, undoubtedly were in use even before the hewing of the rock-cut tombs, yet they made no pretension for monumentality. It was not until the arrival of the Indian idea that the cave ascended to architectural prominence.

In the middle of the fourth century AD, Buddhist believers started hewing caves as places for worship, and the practice was continued till the Ming Dynasty (1368–1644). The high tide was reached during the Northern Wei, Northern Qi, Sui and Tang Dynasties, from the middle of the fifth to the later part of the ninth centuries, assuming the scale of a nationwide "movement" of great popularity. It was only during the earlier years, approximately up till the middle of the seventh century, that the caves were treated architecturally. Gradually the idea of opening up a cave was replaced by that of carving niches on the rock cliffs and became mere objects of sculpture. Architecturally speaking, the most important caves are those at Dunhuang, Gansu Province, Yungang, Shanxi Province, the Maiji Mountains, Tianshui, Gansu Province, Tianlong Shan, Taiyuan, Shanxi Province and Xiangtang Shan, Cixian, Hebei Province.

In most of these caves, with the exception of the last mentioned, the architectural treatment show surprisingly little influence form India and the architecture is essentially Chinese. The only noticeable indications of foreign influence are the concept of the caves itself and the Greco-Buddhist motifs in the ornaments, such as the acanthus leaf, the egg-and-dart, the swastika, the garland, the bead, etc. These motifs have enriched, and have since taken their permanent positions in, the vocabulary of Chinese ornamental motifs.

The architecture of these caves may be studied from two aspects: firstly, the caves themselves, including the architectural treatment of the exterior and interior; and, secondly, contemporary timber and masonry architecture depicted in the reliefs decorating the walls of the caves. Among the latter are depicted numerous halls and pagodas, replicas of the structures that once rose in great numbers all over the plains and hills of North and Central China.

伍 宗教建筑

佛窟

中国如今尚存的最早佛教建筑是佛窟。这种理念当然是从印度引进的，其原型如印度的卡尔利、阿旃陀及其他处的佛窟。汉朝时，可能是公元纪年开始后不久，已有石刻的墓穴，其中一些也有人工营造处理的痕迹，但都是为逝者而建。如前所提，尽管窑洞在石刻墓穴出现之前就已存在了，但当时却没有张扬。直到印度佛教的思想传入之后，石窟才上升到建筑的高度。

4 世纪中期，佛教徒开始为宗教信仰而开凿洞窟，这一举措一直延续到明朝（公元 1368—1644 年）；从 5 世纪中叶至 9 世纪末，即在北魏、北齐、隋朝以及唐朝等朝代达到高潮，在全国掀起了大规模的信佛造佛“运动”。但也只是在约至 7 世纪中期之前的早期，洞窟的建筑风格才有所讲究。之后，在崖壁上雕刻的佛龛逐渐取代了向内开凿的洞窟，并发展成为纯粹的雕塑的创作对象。从建筑角度上讲，最重要的石窟是甘肃省的敦煌石窟、山西省的云冈石窟、甘肃天水的麦积山石窟、山西太原的天龙山石窟以及河北磁县的响堂山石窟。

除上段提到的最后一个响堂山石窟之外，这些石窟的建筑风格很少体现印度的影响，而主要是中国风格。唯一明显受到外国影响的标志，便是石窟的概念本身以及饰品中的希腊—佛教图案，例如莨苕叶纹饰、卵锚饰、万字饰、花环纹饰、串珠纹饰等。这些图案丰富了中国装饰图案的语汇，并自此占据了永久性的地位。

这些石窟的建筑手法，可从两方面加以研究：首先是石窟本身，包括外部和内部的建筑处理；其次是装饰石窟墙体用的浮雕所描绘的同时期的木材及石材建筑。后者包括所绘大殿和佛塔，摹仿了曾经风靡于华北平原和华中山区的建筑风格。

These caves have preserved in stone faithful copies of the wooden architecture of their time. Among the salient characteristics we notice that the columns in most cases are octagonal, with capitals in the shape of a dou (the block in the dougong). Above the capital is placed the architrave, which, in turn, is to receive the principal dou of the set of dougong. This arrangement was in later ages modified by mortising the architrave directly onto the upper end of the column, thus making the dou on the column to function at the same time as the principal dou of the set of dougong.

In the architectural treatment of these caves, the element most informative to posterity is the presentation of the timber construction in stone carving. Here we notice that the dougong is ever the dominant decorative feature. The aesthetic potentialities of the structural system were by this time so much...

这些石窟忠实地保留了当时的木质建筑的风格。我们注意到的最明显的特点，便是柱头呈斗状的八边形立柱的运用。在柱头之上是过梁，用来承托斗拱中的主斗。这一组配方式后来经过修改，用榫将过梁与柱头直接联系起来。这样，柱头的斗状部分就类似于斗拱中斗的构件而且发挥着同样的作用。

这些石窟的建筑处理对后世最大的意义，在于以石雕形式再现了木结构建筑的风格。我们在此注意到，斗拱始终主要起着装饰性的作用。这一构件体系此时已充分显示出其美学蕴涵

（郑文博 任小玫 译 曾俊伟 校）

A Han Terracotta Model of a Three-story House

一个汉代的三层楼陶制明器[1]

[年份不详]

Like most people of the ancient civilizations, the Chinese believed in life after death. He did not think that the soul would come back to the same body, as the Egyptians, but that the deceased was to live in another world where the daily life of this world would be led as usual. He would have to be living in a house, wearing clothes and eating the same grain as he did in his life of this side, and, in an important personage, he would be needing the service and attendance of servants.

The practice of human sacrifice was therefore not uncommon with the early Chinese. But the practice was apparently abandoned later, and, in its place, clay or wooden figures were used to accompany the dead; and, with the figures, undoubtedly all kinds of utensils necessary for a comfortable living.

Even as late as the seventh century BC, we find in *Cho Chuan,* the chronology of the state of Lu, recording the funeral of Chin Mu-kung: "Jen-hao, Court of Chin, died. The three sons of the Tze-chu family, Yen-hsi, Chung-hsing and Tsen-hu, were sacrificed as his attendants. All three were geniuses of Chin. The people were mournful over their death, and composed *The Poem of Huang-niao* (*Yellow Bird*):

'If only their lives could be restored,
Let every man have hundred bodies.
...'"

About seventy years after this song was sung, Confucius was born (551 BC). This master's doctrines never touched anything outside of this world or this life. He evaded all questions concerning the mysterious, such as ghosts, gods, death, etc. His mention of God has always been the vague Shang-ti or T'ien-ti. When he was asked on the question of spirits, his answers was "respect and keep away from them." One of his pupils asked about death, he again cunningly replied, "Not knowing life, what do I know of death?"

During the century after Confucius the Middle Kingdom was producing an amazing number of thinkers. And about the fifth generation after him was Mencius, whom the Sung scholars considered the orthodox of the Confucian school. Among the numerous quotations in *Mencius* is this isolated utterance of a curse: "May the originator of Yung (tomb figures) be forever void of descendants!" which is the greatest of the three infilialities. The cause of this curse is not explained, but it must be either that it was too mysterious and superstitious which was not Confucius' taste to practice, or that the consequent extravagance or its use was in conflict with Mencius' economic principles.

中国人和古代文明中的大多数人一样，也相信人死后有灵魂。他们不像埃及人那样，认为灵魂还会回到原有身体里，而是认为死者会生活在另一世界，那里的日常生活仍同在世时一样。他将会生活在一所住宅里，穿衣、吃饭一如生前，并且他如果是位重要人物，还需要照顾和陪侍的奴仆。

因此，在中国早期，以活人殉葬的做法并不少见。但是这种做法后来明显是废止了，而是代之以泥制或木制的人俑来陪伴死者，同人俑一起当然还有为生活舒适的各种必要用品。

甚至晚至公元前 7 世纪时，我们在鲁国的编年体史书《左传》中，还读到秦穆公葬仪的记载，说到秦穆公任好亡，子车氏三子——奄息、仲行、针虎——皆随而殉葬。这三个人都是秦国的良臣，时人感伤其死，乃制《黄鸟》诗篇，其中说：

"如可赎兮，人百其身。……"

这诗篇唱出后大约七十年，孔子诞生了（公元前551年），这位导师的学说，从未触及现世和今生以外的任何事物。他回避全部神秘的问题，如鬼、神、死亡等等。他提到神的时候，总是模糊的上帝或天帝。当被问到神鬼问题时，他的回答是："敬鬼神而远之。"他的一位弟子问到死亡问题，他又一次巧妙地回答说："未知生，焉知死？"

在孔子之后的世纪中，中国产生了大批的思想家。而孔子后大概经过五代人，出现了孟子，他被宋代学者尊为儒家的正宗传人。在《孟子》书中大量的孟子语录里，有这么一句孤立的咒语，即："始作俑（陪葬偶人）者，其无后乎？"而"无后"居三大不孝之首。这个诅咒的理由没有解释，但它很可能或是过于神秘和迷信，而与孔子的行事风格不合；或是使用过分与奢侈，而与孟子的节俭原则相背。

However, this art, which later flourished to its height during the T'ang Dynasty, was already widely practiced during the early half of the fourth century BC. Although we find no positive record of its practice before Mencius' time, we may with fair justification date it considerably back, even earlier than Chin Mu-kung.

In spite of its popularity, the late Chou tomb utensils, pottery or wood, is yet little known to us. But of the next epoch—the Han—various kinds of funeral accompaniments had been unearthed and a great number of them distributed among these object are some small terracotta models of houses.

These models of houses are not uncommon in American museums. They represent from pig pens to palaces. Among these the new acquisition of the Fogg Museum of Harvard University is indeed a valuable example. Aesthetically it is not a masterpiece, but is of great importance to a student of architectural archaeology.

It is a three-story house or palace, measuring approximately 39½ inches in height. The terracotta is of a reddish buff color baked from the huang tu (yellow earth) that is common in North China. Each story is baked separately with the balcony or roof over it. Thus, the lower-story and the second-story balcony form one section; the second-story and the third-story balcony another; and the third with the roof, another. It was glazed with a coat of green glaze, but now only a few flakes of silver gray glaze are visible. The original color is still recognizable where parts overhang allowing the dripping glaze to collect thick—such as the lower side of the tile ends. The whole house is built up from flat "boards" of clay, of a uniform thickness of approximately 3/8 of an inch, put together at angles. The joints are distinctly visible, and there is not a single bent or curved surface throughout. Where the short flight of steps is attached to the wall, we can still find traces of the scratched surfaces that were made to hole the two pieces securely together. The bracket and the corbels that support them seem to have been produced from molds. The two balconies are made from flat pieces with the open work cut out. The floors of the second and third stories or rather, in our case, the tops of the two lower sections have each a round hole about two inches in diameter, probably for the convenience of the handling of the potter. The round windows on the side of each floor may be explained as an outlet for the hot air in the process of baking, and to prevent the thing from bursting in the kiln. The front window lattice on the second floor is likewise a cut-out piece, but the potter here failed as a draughtsman to lay out the crossing of laths neatly. The grille-like front of the box window on the third floor is produced by a mold.

然而，这种在唐代以后极为盛行的艺术，无论如何在公元前 4 世纪上半叶已经广为使用了。虽然我们尚未发现在孟子以前其被使用的确切记载，我们仍可以有充分理由推前其年代，甚至早于秦穆公。

尽管它早已普及，晚周墓穴中的陶制或木制的随葬品，我们迄今仍知之不多。但是属于下一个朝代——汉代的各式各样的随葬品已经出土，并且其中大量明器等已经散布在欧洲和美国的博物馆里了。其中最令人感兴趣的是一些陶制的房屋小模型。

这些房屋的模型（明器）在美国的博物馆中并不少见，从猪圈到宫室都有所体现。其中哈佛大学福格博物馆的新藏品确实是一件有价值的例子。从美学上说，它或许不是杰作，但是对于一位建筑考古的学者来说，则是非常重要的。

它是一座三层的住宅或宫室，高约 39 又 1/2 英寸。陶器是用中国北方普通的黄土烧成的，呈偏红的暗黄色。每一层楼都是连带着上面的阳台或屋顶一起分别烧成的。因此，底层和二层的阳台形成一部分；二层和三层的阳台是另一部分；三层带着屋顶是又一部分。它原涂有绿釉，但现在只有很少的银灰色残片尚能见到。而在陶器的釉子流淌聚集的部位，如瓦片的最底处，仍能辨认出原来的颜色。整个住宅是用平的泥“板”制成的，泥板的平均厚度约 3/8 英寸，将其以各种角度合在一起。结合处清晰可见，而且任何地方都没有一个折弯或曲面。在台阶与墙体的接触处，我们仍能发现刮平表面的痕迹，那是为了使两者牢固结合。托架和支承它的托臂好像是用模子制成的。两个阳台是用平片做成并切出栏杆孔眼。第二、三层的楼板，更确切说在我们这里是两个下面组件的顶部，各有一个约两英寸直径的圆孔，可能是为了陶工操作的方便。每层楼两侧的圆窗，可以解释为在烧制过程中的热气出口，以避免器物在窑内爆裂。二层楼前窗的网格也是切出来的，但是陶工在这里却没能像绘图员那样使交叉的窗棂排列匀整。三层正面的格栅似的盒窗是用模子制出的。

House models like this must have been produced in the great demand of the surviving sons and daughters who were anxious to provide their parents with a comfortable lodging in the other world.

Architecturally it is of great significance. Of Han Dynasty architecture, no actual edifice has come down to our time, and a future discovery is not probable. In the few reliefs in the Wu Family Tombs near Chiahsiang Hsien, Shantung Province, palaces of one, two, or even three stories were represented. But its drawing can give only a very vague idea of the appearance of the actual building. The other source of information is the numerous stone piers that form the monumental gateways leading to the roads of spirits of the Han tombs. These sculptural pieces almost invariably have each an elaborately carved top in the form of a cornice with a roof over it. It is an imitation of wooden structure and gives a fairly good idea of the system of construction. But the lower portion is a mere tablet, and tells nothing about the habitable part of a house.

The third source, in plastic form, is the clay models that were unearthed. Whether these houses were meant for the deceased to live in the other world or not is uncertain, but outwardly they are fairly good representations of the domestic architecture of its period.

This one in the Fogg Museum has a unique combination of a number of the architectural elements. We may without much doubt assume that there is not more than one room in each story. The first floor, as we may call it, has two doorways in the front. These two doorways open out to a small porch landing which is approached by a short flight of steps running parallel to the front facade. The spirit of the deceased, who is to go in and out of these doorways by way of this porch is prevented from falling over it by a balustrade on two sides. This balustrade on this small landing, as well as the two larger balconies on the two upper floors, distinctly shows its wood structure. It consists, in its scheme, of three horizontals—a hand rail, a base rail, and an intermediate piece—supported by studs at certain intervals. Where the joints occur, nail heads are shown in the form of decorative metal buttons. Where the balustrade of the landing meets the steps, it is ingeniously eased off in a downward curve, as can be seen in the illustration. This interesting way of ending railing is represented also in the Han model house in the Museum of the University of Pennsylvania. It probably was a common treatment of the subject by the architects in those days. At this point on the railing is a peculiar piece of horizontal board of plank, apparently nailed down in the middle on top of the railing. It may be a piece supposed to be pivoted on this rail like a turn-stile, and when turned over, could be locked, so that the advance of any intruding ghosts might be barred.

这种房屋模型想必是为满足孝子贤孙们想给先人提供舒适阴宅的急切愿望而生产的。

在建筑学上，它极有意义。关于汉代建筑，没有真正的大型建筑物保存至今，并且未来的发现也不大可能。在山东省嘉祥县附近武氏祠的少数浮雕中，刻画了单层、双层甚至三层的宫室，但这种描绘只能给予实际建筑形象以非常模糊的概念。另外的信息来源是汉墓神道前形成纪念性入口的石阙。这些雕刻的石阙几乎都有带屋顶檐口形式的精心雕刻的顶部，是木结构的仿制品，而且相当准确地表达出结构系统。但是下面的部分则只不过是块平板，完全没有表现出住宅的使用部分。

第三个在造型上的来源，则是出土的陶制模型（明器）。这些住宅是否原本是为死者准备的在阴间的生活之处虽然难以肯定，但是从外观上，它们却是该时代居住建筑的极好表现。

福格博物馆的这个明器，是许多建筑要素的独特组合器。我们可以不用过多怀疑地设想：它每层至多只有一个房间。我们称之为首层处，前面有两个出入口。这两个出入口开向一座小的门廊平台，从平行于前立面的几步台阶可以通至其上。自这个门廊出入的死者鬼魂，由两面的扶手栏杆保护着，以防其跌落。小平台的栏杆也像上边两层较大的阳台一样，明显是模仿木结构的。它的组成包括三条水平带——一扶手、一基座以及一中间部分——由一定间隔的立柱支承。当出现结合点处，则有表现装饰性金属圆纽形状的钉头。在平台扶手栏杆到台阶处时，巧妙地变成向下的曲线，如插图中可以看到的（见后）。这种结束扶手的有趣方法，也同样表现在宾夕法尼亚大学博物馆所藏的汉代明器上。这大概是当时建筑师们的一般处理方法。在扶手的这个点上是一块特殊的水平板，表面上钉在扶手顶部的中间。它可能是可以在扶手上旋转的一块板，像一个转梃，转动后能将平台锁上，将任何闯入的恶鬼拒之门外。

The house itself is shown in an indication of, if we may call it, "half timber construction," that is, a framework of uprights and lintel is first constructed, and the wall spaces between are filled in with solid masonry or merely plaster on lath. The latter case is still commonly practiced in Japan today, and this model is undoubtedly the miniature of a near ancestor of the architectural forms which were introduced to the Islands at the Suiko period.

The two doorways leading to the porch are expressed structurally with jambs on the sides and a common lintel over head. One of them is left ajar, and the other closed. The closed door is well rendered by a few parallel vertical lines suggesting a wood texture. The open door is slightly lower than the closed one, probably due to the inaccuracy of the potter.

The two side walls have each a round hole like a bull's eye window. The same are also found on the two upper stories. It is possible to explain it as an escape for hot air to prevent the house from bursting during the process of baking. But they show a very consistent architectural scheme not to be overlooked.

On the front wall are two projecting corbels, flanking the two doors. On them are the two brackets which support the second floor balcony. One of these corbels is cleverly merged with the narrow side of the balustrade of the landing. The precise form of these brackets is not yet known to us. They are certainly not the same thing that is commonly seen in Chinese and Japanese architecture, both ancient and modern. It is an upright supporting a horizontal on top, but to assure its rigidity, another horizontal is put across the upright at a little distance down, and the ends of the horizontals are held in place by means of some almond shaped "nuts." The two horizontals are decorated with a simple panel, more likely meant to be painted on, and the short stub between them has a monster's mask with a large ring in its mouth. The short piece supporting the lower horizontal is decorated with a leaf form. These brackets were made from a mold.

Immediately above these brackets is the second-floor balcony, showing the same structural detail as the smaller one underneath; but it is carried around and it overhangs the front and the sides of the house.

It has three bays in front and the ends are strengthened by an extra post, with the intermediate horizontal stopping only at the inner post. Nail heads in form of bosses are used at joints, and, on the base rail, on axis of the bays. This balcony, the ones above and beneath it, as well as the timbers framed in the walls of the first floor, are all decorated with lines crossing each other to make a diamond shape, which is characteristic of many other decorated sculptures of the Han Dynasties.

这个住宅本身表现的样式，我们或可称之为“半木构架”——即先造起由立柱和梁组成的框架，再将其间的墙体部位以实砌体或板条抹灰填充。后面这种作法，在今天的日本仍然普遍实践着，而这个明器无疑是近于初始形式的建筑小模型，该种建筑形式是在推古时期被日本岛国引进的。

通向门廊的两个门，从结构上表现出两边有门框和顶上有一通梁。一个门半开着，另一个关着。关着的门刻画入微，以几条平行的垂直线表现着本材质感。开着的门稍低于关着的门，这可能由于陶工做得不够精确。

两侧墙上各有一个像圆窗似的洞口。同样在上面两层也有。它可能解释为热气出口，以防模型在焙烧的过程中爆裂。但是它们也显示出一种不应忽视的非常协调的建筑设计。

在正面墙上，双门的两旁是两个突出的托臂，其上是两个托架支承着二层阳台。托臂之一聪明地并入了平台扶手栏杆的短边。这些托架的精确形式我们尚不清楚。它们肯定与古代或现代的中国和日本一般见到的斗拱不是同样的东西。它是一根直立件顶上支承着一个水平件，但为了保证其刚性，又有另一水平件穿过垂直件放在稍下边，水平件尽端是用一些扁桃状的“坚果”来固定位置的。两个水平件以简单的镶板装饰，很像本应是上面涂色的，而在其间的短柱则有一个嘴里衔着大环的兽面。支承下面水平件的短件以叶形装饰。这些托架全用模子制成。

紧接在这些托架上的是二层阳台，同下面较小的平台一样表现着同样的结构细部；但是它是环绕房子四周的，并且悬挑在房子前面和边上。阳台在前面分成三个柱间，在端部则另有较粗的立柱加固，只是在内柱之间带有中间水平栏板。凸圆状的钉头用于连接点，在底横杆上和柱间轴线上。这个阳台，以及它上面和下面的阳台，同首层墙上的框架木材一样，都用互交成菱形的线装饰，它是汉代许多装饰性雕刻的特点。

The balustrades at the two ends of the building are left merely a smooth low wall, undecorated. The underside of the second-story balcony is decorated with a series of closely drawn parallel line suggesting the so-called combed line ornament.

There are still two riddles in this balcony which remain unsolved. First, the little extra boards at the corners of the railings, nailed down in the same manner as the "turn-stile" on the lower floor. An excuse for its presence is difficult to find. Second, the two lower corners of the balcony are smoothly sliced off. It is not likely to be a faithful reproduction of the structural detail, as the architects or carpenters of the Han would know well enough not to weaken an important joint. It is probably a potter's technicality. The balcony is much wider on the side than in front. The overhang is also braced at one end to the wall by a diagonal piece. The second-story eave receives the same treatment.

The second story is quite different from the first. There is no doorway on any wall in spite of the balcony around it. There is only a rectangular window on the front, the frame of which projects slightly from the wall surface. Diagonals crossing each other make this a latticed opening. The wood frame and the lattice are ornamented with lines. The ornamental nail heads also appear on the window frame.

The walls of this story have no indication of the timber frame. Two brackets like those of the lower floor project from the wall, at the corresponding position supporting a roof, instead of the balcony, which comes over the roof.

The roof is very interesting. It shows only the tiles. The rafters underneath them are innocently forgotten by the potter. The tiles are apparently similar to those of the orient today. The tubular ridges, the supposed to be concaved spaces between them, the double crested hips, all are precisely the same as those of today. The tile ends are decorated with a simple design of two concentric circles; the band between them is divided into four quadrangles with a little boss in each. Inside of the inner circle is a slightly larger boss. The potter made the tubular ridges too thin for the end design so that the jointing of the two makes a clumsy shape resembling a horse's hoof.

The third or top story has a balcony exactly like that of the second. It is the same in every detail—even the curious corner board on the railing and the sliced off lower corners.

House model, unglazed clay with polychrome, Han Dynasty (206 BC-221 AD), Fogg Museum at Harvard University. 哈佛大学福格博物馆藏汉明器

在建筑物两头的栏杆，则仅处于光溜无装饰的矮墙状态。二层阳台的底面以一系列刻画稠密的平行线加以装饰，使人想到所谓的齿纹饰。

这个阳台仍然有两个谜团没有解开：第一，附加的小板以首层栏杆上同样的方式钉在扶手角上，这难以找出其存在的理由。第二，阳台两个拐角的下边被整齐地切掉了。它不大可能是结构细部的忠实再现，因为汉代的建筑师或木工们也很清楚，不能削弱此重要节点。它大概是某位陶工的技术问题。侧面的阳台比正面的要宽得多。悬挑部分也由墙上伸出的斜撑加固。二层的挑檐也有同样的处理。

二层与首层完全不同。二层虽有阳台环绕，却在任何墙上全没有门。在正面上只有一个长方窗，其窗框稍稍突出于墙面。窗棂斜向交叉而成为斜条格窗。木窗框和斜条全用细线装饰。装饰性钉头也出现在窗框上。

这层墙壁并未表现出木框架的迹象。两个托架像下层一样突出于墙面，而在原阳台的位置上托起了屋檐，阳台则在屋檐的上面。

屋檐非常有趣。它只表现着屋瓦，下面的椽子则被陶工无辜地省略了。屋瓦显然与今天东方的那些类似。筒形的脊背、其间想象应是下凹的空间、双顶饰的斜脊，全部同今天的一模一样。瓦端头（瓦当）简单设计成两个同心圆来装饰，两圆之间分成四个四边形，每个中间有个小凸圆饰，而在内圆的中心则是稍大的凸圆饰。陶工的筒形瓦垄做得太浅了，因而贴上圆形瓦当后成了不规矩的马蹄形了。

第三层或顶层的阳台极像第二层的那样，每个细部完全相同——甚至扶手上奇特的角处板和被切掉的下边拐角。

This floor, too, is doorless, but it has two windows in front. One is a mere rectangular opening, the jambs of which are decorated with diamond cross lines. The other window has a curious cage masking the entire opening. It looks as if a box is put against the wall. The top is taken off, and the front is in the form of a grill or lattice. The enclosed space forms a protruded sill of considerable room. The sweet daughter of the house must have carefully caressed her delicate flowers planted in pots and placed on this sill, or else she must have leaned pensively over this high window meditating about some romantic Prince Charming that might one day come from a distant land to ask her father for her hand.

A pair of brackets is again placed at exactly the same position supporting the crowning roof. This one is not unlike the skirt-like roof dividing the two upper stories except that instead of carrying the balcony, the four sloping sides go up to meet in a ridge, which is in the form of a shallow crescent. The tubular ridges at the sides have no decorative tile ends, as on the second floor. The rear surface of the top roof is left simply plain, with a crude suggestion of the double crested hips. The Han potter, like some American architects of today, must have forgotten or purposely neglected the other three facades.

As a whole, the potter conceived the piece in terms of different architectural elements with no sense of scale whatsoever. The brackets are huge, and also the roof tiles. The balcony is much too narrow, and its railing is heavy. However, it is superfluous to criticize it from such a viewpoint. The innocence and naivety of this ancient craftsman is most entertaining.

The question of multi-story buildings may be of some interest. Although the trick of superposing one house over another was known to the ancient Chinese, the use of such for habitation is found only in a comparatively late date. Ch'in Shih-huang-ti's palace, the O-fang-kung is said to have a sitting capacity of ten thousand on the upper floor, and beneath it, a flag on a fifty-foot pole could be hoisted.

The chronology shows that the early Han emperors built quite a number of t'ai (towers), mainly for sporting or religious purpose. It is not until the great Han Wu-ti that the definite evidence of upper story living has been recorded. Not satisfied with merely a glorious long reign of over fifty years, he became desirous to find the elixir of life, and to get into communication with the immortals. Kung-shun Ch'ing the magician said that the immortals loved living in lo (house of more than one story), so a number of them were ordered to be constructed. Kung-shun Ch'ing was charged to live in them with all ceremonial apparatus to wait for the visit of the immortals.

这层也没有门，但正面有两个窗户。一个不过是一长方形的开口，窗框饰以斜交线。另一个窗户则用奇怪的笼子遮住了整个窗口。它看上去像是个箱子反扣在墙上。它的顶板已经去掉，而正面像网或格栅。闭合的空间形成一间相当大的突出的窗台。这所住宅里的可爱小姐，曾经一定细心抚弄她摆在这个窗台上的娇嫩盆花，或者心事重重地斜倚在窗边，默想着浪漫的白马王子，他可能有朝一日，自远方来请求她的父亲把女儿嫁给他。

再一次置于相同位置上的一对托架，支承着屋面。它与将上面两层隔开的裙状屋檐样子相似，只是不再支承阳台，而是四面坡屋面向上汇于一条微呈新月形的房脊上。侧面的瓦垄没有像二层的屋檐那样有端头瓦当。屋顶的后坡表面是没有装饰的，双顶饰的斜脊也做得粗糙。汉代的陶工，也像今天某些美国的建筑师一样，一定是忘掉或有意忽略其他三个立面了。

从整体看，陶工在构想这些不同的建筑组件时，毫无尺度比例的概念。托架巨大，屋瓦也是这样。阳台过于狭窄，而其扶手却极粗。然而，用这种观点去批评它未免太过分。这位古代匠师的天真和质朴是最有趣的。

多层建筑物的问题可能有点意思。虽然古代中国人已知将房屋叠加起来的手法，而将其用于住房仅发现在较晚时期。据说秦始皇的宫殿（阿房宫）“上可以坐万人，下可以建五丈旗”。

史书记载：汉朝初年的皇帝们曾建了许多台，主要为游乐或宗教目的。直到汉武帝，才有住楼上的确切记载。他不满足于五十多年的盛世王朝，开始渴望长生不老，并且得与诸神交往。方士公孙卿进言说，诸神喜欢住在多层的楼上，因此遵旨建成了许多楼房。皇帝命公孙卿住于楼上，备好全部礼器，静待众神造访。

The reliefs from the Wu family tombs show a number of two- or three-story buildings. Generally the first floor is for service; the second for men, and other social and business affairs, as feast scenes are often shown; and the third is most logically assigned to women, as the sexes had always been most carefully separated since the earliest time.

This model is important for its completeness in showing the architectural elements. Of special significance is the use of brackets, which is a unique feature of Chinese architecture. It must have originated back of history, far beyond the memory of the BC chroniclers.

Curious enough is that every house in the Han reliefs has columns, but none of our Han models has any trace of it. It is not a good excuse to say that the material is not fit for it, as we can see that house models with columns of later periods have been found. Our knowledge may have to stop here for the time being. Some future discoveries may help to throw more light on this, and many other problems. The secret remains always a secret until it is revealed.

武氏祠的浮雕上表现着许多二层或三层建筑物。一般讲，首层是作服务之用的；二层是为男人们提供的，并且是处理社会或其他事务之处，因为经常可见宴会情景；第三层最符合逻辑的是分配给妇女们，因为自古以来，男女从来就是严格分开的。

这个明器的重要性在于其表现建筑物各组成部分的完整性。尤其意义重大的是托架（斗拱）的使用，它是中国建筑中独有的特征。它肯定是大大早于有史书的时代所创始的。

十分奇怪的是：汉代浮雕中每个住宅都有柱子，但是在我们的汉代明器中却没有它的踪迹。如果说这种材料不宜于表现柱子，其理由似难成立，因为我们已经发现较晚时期的有柱子的明器。我们的理解目前仅止于此。某些未来的发现将可能帮助我们更多了解这个疑问以及其他许多问题。秘密在揭露之前总还是秘密。

（英若聪 译 程慕胜 校）

Two Liao Structures of Tu-lo Ssu, Chi Hsien

蓟县独乐寺观音阁山门考[1]

[1932]

1 Sketch of Tu-lo Ssu, Chi Hsien from *The Lo-yang Chia-lan Chi*.

蓟县独乐寺伽蓝配置略图

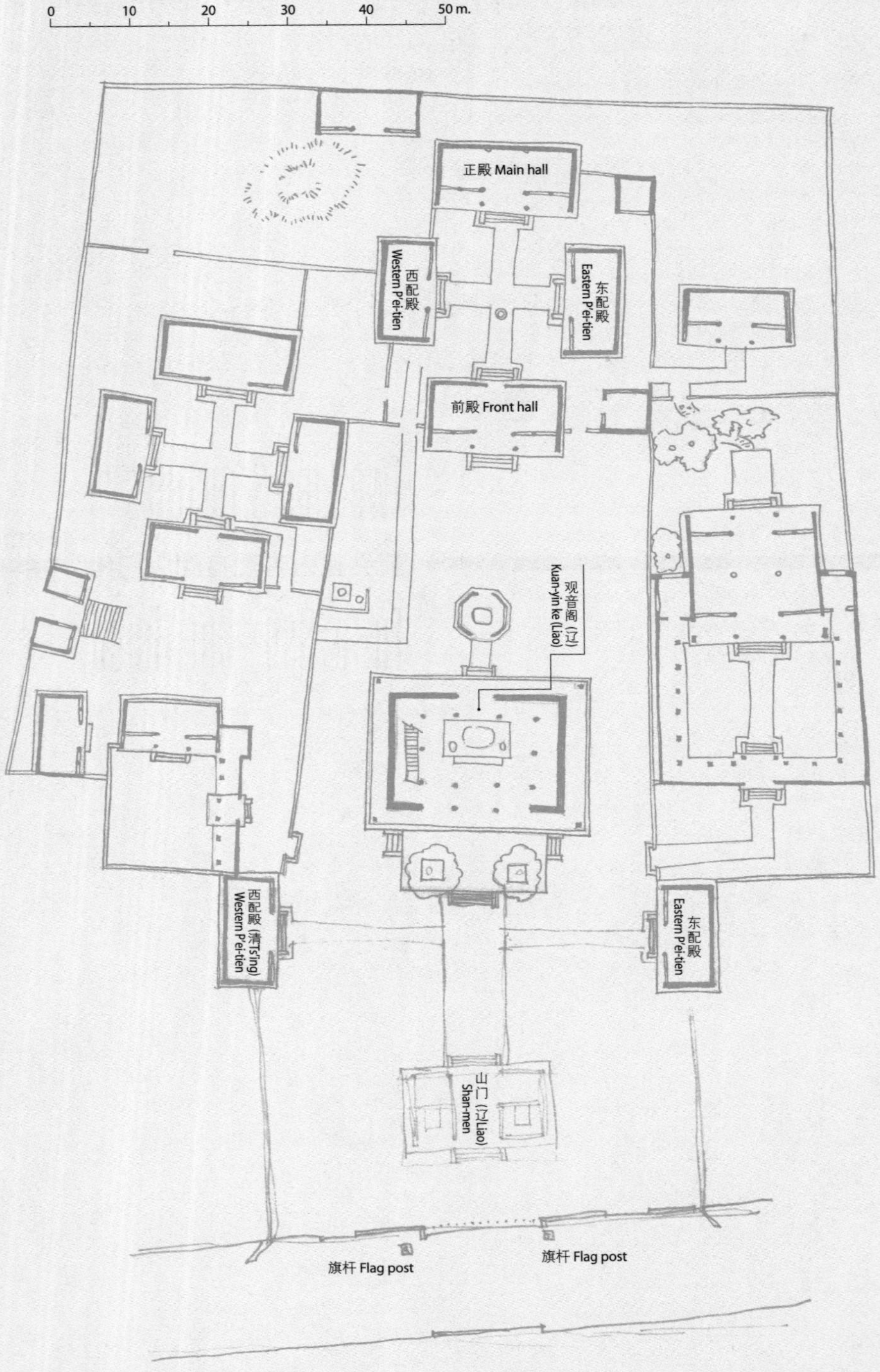

I. INTRODUCTION

Records and descriptions of ancient Chinese architecture are often found in the classics and essays such as *The Kao-kung-chi of Chow-li*[2], *The O-fang-kung Fu*[3], *The Liang-tu Fu, The Liang-ching Fu,*[4] and *The Lo-yang Chia-lan Chi*[5] (Figure 1). In these the palaces and temples of old are described most beautifully and often in exquisite meter, but the impression the reader obtains is merely a hazy picture of the grandeurs, the intricate construction and the elaborate ornaments of these structures. The Ming and Ts'ing Dynasties have handed down more records of old palaces, among which the *Yuan-ku-kung Yi-lu*[6], or *Recollections of the Old Yuan Palaces*, by Hsiao Hsun of the Ming Dynasty, is well known to Chinese scholars. Nevertheless, these records are no more than long lists of names of different buildings, with figures indicating their dimensions, and characters indicating their positions relative to the cardinal point.

壹 绪言

近代学者治学之道，首重证据，以实物为理论之后盾，俗谚所谓“百闻不如一见”，适合科学方法。艺术之鉴赏，就造形美术言，尤须重“见”。读跋千篇，不如得原画一瞥，义固至显。秉斯旨以研究建筑，始庶几得其门径。

我国古代建筑，征之文献，所见颇多，《周礼·考工记》、《阿房宫赋》、《两都赋》、《两京赋》，以至《洛阳伽蓝记》（图 1）等等，固记载详尽，然吾侪所得，则隐约之印象，及美丽之辞藻，调谐之音节耳。明清学者，虽有较专门之著述，如萧氏《元故宫遗录》，及类书中宫室建置之辑录，然亦不过无数殿宇名称，修广尺寸，及“东西南北”等字，以标示其位置，盖皆“闻”之属也。

2 Bronze statue of Veda. 韦驮铜像

To obtain knowledge of the actual appearance of the architecture of its structure through reading these records is as difficult as to try to recognize a person's face from a description. The study of ancient Chinese architecture, like all other plastic arts, must naturally be undertaken with the aid of actual specimens, and not merely through literature.

Wood has since time immemorial been the principal material used in Chinese buildings. It is used as a structural frame, and walls are filled in as "curtain walls." The system is identical with that of the reinforced concrete or steel frame systems of today. When wood is used to form the structural frame, its durability becomes the one factor that determines the length of life of the building. Unfortunately it is an impermanent material and thus a wooden edifice of ancient period is rare and therefore especially valuable. But, under favorable circumstances, wood can easily last over a thousand years or more. The Scientific Expedition to the Northwest that returned to Peiping in 1931, brought back from Chinese Turkestan numerous wooden chien, or thin sheets of wood, of the Han Dynasty, all in a remarkable state of preservation. As they are all over two thousand years old, they can testify to the durability of wood under certain circumstances.

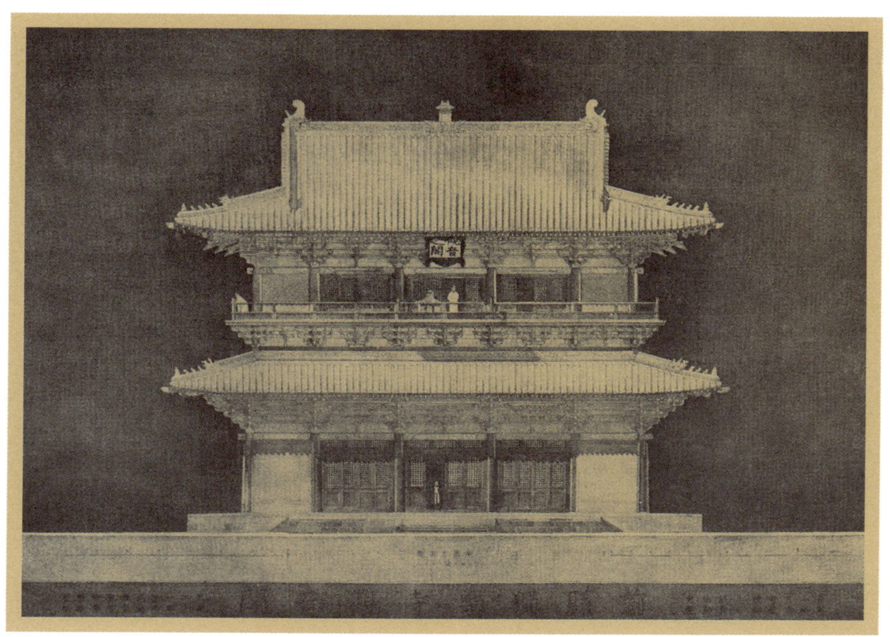

3 Facade of south of Kuan-yin Ke. 观音阁南面立面图

读者虽读破万卷，于建筑物之真正印象，绝不能有所得，犹熟诵《史记》“隆准而龙颜，美须髯，左股有七十二黑子”，遇刘邦于途，而不之识也。造形美术之研究，尤重斯旨，故研究古建筑，非作遗物之实地调查测绘不可。

我国建筑，向以木料为主要材料。其法以木为构架，辅以墙壁，如人身之有骨节，而附皮肉。其全部结构，遂成一种有机的结合。然木之为物，易朽易焚，于建筑材料中，归于“非永久材料”之列，较之铁石，其寿殊短；用为构架，一旦焚朽，则全部建筑，将一无所存，此古木建筑之所以罕而贵也。然若环境适宜，保护得法，则千余年寿命，固未尝为不可能。去岁西北科学考察团自新疆归来，得汉代木简无数，率皆两千年物，墨迹斑斓，纹质如新。固因沙漠干燥，得以保存至今；然亦足以证明木寿之长也。

4 Cross section of Kuan-yin Ke.

观音阁断面图

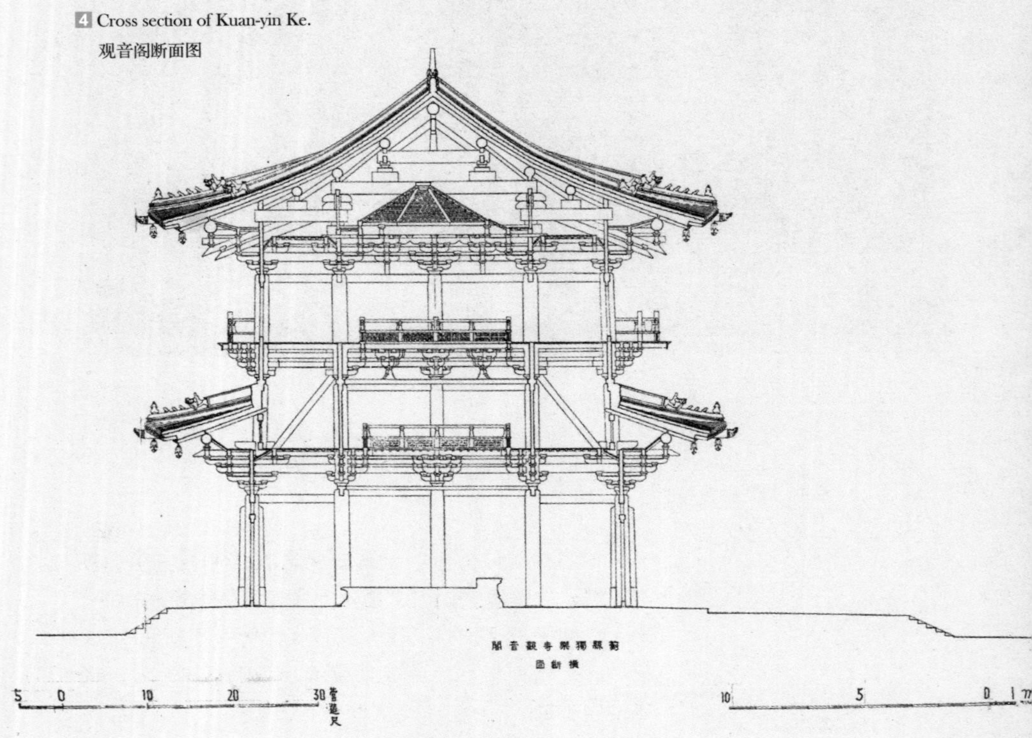

The oldest known examples of wooden architecture are the few Suiko (593–628 AD) structures of Horyuji in Nara, Japan, built some thirteen hundred years ago by Koreans, or even possibly Chinese builders who went to Japan across the Channel from Korea. The climatic conditions of Japan are not particularly advantageous for the preservation of wooden architecture. But the comparative rarity of civil wars, as well as the love for art and antiquity on the part of the Japanese fighting nobility may account for the comparatively large number of wooden structures preserved in Japan. While in China, if any structure escaped destruction at a change of dynasty, it was a matter of sheer luck. Chinese conquerors usually followed the example of Hsiang Yü who set fire to the palaces of the Ch'in Emperors, and the flames, it is recorded in the histories, lasted for three months.

至于木建筑遗例，最古者当推日本奈良法隆寺飞鸟期诸堂塔，盖建于我隋代，距今已千三百载[7]。然日本气候湿润，并非特宜于木建筑之保存，其所以保存至今日者，实因日本内战较少，即使有之，其破坏亦不甚烈，且其历来当道，对于古物尤知爱护，故保存亦较多。至于我国，历朝更迭，变乱频仍，项羽入关而“咸阳宫室火三月不灭”，二千年来革命元勋，莫不效法项王，以逞威风，破坏殊甚。在此种情形之下，古建筑之得幸免者，能有几何？故近来中外学者所发现诸遗物中，其最古者寿亦不过八百九十余岁[8]，未尽木寿之长也。

蓟县独乐寺观音阁及山门，皆辽圣宗统和二年重建，去今（民国二十一年）已九百四十八年，盖我国木建筑中已发现之最古者。以时代论，则上承唐代遗风，下启宋式营造，实研究我国建筑蜕变上重要资料，罕有之宝物也。

翻阅方志，常见辽宋金元建造之记载；适又传闻阁之存在，且偶得见其照片，望而知其为宋元以前物。平蓟间长途汽车每日通行，交通尚称便利。二十年秋，遂有赴蓟计划。行装甫竣，津变爆发，遂作罢。至二十一年四月，始克成行。实地研究，登檐攀顶，逐部测量，速写摄影，以纪各部特征。

Recent researches and discoveries have not yet revealed edifices of wood over a thousand years old in China. Until recently, the oldest known wooden edifice was the Library of Hsia Hua-yen Ssu, Ta-t'ung, built in 1038. But in April, 1932, the author had the good fortune to discover two Liao structures among the buildings of the Tu-lo Ssu of Chi Hsien, in the Province of Hopeh. The Tu-lo Ssu is a temple built in 984 AD—the second year of T'ung-ho, of the reign of Emperor Sheng-tsung of the Liao Dynasty which was contemporary with the Northern Sung Dynasty.

The two above-mentioned buildings are significant not only because they are the oldest wooden structures yet discovered in China, but because stylistically they show the transition between the T'ang and Sung styles, a rare feature that reveals a most interesting chapter in the history of Chinese architecture.

归来整理，为寺史之考证、结构之分析及制度之鉴别。后二者之研究方法，在现状图之绘制；与唐、宋(《营造法式》)，明、清(《工程做法则例》)制度之比较；及原状图之臆造（至于所用名辞，因清名之不合用，故概用宋名，而将清名附注其下）。计得五章，首为总论，将寺阁主要特征，先提纲领；次为寺史及现状；最后将观音阁山门作结构及制度之分析。

除观音阁、山门外，更得观音寺辽塔一座，附刊于后。

此次旅行，蒙清华大学工程学系教授施嘉炀先生[9]惠借仪器多种，蓟县王子明先生及蓟县乡村师范学校校长刘博泉，教员王慕如、梁伯融，工会杨雅园诸先生多方赞助，予以种种便利。而社员邵力工、舍弟梁思达同行，不唯沿途受尽艰苦，且攀梁登顶，不辞危险，尤为难能。归来研究，得内子林徽因在考证及分析上，不辞劳，不惮烦，予以协作。又蒙清华大学工程教授蔡方荫先生[10]在比较计算上予以指示，始得此结果。而此次调查旅行之可能，厥为社长朱先生[11]之鼓励及指导是赖，微先生之力不及此，尤思成所至感者也。

II. GENERAL CHARACTERISTICS

Of the Liao structures of Tu-lo Ssu, only the three-storied Kuan-yin Hall and the Shan-men or Main Entrance still remain. These are not only the oldest examples of wooden architecture known to us, but, as already stated, they are especially important in showing the transition between the T'ang and Sung periods and thus very valuable to the structure of Chinese architecture. The second year of T'ung-ho corresponds to the first year of Yung-hsi, of the reign of Tai-tsung, second emperor of the Northern Sung Dynasty. This was the 24th year of the Sung Dynasty and only 77 years since the overthrow of the T'ang sovereignty.

It was not until 116 years after the erection of these edifices that the famous *Ying-tsao-fa-shih*[12] was first published. It is interesting to note how much nearer style of the Tu-lo Ssu structures are to the late T'ang than to the matured Sung style. Li Chieh, the author of the *Ying-tsao-fa-shih*, better known as Li Ming-chung, was imperial architect to the Emperor Hui-tsung, who was a ruler of no high ability although he was an artist of the first rank. He was later captured by the Chin Tartars, who had by this time conquered the Liao Tartars and become the invaders of the northern border of the Sung domain. With the capture of Ch'in-tsung, Hui-tsung's son and successor, the Northern Sung Dynasty ended in 1127.

贰 总论

独乐寺观音阁及山门，在我国已发现之古木建筑中，固称最古，且其在建筑史上之地位，尤为重要。统和二年为宋太宗之雍熙元年，北宋建国之第二十四年耳。上距唐亡仅七十七年，唐代文艺之遗风，尚未全靡；而下距《营造法式》之刊行尚有百十六年。《营造法式》实宋代建筑制度完整之记载，而又得幸存至今日者。观音阁、山门，其年代及形制，皆适处唐宋二式之中，实为唐宋间建筑形制蜕变之关键，至为重要。谓为唐宋间式之过渡式样可也。

The *Ying-tsao-fa-shih* is the most complete treatise on architecture of the Northern Sung style, a Vignola and a Kidder combined. A comparison of the Kuan-yin Hall and the Shan-men of the Tu-lo Ssu with the specifications and designs of the *Ying-tsao-fa-shih* has revealed to us many hitherto unknown architectural characteristics besides illustrating many statements in the book which have been almost meaningless to us before.

The general arrangement of the whole temple during the Liao Dynasty is unknown. From the old records we learn that Buddhist temples of the Sui and T'ang Dynasties were usually divided into a number of cloisters or yuans surrounded on all sides by colonnades. Examples of such arrangements can still be found in the Horyuji at Nara, Japan. But in the case of Tu-lo Ssu, one can now find no trace of the colonnade that must have once connected the Shan-men with the rear part of the temple. The P'ei-tien or Flanking Hall in front of the Kuan-yin Hall along its east and west sides, as well as the several courtyards to the rear, are all reconstructions. Neither is the courtyard to the east in its original condition as in 1753, during the reign of Emperor Ch'ien-lung of the Ts'ing Dynasty, it was demolished to make room for the erection of an imperial apartment which stood ready for the occasional visits of the Emperor. These changes necessarily affected the general parti of the temple. Only the Hall and the Shan-men survived in these disasters.

The most important characteristic of the Hall and the Shan-men is its striking resemblance to the architecture so faithfully represented in the mural paintings of the Grottoes of Tun-huang (Figure 30). This architecture is mostly of the late T'ang or Wu-tai periods, antedating the Tu-lo Ssu structures by a hundred years or so. In these paintings there are representations of halls, one or two stories in height, with heavy overhanging eaves supported by a system of tou-kung, or brackets, of gigantic proportion. The exterior appearance of both the Hall and the Shan-men is curiously similar to the buildings in the paintings, while it is radically different from not only the Ts'ing buildings we see today, but also from the comparatively nearer style of the *Ying-tsao-fa-shih.*

This resemblance in exterior appearance is neither a coincidence nor a conscious imitation, but the natural consequence of a similar system of construction based upon the wooden structural frame.

The Chinese structural framing system may be divided roughly into three principal parts: the vertical supports, or columns; the horizontal members, or the beams, purlins; and the transitional members, or system of members, the characteristic tou-kung or brackets.

The columns of the Kuan-yin Hall, taking the material used into consideration, are rather stout in proportion, thus giving an impression of stability. The columns of the Shan-men are the same in diameter as those of the Hall while they are shorter. The columns on the second and third stories of the Hall are also the same in diameter, but shorter than those below. It is evident, therefore, that the height of the column is in proportion to the diameter as is the case with the Ts'ing style or the Roman orders. The rounded head (Figure 33) as well as the slight inward inclination of the column are also among the few notable characteristics.

独乐寺伽蓝之布置，今已无考。隋唐之制，率皆寺分数院，周绕回廊[13]。今观音阁山门之间，已无直接联络部分；阁前配殿，亦非原物；后部殿宇，更无可观。自经乾隆重修，建筑坐落于东院，寺之规模，更完全更改，原有布置，毫无痕迹。原物之尚存者惟阁及山门。

观音阁及山门最大之特征，而在形制上最重要之点，则为其与敦煌壁画中所见唐代建筑之相似也。壁画所见殿阁，或单层或重层，檐出如翼，斗拱雄大。而阁及门所呈现象，与清式建筑固迥然不同，与宋式亦大异，而与唐式则极相似。熟悉敦煌壁画中净土图（图 30）者，若骤见此阁，必疑身之已入西方极乐世界矣。

其外观之所以如是者，非故仿唐形，乃结构制度仍属唐式之自然结果。而其结构上最重要部分，则木质之构架——建筑之骨干——是也。

其构架约略可分为三大部分：柱，斗拱，及梁枋。

观音阁之柱，权衡颇肥短，较清式所呈现象为稳固。山门柱径亦如阁，然较阁柱犹短。至于阁之上中二层，柱虽更短，而径不改，故知其长与径，不相牵制，不若清式之有一定比例。此外柱头削作圆形（图 33），柱身微侧向内，皆为可注意之特征。

The tou-kung or bracketing system is a peculiarity unique to the Chinese style architecture—in the broader sense which therefore includes the Japanese style. It is a motif structural in function, while at the same time highly decorative in appearance. It is the transition as well as the connection between the horizontal members above and the vertical supports below. The position it occupies in Chinese architecture is much like that of the order in the Greco-Roman styles. One may justly say that the development of the tou-kung has influenced the development of the Chinese structural system just as the order has influenced Western architectural styles.

The origin of the tou-kung is unknown. As early as the Chou Dynasty, it was often mentioned in literature. Among the sepulchral sculpture of the Han Dynasty one finds the tou-kung in stone, imitating a highly perfected wooden construction. During the T'ang and Sung Dynasties, the tou-kung was used primarily for its structural value—for the support of the heavy overhanging eave; it was logical both in proportion and arrangement. But, during the Ming and Ts'ing Dynasties, the tou-kung gradually lost its original function, became more intricate and delicate, and assumed a weak and frail proportion. Since the Ming Dynasty, the tou-kungs have increased in number and have become almost purely ornamental. The degeneration of the tou-kung has reached the utmost limit.

Returning to the Tu-lo Ssu, the height of tou-kungs of the Hall and the Shan-men is approximately half the height of the column, or one-third of the entire story, while the Ts'ing regulation allowed only a proportion of about one-fourth or one-fifth of the column, or one-sixth of the height of the entire story. A simple comparison of the height of the tou-kung to its height or the column is a fair means of judging the importance of the tou-kung. Structurally, these Liao tou-kungs are also different from those of the Sung or Ts'ing system. They are constructed so as to serve each its particular function, and they are units of an organic, logical whole.

In the case of the Kuan-yin Hall, the tou-kungs support either the eave, the balcony, or the beams and purlins; they are placed either on a column, or between columns, or at a corner; they are used either on the exterior or the interior, on the first, second, or third stories. Each one was designed to fulfill its particular function. These are in all twenty-four different kinds of tou-kung, each kind alone being an exemplification of architectural logic.

The beams and other horizontal members in the Hall and the Shanmen are all laid according to the simple lintel system, involving no complicated theory of mechanics. The only peculiarity of the beams as compared with those of later Chinese structures is the proportions of the cross section.

斗拱者，中国建筑所特有之结构制度也。其功用在梁枋等与柱间之过渡及联络，盖以结构部分而富有装饰性者。其在中国建筑上所占之地位，犹柱式之于希腊罗马建筑；斗拱之变化，谓为中国建筑制度之变化，亦未尝不可，犹柱式之影响欧洲建筑，至为重大。

唐宋建筑之斗拱以结构为主要功用，雄大坚实，庄严不苟。明清以后，斗拱渐失其原来功用，日趋弱小纤巧，每每数十攒排列檐下，几成纯粹装饰品，其退化程度，已陷井底，不复能下矣。

观音阁山门之斗拱，高约柱高一半以上，全高三分之一，较之清式斗拱——合柱高四分或五分之一，全高六分之一者，其轻重自可不言而喻。而其结构，与清式、宋式皆不同；而种别之多，尤为后世所不见。盖古之用斗拱，辄视其机能而异其形制，其结构实为一种有机的、有理的结合。如观音阁斗拱，或承檐，或承平坐，或承梁枋，或在柱头，或转角，或补间，内外上下，各各不同[14]，条理井然。各攒斗拱，皆可作建筑逻辑之典型。都凡二十四种，聚于一阁，诚可谓集斗拱之大成者矣！

观音阁及山门上梁枋之用法，尚为后世所常见，皆为普通之梁，无复杂之力学作用。其与后世制度最大之区别，乃其横断面之比例。

The Ts'ing regulation specifies that the proportion of the width to the height of the cross section of a beam be either eight to ten or ten to twelve, resulting in almost a square. The Sung regulation, as specified in the *Ying-tsao-fa-shih* seems to be more scientific, requiring a proportion of two to three. The Liao proportions, as seen in the Hall and the Shan-men, are one to two, just those most practiced in modern construction. It is incredible that a thousand years of evolution in Chinese architecture has brought us not only to no new knowledge, but positively to greater ignorance in the mechanics of materials.

Another characteristic of importance is the high degree of standardization in the size of the timbers. In the Kuan-yin Hall, there are only six different sizes in its structural members. This extreme degree of standardization must have simplified to a very great extent the processes of designing, cost estimation, as well as construction.

Among the less important characteristics may be mentioned the ceiling of the Hall and the tile ornaments of the roof. The caisson of the Hall has an appearance quite different from the corresponding sections of the Imperial Palaces of the Peiping of today. The check-squares are rather small in proportion to the timbers that are used to form them. This peculiarity is also found in the architecture of the Kamakura period in Japan. The roof-tiles are later substitutes of the Liao original. The ornamental ridge-ends of the Shan-men are particularly interesting. Prior to the Sung Dynasty, this feature was a kind of fish-tail, turned upwards and inwards towards the center of the building, while the post-Sung examples were all in the form of a dragon's head with a small tail turned up and outward. On the Shan-men one finds a combination of both: the lower part is already the dragon-head of today while the top still retains the upward-inward tail of the T'ang manner. This ornament may not be the original of the Liao period, but is probably a Ming reproduction of the original. As a milestone marking a step in the history of architecture, no better example can be found.

The peculiarly low ch'ün-chien or "pedestal" of the masonry

wall is also noteworthy. It is less than half the height of the Ts'ing specifications. The few Liao structures in the northern part of Shansi Province all possess this same characteristic, which must have been particular to that age.

The colossal statue of the Eleven-headed Kuan-yin, although it was remodeled at the time of the reconstruction of the Temple, still retains much of the T'ang flavor. The two smaller Bodhisattvas standing on either side of the central figure are particularly T'ang in character. They could undoubtedly be placed in their due position in the history of Chinese sculpture.

梁之载重力，在其高度，而其宽度之影响较小；今科学造梁之制，大略以高二宽一为适宜之比例。按清制高宽为十与八或十二与十之比，其横断面几成正方形。宋《营造法式》所规定，则为三与二之比，较清式合理。而观音阁及山门（辽式）则皆为二与一之比，与近代方法符合。岂吾侪之科学知识，日见退步耶！

其在结构方面最大之发现则木材之标准化是也。清式建筑，皆以"斗口"[15]为单位，凡梁柱之高宽，面阔进深之修广，皆受斗口之牵制。制至繁杂，计算至难；其"规矩"对各部分之布置分配，拘束尤甚，致使作者无由发挥其创造能力。古制则不然，以观音阁之大，其用材之制，梁枋不下千百，而大小只六种。此种极端之标准化，于材料之估价及施工之程序上，皆使工作简单。结构上重要之特征也。

观音阁天花，亦与清代制度大异。其井口甚小，分布甚密，为后世所不见。而与日本镰仓时代[16]遗物颇相类似，可相较鉴也。

阁与山门之瓦，已非原物。然山门脊饰，与今日所习见之正吻不同。其在唐代，为鳍形之尾，自宋而后，则为吻，二者之蜕变程序，尚无可考。山门鸱尾，其下段已成今所习见之吻，而上段则尚为唐代之尾，虽未可必其为辽原物，亦必为明以前按原物仿造，亦可见过渡形制之一般。

砖墙下部之裙肩，颇为低矮，只及清式之半，其所呈现象，至为奇特。山西北部辽物亦多如是，盖亦其特征之一也。

观音阁中之十一面观音像，亦统和重塑，尚具唐风，其两傍侍立菩萨，与盛唐造像尤相似，亦雕塑史中之重要遗例也。

III. HISTORY

About 180 li directly east of Peiping (Peking) is the old city of Chi Hsien. During the Han Dynasty, it was a part of Yü-yang Chün. It was not until the reign of Emperor Hsuan-tsung, 712–756 AD, of the T'ang Dynasty that the Magistracy of Chi-chou was first founded. The Tsin rulers of the Wu-tai period ceded the land as a bribe to the Liao Tartars, and, thereafter, for a period of nearly four hundred years, the land was under the control of the northern invading tribes. The Chin Tartars once returned Chi-chou to the Sung, only to snatch it back a few years later. Even during the Yuan and Ming Dynasties it continued to be the zone of conflict between the Chinese and the invaders from the North, a city of strategic importance, guarding the entrance to old Peking.

Chi-chou is not only a city of military importance, but also a name that has been dear to artists and poets for over a thousand years. The quaint fortified city is located at the foot of Pan Shan, the beautiful hill that has been the subject of so many poems of the T'ang and Sung Dynasties.

Being a city of no little importance, Chi Hsien is well provided with public buildings of all kinds—offices, schools, garrisons, barns, as well as Taoist and Buddhist temples (Figure 5). And the one temple that had been the religious center, for over a thousand years, to the Chi people, is no other than the Tu-lo Ssu, situated just inside the Western City Gate. Its three-storied Kuan-yin Hall towers over the city wall and is visible miles away. On the fifteenth day of the third moon every year, a fair is always given in the temple; pilgrims from all parts of the hsien will come, to participate in and enjoy the different acrobatic side-shows and tournaments, and to ascend the celestial hall to view the mountains and the plain, and finally to pay homage to the almighty God (or Goddess) of Mercy. This has been the custom for centuries, the origin of which is perhaps as old as the city itself.

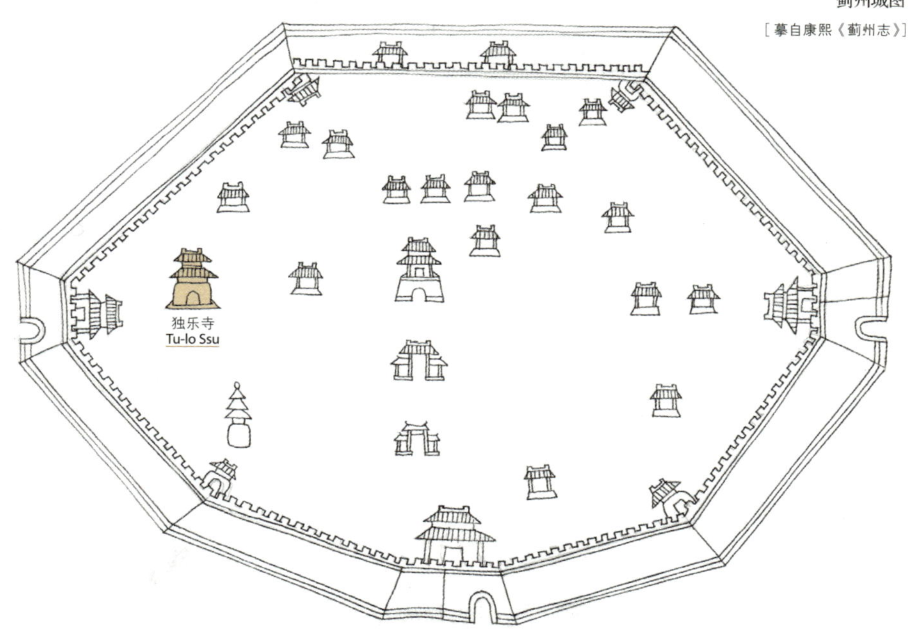

5 Map of Chi-chou.

[Copy of *Chi-Chou Chih* during Kang-hsi Period]

蓟州城图

［摹自康熙《蓟州志》］

叁 寺史

蓟县在北平之东百八十里。汉属渔阳郡，唐开元间，始置蓟州。五代石晋，割以赂辽，其地遂不复归中国[17]。金曾以蓟一度遣宋，不数年而复取之。宋元明以来，屡为华狄冲突之地；军事重镇，而北京之拱卫也。蓟城地处盘山之麓。盘山乃历代诗人歌咏之题，风景幽美，为蓟城天然之背景。

蓟既为古来重镇，其建置至为周全，学宫衙署，僧寺道院，莫不齐备（图 5）。而千数百年来，为蓟民宗教生活之中心者，则独乐寺也。寺在城西门内，中有高阁，高出城表，自城外十余里之遥，已可望见。每届废历[18]三月中，寺例有庙会之举，县境居民，百数十里跋涉，参加盛会，以期“带福还家”。其在蓟民心目中，实为无上圣地，如是者已数百年，蓟县耆老亦莫知其始自何年也。

But, in spite of the religious and social importance of Tu-lo Ssu, the history of the temple is shrouded in mists. Its origin is unknown. It is said that the tablet in the little pavilion placed at the middle of the roof-ridge of the Hall once bore the characters "Built in the Tenth Year of Cheng-kwan" (636 AD); some say that the inscription was "Built under the direction of Yü-ch'ih Ching-teh"; while another version of the story combines these two and the inscription is reported as "Built in the Tenth Year of Cheng-kwan under the direction of Yü-ch'ih Ching-teh." Yü-ch'ih Ching-teh was a general under T'ang T'ai-tsung, and having successfully assisted the Emperor in building the Empire, was later entrusted with the erection of many important palaces and temples. Thus he became a legendary figure, to whom any building that is considered old is attributed. Now the tablet is no longer the original, but a plain one without any inscription, so that the date and the name of the architect if is supposed to have cannot be assumed as authentic. And, even if they are accepted, they mark only the founding of the history of the temple. The Kuan-yin Hall and the Shan-men as they stand today could not have been built at the founding of the temple as they are decidedly of a period later than the T'ang.

The people of Chi Hsien also take delight in telling that the Tu-lo Ssu, the Temple of "Unshared Joy," is the site where An Lu-shan, the rebellious Tartar general, then garrison commander of Yü-yang, took his oath of office before he started his march against the romantic Emperor Hsuan-tsung. The wicked general, it is said, named the temple "Tu-lo" because he did not want his joys shared by others.

To the northwest of the city is a river by the same name. It is a problem whether the temple is named after the river, or the river after the temple, or both named by the selfish Tartar rebel.

The Temple must have been founded no later than the beginning of the T'ang Dynasty. A passage from the *P'an-shan Chih*[19] is quoted in the *Jih-hsia-chiu-wen Kao* as follows:

"Tu-lo Ssu, date of founding unknown; reconstructed in the Liao Dynasty. In the temple is a stele by Liu Cheng, Hsueh-shih of the Han-lin Yuan, erected in the fourth year of T'ung-ho. The inscription reads 'The late Shang-fu, Prince of Ch'in, requested the Great Master T'an-chen to Tu-lo Ssu to repair the Kuan-yin Hall. In the tenth moon, in the winter of the second year of T'ung-ho, the great Hall was reconstructed. It measured two stories in height, and had five bays from east to west, and eight rafters from south to north. The statue of the Eleven-headed Kuan-yin was also remodeled.'"

The reign of T'ung-ho was about three hundred years after the beginning of the T'ang Dynasty which was marked by a hitherto unequalled spread of Buddhism. Many temples and statues were then erected so that it is quite probable that the Tu-lo Ssu was founded then, and for three centuries or more, well protected by the devout public.

独乐寺虽为蓟县名刹，而寺史则殊渺茫，其缘始无可考。与蓟人谈，咸以寺之古远相告；而耆老缙绅，则或谓屋脊小亭内碑文有"贞观十年建"字样，或谓为"尉迟敬德监修"数字，或将二说合而为一，谓为"贞观十年尉迟敬德监修"者，不一而足。"敬德监修"，已成我国匠人历代之口头神话，无论任何建筑物，彼若认为久远者，概称"敬德监修"。至于"贞观十年"，只是传说，无人目睹，亦未见诸传记。即使此二者俱属事实，亦只为寺创建之时，或其历史中之一段。至于今日尚存之观音阁及山门，则绝非唐构也。

蓟人又谓：独乐寺为安禄山誓师之地。"独乐"之名，亦禄山所命，盖禄山思独乐而不与民同乐，故尔命名云。蓟城西北，有独乐水，为境内名川之一，不知寺以水名，抑水以寺名，抑二者皆为禄山命名也。

寺之创立，至迟亦在唐初。《日下旧闻考》引《盘山志》云：

"独乐寺不知创自何代，至辽时重修。有翰林院学士承旨刘成碑。统和四年孟夏立石，其文曰：'故尚父秦王请谈真大师入独乐寺，修观音阁。以统和二年冬十月再建上下两级、东西五间、南北八架大阁一所。重塑十一面观音菩萨像。'"

自统和上溯至唐初三百余年耳。唐代为我国历史上佛教最昌盛时代；寺像之修建供养极为繁多，而对于佛教之保护，必甚周密。在彼适宜之环境之下，木质建筑，寿至少可数百年。

Then came the disturbances of Wu-tai after the overthrow of the T'ang line, when the religious fervor, curiously coincidental with the political and social welfare, sank down to the unprecedentedly low ebb. It was at this time that the Chi district was ceded to the Liao Tartars, and, most probably, the buildings of the Tu-lo Ssu reached a state of deterioration that made reconstruction necessary. The supposition that the Tu-lo Ssu had already had a history of three hundred years or more prior to the reconstruction in 984 AD is not altogether untenable.

The stele of Liu Ch'eng has since long disappeared, while the name of the erector is also unknown to history. Shang-fu, Prince of Ch'in, whose proper name is Yeh-lü Nu-kwa, was a Prince of royal blood and a general, who, more than once, defeated the Sung army in the vicinity of Ting-chou and Wang-tu, situated in the southern part of the Province of Hopeh. Chi-chou, which is nearer to the northern border of the present province, was then considered safe in the interior of the Liao domain, where constructions could be carried on without the danger of being interrupted by the receding Sungs. Yeh-lü Nu-kwa was, therefore, the client or donor of the reconstructed Tu-lo Ssu, while T'an-chen, Buddhist monk of high prestige, supervised the construction.

It has already been noted that, chronologically, the Liao structures of the Tu-lo Ssu belong rather to the late T'ang than to the matured Sung style. It is also interesting to note that, geographically, during the T'ang Dynasty Chi-chou was a part of China, where the cultural influence from Ch'ang-an could not but have dominated, while after the fall of T'ang, it fell into the hands of the "barbarians." There the old cultural sway nevertheless naturally lingered on, and more likely, retained more of the T'ang flavour than in China proper, for the very reason that it was separated from China where new movements in culture continued to develop, sweeping away and replacing the old as time went on. Therefore, the Tu-lo Ssu structures, as is the case with Roman colonial architecture, may be built in a manner older than its accepted date, while further down south in the Sung territory, the Chinese had modified architectural style to something that is more akin to that of the *Ying-tsao-fa-shih.*

The hall that we see today answers well to the description of the Liu Ch'eng stele, "two stories in height, five bays from east to west, and eight rafters from south to north." In reality, the Hall is of three stories but the second story, which is a sort of mezzanine, is invisible from the exterior. The Hall thus has the appearance of a two-storied building, or a building of two principal and a mezzanine stories. "Eight rafters" means that there are nine purlins running from east to west, thus dividing each row of rafters into eight sections.

殆经五代之乱，寺渐倾颓，至统和（北宋初）适为须要重修之时。故在统和以前，寺至少已有三百年以上之历史，殆属可能。

刘成碑今已无可考，而刘成其人者，亦未见经传。尚父秦王者，耶律奴瓜也。[20] 按辽史本传，奴瓜为太祖异母弟南府宰相苏之孙，“有膂力，善调鹰隼”，盖一介武夫。统和四年始建军功。六年败宋游兵于定州，二十一年伐宋，擒王继忠于望都。当时前线乃在河北省南部一带，蓟州较北，已为辽内地，故有此建置，而奴瓜乃当时再建观音阁之主动者也。

谈真大师亦无可考，盖当时高僧而为宗室所赏识或敬重者。观音阁之再建，是在其监督之下施工者也。

统和二年，即宋太宗雍熙元年，公元 984 年也。阁之再建，实在北宋初年。《营造法式》为我国最古营造术书，亦为研究宋代建筑之唯一著述，初刊于宋哲宗元符三年（公元 1100 年）[21]，上距阁之再建，已百十六年，而统和二年，上距唐亡（昭宣帝天祐四年，公元 907 年）仅七十七年。以年月论，距唐末尚近于《法式》刊行之年。且地处边境，在地理上与中原较隔绝。在唐代地属中国，其文化自直接受中原影响，五代以后，地属夷狄，中国原有文化，固自保守，然在中原若有新文化之产生，则所受影响，必因当时政治界限而隔阻，故愚以为在观音阁再建之时，中原建筑若已有新变动之发生，在蓟北未必受其影响，而保存唐代特征亦必较多。如观音阁者，实唐宋二代间建筑之过渡形式，而研究上重要之关键也。

阁之形式，确如碑所载，“上下两级，东西五间，南北八架”。阁实为三级，但中层为暗层，如西式之 mezzanine。故主要层为两级，暗层自外不见。南北八架云者，按今式称为九架，盖谓九檩而椽分八段也。

We are able to trace only four of the numerous restorations that must have occurred to the temple since the T'ung-ho reconstruction. All these restorations occurred not earlier than the beginning of the seventeenth century. For six hundred years since it was, i.e., during the Liao, Chin, Yuan and Ming Dynasties, no record of restoration can be found anywhere.

The earliest of the recorded restorations is that of the Wan-li period, near the end of the Ming Dynasty. Wang Yü-pei, lang-chung of the Treasury, is the principal director of this "good act" as recorded in his essay "Tu-lo Ssu Ta-pei Ke Chi" or "Memoirs of the Hall of Great Mercy of Tu-lo Ssu." No date is given in this essay, but it must have been written very soon after 1595, the year Wang Yü-pei passed his examination for the degree of Chin-shih, after which he was appointed Chu-shih and subsequently promoted to the position of lang-chung. In this early restoration, no alteration was made to the structural parts.

The change of dynasty from Ming to Ts'ing instigated three massacres of Chi-chou city. It is said that the people of the city gathered at Tu-lo Ssu and defended the Holy Structure at the expense of numerous lives, or it would have suffered the same fate as so many other once famous but now destroyed buildings.

In 1658, it was repaired by Wang Hung-tsao, director (Shang-shu) of the Treasury, who also recorded in an essay "Hsiu Tu-lo Ssu Chi" a list of the personnel who participated in the event, among whom were Hu Tso-kuo[22], the magistrate and the monks Chun-shan and Miao-ch'eng. Like the former one, this reparation consisted in merely retouching the paint and ornaments, involving little or no structural changes. It is to be noted that this was the first restoration in the Ts'ing Dynasty.

The *Chi-chou Chih* or the *Chronicle of Chi-chou* mentioned another reparation in 1753, the eighteenth year of Ch'ien-lung, when "an imperial apartment was erected in the Eastern Cloister, with wooden railings and spirit screen at the main entrance to match, thus altering the appearance to a great extent." This must have caused a radical departure from the plan of its original parti, for prior to this date, the temple must have been as usual in the T'ang period, surrounded on all sides by verandas, which led from the Shan-men around the Hall to the rear of the Temple. The Ch'ien-lung addition necessarily caused the destruction of certain parts of the veranda on both the east and west sides, resulting in the plan that is found today.

自统和以后，历代修葺，可考者只四次，皆在明末以后。元明间必有修葺，然无可考。

万历间，户部郎中王于陛重修之，有《独乐大悲阁记》，谓：

"……其载修则统和已酉也。经今久圮，二三信士谋所以为缮葺计；前饷部柯公[23]，实倡其事，感而兴起者，殆不乏焉。柯公以迁秩行，予继其后，既经时，涂暨之业斯竟。因瞻礼大士，下睹金碧辉映，其法身庄严钜丽，围抱不易尽，相传以为就刻一大树云。"

按康熙《朝邑县后志》：

"王于陛，字启宸，万历丁未进士。以二甲授户部主事，升郎中，督饷蓟州。"

丁未为万历二十五年（公元 1595 年）。其在蓟时期，当在是年以后，故其修葺独乐寺，当在万历后期。其所谓重修，亦限于油饰彩画，故云"金碧辉映，庄严钜丽"，于寺阁之结构无所更改也。

明清之交，蓟城被屠三次，相传全城人民集中独乐寺及塔下寺，抵死保护，故城虽屠，而寺无恙，此亦足以表示蓟人对寺之爱护也。

王于陛修葺以后六十余年，王弘祚复修之。弘祚以崇祯十四年（公元 1614 年）"自盘阴来牧渔阳"。入清以后，官户部尚书，顺治十五年（公元 1658 年）"晋秩司农，奉使黄花山，路过是州，追随大学士宗伯菊潭胡公来寺少憩焉。风景不殊，而人民非故；台砌倾圮，而庙貌徒存。……寺僧春山游来，讯予（弘祚）曰，'是召棠冠社之所凭也，忍以草莱委诸？'予唯唯，为之捐资而倡首焉。一时贤士大夫欣然乐输，而州牧胡君[24]，毅然劝助，共襄盛举。未几，其徒妙乘以成功告，且曰宝阁配殿，及天王殿山门，皆焕然聿新矣"（《修独乐寺记》）。

此入清以后第一次修葺也。其倡首者王弘祚，而"州牧胡君"助之。当其事者则春山妙乘。所修则宝阁配殿，及天王殿山门也。读上记，天王殿山门，似为二建筑物然者，然实则一，盖以山门而置天王者也。以地势而论，今山门迫临西街，前无空地，后距观音阁亦只七八丈，其间断不容更一建筑物之加入，故"天王殿山门"者，实一物也。

6 A distant view of Kuan-yin Ke. 观音阁远望

The four posts supporting the eave at the four corners of the Kuan-yin Hall much have been added at this reparation. The corners of the eave were probably found to be tumbling after seven hundred years. The addition of these posts was a necessity without which the entire structure would have been reduced to ruins a hundred years ago. The shan-hua-pan, or "gable board," that covered and concealed the beautiful overhanging gable, of which only a few millions of the grills of the transom are left today, as also the doors and windows, was all added or "restored" at this time.

Ch'ien-lung had the good fortune to be the Emperor when the Ts'ing Dynasty was at its height. The entire Empire enjoyed great prosperity and the Imperial Treasury was full of gold and silver. Being a great traveler and lover of art, the Emperor seldom failed to visit any temple of renown, where he, sometimes ordered the temple to be "restored," but more often pulled down and reconstructed, thus destroying innumerable treasures of T'ang and Sung architecture, especially around the neighborhood of Peking. It is miraculous, and most fortunate for the student of architectural archaeology, that the Kuan-yin Hall, together with the Shan-men, actually escaped the "restoration" of the art-loving Emperor in spite of the erection of the imperial apartment to the east of the temple.

乾隆十八年（公元 1753 年）“于寺内东偏……建立座落，并于寺前改立栅栏照壁，巍然改观”（《蓟州沈志》卷三）是殆为寺平面布置上极大之更改。盖在此以前，寺之布置，自山门至阁后，必周以回廊，如唐代遗制。高宗于“寺内东偏”建立座落，“则寺内东偏”原有之建筑，必被拆毁。不唯如是，于“西偏”亦有同时代建立之建筑，故寺原有之东西廊，殆于此时改变，而成今日之规模。“巍然改观”，不唯在“栅栏照壁”也。

乾隆重修于寺上最大之更动，除平面之布置外，厥唯观音阁四角檐下所加柱，及若干部分之“清式化”。阁出檐甚远，七百余年，已向下倾圮，故四角柱之增加，为必要之补救法，阁之得以保存，唯此是赖。

关于此次重修，尚有神话一段。蓟县老绅告予，当乾隆重修之时，工人休息用膳，有老者至，工人亨以食。问味何如，老者曰：“盐短，盐短！”盖鲁班降世，而以上檐改短为不然，故曰“檐短”云。按今全部权衡，上檐与下檐檐出，长短适宜，调谐悦目，檐短之说，不敢与鲁班赞同。至于其他“清式化”部分，如山花板，博脊及山门雀替之添造，门窗隔扇之修改，内檐柱头枋间之填塞，皆将于各章分别论之。

高宗生逢盛世，正有清鼎定之后，国裕民安，府库充实；且性嗜美术，好游名山大川。凡其足迹所至，必重修寺观，立碑自耀。唐宋古建筑遗物之毁于其“重修”者，不知凡几，京畿一带，受创尤甚。而独乐寺竟能经“寺内东偏”座落之建立，观音阁山门尚侥幸得免，亦中国建筑史之万幸也。

光绪二十七年（公元 1901 年），“两宫回銮”之后，有谒陵[25]盛典，道出蓟州，独乐寺因为座落之所在，于是复加修葺粉饰。此为最后一次之重修，然多限于油漆彩画等外表之点缀。骨干构架，仍未更改。今日所见之外观，即光绪重修以后之物。

On their return to Peking in 1901, after the "Boxer Rebellion," Emperor Kwang-hsü and the Empress Dowager visited and paid homage to the Imperial Tombs at Tsun-hua Hsien, east of Chi-chou. Being the site of the imperial apartment, the Tu-lo Ssu then received its last "restoration" which consisted mostly in the retouching of the painted ornament on the inside of the building giving the structures the appearance that we see today.

After the erection of the imperial apartment, the Tu-lo Ssu became a forbidden ground. The annual fair was held in front of the temple throughout the Ts'ing Dynasty instead of in the temple grounds.

Since the overthrow of the Manchu monarchy in 1911, the temple has become once more the monument of the people. It enjoyed for a time an overwhelming popularity expressed in incense and sacrifice. A country normal school was established in the western courtyards in 1917. From 1924 to 1929, the central and eastern portions were occupied by different armies that caused a tremendous amount of damage to the various buildings, especially to the windows and doors, as well as to the ceiling boards, which were broken and used as fuel.

In 1930, the entire property was given into the charge of the Normal School, which turned all the modern parts into school buildings, but left the two Liao structures untouched. Fortunately, the school authorities are now beginning to realize the significance of the two invaluable treasures they have in their custody, and are anxious to do whatever they can to protect and conserve these ancient monuments.

有清一代，因座落之关系，独乐寺遂成禁地，庙会盛典，皆于寺前举行。平时寺内非平民所得入，至清末遂有窃贼潜居阁顶之轶事。贼犯案年余，无法查获。终破案于观音阁上层天花之上；相传其中布置极为完善，竟然一安乐窝。其上下之道，则在东梢间柱间攀上，摩擦油腻、尚有黑光，至今犹见。

7 Rear hall and censer. 后殿及香炉

鼎革以后，寺复归还于民众，一时香火极盛。民国六年，始拨西院为师范学校。十三年，陕军来蓟，驻于独乐寺，是为寺内驻军之始。十六年，驻本县保安队，始毁装修。十七年春，驻孙殿英部军队，十八年春始去。此一年中，破坏最甚。然较之同时东陵盗陵案，则吾侪不得不庆独乐寺所受孙部之特别优待也。

北伐成功以后，蓟县党部成立，一时破除迷信之声，甚嚣尘上，于是党部中有倡议拍卖独乐寺者。全蓟人民，哗然反对，幸未实现。不然，此千年国宝，又将牺牲于“破除迷信”美名之下矣。

民国二十年，全寺拨为蓟县乡村师范学校，阁、山门并东西院座落归焉。东西院及后部正殿，皆改为校舍，而观音阁、山门则保存未动。南面栅栏部分，围以土墙，于是无业游民，不复得对寺加以无聊之涂抹撕拆。现任学校当局诸君，对于建筑，保护备至。观音阁山门十余年来，备受灾难，今归学校管理，可谓渐入小康时期，然社会及政府之保护，犹为亟不容缓也。

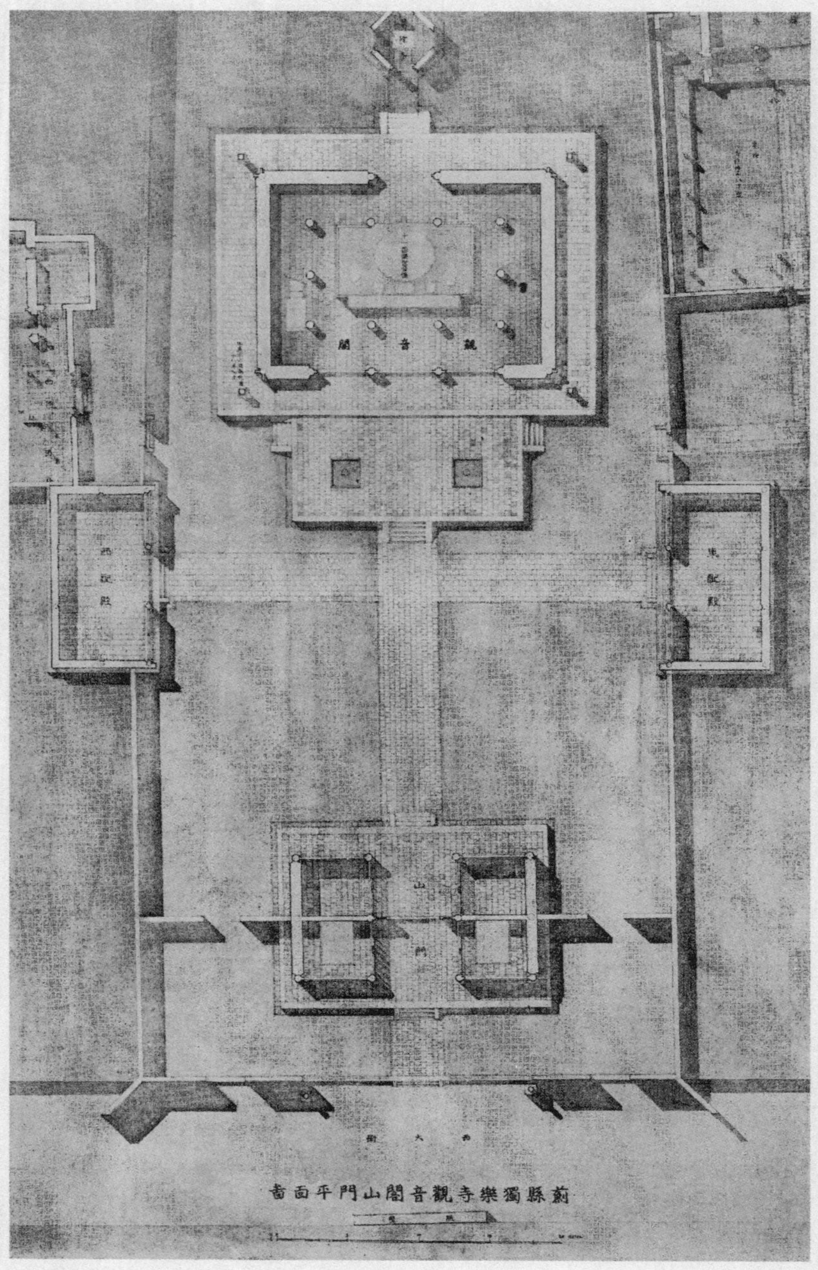

8 Plan of Main Gate (Shan-men), Kuan-yin Ke, Tu-lo Ssu.

独乐寺观音阁山门平面图

- **现状**

统和原构，唯观音阁及山门尚存，其余殿宇，殆皆明清重建。今在街之南，与山门对峙者为乾隆十八年所立照壁。街之北，山门之南为墙，东西两端辟门道，而中部则用土坯垒砌，与原有红墙，显然各别。此土墙部分，原为乾隆十八年立栅栏所在，日久栅栏朽坏，去岁蓟县乡村师范学校接收寺产后，遂用墙堵塞，以防游民入校。虽将山门遮掩，致使瞻仰者不得远观前面立面之全部，然为古物之保存计，实亦目前所不得不尔者。栅栏之前有旗杆二，一杆虽失，而石座夹杆则并存。旗杆与栅栏排列并非平行，东座距壁 0.28 米而西座距壁 0.73 米。座高 1.57 米，见方约 0.84 米。与北平常见乾隆旗杆座旨趣大异。且剥蚀殊甚，殆亦辽物也。

栅栏之内为山门（图 12），二者之间，地殊狭隘。愚以为山门原临街，乾隆以前未置栅栏，寺前街道，较他部开朗，旗杆立于其中，略似意大利各寺前之广场，其气象庄严，自可想见。山门面阔三间，进深二间[26]，格扇装修，已被军队拆毁无存、仅存楹框。南面二梢间[27]，立天王像二尊，故土人亦称山门曰“哼哈殿”。天王立小砖台上。然砖已崩散，天王将无立足之地矣！北面二梢间东西壁画四天王，涂抹殊甚，观其色泽，殆光绪重修所重摹者。笔法颜色皆无足道。

山门之北为观音阁，即寺之主要建筑物也。阁高三层，而外观则似二层者。立于石坛之上，高出城表，距蓟城十余里，已遥遥望见之（图 6）。经千年风雨寒暑之剥蚀，百十次兵灾匪祸之屠劫，犹能保存至今，巍然独立。其完整情形，殊出意外，尤为难得。

9 Longitudinal section of Kuan-yin Ke.

观音阁纵断面图

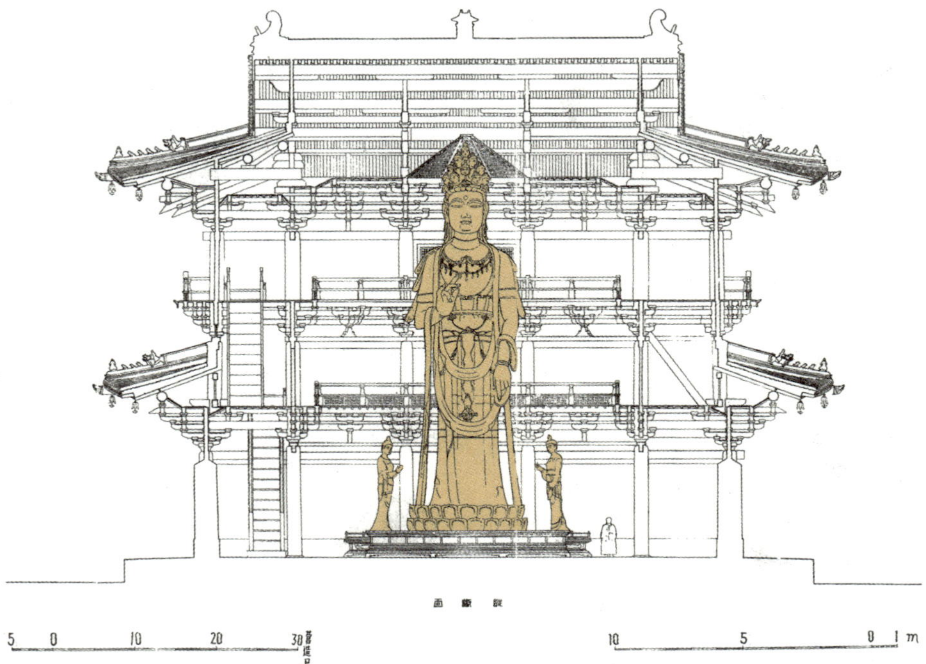

阁檐四隅，皆支以柱，盖檐出颇远，年久昂腐，有下倾之虞，不得不尔。阁中主人翁为十一面观音像，高约 16 米，立须弥坛上，二菩萨侍立（图 9）。法相庄严，必出名手，其年代或较阁犹古，亦属可能。与大像相背，面北部分尚有像，盖为落伽山中之观音。此数像者，其意趣尚具唐风，而簇新彩画，鲜艳妖冶，亦像之辱也。坛上除此数像外，尚有像三躯，恐为明以后物。北向门额悬铁磬一，万历间净土庵物，今为学生上课敲点用。庵在县城东南，磬不知何时移此。

阁与山门之间，为篮球场，为求地址加宽，故山门北面与观音阁前月台南面之石阶，皆已拆毁，其间适合球场宽度。球场（即前院）东西为配殿，各为三楹小屋，纯属清式。东配殿门窗全无，荒置无用，西配殿为学校接待室。

阁之北，距阁丈余为八角小亭，亦清构。亭内立韦驮铜像（图 2），甲胄武士，合掌北向立，高约 2.30 米，铸刻极精。审其手法，殆明中叶所作。光绪重修时，劣匠竟涂以灰泥，施以彩画，大好金身，乃蒙不洁，幸易剔除，无伤于像也。

10 Iron bell. 铁钟

亭北空院为网球场，场北为本寺前殿，殿三楹，殊狭小，而立于权衡颇高之台基上。弦歌之声，时时溢出，今为音乐教室。前殿之后为大殿，大小与前殿略同，为学校办公室。东西配殿为学生宿舍，此部分或为明代重修。然气魄极小，不足与阁调和对称（图 7）。庭中有铁香炉一座，高约 2.60 米，作小圆亭状，其南面檐下斗拱间文曰：

顺天府蓟州
独乐寺大殿前进
□炉一座
本寺僧正　□僧□
□□　□□ (?)
元成 (?)
□智
□□
宽龙 (?)
普福
普祥

惜僧正名无可读。西南二门之间文曰：

信士　平治　陈□程元忠魏邦治
铸匠　王之禄　王之富　王之屏　王之蒲　男王有文等
崇祯拾肆年拾壹月吉日造

韦驮亭西有井一口，据县老绅士王子明先生言，幼时曾见寺有残碑，于光绪重修时用作垒砌井筒之用，岂即刘成碑耶？井口现有铁钟一口（图 10），系于井架，高 0.83 米。钟分八格，其中二格有左列文字：

蓟州独乐　口二百斤
寺募缘比　弘治二年
丘戒莲诚　四月□日
资铸钟一　首座戒宗
皇图永固　匠人邓华
帝道遐昌　信女惠成
佛日增辉　妙真妙全
法轮常转　刘氏刘氏
惠贤
惠荣
铸钟信人
王璩

藉此得知明孝宗时首座之名。

11 Main Hall located in the eastern yard.
东院座落正厅

前院东配殿之北，墙有门，通东院，即乾隆十八年所建之“座落”也。入门有空院，其北为垂花门，内有围廊，北面广厅，东西三楹，南北二间，其一切形制，皆为最合规矩之清式。厅现为大讲堂（图 11）。其后空院，石山大树犹存，再后则小屋三楹，荒废未用。

前院西配殿之北，墙亦有门，通两院，殆亦同时建。入门为夹道，垂花门东向，内有小廊，小屋三楹，他无所有。现为校长及教员宿舍。

此部之后面，尚有殿二进，东西配殿各一座，皆三楹。现为学生宿舍及食堂。其西尚有大门三楹，外临城垣，内有礓䃰[28]，颇似车骑出入之门。在寺产完全归校以前，此即学校正门也。

总之，寺之建筑物，以观音阁为主，山门次之，皆辽代原构，为本次研究主物。后部殿宇，虽属明构，与清式只略异，东西两院，则纯属极规矩之清式，无特别可注意之点也。

12 The Shan-men. 山门

IV. THE SHAN-MEN

A General Appearance

The Shan-men of the Tu-lo Ssu is a one-story building of moderate size but monumental proportions, and is the propylaea or main entrance to the temple. The longer facades are on the north and are each divided into three bays. The central and slightly wider one with its gigantic doors is the main thoroughfare and the side ones with windows and railings as rooms for the guardian Lokapalas. The Shan-men is covered by a gray tile roof, sloping on all four sides, with heavy overhanging eaves. It is supported by a system of tou-kung, or brackets, of bold proportion. The general proportion is altogether different from that of the Ming and Ts'ing styles, giving an impression of vigor, stability and dignity. The use of the "four sloped roof" on a building of secondary importance and size is unknown to later styles (Figure 26). The pien, or sign board, under the southern eave, bearing the characters for "Tu-lo Ssu" is attributed to Yen Sung, one of the best known treacherous prime ministers of the Ming Dynasty.

 山门

❶ 外观

山门为面阔三间、进深二间之单层建筑物。顶注四阿[29]，脊作鸱尾，青瓦红墙。南面额曰“独乐寺”，相传严嵩手笔。全部权衡，与明清建筑物大异，所呈现象至为庄严稳固。在小建筑物上，施以四阿，尤为后世所罕见（图 26）。

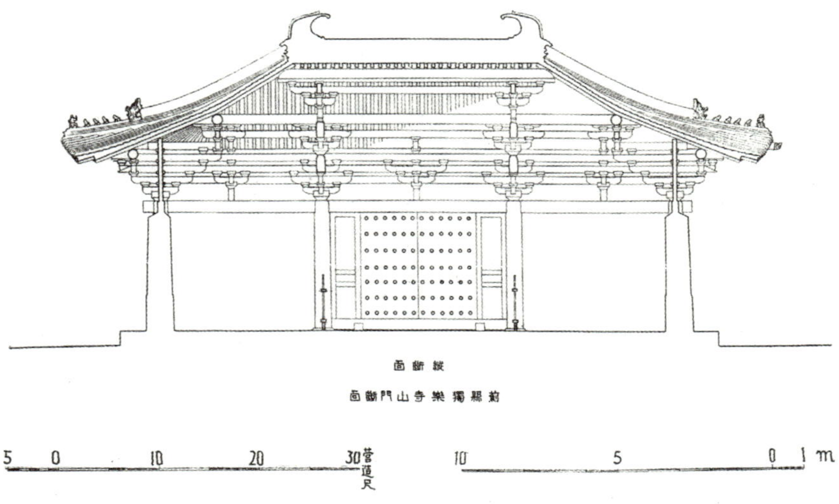

13 Longitudinal section of the Shan-men. 山门纵断面图

Ⓑ Plan

The plan of the Shan-men is a rectangle, three chiens or bays long and two chiens wide, formed by twelve columns arranged in three rows of four in each row. The tang-hsin-chien or central bay, measuring 6.10 m. from center to center of columns, is the main thoroughfare. It can be shut off with the doors between the chung-chus, or columns on the longitudinal axis. The shao-chiens, or end bays, are smaller than the tang-hsin-chien; in the two southern chiens are two statues of guardian Lokapalas, practically filling the entire chien, while on the walls of the two northern chiens are mural paintings of the four Lokapalas. The distance between the chung-chus and the yen-chus, or columns under the eave, is smaller than the width of the shao-chien, resulting in the intersection of the main ridge of the roof with the two hips at a point somewhere in the shao-chien instead of on the chung-chu.

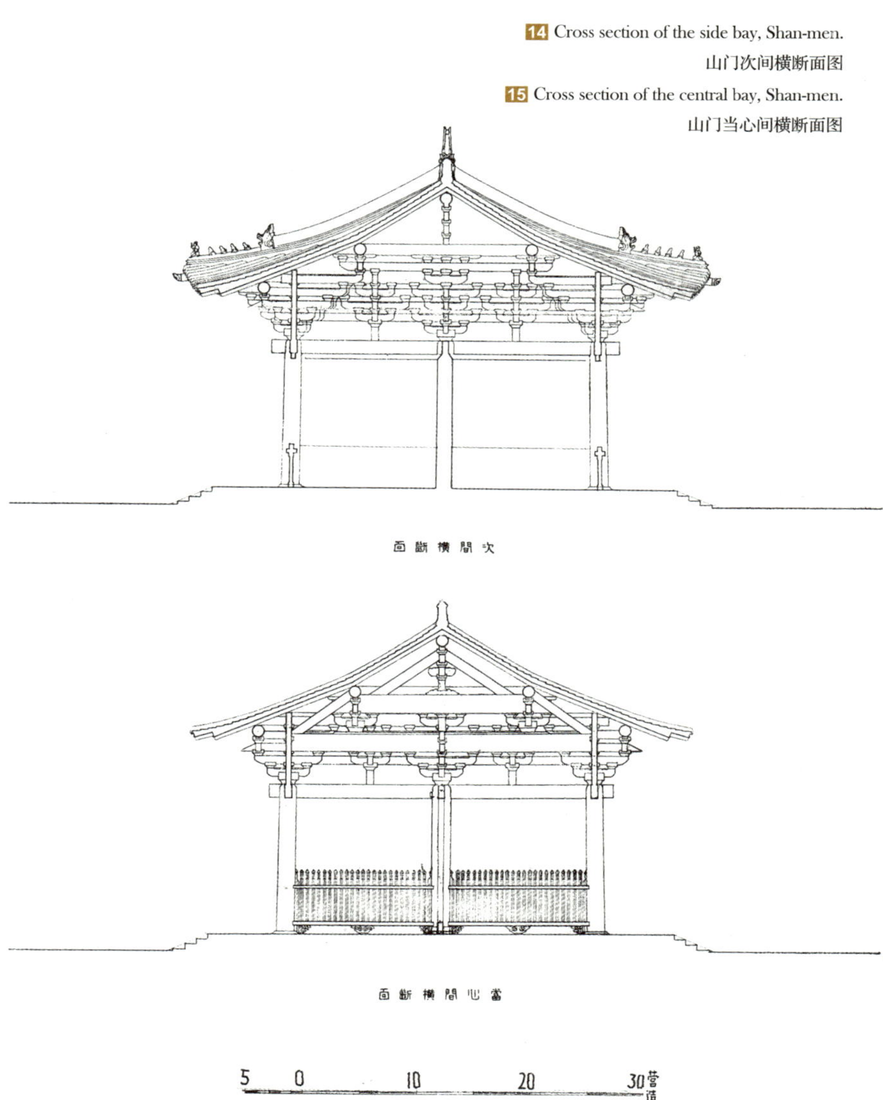

14 Cross section of the side bay, Shan-men.

山门次间横断面图

15 Cross section of the central bay, Shan-men.

山门当心间横断面图

❷ 平面

面阔三间，进深二间，共有柱十二。当心间（今称明间）面阔 6.10 米，中柱[30] 间安装大门，为出入寺之孔道。梢间面阔 5.23 米，南面二间立天王像，北面二间原来有像否，尚待考。中柱与前后檐柱间之进深为 4.38 米。因进深较少于梢间面阔，故垂脊与正脊相交乃在梢间之内而不正在中柱之上也（图 8）。

Ⓒ Base and Steps

The Shan-men stands on a stone base, or terrace, of low proportion paved with square brick tiles. The distance from the yen-chu to the edge of the terrace is wider on the front and rear than on the sides of the building. Thus the border around the yen-chu is not equally wide on all sides, contrary to the practice of the Ming and Ts'ing styles. This was probably because it was not designed to accommodate circulation around the building. It should be remembered that the Shan-men in its original surroundings was not a free-standing building like the one we see today, but connected with the rear of the temple by colonnades leading from the two narrow sides, and it was therefore only natural to narrow down the terrace slightly at those sides. On the southern side there are steps leading from the street level up to the terrace and these, according to the practice from the Sung Dynasty until today, should be as long as the width of the tang-hsin-chien. But the present steps are only a dingy narrow "restoration" of modern times. The steps to the north of the base have been destroyed.

Ⓓ Columns and Bases

The columns of the Shan-men, twelve in number, form the main supports of the heavy roof above. The height of the columns is about 8.6 times the diameter, slightly shorter than that of the Ionic order. Considering the material used, this proportion seems rather heavy, especially when compared to the wooden columns of American colonial architecture. The column has a very slight entasis of about 2.5 per cent of the length. The tapering from the bottom towards the top is almost imperceptible and nothing like the very marked entasis of the Greco-Roman orders.

Measurements taken cross-section-wise show that the distance between the top of the columns is smaller than that between the bases by about two per cent of the height of the column. In Chapter V of the *Ying-tsao-fa-shih,* the following passage occurs.

"In the erection of a column, the top should incline slightly inward, with the roof protruding out, this is called ch'e-chiao (meaning 'tilted-foot'). On the front and rear of the building, the ch'e-chiao should be 1 fen to every ch'ih of the height of the column (1%); while on the sides of the building it should be 8 li (0.8%). [31] When it comes to a corner column, the inclination should be in both directions in accordance to this rule (diagonally)."

The columns of the Shan-men were undoubtedly erected in the manner described above, but with an even greater inclination, so marked that it is noticeable to the naked eye (Figure 26).

❸ 台基及阶

台基为石质，颇低；高只 0.50 米。前后台出[32] 约 2.20 米，而两山 [33] 台出则为 1.30 米，显然不备行人绕门或在两山檐下通行者。南面石阶三级，颇短小，宽不及一间，殆非原状。盖阶之"长随间广"，自李明仲至于今日，尚为定例，明仲前百年，不宜有此例外也。北面石阶已毁，当与南面同。

❹ 柱及柱础

山门柱十二，皆《营造法式》所谓"直柱"者是。柱身与柱径之比例，虽只为 8.6 与 1 之比，尚不及罗马爱奥尼克式[34] 柱之瘦长，而所呈现象，则较瘦；盖因抱框[35] 等附属部分遮盖使然。柱之下径较大于上径，唯收分[36] 甚微，故不甚显著，非详究不察；然在观者下意识中，固已得一种稳固之印象。兹将各柱之平均度量列下：

柱高	4.33 米	下径	0.51 米
上径	0.47 米	高：径	8.65 : 1
收分	25‰		

前后柱脚与中柱脚之距离为 4.38 米，而柱头间则为 4.29 米，柱头微向内偏，约合柱高 2%。按《营造法式》卷五：

"凡立柱，并令柱首微收向内，柱脚微出向外，谓之侧脚。每屋正面，随柱之长，每一尺即侧脚一分；若侧面，每长一尺，即侧脚八厘。至角柱，其柱首相向各依本法。"

山门柱之倾斜度极为明显，且甚于《营造法式》所规定，其为"侧脚"无疑（图 26）。

16 Plan and cross section of the Shan-men

山门平面和断面图

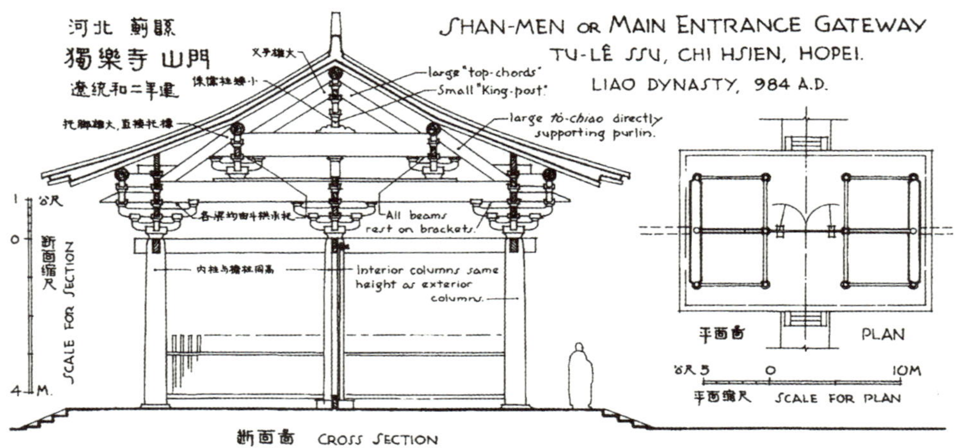

This refinement is identical with that of the Parthenon, another important but unnoticed evidence of the influence of Greco-Buddhist art in China.

The chu-ch'u, or base of the column, is of local greenish slate stone, measuring less than twice the diameter on its side, differing from both Sung and Ts'ing regulations that call for a base the side of which is twice the diameter. This dimension refers to the plinth of the base, which is usually sunken in the ground with the top of the plinth flushing with the finished floor. On the top is the part corresponding to the torus and the moldings in the Roman columns, called fu-p'en, the "upset basin." The fu-p'en of the *Ying-tsao-fa-shih* is very similar to the torus and the fillet in the base of a Roman order, but usually decorated with elaborate carvings. But in the case of the Shan-men, the fu-p'en is merely a slightly rased disc with no carving, more like those of the Ts'ing style.

E The Tou-kung, or Bracketing System

Structurally analyzed, the tou-kung is merely a system of corbelling, consisting of a number of kungs or horizontal "arms," put one on top of another—the higher the position, the longer the "arm"—with tous, or blocks, or "cushions" as Dr. Siren calls them, at the end and center of each lower kung to support the upper one. The kungs are put often both parallel and perpendicular to the facade, the former to enable a far overhang of the eave and the latter to take care of the load of the purlins. The kungs perpendicular to the facade are called hua-kung, and each "step" of the corbel is called a t'iao, and, starting from the bottom, each t'iao is given a numeral "first," "second," etc. to designate its position. The kungs parallel to the facade, and on the center-line of the column, are of only two lengths: the shorter and lower one is called the ni-tao-kung, while the longer and upper one is called the man-kung. Those parallel to the facade, but supported on the end of a hua-kung, are called the ling-kung if they are on the end of the uppermost, and, therefore, longest hua-kung. Those on any other hua-kung but between the ling-kung and the center-line of the column are called the kua-tzu-kung.

Under the intersection of the 1st hua-kung and the ni-tao-kung is the large lu-tou, the foot of the entire p'u-cho, or set of tou-kung, standing right on top of the column. On the ends of all kungs are smaller tous called san-tou, and at the intersection of kungs, chiao-hu-tou.

On the exterior of the Shan-men, supporting the eave, are three different kinds of tou-kungs: 1. chu-t'ou-p'u-cho; 2. chuan-chiao-p'u-cho; 3. pu-chien-p'u-cho.

柱身经历次重修，或坎补，或涂抹，乃至全柱更换，亦属可能。观音阁柱头，皆"卷杀[37]作覆盆样"（图 33），而山门柱头乃平正如清式，其是否原物，亦待考也。

柱础[38]为本地青石造，方约 0.85 米不及柱径之倍，而自《营造法式》至清《工程做法》皆规定柱础"方倍柱之径"，此岂辽宋制度之不同欤？础上"覆盆"较似清式简单之"古镜"，不若宋式之华丽也。

❺ 斗拱

山门外檐斗拱，共有三种，分述如次：

17 Chu-t'ou-p'u-cho, Shan-men.

山门柱头铺作侧样

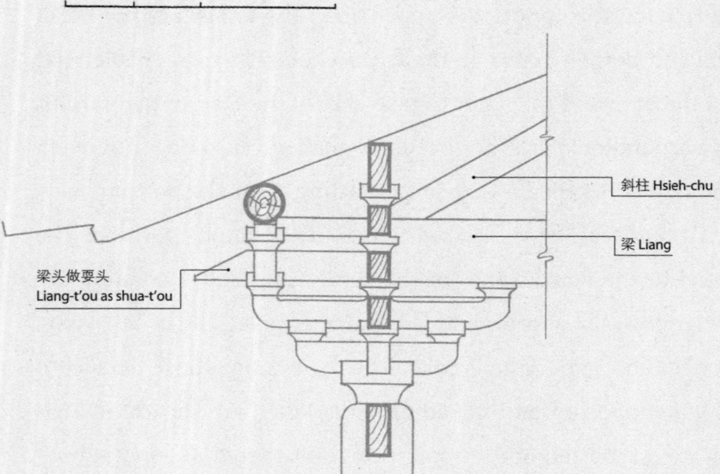

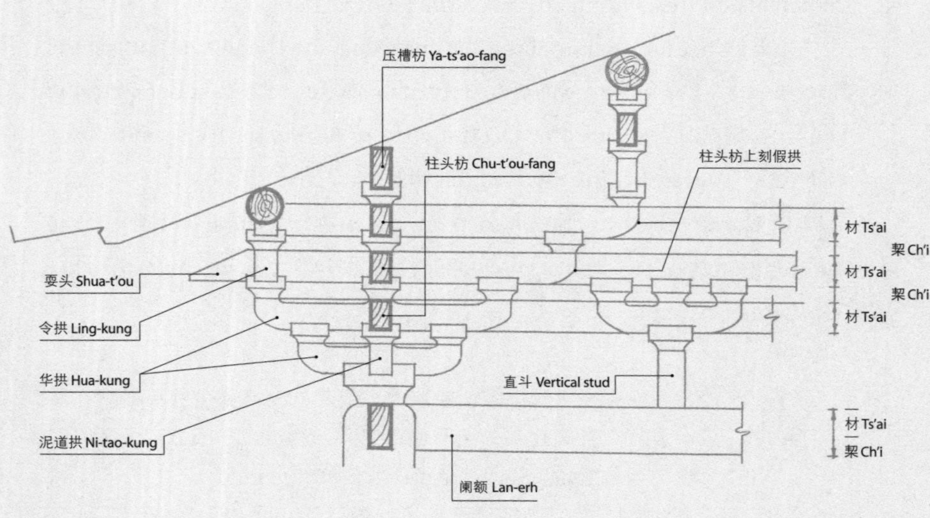

1. Chu-t'ou-p'u-cho or "the set of tou-kung on the column"

The lu-tou stands right on top of the column instead of on a p'u-p'ai-fang, or plate, differing from the practice of the Ming and Ts'ing styles (Figures 16, 17). From the lu-tou extending two hua-kungs, one on top of the other. At the end of the second hua-kung is a ling-kung, intersecting with the shua-t'ou, a member parallel to, above, and of the same size as a hua-kung, but instead of the rounded curve near the end, it is beveled off from the upper surface into a wedge, with the inclined surface making an angle of 30 degrees with the ground. On the ling-kung are placed three shua-t'ous, in which is the t'i-mu, which in turn supports the liao-yen-ch'uan, or eave supporting purlin. The t'i-mu is a member unseen in later structures, the term occurs in the *Ying-tsao-fa-shih*, with dimensions and proportion, but its function and position is not defined. From the passage "the lower surface is rounded off by four fens...and when it is used in gable construction, it should follow the length of the purlin," a rough idea of its shape can be gathered, and its position is found to be related to the purlin. This unknown member in this p'u-cho, as well as in the gable of the Hall, seems to answer very well to the description. And since there is no reason to contradict its being something else, I call it the t'i-mu, for the time being at least, till evidence is brought up to contradict it.

1. 柱头铺作[39]　　清式称柱头科（图 16，17）。其栌斗（今称坐斗）“施之于柱头”，不似清式之将“坐斗”施于“平板枋”上。自栌斗外出者计华拱（今称翘）两层，故上层长两跳[40]。上层跳头施以令拱（今称厢拱），与耍头相交，置于交互斗（今称十八斗）内。其耍头之制，将头作成约三十度向外之锐角，略似平置之昂，不若清式之作六十度向内之钝角者。令拱之上，置散斗（今称三才升）三个，以承拱形小木，及其上之槫（今称桁）按《营造法式》卷五，有所谓“替木”者，其长按地位而异，“两头各下杀四分……若至出际，长与槫齐”。此拱形小木，殆即“替木”欤？与此“替木”位置功用相同者，于清式建筑中有“挑檐枋”，长与檩同，而此处所见，则分段施于各铺作令拱之上，且将两端略加卷杀，甚足以表示承受上部分散之重量，而集中使移于柱头之机能，堪称善美。

18 Chuan-chiao-p'u-cho and the rear of the pu-chien-p'u-cho, Shan-men. 山门转角铺作并补间铺作后尾

Intersecting with the first hua-kung is the ni-tao-kung, and with the second hua-kung is the man-kung. It is interesting to note in this case that the man-kung is not a kung in the real sense, but a fang, here called the chu-t'ou-fang, of the same size as the kung, but extending through the entire length of the facade. In later styles, the chu-t'ou-fang, supported by the man-kung, usually intersects with the third hua-kung, or shua-t'ou as the case may be. But here the chu-t'ou-fang is supported on the ni-tao-kung, with the man-kung carved in relief on the fang, a characteristic not found in the representations of buildings in the mural paintings of Tun-huang (T'ang), or in the specifications of the *Ying-tsao-fa-shih* or in still existing old buildings such as the Ch'u-chu-an in Shao-lin Ssu, Sung-shan, or in late Northern Sung, or any of the Ming and Ts'ing structures. But, this characteristic is common to the approximately contemporary Upper and Lower Hua-yen Ssu at Ta-t'ung and the Wooden Pagoda of Fo-kung Ssu at Ying Hsien, Shansi Province. The above-mentioned characteristic therefore must have been peculiar to the Liao period.

On the end of the second hua-kung is a ling-kung, a transverse member supporting the eave-purlin, but on the end of the first hua-kung, such a member is absent, another peculiarity not found in later styles. In Chapter IV of the *Ying-tsao-fa-shih*, there is the following statement describing the "ensemble of the p'u-cho":

"If a transverse kung is used on every t'iao, the p'u-cho is called chi-sin; if used on every other t'iao, it is called t'ou-sin."

In the very few existing structures contemporary to the *Ying-tsao-fa-shih* only the chi-sin system is used. To the builder of the Ming and Ts'ing Dynasties, even the term t'ou-sin was unknown. It is only in these Liao structures that we see an actual example and possibility of such a system of construction.

与华拱相交而与建筑物表面平行者为泥道拱（今称瓜拱）及与今万拱相似之长拱。然此长拱者，有拱之形，而无拱之用，实柱头枋（清式称正心枋）上而雕作拱形者也。就愚所知，敦煌壁画、嵩山少林寺初祖庵、[41]营造法式及明清遗构，此式尚未之见，而与独乐寺约略同时之大同上下华严寺、应县佛宫寺木塔皆同此结构，殆辽之特征欤?

华拱二层，其上层跳头施以令拱，已于上文述及；然下层跳头，则无与之相交之拱，亦为明清式所无。按《营造法式》卷四，《总铺作次序》中曰：

"凡铺作逐跳上安拱谓之'计心'。若逐跳上不安拱，而再出跳或出昂者谓之'偷心'。"

山门柱头铺作，在此点上适与此条符合，"偷心"之佳例也。

前后檐柱柱头铺作后尾为华拱两跳，跳头不安拱，而以上层跳头之散斗承托大梁之下。使梁之重量全部由斗拱转达于柱以至于地，条理井然，为建筑逻辑之最良表现（图 13–15）。

山柱柱头铺作后尾，则唯华拱四跳，层层叠出，以承平槫。跳头皆无横拱，为明清制度所无（图 17，18）。此式《营造法式》亦未述及。然考之日本镰仓时代所建之奈良东大寺南大门，及伊东忠太博士发现之怀安县照化寺掖门[42]，皆作此式，虽内外之位置不同，而其结构法则一。此式在日本称"天竺样"，虽称"天竺"，亦来自中土，不过以此示别于日本早年受自中国之"唐样"，及其日本化之"和样"耳。

服部胜吉《日本古建筑史》所引《东大寺造立供养记》关于寺中佛像之铸造，则有"……铸物师大工陈和卿也，都宋朝工舍弟陈佛铸等七人也，日本铸物师草部是助以下十四人也。……"等句，是此寺所受中土影响，毫无疑义。前此只见于日本者，追溯其源，伊东先生得之于照化寺，今复见之于蓟县遗物，其线索益明瞭矣。

At the rear of the chu-t'ou-p'u-cho are two t'iaos of hua-kung, with no transverse kungs at the ends; on the shua-t'ou at the end of the second hua-kung is supported the principal beam, the ends of which are made into the shape of shua-t'ous, intersecting with other kungs of the p'u-cho, thus making a strong and logical union between the beam and the tou-kung (Figures 13-15).

On the narrow side of the building, the rear of the chu-t'ou-p'u-cho is different from these of the longer facade in the following respect. It does not support any beams which are all placed parallel with the transversal axis of the building. Here the second hua-kung, the shua-t'ou, and another similar member above, all have the rear ends prolonged into fangs on the longitudinal axis, with the form of kungs carved on the fang in relief, four successive t'iaos without a single transversal kung. This characteristic will be discussed under the topic "pu-chien-p'u-cho."

From the structural point of view, to disguise a fang in the form of a kung may be considered an architectural dishonesty. Existing examples as well as diagrams in the *Ying-tsao-fa-shih* all show the use of a fang immediately above the man-kung; no instance of the fang carved with a kung is found in later structures. But the logical development of such a system is easily traced in the T'ang engraved drawing of a temple on a stone lintel over the western doorway of the Ta-yen T'a of Sian Fu. A set of ni-tao-kung is represented there as supporting a chu-t'ou-fang superposed on another set of ni-tao-kung and chu-t'ou fang identical to those below (Figure 19). Should one imagine the ni-tao-kung of the upper set as elongated into a fang, while still retaining the kung in relief, while the chu-t'ou-fang of the lower set is carved with a man-kung, the result would be exactly a tou-kung of the Liao style, as those found in the Shan-men and the Kuan-yin Hall of the Tu-lo Ssu.

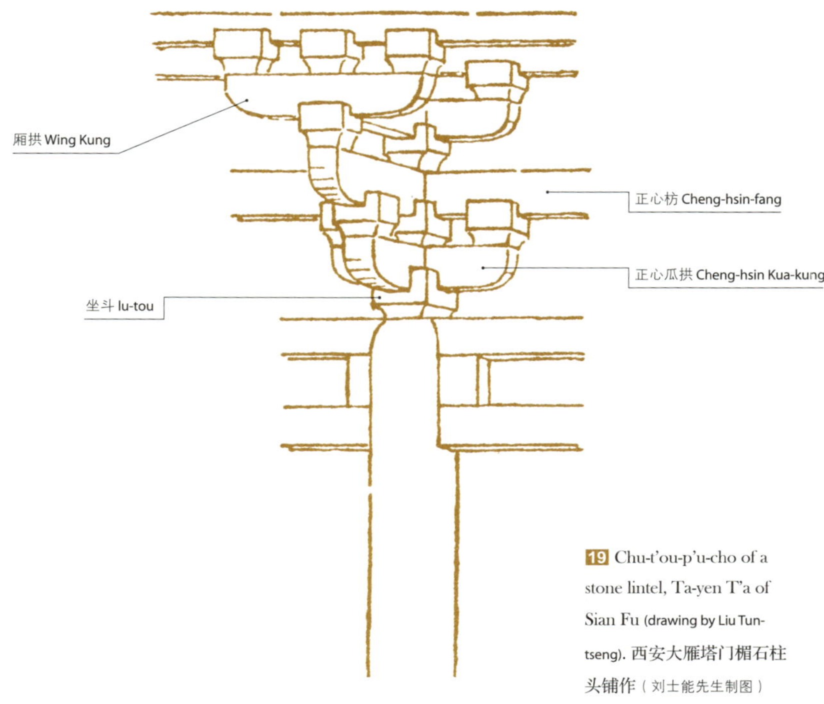

19 Chu-t'ou-p'u-cho of a stone lintel, Ta-yen T'a of Sian Fu (drawing by Liu Tun-tseng). 西安大雁塔门楣石柱头铺作（刘士能先生制图）

至于斗拱之正面，则栌斗之内，与华拱相交者，有泥道拱（今称正心瓜拱），其两端施以散斗（散斗之在正心上者今称槽升子）；其上则为柱头枋，枋上刻成长拱形。再上为第二层柱头枋，亦刻作拱形，长与泥道拱同，其上为第三层柱头枋，又刻作长拱形。其全部所呈现象，为短拱上承长拱之结合共二层，各拱头皆施以散斗。

上述泥道拱，即今之正心瓜拱。其长拱殆即《营造法式》所谓“慢拱”是。《营造法式》卷四有各拱名释，谓“造拱之制有五”，而所释只四。同卷中又见“慢拱”之名，慢拱盖即第五种拱而为李所遗者。但卷三十大木作图样中，又有慢拱图，其形颇长。清式建筑中，与之位置相同者称“万拱”，南语慢万同音，故其名称无可疑也。

在结构方面着眼，将多层枋子雕作拱形，殊不合理。《营造法式》以至明清制度，皆在慢拱之上施以枋子，无将枋上雕作拱形者。然追溯古例，其所以如此之故，颇易解释。按西安大慈恩寺大雁塔门楣雕刻所见，乃正心瓜拱上承正心枋，正心枋上又有小坐斗（《营造法式》所称“齐心斗”？），斗上又有正心瓜拱及正心枋。是同一物而上下两层叠叠者也（图 19）。今若将此下层正心枋雕以慢拱之形，再将上层正心瓜拱伸引成枋，则与山门所见无异。其来历固极明显也。

2. Chuan-chiao-p'u-cho or "the set that turns the corner"

The chuan-chiao-p'u-cho may be considered an intersection of two sets of chu-t'ou-p'u-cho (Figure 20). As the adjacent sides are identical, either may be taken for the front. Therefore, on the center-line of the column, both on the front and side, are two t'iaos of hua-kung. In the first t'iao, the rear of the hua-kung is at the same time the ni-tao-kung on the other side, and vice versa when viewed from around the corner. The rear of the second t'iao, likewise extends to become the first chu-t'ou-fang on the other side, while the shua-t'ou becomes the second chu-t'ou-fang. The third chu-t'ou-fang, in this case, does not reveal its end, but intersects with the one on the other side that is hidden behind the eave-purlin. This system of extending the rear of a member to form another member on the adjacent facade is called lieh-kung in the *Ying-tsao-fa-shih*. On the end of each t'iao of hua-kung is placed a transversal kung in the "chi-sin" manner.

On the mitre-line of the building, bisecting the right angle, formed by the intersection of the kungs and fangs of the adjacent facades, and perpendicular to each other, are three t'iaos of chiao-kung or corner kungs. The uppermost t'iao is on the level of the ling-kung, supporting the chiao-liang, or hip-rafter, above. On the same level is another long kung, on the axis of the column, but making a right angle with the mitre kungs, with shua-t'ous on its ends to support the t'i-mu. The author takes the liberty to call this characteristic mo-chiao-man-kung, or "diagonal man-kung."

The rear of the chuan-chiao-p'u-cho is formed by the rear ends of the chiao-kungs, five t'iaos altogether in number, corbelling out one above and beyond the other. The uppermost or fifth t'iao is just in position to receive the intermediate purlin or hsia-p'ing-chuan.

This will be discussed more fully under the next topic.

2. 转角铺作　清式称“角科”。其结构较柱头铺作为复杂，盖两朵[43]柱头铺作相交而成（图 20）。于柱之中线上，其正面及侧面皆有华拱二层。上层华拱之上，正面侧面皆各出耍头，与柱头铺作上者同。而此面耍头之后尾，则为他面第二层柱头枋，换言之，则正侧二面第二层柱头枋相交后伸出而为耍头也。此面第一层华拱之后尾为彼面泥道拱，第二层华拱后尾则为彼面刻成慢拱形之第一层柱头枋。此种做法，即清式所谓“把臂”，宋式称为“列拱”者是，每层华拱跳头，皆施以拱，成所谓“让心”者。

屋角四十五度斜线上，有角拱三层，最上者与跳头令拱平，以支角梁。与角拱成正角，而施于柱中线上者，有长拱一道，与令拱平，唯安于二层跳头之瓜子拱（今称外拽瓜拱）上，姑名之曰“抹角慢拱”。其拱端亦安散斗，以承槫下之替木。

转角铺作之后尾乃由角拱后尾五层叠成，与山柱头铺作后尾同其形制，其最上一跳则以承正面及山面下平槫（今称下金桁）之相交点。

3. Pu-chien-p'u-cho or "the set that fills the bay" (Figures 16, 21)

The function of the pu-chien-p'u-cho is to prevent the sagging of the middle portion of the purlin which is supported at the two ends by the chu-t'ou-p'u-chos. It is placed midway, or nearly midway, between the columns. The lowest member of the set, a short stud, stands on the lintel, or lan-erh; on the stud is placed a large tou, which holds two t'iaos of hua-kung. The upper hua-kung has a short t'i-mu on its end, immediately beneath the eave-purlin. Intersecting with the lower hua-kung in the large t'ou is the first chu-t'ou-fang, which is carved with a ni-tao-kung in relief, while the upper hua-kung intersects with the second fang in which the man-kung is carved. The third chu-t'ou-fang is again carved with a ni-tao-kung. The distribution of these carved fangs is such that the lengths of the kungs of the pu-chien-p'u-cho is just the reverse of that of the chu-t'ou-p'u-cho, fitting but not interfering each other. This distribution would have been impossible if the kungs had been real, instead of being carved as the fangs.

3. 补间铺作（图 16，21） 清式称“平身科”。其机能在防止两柱头间之檩及上部向下弯坠。其位置在二柱头之间。其最下层为“直斗”，立于阑额（今称额枋）之上，直斗之上置大斗，大斗之上安华拱两跳，上层跳头施以替木，以承檐檩（今称挑檐桁）。下层华拱与第一层柱头枋相交安于大斗口内。此第一层柱头枋雕作泥道拱（瓜拱）形，其上第二层柱头枋则雕作慢拱，第三层又雕作泥道拱。与柱头铺作上各层枋上所雕拱，长短适相错。若皆为真拱，则此相错排列，为事实上所不能，亦其不合理处也。

此种补间铺作，与明清制度固极不同，而与《营造法式》亦迥然异趣。明清式之补间铺作，多者可至七八攒——如太和殿。《营造法式》卷四《总铺作次序》则谓：

“当心间须用补间铺作两朵，次间及梢间各用一朵。其铺作分布，令远近皆匀。”

而独乐寺观音阁及山门，补间铺作皆只一朵（即一攒），虽当心间亦无两朵者。

21 Pu-chien-p'u-cho, Shan-men.

山门补间铺作侧样

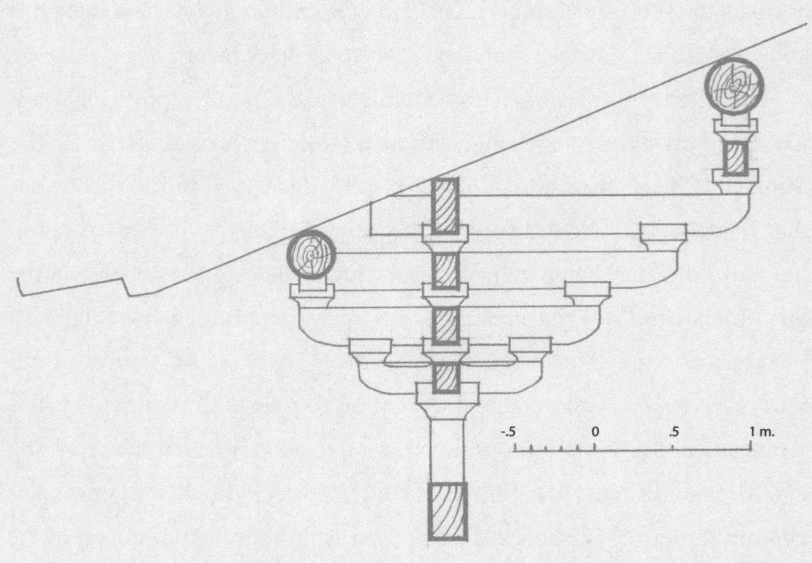

Here we have another motif that is unknown, or at least not used, in later ages, namely, the short stud. The use of such a stud was quite commonplace in the pre-T'ang dynasties, as exemplified in the mural paintings and cave sculptures of Tun-huang, Yun-kang, Lung-men and T'ien-lung Shan. But in the *Ying-tsao-fa-shih,* the stud is not even mentioned, thus leaving us in total ignorance of the name of a once very popular architectural motif. But in Japan, the short stud has been retained in later monuments, and there it is known as 束. The Chinese equivalent is yet to be determined.

In earlier examples, the short stud is usually found supporting a tou which in turn supports the fang, with no intersecting hua-kungs. But in the Ming and Ts'ing styles, the pu-chien-p'u-cho developed to such an extent that it was actually identical with the chu-t'ou-p'u-cho in construction, the only difference being in its position. But in the case we see here in the Shan-men, two t'iaos of hua-kung are placed in the tou, intersecting with the chu-t'ou-fang. At the end of the second t'iao is placed a short t'i-mu that receives the purlin above it. As far as complexity is concerned, this arrangement may be fairly considered as a transition between the pre-T'ang and Ming or Ts'ing styles. This short stud is preserved only in the two p'u-chos on the eastern facade, but it has been sadly abused by restorers of the Kwang-hsü period who painted it over with an all-over pattern of frets, together with the wall between the p'u-chos, ignoring totally its structural function. To an unobservant eye, it is as good as lost.

The point of greatest significance in the pu-chien-p'u-cho is the arrangement of the rear ends of the hua-kungs. Four t'iaos of hua-kungs are placed one on top of the other till the uppermost is high enough to support the p'ing-ch'uan, or intermediate purlin. With the exception of the uppermost t'iao, which carries a p'an-chien, or long fang on its end, not one of these hua-kungs carries any transversal member, either the kung or the fang. This system is again unknown to later ages, and not even mentioned in the *Ying-tsao-fa-shih*. But on the Nandaimon of the Todaiji at Nara, Japan, a structure of the Kamakura period, as well as the Chao-hua-ssu at Huai-an Hsien, an identical treatment of the hua-kung is seen. It was undoubtedly a feature once very common in China and later taken up and much used in Japan where it is known as the Tenjiku style. Although nominally from India, its Chinese origin can never be denied. The discovery of such a construction here is another evidence of its genealogy.

On the interior of the Shan-men are two different kinds of tou-kungs:

4. Chu-t'ou-p'u-cho on the chung-chu

The chung-chu, whose literal translation is the "central column," is a column on the longitudinal axis of a building and at the same time in the interior. (Those on the exterior being called shan-chu, or "gable columns.") The p'u-cho on the chung-chu is used to support the middle of the principal beam, the two ends being supported by the yen-chus. Parallel with the beam and beneath it, are two t'iaos of hua-kung, extending from the lu-tou, like the rear of the exterior chu-t'ou-p'u-cho. Intersecting with these hua-kung, and also with the beam, are one ni-tao-kung and three tiers of chu-t'ou-fang, which are also carved with kungs in relief, like those on the exterior.

至于其结构，则与宋元明清更异，如直斗一物，在六朝隋唐遗物中，固所常见；在《营造法式》中则并其名亦无之；日本称之曰“束”，刘士能先生称之曰“直斗”，今沿刘先生称。隋唐直斗上多安一斗以承枋，而无拱交于其口内。明清补间铺作则似柱头铺作，以栌斗安于平板枋上。此处所见，则直斗之上，施以华拱二跳，以承檐桁，盖二者间之过渡形式，关键至为明显。今南北西三面直斗皆已失，唯东面尚存，劣匠施以彩画，竟与垫拱板画成一片，欲将其机能之外形一笔抹杀；幸仔细观察，原形尚可见也。

补间铺作之后尾，与山柱柱头铺作后尾略同，为四层华拱，跳头无横拱，层层叠出以承下平榑。其梢间铺作与山面铺作皆不在二柱之正中，与《法式》“令远近皆匀”一语不符，前者偏近角柱，后者偏近山柱，而二者与角柱间距离则同，盖其后尾与转角铺作之后尾共同承支前后下平榑及山下平榑之相交点，其距离乃视下平榑而定也。

山门内檐斗拱，则有：

4. 中柱柱头斗拱 其机能在承托大梁之中段，将其重量转达于柱。华拱二跳自栌斗伸出，与外檐柱头铺作后尾同，前后二面皆如此。正面则泥道拱一道，上承三层枋，枋上亦雕拱形，如外檐所见。

5. Interior pu-chien-p'u-cho

Structurally, the pu-chien-p'u-cho in the interior is practically of no value. It is composed of the three fangs extending from the rear of the chu-t'ou-p'u-cho of the narrower facade. Near the center of each bay, these fangs are carved into the forms of different kungs like those on the exterior chu-t'ou-fangs, and the spaces between each tier of the kungs are taken care of by tous, while the lowest fang is supported by a larger tou which is placed on top of a short stud standing on the lan-erh. Having no overhanging roofs for them to support, intersecting hua-kungs are totally absent in this particular case, which is similar to many of the pre-T'ang examples.

Before leaving the subject of the tou-kung, it may be interesting to make an analysis of the dimensions and proportion of the different members of the entire p'u-cho, and also to compare them with those of the Sung and Ts'ing styles.

In Chapter IV of the *Ying-tsao-fa-shih*, on the making of the tou, it is specified that:

"The lu-tou...should be thirty-two fen square...by twenty fen in height. The upper eight fen of the height compose the erh, the middle four fen the p'ing, and the lower eight fen the i. The kou (mortise on the tou to receive the kung) should be ten fen wide by eight fen deep."

From this passage it is clear that the proportion of the length or width to the height is 8:5. The Shan-men, in this particular respect, is similar to the Sung style while differing from the 3:2 of the Ts'ing regulations. The proportion of the erh, p'ing and i, which are called the tou-erh, sheng-yao and tou-ti respectively in the Ts'ing style, is however definitely different to both the Sung and Ts'ing regulations which specified that it should be 2:1:2. In the Shan-men under consideration the approximate proportion is 6:4:7. The depth of the kou is slightly less than either the Sung or Ts'ing lu-tous, causing a great influence on the proportion of the entire p'u-cho. The proportions of the chiao-hu-tou and the san-tou are also slightly different from the *Ying-tsao-fa-shih* proportions, but being much smaller in size, their influence on the appearance of the p'u-cho is far less prominent.

All the kungs, regardless of their lengths, are the same in their cross sections, about 16.5 cm. × 24 cm., which is in accordance with the 2:3 proportion of the *Ying-tsao-fa-shih*. The Ts'ing proportion was 1:2.

5. 补间铺作 内檐补间铺作乃将外檐补间铺作而去其华拱所成。其直斗立于阑额上，其上承枋三层，枋亦雕成拱形。当心间铺作上，第一层枋雕作泥道拱，第二层则雕作慢拱，第三层不雕。梢间唯第一层雕作拱形，二三层不雕。此三层枋子者，实山面柱头铺作后尾伸引而成，亦有趣之结构法也。

大梁以上尚有斗拱数种，当于下节分析之。

至于斗拱各部尺寸，亦饶研究价值，兹先表列如左：

	长（米）	宽（米）	高（米）
栌斗	0.51	0.51	0.32
交互斗	0.27	0.22	0.165
散斗	0.22	0.22	0.165
补间铺作大斗	0.43	0.43	0.25
华拱	按跳定	0.165	0.24
泥道拱	1.17	0.165	0.24
慢拱	1.90	0.165	0.24
令拱	1.08	0.165	0.24
替木	1.83	0.165	0.105

考之《营造法式》，卷四有造斗之制：

"栌斗……长与广皆三十二分……高二十分；上八分为耳，中四分为平，下八分为欹，开口广十分，深八分。底四面各杀四分，欹䫜一分。"

其长广与高之比例为八与五之比；0.51 米与 0.32 米亦适为八与五之比，故在此点，与宋式同，而异于清式之三与二之比。宋式之耳、平、欹，及清式之斗口、升腰、斗底，皆为二一二之比；而山门栌斗此三部乃 0.37、0.26、0.43 米[44]。其开口之深度，较宋清式略浅，而其影响于全朵之权衡则甚大。

交互斗及散斗与法式所述亦略有出入，然因体积较小，故对于全朵权衡之影响亦较小也。

关于拱之横断面，《法式》所定宽与高为二与三之比，此处所见虽略有不同，大致仍符合。而清式则为一与二之比。

In both the Sung and Ts'ing styles, the lengths of the different kungs are set in definite proportion to the width of the k'ou, i.e., the width of the kung. The Ts'ings required a length of 6.2 times the k'ou for the kua-kung (called ni-tao-kung by the Sungs) and 9.2 times the k'ou for the wan-kung (called man-kung by the Sungs), while in the *Ying-tsao-fa-shih,* with the width of the k'ou set as 10 fen, the length of the ni-tao-kung was specified as 62 fen, the kua-tze-kung 62 fen, the ling-kung 72 fen while the man-kung is not mentioned. Judging from the similarity of lengths in the Sung and Ts'ing kungs, it is fairly safe to assume the man-kung would have been specified to be 92 fen long. The measurements of the Liao kungs in the Shan-men however revealed to us something quite different; the ni-tao-kung is slightly less than 71 fen long while the man-kung reached the tremendous length of more than 115 fen. It is evident that the Liao kungs assume a much slenderer proportion than those found in later architecture.

The lengths of the hua-kungs are rather indefinite, depending entirely upon the distance of each t'iao, which seems to be rather irregular. The first t'iao measures 45 cm., and the second t'iao, 35 cm., unlike the even extension of the Ts'ing t'iaos.

The gentle curve at the ends of the kungs is formed by a series of straight planes. There are four such planes on the hua-kung and three on the ni-tao-kung. This particular process of making the curve is termed chüan-sa.

F Liang and Fangs, the Horizontal Members

1. The Lan-erh

On the heads, and connecting, the columns are horizontal lintels, whose upper surfaces flush with the tops of the columns, and the ends are fitted into mortises cut out from the columns. These lintels are known in the *Ying-tsao-fa-shih* as lan-erh, and later as eh-fang. Originally they were not intended to carry any weight, their sole function being to hold the columns in position. When the pu-chien-p'u-cho was introduced, the lan-erh began to assume another duty until in the Ming and Ts'ing periods, the pu-chien-p'u-cho became so numerous that the size of the lan-erh was necessarily enlarged to a stupendous dimension. And in addition the p'ing-pan-fang, or plate, which was placed on top of it, was introduced to carry the tou-kungs.

In the case of the Shan-men, the lan-erh measures 37 cm. × 15 cm., which is a rather slender dimension. The p'ing-pan-fang, whose use the Liao builders undoubtedly knew, is not in evidence. The pu-chien-p'u-cho is placed directly on the lan-erh.

2. The Liang-chia or the "Truss"

The central portion of the roof is held up by two "trusses," placed on the chu-t'ou-p'u-cho. They are not trusses in the true sense, being a series of lintels on posts supported by the longer lintel below, exerting no thrust as a true truss does. In the Shan-men, the "truss" is formed by the combination of two liangs, or beams, the shorter one with its two t'o-tuns or beam-supports, is placed on the longer and lower one, which is in turn supported by the chu-t'ou-p'u-cho.

宋式口广十分，泥道拱长六十二分，慢拱长无可考[45]。清式瓜拱之长与斗口之比亦六十二分，而万拱则为九十二分。山门泥道拱长 1.17 米，口广 0.165 米，其比例约为七十一分弱；慢拱长 1.90 米，约合一百十五分强，故辽拱之长，实远甚于宋以后之拱。

华拱之长，视出跳之数及其远近而定。然出跳似无定制，第一跳长 0.49 米，第二跳则长 0.35 米，耍头则长 0.47 米，不若清式之各跳均匀也。华拱卷杀，每头四瓣，每瓣长约 0.075 米；泥道拱则每头三瓣，与宋清制度均同。

❻ 梁枋

阑额横贯柱头之间，清名额枋。其广 0.37 米，厚 0.15 米。厚约当广之五分之二。额上无平板枋，异于清制。补间铺作即置于阑额之上。

山门有梁二架（图 13–15），置于柱头铺作之上，梁端伸出，即为耍头，成铺作之一部分。清式耍头只用于平身科（即补间铺作），柱头科上梁头则大几如梁身，不似辽式之与拱同大小也。

The portion of the beam that extends beyond the center-line of the column below is shaped into a shua-t'ou, forming a part of the p'u-cho. The shua-t'ou is found only on the chu-t'ou-p'u-cho in the Ts'ing style; while on the chu-t'ou-p'u-cho, the end of the liang is almost as big as the liang itself. Since the shua-t'ou, the end of the beam, is at the same time a part of the tou-kung, the connection between the two parts cannot but be strong, and the transition logical. Moreover, the shua-t'ou is made to intersect with ling-kung for the supporting of the t'i-mu and the eave-purlin, resulting in the organic union of the different parts.

The beam is supported at the middle by the chu-t'ou-p'u-cho on the chung-chu, reducing the span of the beam by half, although, judging from its size, it could without difficulty stand the load for the last thousand years without the intermediate support.

The t'o-tun, or beam-support, which lifts the shorter and upper beam on the longer and lower beam is a simple p'u-cho in form and construction. Two intersecting kungs are placed in a large tou; the one parallel with the beam supports the shorter beam above, and the one perpendicular to the beam supports the p'an-chien, an auxiliary horizontal member, usually of the size as the kung, and running parallel and beneath the purlin (Figure 22). It is to be noted that the t'o-tun is not placed directly on the main beam, but on a thin plate, measuring 21 cm. × 6 cm. Its position is not mid-way between the center-line of the ridge and the external columns, but nearer to the latter; the distances to the two center-lines being 2.41 m. and 1.88 m. respectively.

The upper beam, called the san-chia-liang, or the beam of three supports, is placed on the above mentioned t'o-tun. Its ends are also shaped like the shua-t'ou. The middle of the san-chia-liang is supported by a short stud, standing on the middle of the wu-chia-liang. Above it, and on the san-chia-liang is the t'o-feng or "camel's back," forming the base of the chu-ju-chu or "dwarf column," which supports the tou, the ni-tao-kung with its intersecting wing-shaped kung, the p'an-chien, the t'i-mu, and ultimately the ridge-purlin. The ridge-purlin is supported on the sides by two hsieh-chus,

22 The T'o-tun, Shan-men. 山门大梁柁橔

23 The chu-ju-chu, Shan-men. 山门侏儒柱

or inclined columns, forming a sort of bracing to prevent the purlin from inclining to either side. The triangular spaces beneath the hsieh-chu were originally empty, but are now filled up with brick and plaster, the original light effect therefore becoming totally lost (Figure 23).

耍头既为梁头，而又为斗拱之一部分，梁与斗拱间之联合乃极坚实。同时耍头又与令拱交置，以承替木及“橑檐榑”[46]（今称挑檐桁），于是各部遂成一种有机的结合。梁之中段，置于中柱柱头铺作之上，虽为五架梁，因中段不悬空，遂呈极稳固之状。梁上檐柱及中柱之间置柁橔，然其形不若清式之为“橔”，乃由大斗及相交之二拱而成，实则一简单铺作（图 22）；其前后拱则承上层之三架梁，左右拱则以承襻间（今称枋）。然此铺作，不直接置于梁上，而置于梁上一宽 0.21 米、厚 0.06 米之缴背上。其位置亦非檐柱及山柱之正中，而略偏近檐柱。距檐柱 1.88 米，距中柱则 2.41 米。

三架梁与下平榑相交于此铺作上，梁头亦形如耍头。枋上复有散斗及替木以承平榑。梁之中段则置于五架梁上直斗之上；其上则有驼峰，驼峰上又为直斗，直斗上为交互斗（或齐心斗），口内置泥道拱及翼形拱一。泥道拱上为襻间（今称脊枋），枋上置散斗，枋端卷杀作拱形，以承替木及脊榑。自枋之前后，有斜柱下支于三架梁，平榑之前或后，亦有斜柱下支于五架梁。斜柱下空档，现有泥壁填塞，原有玲珑状态为此失去不少（图 23）。

The wu-chia-liang is known in the *Ying-tsao-fa-shih* as the ssu-ch'uan-fu or the beam of four rafters' length, while the san-chia-liang is called the p'ing-liang. The wing-shaped kung is not named in the famous book, but on page 22, Chapter XXXI, in the drawing of the cross section of a small building, is shown a motif very similar to it; judging from its position, it may well be considered the prototype of the p'eng-liang-yün of the Ts'ing style.

In Chapter V of the *Ying-tsao-fa-shih,* on the making of the chu-ju-chu, it is specified that:

"If the truss construction is exposed, a tou should be placed on the chu-ju-chu; on the t'ou should be placed one or two pieces of p'an-chien. The size of the p'an-chien should be the same as the ts'ai, and its length in accordance with the width of the bay. Its end should be made into a half kung extending beyond the chu-ju-chu with the other half in the p'an-chien itself..."

The chu-ju-chu construction of the Shan-men answers very well to the above specifications (Figure 24).

The beams, which are the principal members of the "truss," are also worth studying. Beams are divided into two main categories in the *Ying-tsao-fa-shih*: the yüeh-liang or "crescent beam" and the chih-liang or "straight beam." Those used in the Shan-men and the Kuan-yin Ke are of the latter kind. Their peculiarity lies in the cross section of the beams. The Ts'ing regulations required the proportion between the depth and the width of the beam to be 10:8 or 12:10; the cross section resulting in almost a square. They did not know that the strength of the beam lies in the depth rather than in the width. The *Ying-tsao-fa-shih* set the proportion of 3:2, a much more logical shape. But in the case of the Shan-men, the wu-chia-liang measures 54 cm. × 30 cm., and the san-chia-liang measures 50 cm. × 26 cm., both being very near the modern practice of the 2:1 proportion. It seems that the Chinese builders of the Ts'ing Dynasty compared to their ancestors had a very poor knowledge of the strength of materials.

Refinement is also evident on these beams. They were shaped with a slight bulge near the middle on the sides of the beam. This was certainly done not for structural value, but in order to soften the mechanical harshness of the straight lines as the slightly curved face of the Parthenon. It may not be altogether incredible to suppose that the T'ang and Sung architects learnt delicate techniques of this kind, indirectly, of course, through Gandara and India, from Greece.

Ⓖ The Heng or Purlin

At the end of the beams and on the chu-ju-chu are placed hengs, (also termed lins), or purlins. The Chinese purlin, unlike those of the Western method of constructions are round in cross section. The Ming and Ts'ing methods of construction placed these hengs, in addition to the above-mentioned places, also on the center-line of the columns. They were then termed cheng-hsin-heng or "center-line purlins," and if on the end of the uppermost hua-kung, they were called the t'iao-yen-heng or "eave-lifting purlins."

五架梁于《营造法式》称“四椽栿”，三架梁称“平梁”。平梁上之直斗称“侏儒柱”。斜柱亦称“义手”，见《法式》卷五《侏儒柱》节内。翼形拱不知何名，《法式》卷三十一第 22 页图中有相类似之拱；以位置论，殆即清式所谓“捧梁云”之前身欤？

《营造法式》卷五《侏儒柱》节又谓：

“凡屋如彻上明造，即于蜀柱之上安斗，斗上安随间襻间，或一材或两材。襻间广厚并如材，长随间广，出半拱在外，半拱连身对隐。……”

“彻上明造”即无天花。柱上安斗，即山门所见。襻间者，即清式之脊枋是也[47]。今门之制，则在斗内先作泥道拱，拱上置襻间。其外端作拱形，即“出半拱在外，半拱连身对隐”之谓欤？（图 24）。

此部侏儒柱之结构，合理而美观，良构也。然至清代，则侏儒改称脊瓜柱，驼峰斜柱合而为一，成所谓“角背”者，结构既拙，美观不逮尤远。

❼ 桁

侏儒柱之机能在承脊槫，而槫则所以承椽。而用槫之制，于檐槫——清式称檐桁或檐檩——一部，辽宋清略有不同，特为比较。

Of the twenty-two cross section drawings in Chapter XXXI of the *Ying-tsao-fa-shih*, five include the cheng-hsin-heng but omit the t'iao-yen-heng, in place of which is represented a fang, rectangular instead of round in cross section. In the remaining seventeen drawings no heng are represented in either position, but fangs are indicated.

The Hall of Ch'u-chu-an, of the Shao-lin Ssu in Sung-shan, was built in the seventh year of Hsuan-ho (1125), contemporary to the publication of the famous book on Chinese architecture. In the structure of this hall only cheng-hsin-heng were employed. It is evident that it was customary in the Sung period to omit either t'iao-yen-heng, or both the t'iao-yen and the cheng-hsin-heng. But in the Shan-men and Kuan-yin Ke of Tu-lo Ssu, the placing of the heng and the fang is just contrary to the Sung method. Here it is the cheng-hsin-heng that has been omitted while on the end of the uppermost hua-kung is placed a large, round t'iao-yen-heng (Figure 17).

清式于正心枋上置桁（即槫），称“正心桁”，而于斗拱最外跳头上亦置桁，称“挑檐桁”。

《营造法式》卷三十一殿堂横断面图二十二种，其中五种有正心桁而无挑檐桁，其余则并正心桁亦无之，而代之以枋。嵩山少林寺初祖庵，建于宣和间，正与《营造法式》同时，亦只有正心桁而无挑檐桁，其为当时通用方法无疑。

独乐寺所见，则与宋式适反其位置，盖有挑檐桁而无正心桁者。同一功用，面能各异其制如此，亦饶趣矣（图17）。

《营造法式》造梁之制多用月梁，于力学原则上颇为适宜。《法式》图中亦有不用月梁而用直梁者。山门及观音阁所用亦非月梁。其最异于清式者，乃在梁之横断面。《工程做法则例》规定梁宽为高之十分之八，其横断面几成正方形。不知梁之载重力，视其高而定，其宽影响甚微也。《营造法式》卷五则规定：

“凡梁之大小，各随其广分为三分，以二分为厚。”

Ⓗ The Chiao-liang or Hip-rafter

In the construction of a hipped roof, the Chinese method had always been to place the hip-rafter on the purlins, contrary to the practice in modern construction. But the function of the hip-rafter is no different from that of the purlin, that is, to support the rafters. The hip is built in sections spanning the spaces between the purlins, running in a direction bisecting the right angle of the two adjacent walls. The lowest section is longer than the span and overhangs a considerable distance beyond the corner column on the mitre-line. This is the lao-chiao-liang or "old corner beam." On top of the lao-chiao-liang and extending even further out, forming a corbel, is the tze-chiao-liang or "little corner beam."

其广与厚之比为三与二，此说较为合理。今山门大梁（《法式》称"檐栿"）广（即高）0.54 米，厚 0.30 米，三架梁（《法式》称"平梁"）广 0.50 米，厚 0.26 米，两者比例皆近二与一之比。梁之载重力既不随其宽度减小而减，而梁本身之重量，因而减半。宋人力学知识，固胜清人；而辽人似又胜过宋人一筹矣！

梁横断面之比例既如上述，其美观亦有宜注意之点，即梁之上下边微有卷杀，使梁之腹部，微微凸出。此制于梁之力量，固无大影响，然足以去其机械的直线，而代以圜和之曲线，皆当时大匠苦心构思之结果，吾侪不宜忽略视之。希腊雅典之帕蒂农神庙亦有类似此种之微妙手法，以柔济刚，古有名训。乃至上文所述侧脚，亦希腊制度所有，岂吾祖先得之自西方先哲耶？

❽ 角梁

垂脊之骨干也。于屋之四隅伸出者，计上下二层，下层较短，称老角梁或大角梁，上层较长者为仔角梁，置于老角梁之上。

The sections of the hip-rafter spanning the spaces between the higher purlins are termed the yin-chiao-liang or "hidden corner beam" in the *Ying-tsao-fa-shih*, but it was known to the Ts'ing architects as the yiu-ch'iang. When the point of intersection of the two hips and the ridge is directly above a chung-chu, as in most cases, the load is carried down straight to the column. But in the Shan-men, the shao-chien or end bay is smaller than half the width of the building, so the mitre-lines and the longitudinal axis meet at a point quite far in the shao-chien. This necessitates the use of two kungs extending from the chu-ju-chu to transmit the load to the column (Figure 24).

The end of the lao-chiao-liang is finished in two fine, restrained curves, architecturally far superior to the complicated pa-wang-ch'uan curve of the Ts'ing style. The tze-chiao-liang is smaller than the lao-chiao-liang in cross section, but much longer. Its outer end is terminated by a t'ao-shou, the head of a monster, in terracotta; and from underneath is hung a bronze bell. Both ornaments are believed to be not earlier than the Ming Dynasty.

Ⓘ Chü-che

Chü-che, literally meaning "raise and bend," is the method used in deciding the pitch and in plotting the curve of the Chinese roof (Figures 13-15). In Chapter V of the *Ying-tsao-fa-shih* is the following rule:

"For raising the roof: For Palaces, halls, multiple-storied buildings and towers, the distance between the front and rear liao-yen-chuans" should be taken and divided into three equal parts. The altitude measuring from the top of the liao-yen-chuan to the top of the chi-ch'uan should be equal to one part. For halls and buildings covered with tubular tiles, the distance should be divided into four parts, and the altitude should be equal to one part; this may be further increased by eight-one hundredth...

For bending the roof: The first bend from the top should be one-tenth the height of the raise, and each bend below is lessened by half. For instance, if the raise is twenty feet in height, a straight line is drawn from the top of the chi-ch'uan to the top of the liao-yen-ch'uan. The first bend

24 The ridge-purlin, chu-ju-chu and pu-chien-p'u-cho, interior tou-kungs of the Shan-men. 山门脊槫与侏儒柱并内檐补间铺作

from the top is bent down two feet. Again a straight line is drawn from the top of the ch'uan of the first bend to the top of the liao-yen-ch'uan, and the second bend is bent down one foot...and so forth..."

A few words of explanation are perhaps necessary to make these passages clear. The liao-yen-ch'uan is called t'iao-yen-heng in the Ts'ing style, and the chi-ch'uan is the chi-heng or ridge-purlin.

由平槫以达脊槫者今称“由戗”，《法式》卷五则称为“隐角梁”。大角梁及隐角梁皆置于槫（即桁）上，前后角梁相交于脊槫之上。清式往往使梢间面阔作进深之半，使其相交在梁之中线上。山门因面阔较大，故相交在梢间之内，而自侏儒柱上伸出斗拱以承之（图 24）。

大角梁头卷杀为二曲瓣，颇简单庄严，较清式之“霸王拳”善美多矣。仔角梁高广皆逊大角梁，而长过之。头有套兽，下悬铜铎，皆非辽代原物。

❾ 举折

今称“举架”，所以定屋顶之斜度，及侧面之轮廓者也（图 13–15）。山门举折尺寸，表列如下：

部位	长（米）	举高（米）	高长之比
橑檐槫中至平槫中	2.72	1.11	十之四强
平槫中至脊槫中	2.41	1.46	十之六强
橑檐槫中至脊槫中	5.13	2.57	十之五强

The method for-plotting the curve is first to draw a straight line from the top of the ridge-purlin to the top of the eave-lifting purlin, and at the line of the first intermediate purlin from the top, a vertical line, perpendicular to the ground, is dropped down. One-tenth the total altitude is measured off on this line, deciding the height of the top of the first intermediate purlin. From the top of this purlin, another straight line is drawn to the top of the eave-lifting purlin, and at the line of the second intermediate purlin, a vertical line is also dropped. One-twentieth of the total altitude is measured off to give the top of the next purlin below. The same process is repeated until the top of the lowest intermediate purlin is reached, and every bend is half the height of the one above.

The measurements of the roof of the Shan-men revealed to us an example that was built almost in exact accordance to the *Ying-tsao-fa-shih* rules, entirely different from the rules of the Ts'ing style, according to which the roof is "built up" by a series of rafters each put in an angle greater than the one below. Thus the height of the ridge is therefore a consequence of the meeting of the two "built-up" slopes of the roof, contrary to the earlier method, according to which the pitch is first decided and the curved slope is the consequence of the "bends."

The distance between the front and rear liao-yen-ch'uan is 10.26 m., while the "raise" is 2.57 m., just one-fourth of the distance; but the additional raise of eight per cent was apparently ignored. The intermediate purlin—there is only one in this case—whose center line is horizontally 2.72 m. from the projection of that of the liao-yen-ch'uan, is raised 1.11 m. The figure drawn from these dimensions gives at the line of the intermediate purlin a "bend" of about 0.257 m. below the straight line drawn from the ridge to the eave-purlin, a perfect example of the "bending" method described in the *Ying-tsao-fa-shih.*

The general effect resulting from this method of chü-che is radically different from that of the Ts'ing methods. In the Ts'ing structures, the slope of the roof near the ridge is often set at 45 degrees to the ground, whereas in the earlier examples, the pitch is usually set at a proportion of 6 to 10, or about 30 degrees. The earlier edifices, therefore, often give an impression of gentility and ease in swing which is totally lacking in later structures.

J The Eave

In close relation to the chü-che, and influencing the external appearance of the building is the overhang of the eave. The Ts'ing regulations call for an overhang of approximately three-tenths or one third the height from the ground to the eave, giving an impression of restraint. But in the *Ying-tsao-fa-shih* the overhang of the eave is specified as from 9 to 11 times the diameter of the rafter, regardless of the height of the building. But on account of the comparatively large size of the tou-kung, the overhang is usually great, often reaching half the height of the eave from the ground. The impression it gives is that of the vigor and freedom which one often senses in front of an Early Renaissance Italian Palazzo.

此第一举（即橑檐槫至平槫）之斜度，即今所谓“四举”；第二举（平槫至脊槫）之斜度，即今所谓“六举”。而全举架斜度，由脊至檐，为二与一之比，即所谓“五举”是。其义即谓十分之长举高四分、五分或六分是也。《法式》卷五：

“举屋之法，如殿阁楼台，先量前后橑檐方相去远近，分为三分，从橑檐方背至脊槫背，举起一分。如甋瓦厅堂，即四分中举起一分。又通以四分所得丈尺，每一尺加八分……”

若由脊槫计，则甋瓦厅堂之斜度，实乃二分举一分，即今之五举[48]。山门举架之度，适与此合。宋式按屋深而定其“举”高，再加以“折”，故举为因而折为果。清式不先定屋高，而按步数（即宋式所谓椽数）定为“五,七,九”或“五,六五,七五,九”举，此若干斜线连续所达之高度，即为建筑物之高度。是折为因而举为果。清式最高一步，互折达一与一之比，成 45 度角，其斜度大率远甚于古式，此亦清式建筑与宋以前建筑外表上最易区别之点也。

⑩ 椽

与举折有密切关系，而影响于建筑物之外观者，则椽出檐之远近是也。清式出檐之制，约略为高之十分之三或三分之一，其现象颇为短促谨严。《营造法式》檐出按椽径定，而椽径按槫数及其间距离定，与屋高无定比例[49]。然因斗拱雄大，故出檐率多甚远，恒达柱高一半以上。其现象则豪放，似能遮蔽檐下一切者。与意大利初期文艺复兴式建筑颇相似。

The height from the top of the liao-yen-fang to the top of the terrace is 6.09 m., while the distance from the center-line to the tip of the eave is 2.63 m., about 4.32/10 or 1/2.31 of the height. This great overhang together with the gentle slope of the roof, is one of the important factors that constitute the character of the building.

The shaping of the rafter-ends is also worth noticing. The ends of the ch'uan or rafter and the fei-tzu or flying rafter are all slightly tapered. It is specified in Chapter V of the *Fa-shih* that:

"for all fei-tzu, the width should be eight-tenths, and the depth seven-tenths, the diameter of the ch'uan; both the width and the depth are each again divided into five parts; on each of the two sides, one part is tapered off, but from the bottom, two parts are tapered while the top is uncut...."

The rafters of the Tu-lo Ssu structures were apparently shaped in accordance with the above quoted method, or some method similar to it. This particular kind of refinement was totally unused in buildings of the Ts'ing Dynasty.

Ⓚ Roof-tiles and Ornaments

The writer was informed by an old gentleman of Chi Hsien that the original tiles of the Kuan-yin Ke and the Shan-men were very large, measuring about a foot and half in width and four feet in length. They were replaced by smaller ones during the repair of the Kwang-hsü period. A certain gentleman of the town was in possession of a piece of the original tiles, but the author was disappointed when he asked to be allowed to see it. The tremendous length of four feet of the original tile is certainly doubtful, but that the present tiles are not the original ones is unquestionable. However, the most important and noticeable parts of the roof-tiles are the two ridge-end ornaments or tz'u-wei (Figure 25). The tz'u-wei is a motif first introduced by a Taoist monk into Chinese architecture during the time of Han Wu-ti for the superstitious reasons. T'ang examples can still be seen in mural paintings of Tun-huang and on the roof of the Toshodaiji in Nara, Japan, where it assumes the form of a fin-shaped tail, rising from the end of the ridge, and turning up and pointing in towards the center of the building. During the Ming and Ts'ing Dynasties, its name was changed to wen or lips, where it assumes the form of a dragon's head, facing in and biting the ridge in its mouth as though trying to swallow it, while the "tail" turns up and outward.

25 Tz'u-wei, Shan-men. 山门鸱尾

山门自台基背至橑檐槫背高为 6.09 米，而出檐自檐柱中线度之，为 2.63 米，为高之十分之四・三二或二・三一分之一。斜度既缓，出檐复远，此其所以大异于今制也。

椽头做法，亦有宜注意者，椽头及飞椽头（即飞子）皆较椽身略小。《营造法式》卷五檐节下：

"凡飞子，如椽径十分，则广八分厚七分；各以其广厚分为五分，两边各斜杀一分。底面上留三分，下杀二分。……"

此种做法，于独乐寺所见至为明显。且不惟飞子如是，椽头亦加卷杀，皆建筑上特加之精致也。

梢间檐椽，向角梁方面续渐加长，使屋之四角，除微弯向上外，还要微弯向外，《营造法式》称为"生出"，清式亦有之，但其比例略异耳。

⓫ 瓦

蓟县老绅士言，观音阁及山门瓦，原皆极大，宽一尺余，长四尺，于光绪重修时，为奸商窃换。县绅某先生，曾得一块，而珍藏之。请借一观则谓已遗失。其长四尺，虽未必信，而今瓦之非原物，固无疑义。其最可注意者，则脊上两鸱尾，极可罕贵之物也（图 25）。鸱尾来源，固甚久远，唐代形制，于敦煌壁画及日本奈良唐招提寺见之，盖纯为鳍形之"尾"，自脊端翘起，而尾端向内者也。明清建筑上所用则为吻，作龙头形，其尾向外卷起，故其意趣大不相同。

The name "tz'u-wei" is used in the *Ying-tsao-fa-shih,* but no drawing can be found to identify its actual appearance, except in Chapter XXXII, in "the drawings for Cabinet Works," a number of Buddhist shrines are shown with wens identical to the later wens. But here in the case of the Shan-men, the dragon's head is similar to the modern designs, but the inward turn of the tubular "tail" is something unseen in later models. It is probably a Liao original, or a later replica of a Liao original, an interesting evidence of the transition.

About midway down the hip is the shou-t'ou or beast's head. It is known in later periods as the ch'ui-shou, the sloping beast. At the end of the hip, i.e., the corner of the roof, is the hsien-jen or immortal whose correct name is pin-chia or lady-in-waiting in *Fa-shih*; but here she is represented as a fierce, bearded, armored warrior, in a dignified sitting pose, with his right arm raised as though getting ready to strike any sparrow that might happen to perch in front of him!

In between the shou-t'ou and the pin-chia are a number of chou-shou or running beasts, known in the *Fa-shih* as the tsun-shou or sitting beasts. Whether they are running or sitting depends upon the designer, and in many cases on the spectator who views them from below. There are four of them at each corner and even members are employed unlike the Ts'ing image of odd numbers. The distribution of these beasts is here different from both the later practice of putting them close to each other, and the excessively scanty spacing of putting three tiles between each beast as specified in the *Fa-shih.* They are here spaced with one tile between, and a happy medium seems to have been stuck between the two extremes.

Ⓛ The Masonry Walls

The two narrower facades and the spaces in between the chung-chu and shan-chu, i.e., in the two end bays on the longitudinal axis, are all built in with brick walls. They were undoubtedly built in during one of the Ts'ing restorations. It is therefore all the more interesting to note that they were not built in accordance with Ts'ing regulations, in which the ch'ün-chien, the lower part of the wall, is specified to be one-third the total height of the wall, while here it is only 97 cm. high in relation to the 4.33 m. of the height of the wall, that is less than one-fourth (Figure 12).

There are traces of brick walls between the lower parts of the columns in the front and rear in the end bays. They were recently destroyed.

《营造法式》虽有鸱尾之名，而无详图，在卷三十二《小木作制度图样》内，佛道帐上有之，则纯为明清所习见之吻，非尾也。此处所见，龙首虽与今式略同，而其鳍形之尾，向内卷起，实后世所罕见；其辽代之原物欤？即使非原物，亦必明代仿原物所作。于此鸱尾中，唐式之尾与明清之吻，合而为一，适足以示其过渡形制。此后则尾向外卷，而成今所习见之吻焉。

正脊与垂脊，皆以青砖垒成，无特殊之点。但《营造法式》以瓦为脊，日本镰仓时代建筑物亦然，是独乐寺殿堂原脊之是砖是瓦，将终成永久之谜。垂脊之上有兽头（今称垂兽），脊端为“仙人”，《法式》称“嫔伽”，而实则甲胄武士也！嫔伽与垂兽间为“走兽”，《法式》亦称“蹲兽”，其数为四。宋式皆从双数，而清式从单。其分布则不若清式之密，亦不若宋式“每隔三瓦或五瓦安兽一枚”之疎，适得其中者也。

⓬ 砖墙

两山及山柱与中柱间皆有砖墙，其为近代重砌，毫无可疑，然其制度则异于清式。清式以墙之最下三分之一为“裙肩”，此处则墙高 4.33 米，而裙肩高只 0.97 米，约为全高之 1/4.5，其现象亦与清式所习见者大异（图 12）。此外则别无特殊可志者。姑将其各部尺寸列下：

墙高	4.33 米	外裙肩高	0.97 米	山墙厚	约 0.97 米	收分	2%
里裙肩高	0.38 米	墙肩高	0.31 米	中墙厚	0.44 米		

梢间檐柱与角柱间，尚有槛墙痕迹，高 1.13 米，厚 0.43 米，亦清代所修，而近数年始失去者。

Ⓜ Windows and Doors

Not a trace of the Liao original windows or doors is conserved. Even the windows that once sheltered the end bays are missing. The only thing of the sort that can be seen is the two large gates, the design of which tells its date of construction—Ts'ing. A few of the transoms are still left with grills of geometrical patterns, similar to those of the Imperial Palaces in Peiping. Separating the central bay, which was the main thoroughfare, from the end bays, which were rooms for the Lokapalas, were originally wooden railings. Probably they were destroyed only recently.

26 General view of the Shan-men. 山门全貌

⓭ 装修

辽代原物，一无所存。清物则大门二扇，尚称完整。考其痕迹，南北二面梢间之外面，清代曾有槛墙，上安槛窗。今抱框及上中槛尚存，横披花心亦在，其楞子为清故宫内最常见之“菱花”几何形纹样。檐柱与中柱间，当曾有栅栏，想已供数年前驻军炊焚之用矣。

◀ 27 A Lokapala in the end bay, Shan-men. 山门东间天王塑像

▶ 28 Mural paintings of Heavenly Kings on the west wall, Shan-men. 山门西壁天王画像

▼ 29 The pien of Tu-lo Ssu, Shan-men. 山门匾

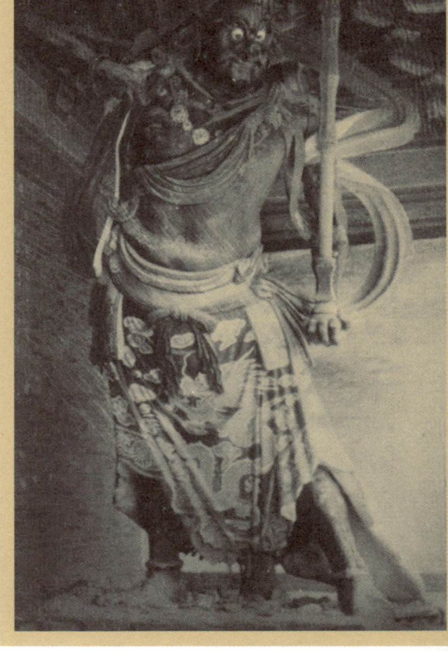

N Painting

The painting is the worst part of the modern touches. It was probably done during the Kwang-hsü restoration in accordance with paintings of the Chien-lung period. The painters were totally ignorant of the functions of the different components of the architecture, and taste was altogether lacking in their distribution of colors. With the exception of the tou-kungs, which are tolerable and not too outrageous, the entire painted decoration is merely an exhibition of the lowest degeneration of decorative art. Because of the difference in structure, the Ts'ing system of painted ornaments could not be very well applied to a Liao building, while the lack of creative ability prevented the painters from inventing something new. The Ts'ing system of ornamentation was thus forced onto the Liao structure, making a clown of the dignified old monument. The filled-in spaces between the tou-kungs are treated with an all-over pattern of frets. This pattern was carried right across and over

the short stud of the pu-chien-p'u-cho, as if purposely trying to disguise its structural value. To paint a religious building in a ridiculous manner like this is not only sacrilegious but mocks the functional value of the architectural parts.

⓮ 彩画

彩画之恶劣，盖无与伦。乃光绪末年所涂者。画匠对于建筑各部之机能，既毫无了解，而于颜色图案之调配，更乏美术。除斗拱所施，尚称合宜外，其他各部，皆丑劣不堪。因结构之不同，以致清式定例不能适用，而画者又乏创造力，于是阑额作和玺，檐槫（桁）作“大点金”，大点金而间以万字“箍头”又杂以“苏画枋心”。数层柱头枋上彩画亦如是，而枋心又不在其正当位置。替木上又加以卍纹。尤为荒谬者则垫拱板上普遍之万字纹上添花，竟将补间铺作之直斗亦置于其掩盖之下，非特加注意，观者竟不知直斗之存在。喧哗嘈杂，不可响尔。夫名刹之山门，乃法相庄严之地，而施以滑稽如彼之彩画，可谓大不敬也矣。

⑮ 塑像

南面梢间立塑像二尊，土人呼为哼哈二将，而呼山门为“哼哈殿”。像状至凶狞，肩际长巾，飘然若动。东立者闭口握拳，为哼（图27）。西立者开口伸掌为哈。实为天王也。像皆前倾，背系以铁索。新涂彩画甚劣。

⑯ 画像

北半梢间山墙，画四天王像。东壁为增长（南）持国（北），西壁为多闻（北）广目（南）（图28）。笔法平庸，而布局颇有意趣，盖近代重修而摹画者耶？驻军曾以纸糊墙，今虽撕去，而画受损已多矣。

⑰ 匾

山门南面额曰“独乐寺”，匾长2.17米，高1.08米，字方约0.9米。相传为严嵩手笔（图29）。

Ⓞ Statues

In each of the two end bays is a colossal figure of a Lokapala, modeled in clay. They are the familiar conventional figures often seen at the entrances of Chinese temples. Their expressions are fierce, and their draperies suggestive of violent movement. Both figures are beginning to fall forward, and are held in position by iron chains and rods from behind. The painting on the figures is new (Figure 27).

Ⓟ Mural Paintings

On the two end walls, in the northern end bays, are painted the Four Heavenly Kings. On the east are Tseng-ch'ang-t'ien (Virûdhaka) and Ch'ih-kuo-t'ien (Dhritarâshtra) on the west wall are To-wen-t'ien (Vais'ravana) and Kwang-mu-t'ien (Virupâksha). The paintings show very little merit from point of view of the technique of the painter, but the composition is fairly interesting. It is quite possible that they are older originals retouched and traced over in one of the later restorations. The murals were packed over with paper and have been much defaced and marred by its removal (Figure 28).

Ⓠ The Pien

Under the eave on the southern (front) facade is the signboard with the characters 獨樂寺 ("Tu-lo Ssu"). The board measures more than two meters by one while each character is about 90 cm. square. The calligraphy is attributed to Yen Sung, a treacherous prime minister of the Ming Dynasty (Figure 29).

V. THE KUAN-YIN KE

A Exterior Appearance

The Kuan-yin Ke is a three-storied building of two main floors and a mezzanine which is not visible from the exterior. It resembles strikingly the two- or three-storied buildings represented in the T'ang mural paintings of the caves of Tun-huang (Figure 30). The bold proportions of the tou-kungs, the heavy overhang of the eaves, together with the gentle pitch of the roof line, endow it with an air of dignity and composure that nevertheless is full of vitality, a characteristic found only in architecture of a new and growing epoch. The three tiers of tou-kungs on the exterior vary in form and structure according to their respective position and function. The roof is of the hsien-shan kind, a combination of the pitched and gabled roof.

30 Mural paintings of the caves of Tun-huang. 敦煌壁画净土图

伍 观音阁

❶ 外观

阁高三层，而外观则似二层；其上下二主要层之间，夹以暗层，如西式所谓 mezzanine 者，自外部观之不见。阁外观上最大特征，则与唐敦煌壁画中所见之建筑极相类似也（图 30）。伟大之斗拱，深远之檐出，及屋顶和缓之斜度，稳固庄严，含有无限力量，颇足以表示当时方兴未艾之朝气。其三层斗拱，各因其地位而异其制。

31 Southern side of Kuan-yin Ke. 观音阁南面

The recess of the gable from the eave, technically termed shou-shan, is greater than that of the Ts'ing style, resulting in a comparatively short ridge and small triangular gable, or shan-hua. Surrounding the third story on the exterior is a balcony, commanding an admirable view of the surrounding landscape. At the four corners on both stories are posts supporting the heavy overhanging eaves which threaten to fall down. This entire structure stands on a low base or terrace of stone, called the t'ai-chi, in front of which is another terrace one step lower, called the yueh-t'ai. On this yueh-t'ai are two square "beds," in one of which still stands an old cypress tree (Figure 31).

屋顶为"歇山"式[50]，而收山殊甚，正脊因之较清式短，而山花[51]亦较清式小。上层周有露台，可登临远眺。今檐四角下支以方柱，以防角檐倾圮。阁立于低广石台基上，其前有月台，台上有花池二方，西池内尚有古柏一株（图 31）。

Ⓑ The Plan

The Kuan-yin Ke is a peristylar hall of five bays by four, with the longer facade facing south. The columns on the exterior are 18 in number, while in the interior there are 10 (Figure 8), forming the cella of the Hall. Within the area bound by the inner columns is a platform, situated slightly to the northern half of the space. On the platform is the colossal standing figure of an Eleven-headed Kuan-yin, with two Bodhisattvas in attendance, all three statues resembling strongly the sculptures of the T'ang period. There are three other seated figures on the platform, apparently of a much later date. On the northern side of the platform, back to the colossal figure is another figure of a Kuan-yin, sitting on a hilly setting. In the bay on the western end is the stairway that gives access to the mezzanine and upper floors.

The mezzanine floor is situated between the ceiling of the lower story and the floor of the upper story. It is not visible from the exterior. Being behind the roof of the lower story and the brackets of the balcony above, fenestration is almost totally illuminated. With the exception of the western end bay, which is used as the hall leading to the stairs, the entire space between the exterior and interior rows of columns is left unused. The central space, bound on the four sides by the inner columns is unfloored, but provided with a balcony which enables the worshipper to go around the body of the figure, which pierces through all the three stories (Figure 9). The stairway from below is accessible at the northern end of the stair-hall, while to the south is another flight of stairs leading to the upper floor.

❷ 平面

阁东西五间，南北四间；柱分内外二周。外檐柱十八，内檐柱十（图 8）。最中为须弥坛，坛略偏北，上立十一面观音像一，侍立菩萨像二，其他像三；与大像相背有山洞及像。西梢间内为楼梯，可达中层。

中层位于下层天花板之上，上层地板之下，其外周为下檐及平坐铺作所遮蔽，故无窗。其檐柱以内，内柱（清称金柱）以外一周，遂空废无用。内柱以内上下空通全阁之高，而有小台可绕像身一周（图 9）。楼梯在西梢间北端，至中层后折而向南，可达上层。

32 Plan of Kuan-yin Ke.

观音阁平面图

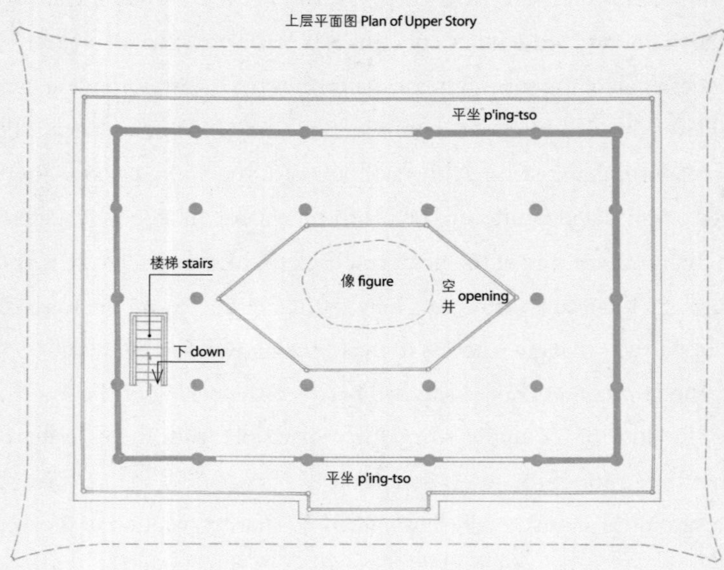

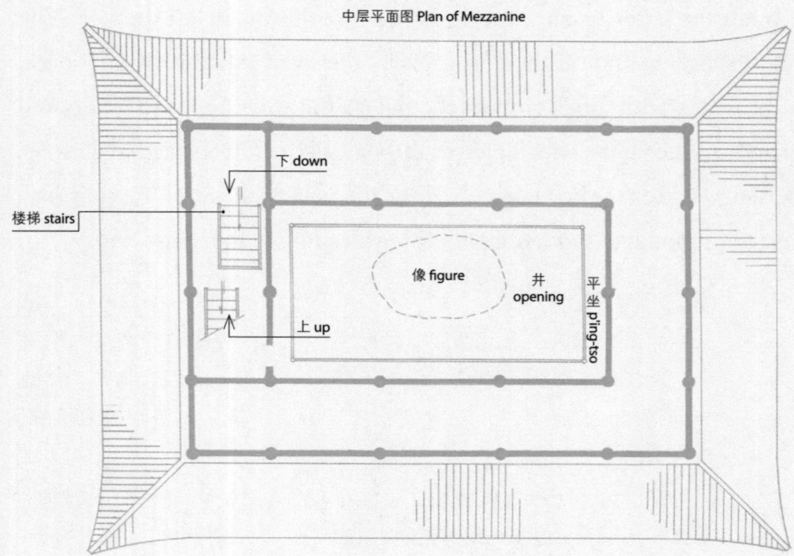

The upper story is one spacious room with the three middle bays open. Now that the doors are destroyed, it gives more than ever a feeling of spaciousness and loftiness. The entire upper story is surrounded on the exterior by a balcony, supported on a series of tou-kungs, commanding a magnificent vista of the city in front and the hills at the rear. In the center of the room is a hexagonal opening, surrounded by balustrades, from which one can obtain an excellent view of the figure, particularly the head and the bust (Figure 32). The bays that are not open are filled in by walls of earthen plaster on laths of twigs.

The inter-columniation of the different bays is not equal, but wider in the center and narrower at the ends. The width of the end bays in both facades is the sauce, that is to say, the inner columns are all equidistant from their corresponding outer columns forming an aisle all the way around the nave. It is interesting to note that the three superposed "orders" of the inner peristylar columns are placed directly one on top of the other, on the same center line, while the two upper "orders" on the exterior columns are placed not directly on the lower columns, but on the beam spanning the space between the inner and outer columns. This moves the outer columns on the two upper stories a little distance back of the lower rows, thus making the upper stories considerably smaller than the lower one and thus giving an appearance of stability.

上层极为空朗，周有檐廊[52]，可以远眺崆峒盘谷。内柱以内，地板开六角形空井，围绕佛身，可以凭栏细观像肩胸以上各部（图32）。南面居中三间俱辟为户，可外通檐廊，北面唯当心间辟户。其余各间则皆为土壁，梯位置亦在西梢间，可以下通中下二层。

下层面阔，当心间较阔于次间，次间又阔于梢间；进深则内间较深于前后间。而梢间之阔与前后间之深同，故檐柱金柱之间乃成阔度相同之绕廊一周。而内部少二中柱，为佛坛所在。其特可注意者，乃中上二层之金柱，立于下层金柱顶上，而上中层檐柱乃不立于下层檐柱顶上，而向内立于梁上，故中上二层外周间较狭，而阁亦因之呈下大上小之状。

Ⓒ The Terrace

The sub-structure to the entire Kuan-yin Ke is the stone t'ai-chi forming that the footing to the Hall, and is the transition between the structure and the ground. In relation to the entire building, the terrace seems rather low. The exterior appearance of the Hall would be greatly improved if the terrace were increased to double its height. But whether the present height is that of the original or not is doubtful. The stone used for the side walls of the terrace is local granite, roughly dressed. The top of the terrace is paved with square brick tiles. The space within the peristyle is on the same level as the outer part of the terrace, forming the floor height of the lower story.

In front of the t'ai-chi, and lower by one step, is the yueh-t'ai, a little more than three bays in length, with its width less than half its length. The side walls are of the same material as the t'ai-chi, and the top paved with the same tile. Two unpaved squares on the yueh-t'ai from the "flower-beds," in one of which may still be seen an old cypress tree.

On both the east and west of the yueh-t'ai, and butting against the side of the t'ai-chi, is a flight of steps. The steps to the southern side, once the main access to the terrace and the Hall, were destroyed in 1931. The stones for the steps are still piled up nearby. A similar flight of steps is provided on the northern side of the terrace.

Ⓓ The Column and the Base

In form the columns of the Kuan-yin Ke are quite similar to those of the Shan-men. After a thousand years' reparation and restoration, in addition to the natural shrinkage and expansion of the wood, the columns have become quite un-uniform in size, and to obtain an accurate measurement is impossible. However, the average of the dimensions taken show definitely that there is no definite proportion between the diameter to the height of the column. This differs from both the Greco-Roman and Ts'ing styles. In Chapter V of the *Ying-tsao-fa-shih* on the making of columns, no definite proportion is given between the diameter and height of the column. In the case of the Shan-men and the Kuan-yin

Ke, although there is no definite diameter to the columns, they nearly all measure half a meter across. It may not be altogether without justification to presume that they were all meant to be of the same size regardless of their height and position. The slight variation in size found today is due to inexact workmanship or the shrinkage of materials in past ages.

兹将各层各柱脚间尺寸列下：

	下层（米）	中层（米）	上层（米）
明间面阔	4.75	4.75	4.75
次间面阔	4.35	4.35	4.35
梢间面阔	3.39	3.03	2.98
前后间进深	3.39	3.03	2.98
内间进深	3.74	3.74	3.74

以上度量，不唯可见中上二层檐柱之内移，且可见柱侧脚之度[53]。

❸ 台基及月台

观音阁全部最下层之结构为台基，全部之基础，而阁与地间之过渡部分[54]也。台基为石砌，长 26.66 米，宽 20.45 米，高 1.04 米。以全部权衡计，台基颇嫌扁矮，若倍其高，于外观必大有裨益。然台基今之高度，是否原高度，尚属可疑，惜未得发掘，以验其有无埋没部分也。砌台基之石，皆当地所产花刚石，虽经磋琢，仍欠方整，殆亦原物而经重砌者。台基之上面，墁以方砖；檐柱以内，即为下层地面。

台基之前为月台，长 16.22 米，占正面三间有余，宽 7.70 米，而较台基低 0.20 米。月台亦石砌，与台基同。上墁方砖。台上左右有花池二，方约 2 米，西池内尚有古柏一株，而东池一株并根不存矣。

月台东西两方，与台基邻接处，有阶五级，可下平地。南面原亦有阶，然因有碍球场，已于去岁拆毁。今阶石尚存月台东阶下，拆毁痕迹尚可见。台基北面亦有阶。

❹ 柱及柱础

观音阁柱与山门柱形制相同，亦《营造法式》所谓直柱者也。山门诸柱，原物较少，而观音阁殆因不易撤换，故皆（？）原物，千年来屡经修葺，坎补涂抹之处既多且乱，致使各柱肥瘦不同，测究非易。

The entasis on the columns of the Ke is peculiarly slight. It is difficult to make any measurement on account of the unevenness and inexactitude of the columns.

However, the ch'e-chiao or slanting of the columns can generally be easily seen. A passage from the *Ying-tsao-fa-shih* has already quoted in discussing the columns of the Shan-men. Referring to the ch'e-chiao of multiple-story buildings, the handbook says that the degree of inclination should be carried all the way up. Measurements taken at different levels show that the ch'e-chiao is strictly observed in the Ke columns, as the distances between the outer and inner columns steadily diminish from the lower to the upper ends. This is plainly visible even to the naked eye (Figure 31).

It is to be noted that the three-story height of the Kuan-yin Ke is actually composed of three separate stories of structural framework, each complete in itself with its "order" of columns, tou-kungs, and horizontal liangs and fangs. Therefore, the superposition of the different stories is worth studying. It has already been mentioned in a previous paragraph that the outer columns of the mezzanine do not stand directly on top of the lower-story columns, but on a beam, and the distance between the center lines of the lower and upper columns is 0.355 m. The column on the beam does not stand directly on the beam, but interposed by a base which is merely an old kung put upside down. This kung is at least as old as the end of the T'ang Dynasty, as it is evident that it must have been taken from some old buildings that were destroyed prior to the building of the Kuan-yin Ke in 984 AD. The function of this interposition is primarily to take care of the strong shear exerted on the beam on account of the closeness of the columns above and below. But the two t'iaos of hua-kungs under the beam have reduced greatly the actual span of the beam on which the upper column stands, and the successive tiers of corbelling are made to react as one single member, transmitting the load to the column below.

然测究之结果，乃得知各柱因位置之不同，尺寸略约，姑列如下表：

	高（米）[55]	下径（米）	上径（米）	收分	高与径比
下层檐柱	4.35	0.48	—	—	9.1:1
下层内柱	4.58	0.505	—	—	9.1:1
上层檐柱	2.75	0.49	0.49	无	5.6:1
上层角柱	2.75	0.52	0.52	无	5.3:1
上层内柱	2.75	0.54	0.52	7‰	5.1:1
上层中柱	2.75	0.47	0.45	7‰	5.85:1

综上列诸度量及山门柱度量，得知柱径与高无一定之比例。清式定例，柱高为柱径之十倍，而独乐寺所见，则绝无定例。考之《营造法式》卷五，用柱之制，亦绝无以柱高或径定其比例及尺寸者。山门及观音阁，其柱径虽每柱不同，然皆约略为 0.5 米，愚意以为原计划必每柱皆同径，不分地位及用途；其略有大小不同者，乃选材不当或施工不准及后世斫补所使然耳。

阁柱收分尤微，虽有亦不及 1%。然因各柱尺寸不同，亦难得知确为何如。

其最显而易见者，则柱之侧脚度也。关于此点，上文已详加申述，然于楼阁柱侧脚之制，则《法式》有下列一段：

“若楼阁柱侧脚，只以柱以上为则，侧脚上更加侧脚，逐层仿此。”

按前页各层面阔进深尺寸表，梢间面阔及前后间进深，向上层层缩减，可知其然；即未测量，肉眼描视，亦显现易见也（图 31）。

阁高既为三倍，柱亦为三层垒叠而上达，而各层于斗拱檐廊等部，各自齐备；故阁之三层，可分析为三个完整之结构垒叠而成[56]。然则各层相叠之制，亦研究所宜注意。中层檐柱，不立于下层檐柱之上，而立于其上之梁上，二柱中线相距 0.355 米。惧其不固也，更以横木承之。而此横木，乃一旧拱，其必为唐以前物无疑。上下二柱既不衔接，则其荷重下达亦不能一线直下，而藉梁枋为之转移，此转移荷重之梁枋，遂受上下二柱之切力[57]，为减少切力之影响，故加旧拱以增其力。但枋下梁拱叠出，最上受柱重之枋，已将其重量层层移向下层柱心，而切力亦在拱之全身，而不独在受柱之枋。此法固非极善，然因斗拱结构完善，足以承重不敧也（图 9）。清式楼阁有童柱之制，与此略同。然因童柱立于梁中，而不在梁之一端，故其应力亦不同也。

The outer columns of the top story are placed directly on those of the mezzanine story. The foot of the upper column is mortised and jointed to form a part of the chu-t'ou-p'u-cho beneath it, with its foot standing on the lu-tou, as if standing on a regular base. The inner columns are also superposed in the same manner. Many of the mortised feet of the upper columns have split and threaten to give way under the slightest access of load (Figure 46).

The heads of the columns are rounded off like a fu-p'en or "in the shape of an inverted bowl." This characteristic is especially noticeable in the dark parts of the mezzanine, where the contours of the columns are not deformed by the plaster and paint of later ages (Figure 33).

The base of the column of the lower story is of the same material as that of the Shan-men. It is about 90 cm., less than twice the diameter of the column, but considerably larger than the Shan-men bases. The fu-p'en of the base is also treated in the same manner as that of the Shan-men.

Ⓔ Tou-kungs

There are twenty-four different kinds of tou-kung in the structure of the Kuan-yin Ke. Each kind is specially constructed to fit the position and suit the function of each particular case.

1. Exterior Tou-kungs of the Lower Story

ⓐ Chu-t'ou-p'u-cho, the Brackets on the Column On the column the lu-tou is placed from which extend four t'iaos of hua-kungs and the shua-t'ou. Intersecting with these are a ni-tao-kung, three tiers of chu-t'ou-fangs, and a ya-ts'ao-fang above in all five tiers. The three tiers of chu-t'ou-fang are all carved with false kungs in relief, like the Shan-men. On the ends of the second and fourth t'iaos of the hua-kung, are placed a transversal kung, in the t'ou-hsin manner. The kung on the second t'iao is called the kua-tze-kung, on which is placed a man-kung, supporting a long horizontal member, called the lo-han-fang (Figures 34, 35). Concerning constructions of this kind, it is stated in Chapter IV of the *Ying-tsao-fa-shih,* on the "Ensemble of the P'u-cho":

"...when the shu-fang is supported by the ling-kung on the end of the t'iao, it is called the single kung method.... When a man-kung is placed on the kua-tze-kung, which is on the end of the t'iao, and the shu-fang placed on the man-kung, it is called the double-kung method."

33 The heads of the columns in the dark parts of the mezzanine. 观音阁暗层内柱头

34 Exterior tou-kungs of the lower story. 观音阁下层外檐柱头及补间铺作

至于上层檐柱，乃立于中层柱头栌斗之上，上中层内柱，亦立于中下层内柱柱头栌斗之上；与各拱相交，似成为斗拱之中心然者，因与各拱交置，故各柱脚竟多劈裂倾斜，亦非用木之善法也。此种作法，当于下文平坐铺作题下详论之（图 46）。

至于柱之形式，上径下径相差无几，其收分平均不过 1%，故其所呈现象颇长而直。所谓直柱者是。其柱头卷杀作覆盆样，亦为特征，此点于在暗层内之中层内柱，未经油饰诸部分最为明显（图 33）。

柱基石料与山门同，亦当地青石造。方 0.90 米，亦不及柱径之倍，然比例较大于山门柱础。其上覆盆之制亦与山门同。[58]

❺ 斗拱

观音阁上下内外计有斗拱二十四种，各因其地位及功用之不同，而异其形制。

下层外檐斗拱四种：

1. 柱头铺作　栌斗施于柱头，斗上出华拱四跳，并耍头共计五层。与华拱耍头相交者计泥道拱一层，柱头枋四层，共计亦五层。下三层柱头枋皆雕作假拱形，如山门之制。跳头每隔一跳，上安横拱，作“偷心”之制，故华拱四跳中，唯第二跳及第四跳跳头上安横拱，拱上承枋（图 34，35）。关于此部结构，《法式》卷四《总铺作次序》谓：

“……每跳令拱上只用素方一重，谓之单拱。……每跳瓜子拱上施慢拱，慢拱上用素方，谓之重拱。”

35 Chu-t'ou-p'u-cho and pu-chien-p'u-cho, exterior tou-kungs of the lower story, Kuan-yin Ke. 观音阁下层外檐柱头及补间铺作

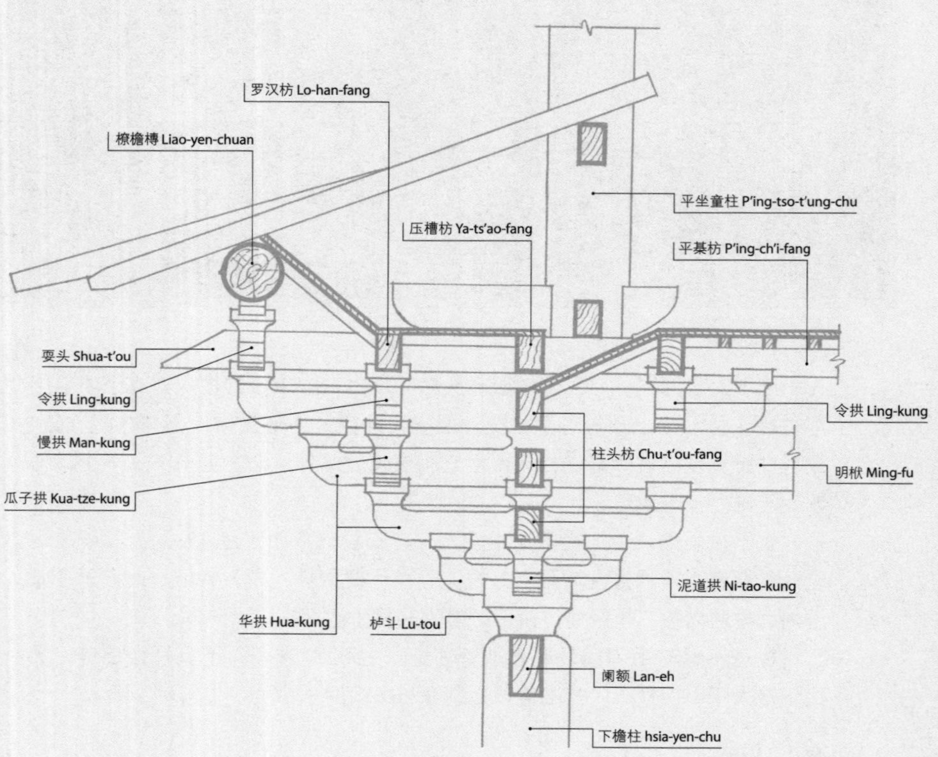

36 T'i-mu of chu-t'ou-p'u-cho, exterior tou-kungs of the lower story, Kuan-yin Ke.
观音阁下层外檐柱头铺作之替木

But in an explanatory note to this passage, the following definitions are given:

"The su-fang (meaning plain fang) above the ni-tao-kung is called the chu-t'ou-fang, while the one on the t'iao is called the lo-han-fang on which is placed the che-ch'uan-pan (rafter-hiding board) in a sloping position."

Here we have on the end of the second t'iao a kua-tze-kung supporting a man-kung, on which is placed a lo-han-fang, answering exactly to the description of the double-kung method; while on the end of the fourth t'iao, the ling-kung with the t'i-mu and eave-purlin above give an excellent example of the single kung construction (Figure 36).

It is interesting to note that the second and fourth t'iaos are slightly longer than the first and third, because in a p'u-cho of the t'ou-hsin manner, the second and fourth t'iaos, on which the transversal kungs are placed, are apparently of greater importance than the other two t'iaos.

而此段小注中则谓：

"素方在泥道拱上者谓之柱头方，在跳上者谓之罗汉方[59]，方上斜安遮椽板。"

第二跳跳头计瓜子拱慢拱各一层，上用罗汉枋，即所谓重拱之制。此制至清代仍沿用之。第四跳跳头上则只用单拱，唯令拱一层，与耍头相交，清代亦同此制。唯清式于令拱（清称厢拱）上散斗（清称三才升）内安挑檐枋，上承挑檐桁。宋式则无桁而用橑檐枋，辽式则以替木代挑檐枋（图 36），上加橑檐槫（挑檐桁）。此节上文虽已论及，唯为清晰计，故重申述之。

至于各跳长度，亦因地位功用而稍异。第一第三两跳出跳较长，而第二第四两跳出跳较短，盖因偷心之制，二四两跳较重要于一三两跳，故使然也。

37 The rear of chu-t'ou-p'u-cho and chuan-chiao-p'u-cho, exterior tou-kungs of the lower story, Kuan-yin Ke. 观音阁下层外檐柱头铺作及转角铺作后尾

The rear of the p'u-cho (Figure 37) consists of two t'iaos of hua-kung supporting a small beam, called the ming-fu, on which is placed the rear of the fourth hua-kung, in the form of a kung, intersecting with a ling-kung. The shua-t'ou is extended at the rear right across the aisle, above and parallel to the ming-fu, known as the p'ing-ch'i-fang or the fang of the coffer ceiling.

The function of these two horizontal members is primarily for the tying together of the inner and outer peristylar columns, and not for the carrying of any load above, although the p'ing-ch'i-fang is made to carry the ceiling which is not very heavy.

The spaces between the inner and outer su-fang are covered by the che-ch'uan-pan, known as the kai-tou-pan in the Ts'ing style. As the spaces are comparatively wider than those of the later styles, the che-ch'uan-pan is supported by a number of small rafters, a treatment not seen in Ts'ing structures but quite usual in Japanese structures of the Heian and Kamakura periods, when T'ang and Sung influence were most dominant in Japan.

ⓑ **Chuan-chiao-p'u-cho** As discussed in a previous paragraph, the set that turns the corner may be analyzed as the intersection of two chu-t'ou-p'u-cho each facing a direction that makes an angle of 90 degrees with

38 Chuan-chiao-p'u-cho and chu-t'ou-p'u-cho, exterior tou-kungs of the lower story, Kuan-yin Ke. 观音阁下层外檐转角铺作及柱头铺作

the other (Figure 38). Here on the exterior of the lower story of the Kuan-yin Ke, the lu-tou is found with intersecting hua-kungs, the rear ends of which are simultaneously the ni-tao-kungs of the adjacent side. Above each of these intersecting kungs are three t'iaos of hua-kungs, all being the extension of the ends of the chu-t'ou-fangs of the adjacent sides.

铺作后尾之结构（图 37），亦殊饶趣味。最下华拱两层，与前面相同，唯长 0.02 米。第三跳前为华拱尾为梁，直达内柱拱头铺作上。第四跳为拱，顺安于梁上，长只如三跳，而于二跳中线上施以令拱，以承内罗汉枋。更上则为耍头后尾，直达内檐柱头铺作上。

檐柱与内柱之间，遂有联络材二件，梁枋各一。二者功用皆在平的联络，而不在上面负重者也。

各跳间素枋上皆有遮椽板，清称盖斗板者是。因枋间相距颇远，故板下以小楞木承之，为清式所无，然多见于日本，亦隋唐遗制也。

铺作正面立面为重拱两叠，令拱一层，其在柱上者，除泥道拱外，皆由柱头枋雕成假拱，第二跳跳头为重拱；第四跳跳头为令拱。其偷心之结构，特长之慢拱，及全铺作雄大之权衡，遂使建筑物全部之现象，迥异于明清建筑矣。

2. 转角铺作　转角铺作者，实两面之柱头铺作，前已述及。故仍当按此原则分析之（图 38）。栌斗口中，泥道拱与华拱相列之列拱二件相交，其上华拱三跳，皆由三层柱头枋伸出，即柱头枋与华拱相列也。

On the mitre-line are five t'iaos of chiao-kungs, corresponding to the four t'iaos of hua-kungs and the shua-t'ou on the two sides. The kua-tze-kung on the end of the second hua-kung on either side is made to intersect with that of the other side on the end of the second chiao-kung, and then carried beyond the point of intersection to become the double-kung of the corresponding level on the other side, whereon is supported the lo-han-fang. The end of the lo-han-fang, in a position similar to that of the shua-t'ou, is shaped into a wing-like curve, with no transversal kung on its end. On the end of the fourth chiao-kung are two intersecting ling-kungs, supporting two intersecting t'i-mu under the eave-purlins which also intersect at this point. On the same level as the shua-t'ou on the mitre-line is the fifth chiao-kung, on the end of which sits a pao-p'ing or "treasure bottle" to support the chiao-liangs above.

The rear of the p'u-cho consists of nothing but the rear ends of the chiao-kungs, bisecting the inner angle. The two lower t'iaos, like those of the chu-t'ou-p'u-cho, are made to support the beam above, running from the outer to the inner corner columns of the peristyle. The third chiao-kung on the exterior is extended in the rear into a diagonal beam, spanning the corner columns. The fourth tier is again a kung parallel to the beam and resting on it. The fifth and uppermost tier is a diagonal fang, forming another tie between the corner columns. The construction of this part is identical to that of the chu-t'ou-p'u-cho, but diagonally put; the only difference being in the ling-kung under the inner lo-han-fang, the outer end of which is made to butt against the chu-t'ou-fang of the corresponding level.

This chuan-chiao-p'u-cho has the appearance of something very complicated, but a little analyzation reveals it to be an ensemble of nothing but logic and order, a natural outcome of the structural system.

ⓒ The Pu-chien-p'u-cho on the Front Facade

It is applied only in the three central bays. It hardly functions as a structural unit. The p'u-cho is only a composition of false kungs carved on the chu-t’ou-fangs, with the spaces between filled in with a few tous. The two lower fangs are carved with the ni-tao-kung and man-kung combination, while the upper fang is treated with a ling-kung. There are no hua-kungs extending out to support the overhanging eave like that of the Shan-men. The large t’ou under the ni-tao-kung was probably supported by a short stud or a t’o-feng which is now missing (Figure 34).

斜角线上，亦安角拱，与各华拱及耍头相垺者五层。正面及侧面华拱第二跳跳头之瓜子拱及慢拱相交于第二跳角拱跳头之上，其另一面遂成罗汉枋下之华拱第三四跳，瓜子拱或慢拱与华拱相列者也。最上一层之柱头枋，在彼一面伸出为耍头，与令拱相交于华拱第四跳跳头之上。而罗汉枋亦在彼一面伸出，与耍头并列，但上不施拱，其端则斫作翼形。角华拱第四跳跳头上则有令拱二件相交，上施散斗，斗上承长替木，达正令拱之上。而与耍头相垺之角枋，则端亦作拱形，成第五层角华拱，拱端斗上安“宝瓶”，以承大角梁。

其后尾唯角华拱二层。第三层为斜梁，达内角柱。第四层为拱，顺安梁上。第五层为斜枋，即外端上置宝瓶之最上层角华拱后尾也。此部结构与柱头铺作后尾完全相同，唯位置斜角；其唯一不同之点，乃内罗汉枋下令拱，其一端为拱，而另一端乃与第三层柱头枋相交，《法式》所谓令拱与切几头相列者是也。

此转角铺作，骤观颇似复杂不堪者，但略加分析，则有条不紊，逻辑井然，结构法所自然产生之结果也。

3. 正面补间铺作　下檐唯当心间及次间有补间铺作，而梢间无之。由结构上言，谓下檐无补间铺作可也。盖柱头铺作与柱头铺作之间，有柱头枋四层互相联络，而所谓补间铺作者，徒在枋上雕作拱形；其在下一层为泥道拱，其上为慢拱，再上为令拱，无华拱出跳，非所以承檐者也。各拱上置散斗三，以承上层之柱头枋，而最下层之下，则有一小斗及直斗，置于阑额之上。今直斗已失，其形制幸自山门东面得见之；而大斗则至今尚虚悬枋下也（图 34）。

39 Tou-kungs on the western side of Kuan-yin Ke. 观音阁西面各层斗拱

40 P'ing-tso-p'u-cho, interior tou-kungs of the lower story. 观音阁下层内檐平坐铺作

ⓓ The Pu-chien-p'u-cho on the End Facade

It is also applied only to the two inner bays, and the spaces between the chu-t'ou-p'u-cho and the chuan-chiao-p'u-cho are left without any p'u-cho. Although, like the pu-chien-p'u-cho of the front and the rear, the p'u-cho is nothing more than a number of carved kungs on the chu-t'ou-fangs, it is yet slightly different in the combination of kungs on account of the slightly smaller inter-columniation. The lowest fang is carved into the form of a wing-shaped kung, supported at its middle by a large tou on a short stud. The second fang is carved into a ni-tao-kung on which is the man-kung, also carved on the fang. It is to be noted here that the carved man-kung of the pu-chien-p'u-cho is connected with that of the chu-t'ou-p'u-cho on account of the narrow space. Such an arrangement is known in the *Ying-tsao-fa-shih* as lien-kung-chiao-yin or the inter-locking hidden kungs (Figure 39).

It was only after the Sung Dynasty that the pu-chien-p'u-cho began to develop into one more complicated form. Sui and T'ang examples are found mostly as the kungs or short vertical studs. The function of these earlier pu-chien kungs or studs was primarily to keep the fangs of different levels in rigid relation to each other, and had little or nothing to do with the supporting of the overhanging eave. The pu-chien-p'u-cho of the other stories of the Kuan-yin Ke and of the Shan-men are all more complicated and "modern." The simple examples like those discussed here that have in very rudimentary form the later combination while still purely Sui-T'angish in function are certainly rare examples of a transitional construction.

2. Interior Tou-kungs of the Lower Story (Figure 40)

ⓔ **Chu-t'ou-p'u-cho** Instead of being supported directly by the inner peristylar column, the chu-t'ou-p'u-cho is placed on a p'u-p'ai-fang or plate which in turn is placed on top of the column. The front of the p'u-cho is made to face the center of the building, while the rear is directed towards the exterior.

4. 山面补间铺作 亦唯内间有之，而前后间不置。虽与正面补间铺作同在枋上雕成假拱形，然因间之进深较小，故拱形亦略异。其最下层为翼形拱，上置一散斗，其上为泥道拱，再上为慢拱，与柱头铺作同层之慢拱“连拱交隐”（图 39）。各层枋间，亦垫以散斗，最下则支以直斗，如正面及山门之制。

补间铺作，自宋而后始见繁杂，隋唐遗例，殆多用人字形或直斗者。人字形及直斗之功用在各层枋间上下之联络，于檐之出跳无与也。观音阁他层及山门虽有较繁杂之补间铺作，而简单如阁之下檐，只略具后代补间铺作之雏型，而于功用上仍纯为“隋唐的”者，实罕见之过渡佳例也。

下层内檐斗拱三种：

5. 柱头铺作（图 40） 立于内柱柱头上平板枋上，其内向者为铺作之正面，而向外一面乃其后尾。

The function of these interior tou-kungs is to support the narrow balcony that is carried around the colossal figure at the mezzanine floor height. The chu-t'ou-p'u-cho consists of two t'iaos of hua-kungs, which, with the assistance of kungs, carry two shu-fangs, forming the immediate support of the overhanging portion of the balcony.

The first hua-kung carries a "double-kung" and the second hua-kung, a single ling-kung. Intersecting with the first hua-kung in the lu-tou is the ni-tao-kung, carrying three chu-t'ou-fangs above, which are also carved into kungs in relief. On the same level with the two upper fangs, and intersecting with them, are two members, the lower one being a shua-t'ou without the projecting tip, while the upper one is a small beam spanning the space between the inner and outer peristylar columns supporting the floor, and at the same time intersecting with the two shu-fangs.

The construction of this p'u-cho answers precisely to the following passage from the *Ying-tsao-fa-shih*:

"In the construction of this p'ing-tso (balcony), the p'u-cho should be one or two t'iaos less than the upper story, with double-kung and built in the chi-hsin manner. Underneath the p'u-cho a p'u-p'ai-fang should be used..."

此斗拱者，所以承中层内平坐：华拱两跳，每跳上安素枋，枋上铺地板，置栏杆，可绕佛身中段一周。而中层内柱，亦立于同柱头之上。重拱计心，与《营造法式》下列数段符合：

“造平坐之制，其铺作减上屋一跳或两跳，其铺作宜用重拱及逐跳计心造作。”

“凡平坐铺作下用普拍方，厚随材广或更加一栔……”

而普拍枋者，盖即清式所谓平板枋；清式凡斗拱皆置于平板枋上，无将栌斗直接置于柱头者，而此处所见于普拍枋之用，只限于平坐铺作之下，与宋式适同。

铺作后尾。第一层为拱，第二层为梁，即外檐第三跳后尾之梁也。第三跳又为拱，第四层为枋。即外檐耍头后尾伸引部分也。

铺作正面，栌斗之内，泥道拱与华拱相交，第二层为慢拱，乃由柱头枋雕成假拱形，柱头枋共计三层，第二层亦雕泥道拱形。第一跳跳头施重拱，上安素枋，第二跳跳头施令拱，上安散斗三枚，以承素枋。

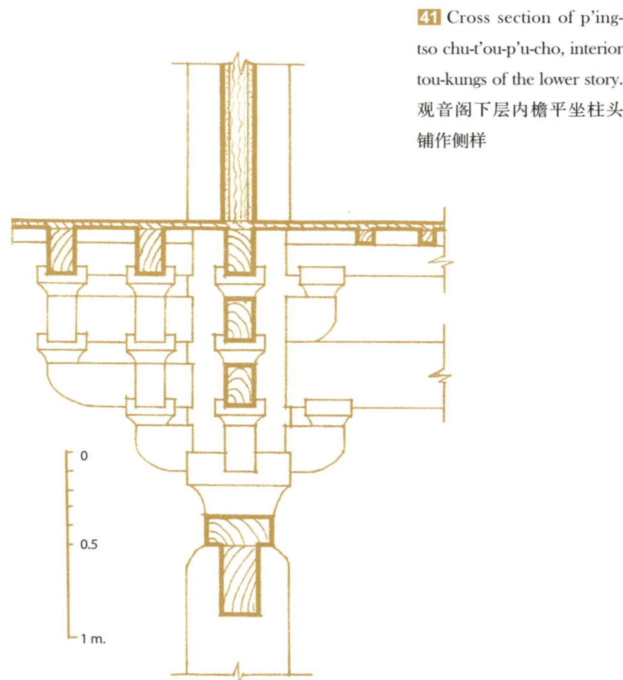

41 Cross section of p'ing-tso chu-t'ou-p'u-cho, interior tou-kungs of the lower story.
观音阁下层内檐平坐柱头铺作侧样

The p'u-p'ai-fang or plate is called the p'ing-pan-fang in the Ts'ing style, where it is seldom missing, while here, as specified in the Sung official book, it is used only under p'u-chos of the balcony.

Besides being the support for the balcony, it is important to note that the chu-t'ou-p'u-cho here is at the same time the base for the second tier of the superposed "orders." The lower end of the column is mortised to join with the kungs and fangs of the p'u-cho of which it seems to form an integral part (Figure 41). Such construction is also specified in the *Ying-tsao-fa-shih*.

中层内柱，立于下层内柱上栌头之上，与各层拱枋相交，似成为斗拱之一部分者（图 41）。《法式》卷四造平坐之制：

“凡平坐铺作，若叉柱造，即每角用栌斗一枚，其柱根叉于栌斗之上；若缠柱造，即每角于柱外普拍方上安栌斗三枚。”

平坐铺作与上层柱之不能分离，于此已可见；故上一层柱根，实已为下层平坐铺作之一部分。观音阁所见，显然非缠柱造，然是否即为叉柱造，愿以质之贤者。

ⓕ **Chuan-chiao-p'u-cho (Figure 40)** The construction of the set at the corner is different from the one on the exterior corner because the front of the p'u-cho is made to face the center of the building. The two principal sides consist of the intersection of ni-tao-kungs and man-kungs with the corresponding members of the other side, while the rear end of the ni-tao-kung becomes the hua-kung and that of the man-kung becomes a beam. Two t'iaos of chiao-kungs bisect the right angle formed by the intersecting kungs. The intersecting ling-kungs are placed at the end of the second chiao-kung, while at its rear is the diagonal beam that spans and braces the inner and exterior corner column thus building them together. Being the point of intersection of beams from three directions, the interior chuan-chiao-p'u-cho is of vital importance in the structure.

ⓖ **Pu-chien-p'u-cho (Figure 40)** Applied only to the front and rear bays. Like the pu-chien-p'u-cho of the exterior, it consists merely of a number of carved kungs with tous filling the spaces in between. It has nothing to do with the support of the balcony. This holds true of the pu-chien-p'u-chos of the first story, whether interior or exterior.

3. Exterior Tou-kungs of the Mezzanine Story

There are five different kinds of tou-kungs on the exterior of the mezzanine. In spite of their similar function, i.e., the support of the exterior balcony, their construction varies according to the positions in which they are placed (Figures 39, 41).

ⓗ **Chu-t'ou-p'u-cho** Like those of the interior p'u-chos of the lower story, the lu-tou is placed on the p'u-p'ai-fang. There are three t'iaos of hua-kungs corbelling out from the lu-tou; the kungs are arranged in the chi-hsin, double-kung manner. The double-kung is placed on the end of the first t'iao, while the second t'iao supports only one ling-kung. The third t'iao has no kung on its end, but merely a small tou, into which the outermost su-fang is placed. The latter, together with the other two su-fangs, which are placed parallel and on the same level with it, form the immediate support for the balcony floor. Intersecting with these su-fangs on the same level is the shua-t'ou, the end of which is not beveled off like those of the lower p'u-chos. The balcony of the central bay on the southern side is widened by lengthening the shua-t'ou considerably to enable an easier view of the main tablet, the penmanship of which was attributed to Li T'ai-po, illustrious poet of the T'ang Dynasty.

To the rear of the p'u-cho, the first and third t'iaos are short hua-kungs, while the second and fourth t'iaos are lengthened into fangs, reaching the tou-kungs of the inner peristylar columns. In Chapter V of the *Ying-tsao-fa-shih,* on the construction of the p'ing-tso we read:

6. 转角铺作（图 40）　其正面向内，故其结构亦与向外之转角铺作不同。其正侧二面各有泥道拱、慢拱，泥道拱与后尾之华拱相列，慢拱与后尾之梁相列，斜角上华拱二跳。第一跳跳头正侧二面重拱相交，重拱之后尾为切几头，接于柱头枋上。第二跳跳头为二面令拱相交，其后尾亦为切几头，与第一跳上慢拱相交于瓜子拱端斗内。斜角华拱后尾为华拱及梁，与柱头铺作同，亦为外檐转角铺作之后尾。外檐转角铺作及次梢间正面山面二柱头铺作后尾，三面梁枋会于此柱头之上，于结构上，其位置殊为重要也。

7. 补间铺作（图40）　唯正面有之，山面则无。其形制似外檐山面补间铺作，只各层柱头枋间之联络，与出檐结构无关系。下层内外檐补间铺作皆如此，制度一致，非偶然也。

中层外檐铺作五种：

皆平坐铺作也；同在一平坐之下，因功用及地位之不同，而各异其结构（图39，41）。

8. 柱头铺作　栌斗安于普拍枋上。华拱三跳，计心重拱：第一跳跳头安重拱，第二跳跳头安令拱，第三跳跳头无横拱，唯安散斗以承素枋及耍头；重拱、令拱上亦施素枋，故共有素枋三道；枋上铺板，即上层外平坐也。耍头之头，不斜斫作耍头形，而南面正中一间，且将此耍头加长约 0.5 米，以增加平坐之深度，俾登临者可瞻李太白题额。泥道拱上为柱头枋三层，上雕假拱形。铺作后尾第一三两层锯齐无卷杀，第二层为枋，直达内檐中层柱头，铺作之上；第四层即耍头后尾，亦为枋以达内柱柱头。耍头端外即为挂落板。《法式》卷五平坐之制末条谓：

42 Cross section of exterior p'ing-tso chu-t'ou-p'u-cho & pu-chien-p'u-cho of Kuan-yin Ke.

观音阁外檐平坐柱头铺作、补间铺作侧样

0 0.5 1 1.5 2 m.

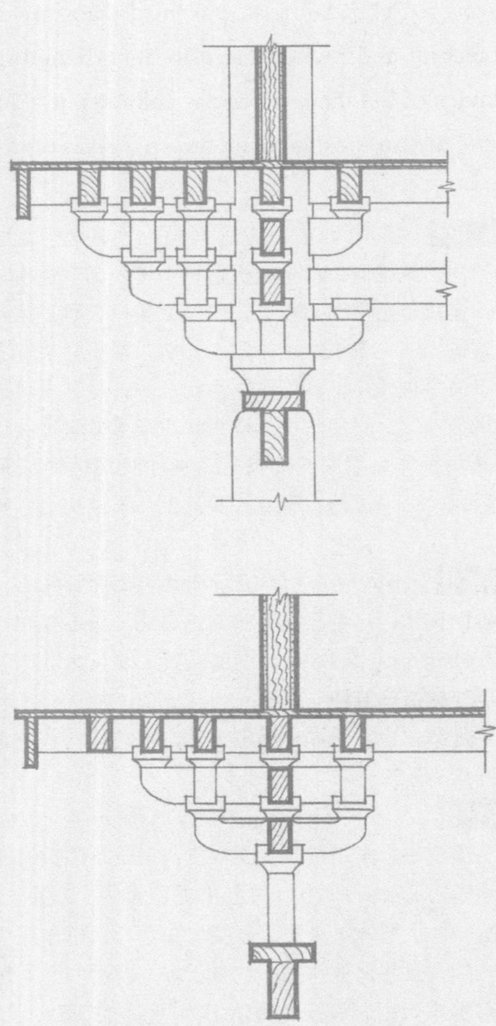

"Beneath the ts'ao-fu, front-and-back-wise, the ti-mien-fang are used to hold the front and rear p'u-chos in position; on the p'u-cho is placed the p'u-pan-fang, one ts'ai in size; all the way around is the yen-ch'ih-pan, twice the ts'ai in width, and four to five fen in thickness."

It is not altogether unjustifiable to call the rear of the second t'iao the ti-mien-fang and that of the fourth t'iao the p'u-pan-fang. The yen-ch'ih-pan is known in the Ts'ing style as the ti-chu-pan. (Figure 42)

ⓘ **Chuan-chiao-p'u-cho** The p'u-cho at the corner is plainly the intersection of the different fangs and kungs of the two adjacent sides. The three t'iaos of hua-kung, together with the shua-t'ou above are extended at the rear to form the ni-tao-kung and the three tiers of chu-t'ou-fangs on the other side. The kua-tze-kung, man-kung, and ling-kung are all extended to form auxiliary hua-kungs on the other side. The intersection of these is supported by three t'iaos of chiao-kungs on the mitre-line. The entire p'u-cho may be considered a very logical and "regular" ensemble (Figure 39).

"平坐之内，逐间下草栿前后安地面方，以拘前后铺作；铺作之上安铺板方，用一材；四周安雁翅板，广加材一倍，厚四分至五分。"

第二跳后尾盖即地面枋，耍头后尾盖即铺板枋耶？清式称为挂落板者，即雁翅板也。西面铺作后尾，虽在暗层，适当梯间，故第一三两层作拱形，拱端施斗。（图 42）

9. 转角铺作 华拱三跳，计心，重拱，各拱平正相交相列，角拱亦三跳，绝无不规则之结构（图 39）。

ⓙ **Pu-chien-p'u-cho of the Three Central Bays on the Front and Rear Facade** Like the chu-t'ou-p'u-cho, it also consists of three t'iaos of hua-kung, with double-kung and built in the chi-hsin manner. From the exterior, it appears to be identical to the chu-t'ou-p'u-cho both in appearance and construction except that it is not burdened from above with a column the foot of which is worked into the p'u-cho (Figure 31). But a careful study of its rear revealed to us that lu-tou is merely a false "applique." The real member on which the entire load of the pu-chien-p'u-cho is concentrated is not the lu-tou, but a t'o-feng or "camel's back" (Figure 43). The rear ends of the hua-kungs are left unfinished.

ⓚ **Pu-chien-p'u-cho of the Two Inner Bays of the End Facades** The short stud, standing on the p'u-p'ai-fang is the foot of the p'u-cho, which is formed by intersecting two hua-kungs with the chu-t'ou-fangs. On the end of each t'iao of the hua-kungs is placed a su-fang. Since there are three su-fangs for the three t'iaos on the chu-t'ou-p'u-cho, and there are only two t'iaos on the pu-chien-p'u-cho, the outermost su-fang is left unsupported at the middle. But the shua-t'ou or p'u-pan-fang comes in conveniently to intersect with it, thus supporting it at the middle.

The short stud as well as the large t'ou on its top are now lost.

The pu-chien-p'u-cho of the end facade on account of the narrower space into which it is put is constructed differently from those of the front and rear facades.

ⓛ **Pu-chien-p'u-cho of the End Bays** On account of the even narrower space, the p'u-cho in the end bay is deprived of even the carved ni-tao-kung, and given a wing-shaped kung instead. The ling-kung on the end of the second hua-kung is forced to join with the man-kungs of the adjacent p'u-chos in the method called the "lien-kung-chiao-yin" (Figures 31, 39).

4. Interior Tou-kungs of the Mezzanine Story

Like the interior tou-kungs of the lower story, they are placed with the front side facing the center of the building. The rear of the tou-kungs is visible only from the dark aisle. They are, therefore, unfinished except in the aisle on the western end which is the staircase. There are also five different kinds of tou-kung in the interior of the mezzanine story. (Figure 32)

43 The rear of tang-hsin-chien, pu-chien-p'u-cho, interior tou-kung of the mezzanine story. 观音阁中层内檐当心间补间铺作后尾

10. 正面当心间及次间补间铺作 亦华拱三跳，计心，重拱。其外形与柱头铺作相同，结构亦极相似，唯栌斗上无斗（图31）。今自外视之，其栌斗与柱头铺作栌斗同，然其背面，则次间无栌斗，而代以驼峰（图43）。其后尾唯第三跳作地面枋（?）直达内檐铺作上，“以拘前后铺作”。

11. 山面补间铺作 指山面居中两间而言。其泥道拱雕于下层柱头枋上，华拱与之相交，计二跳，第一跳跳头横施令拱，上承最内罗汉枋，第二跳无拱，唯安斗以承中罗汉枋，至于外罗汉枋则由柱头达柱头，其间无承支之者。其泥道拱上未雕慢拱形，盖单拱计心造也。下跳华拱与泥道拱之下，盖有大斗及直斗以置于普拍枋者，今皆毁无存。山面补间铺作之必须异于正面者，盖因山面柱间距离较小，不足以容全部之阔也。

12. 梢间补间铺作 柱间距离较山面尤小，并单拱而不能容，故下层柱头枋上雕云形拱，跳头令拱则与并列之柱头铺作及转角铺作之第一跳上慢拱“连拱交隐”（图31，39）。

中层内檐铺作五种：

如下层内檐铺作，以内向一面为正面，外向一面为后尾。外向一面，即为暗层之内，故其中除抹角铺作及西面与梯相近之铺作外，其后尾皆如外檐平坐铺作之后尾，拱头概无卷杀，不加修饰。

斗拱之功用，即在承上层之结构，故此部斗拱，亦因上层特殊之布置（图32），而有特殊之形制。

ⓜ **Chu-t'ou-p'u-cho of the Front and Rear** The large hole on the upper floor through which the figure of the Kuan-yin is hexagonal in shape. The angles at the eastern and western ends are of approximately 50 degrees and those of the northern and southern sides are of 130 degrees. But the hole through the mezzanine floor is a rectangle. The hexagonal shape of the upper floor has been obtained by spanning the spaces between the front columns connecting them to the center columns of the sides. This diagonal span imposes an extra set of fangs on the chu-t'ou-p'u-chos of the front and the end sides. Therefore, besides the intersection of chu-t'ou-fangs and hua-kungs, the p'u-cho is further complicated by the introduction of intersection of the extra fang. This peculiar construction may in a sense be called a chuan-chiao-p'u-cho (Figure 44).

Judging from its function and position, it is really a p'u-cho for the support of a balcony. According to the *Ying-tsao-fa-shih*, it should have been built in the chi-hsin manner, but because of the imposition of the diagonal fangs, the t'ou-hsin manner has been employed to ensure simplicity in construction.

13. 当心间两旁柱头铺作 上层地板围绕像身之空井为六角形，东西两端成较正角略小之锐角，其余四角则成约一百三十度之钝角；然中层空井则为长方形。此六角形者，实由自当心间与次间之间之内柱上至中柱上抹角所成。而此抹角之结构，与其他部分两柱头间之结构相同，其各层枋与柱头上各层枋相交于柱头而成铺作；而铺作上除正角相交之华拱与柱头枋外，乃沿约一百三十度之钝角线上，加交各层枋，此乃中层内檐柱头铺作之特点也。谓为转角铺作亦未尝不可（图 44）。

以位置及功用论，则此部实为平坐；既为平坐，则按法式之制，须用计心造；然因抹角之故，计心颇为不便——结构不便即不合理——故从权用偷心造也。

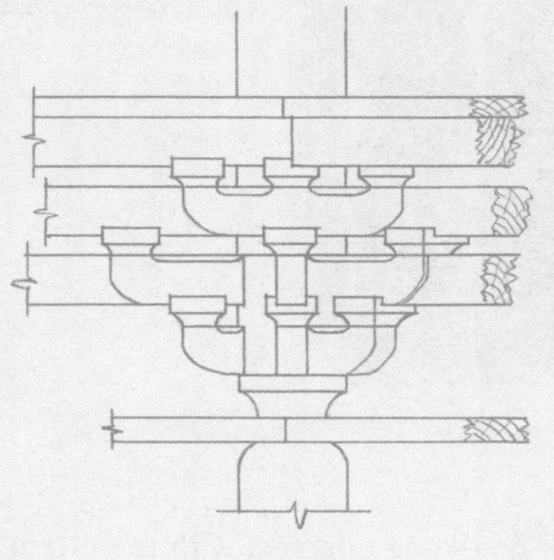

正样 facade

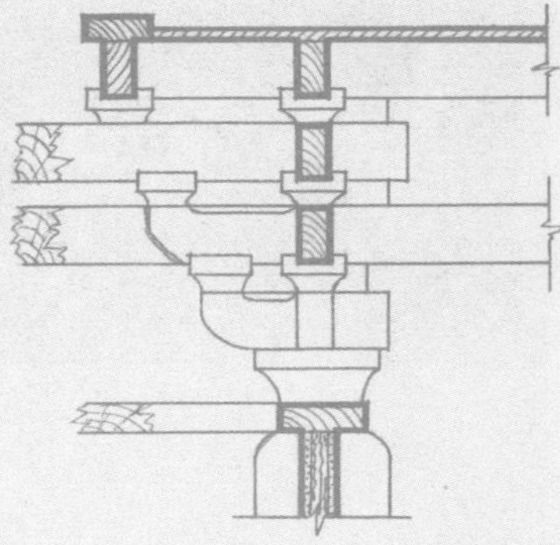

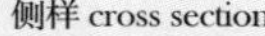

侧样 cross section

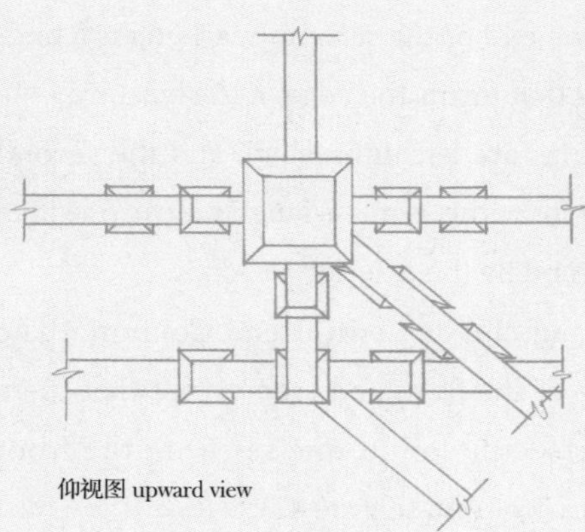

仰视图 upward view

44 Chu-t'ou, interior tou-kungs of the mezzanine story.

观音阁中层内檐柱头斗拱

-.5 0 .5 1 m.

45 Side bays of pu-chien-p'u-cho and chuan-chiao-p'u-cho, interior tou-kungs of the mezzanine story.
观音阁中层内檐次间补间铺作及转角铺作

From the lu-t'ou, two t'iaos of hua-kung intersect with the ni-tao-kungs of both directions, on which are chu-t'ou-fangs, also from both directions. All the chu-t'ou-fangs are carved into kungs in relief exactly as those of the other p'u-chos. On the end of the second hua-kung is a ling-kung, which supports the su-fang that forms the edge of the balcony.

The rear ends of the hua-kungs are left unfinished, and the second and fourth t'iaos are extended to form the ti-mien-fang and p'u-p'ai-fang which are supported at the outer end by the exterior p'u-chos.

ⓝ **Chu-t'ou-p'u-cho of the Chung-chu or Central-end Column** The construction is identical to those of the front and rear, except that there are two extra sets of fangs intersecting on it, one set from the front column and the other from the rear column (Figrue 47).

ⓞ **Pu-chien-p'u-cho** On the p'u-p'ai-fang is the lu-tou, from which spring two t'iaos of hua-kung, built in the t'ou-hsin manner. On the end of the second hua-kung is a ling-kung, supporting the lo-han-fang, on which rests the upper floor (Figure 45). A study of the p'u-cho from the rear reveals that the set rests on a t'o-feng (camel's back) instead of what is seen in the front, a lu-tou, which therefore must have been an alteration in one of the later repairs. The t'o-fengs of the central bay are shaped differently from those of the side bays (Figures 43, 46).

46 The rear of pu-chien-p'u-cho from side bays, interior tou-kungs of the mezzanine story. 观音阁中层内檐次间补间铺作后尾

ⓟ Chuan-chiao-p'u-cho

Being in the t'ou-hsin manner, the construction is extremely simple without the transversal kungs. Besides the ni-tao-kung and the chu-t'ou-fangs of the two sides, there is only the set of three chiao-kungs or corner-kungs for the support of lo-han-fangs from three different directions that intersect on the end of the third chiao-kung (Figure 45).

其结构为华拱二跳，偷心造，跳头横施令拱，拱上置斗，斗上承罗汉枋。与华拱正角相交者为泥道拱及柱头枋三层，枋上雕假拱形，本平平无奇。乃于百三十度斜线上加普拍枋、泥道拱以及柱头枋三层，全部斜加一份，此其所以异也。

铺作后尾则锯齐如外檐平坐铺作，而第二、第四两层则伸长成地面枋及铺板枋焉。

14. 中柱柱头铺作　其结构与13同，唯各层抹角枋自两面来交（图47）。

15. 补间铺作　栌斗安于普拍枋上，华拱二跳，偷心造，第二跳跳头施令拱，拱斗上承罗汉枋，枋上为上层地板（图45）。今栌斗作斗形，然自后尾观之，则作驼峰形；当心间驼峰（图43）与次间驼峰（图46）复略异，正面所见之栌斗，恐非原物也。

16. 转角铺作　结构殊简单，角拱三跳，上承三方面之罗汉枋。第二层柱头枋上雕翼形拱，适在慢拱头散斗上，其上复置交互斗以承罗汉枋（图45）。

47 Pu-chien-p'u-cho on the diagonal fang, interior tou-kungs of the mezzanine story.
观音阁中层内檐抹角补间铺作

It is to be noted that these chiao-kungs do not bisect the right angle into two angles of 45 degrees each, because the outer end of the su-fang is supported by the pu-chien-p'u-cho which is placed midway between the front and rear column and the chung-chu, and consequently, the line of this su-fang is one drawn from the apex of a right-angled triangle of legs of different lengths to the mid-point of its hypotenuse.

ⓠ **Pu-chien-p'u-cho on the Diagonal Fang** Structurally, this pu-chien-p'u-cho differs in no way whatsoever from any other pu-chien-p'u-cho, being placed on a p'u-p'ai-fang or lan-erh which is supported at the two ends by the columns. But, because the space under the p'u-p'ai-fang and lan-erh is left unfilled by a curtain wall, the p'u-cho gives the impression of being suspended in space instead of resting on a solid wall, and the whole effect is one of lightness and ethereal quality (Figure 47).

A t'o-feng, rather tall in proportion, is placed on the p'u-p'ai-fang. In the large tou above it intersect the chu-t'ou-fangs and the two t'iaos of hua-kung. The fangs are carved with kungs in relief as usual. The t'ou-hsin manner is again applied here, eliminating even the ling-kung which is usually used on the end of the uppermost t'iao.

5. Exterior Tou-kungs of the Upper Story

From both the structural and ornamental points of view, the tou-kungs of the upper story are undoubtedly of supreme importance. It is they that give the Kuan-yin Ke its expression and character, and bring us into a closer contact and better understanding with building and builders of the Liao Dynasty. There are three kinds of tou-kung on the exterior of the upper story.

ⓡ **Chu-t'ou-p'u-cho** Here the lu-tou is placed directly on top of the column, the p'u-p'ai-fang being eliminated. From the lu-tou spring four t'iaos for the support of the overhang, the two lower t'iaos being hua-kungs and the two upper t'iaos, angs. The whole ensemble is known in the *Ying-tsao-fa-shih* as ch'ung-ch'ao-ch'ung-ang. The transversal kungs on these t'iaos are distributed in the t'ou-hsin, double-kung manner. On the end of the second hua-kung are a kua-tze-kung and a man-kung, on which is the lo-han-fang. Intersecting with these two kungs are two angs, which may be defined as hua-kungs set in a slanting position. On the end of the second ang is placed the ling-kung with its t'i-mu and liao-yan-ch'uan above (Figure 48).

此角拱中线，非将角平分而成四十五度者[60]。盖角拱上素枋之彼端，乃承于抹角枋正中之铺作上，而素枋非将角平分，则角拱须随枋略偏也。

17. 抹角枋上补间铺作 自结构方面观之，各层枋皆置于柱头之上，而铺作居枋之中，与普通补间铺作无异，唯因悬空而过，下无墙壁，故其所呈现象，殊觉玲珑精巧。驼峰置普拍枋上，上置交互斗；华拱与雕作泥道拱形之柱头枋相交于交互斗内。华拱计共两跳，偷心造，第二跳跳头置散斗，斗上承素枋，而不施横拱。结构至简（图47）。

观音阁全部结构中，除中层内外檐当心间及次间平坐补间铺作外，其余各铺作，泥道拱皆雕于第一层柱头枋上，而于其下置直斗或驼峰；此类部分，内外上下皆毁，唯此抹角铺作上尚存，良可贵也。

上层外檐斗拱三种：

在结构上及装饰上皆占最重要位置，观音阁全部之性格，可谓由此部斗拱而充分表现可也。

18. 柱头铺作 栌斗施于柱头，其上出四跳，下两跳为华拱，上两跳为昂，即《法式》所谓“重杪重昂”[61]者是。其跳头斗拱之分配为重拱，偷心造。第二跳华拱跳头施瓜子拱及慢拱，慢拱上为罗汉枋。与瓜子拱及慢拱相交者为下昂二层，第二层昂上施令拱，以承替木及橑檐槫。其正面立面形与下檐略同，而侧面因用昂而大异（图48）。

48 Chu-t'ou-p'u-cho and pu-chien-p'u-cho of exterior tou-kungs of the upper story, Kuan-yin Ke. 观音阁上层外檐柱头铺作及补间铺作

The rear of the first t'iao is a hua-kung, and that of the second t'iao is lengthened to form a tie beam which is supported by the interior chu-t'ou-p'u-cho in exactly the same manner at both ends. Above the tie beam is another hua-kung, the outer end of which is beveled off to butt against the lower surface of the ang. On this hua-kung is placed a ling-kung, supporting the p'ing-ch'i-fang or the fang that supports the ceiling. This p'ing-ch'i-fang is in a sense a lo-han-fang, the only difference being that it is used in the interior while the latter is used in the exterior. Intersecting with the p'ing-ch'i-fang is another su-fang which would have been the rear of the fourth hua-kung had it been placed horizontally. The exterior end of this su-fang is also beveled to against the bottom of the ang.

The lower support for the lower ang is the end of the second hua-kung, on which the ang is placed in a slanting position with the lower end pointing downward. The bottom of the ang is carried to the same level and therefore intersects with the third chu-t'ou-fang. The angle the ang makes with the ground is approximately 30 degrees. The upper or second ang is made to rest directly on the lower one, and runs parallel to it.

49 Chu-t'ou-p'u-cho of exterior tou-kungs of the upper story, Kuan-yin Ke. 观音阁上层外檐柱头铺作侧样

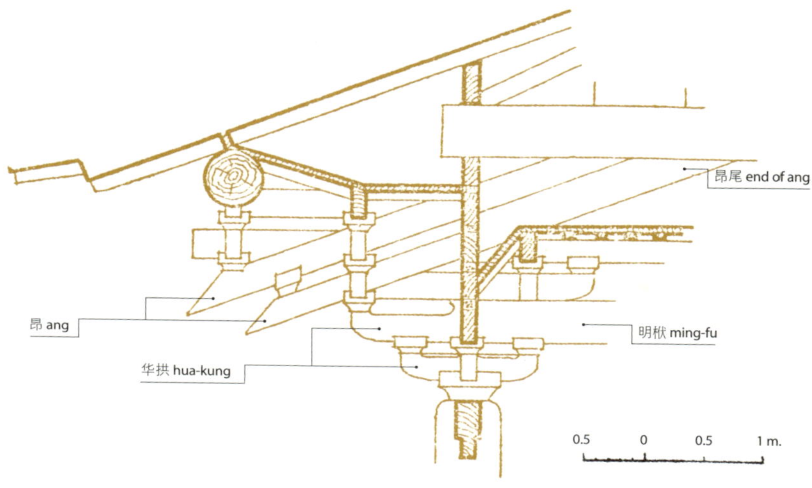

On the end of the upper ang is the ling-kung, on exactly the same level as the man-kung of the second hua-kung, and two t'iaos further out. Thus a greater overhang is achieved without an excessive raise in height, because the outward stretch of two t'iaos is gained with a corresponding raise of one t'iao only. On the upper ang, and intersecting with the ling-kung in a horizontal direction is a small shua-t'ou, the rear end of which is beveled to rest on the sloping surface of the upper ang, while the outer is left angular and square (Figure 49).

华拱第一跳后尾为华拱；第二跳后尾伸引为梁，直达内柱柱头铺作上。梁以上又为华拱，与令拱相交；令拱上承平棊枋（井口枋），与又一素枋相交。此第三层拱之外端，长只及第二跳跳头，第四层枋则长只及柱头枋，二者背上皆斫截成斜尖，以承第一层下昂。下昂下部承于第二跳跳头交互斗内，斜向后上伸，至与柱头枋相交处，其底适与第三层柱头枋之底平，昂之斜度，与水平约略成三十度。第二层昂在第一层昂之上，而与之平行，昂端横施令拱，与第二跳跳头上之慢拱平。其向外伸出较第二跳长两跳，而向上升高，则只较之高一跳。故其出檐较远而不致太高；盖伸出如华拱两跳之远，而上升只华拱一层之高也。与令拱相交者为耍头，与华拱平行，虽平出在第四跳之上，而高下则与第四跳平。其后斫斜，平置昂上（图49）。

The rear end of the ang is really the most important as well as the most interesting part of the chu-t'ou-p'u-cho. After intersecting with the third and fourth chu-t'ou-fang, the two angs are carried straight back until the rear ends hit again the bottom of the beam which the p'u-cho is carrying. The angs are also beveled here to butt against the bottom of the beam. Thus the ang acts as a lever arm, supported at the middle by the chu-t'ou-fang, loaded at the outer and with the liao-yen-ch'uan and the eave above, and held in equilibrium by the beam and its heavy load from above. This enables the eave overhang to become much greater than otherwise. This is also in accordance with the specification in Chapter IV of the *Ying-tsao-fa-shih* on "the making of the ang": "that when it is on the column, it is to be held down by the ts'ao-fu or ting-fu." Before the Sung Dynasty, the ang had always been a structural member, but in Ming and Ts'ing examples, although the term "ang" was still used to designate a certain member of the tou-kung, it was no longer the lever arm that it had been hitherto, but a horizontal hua-kung with the end shaped into the beak form of the ang. The organic function of the original ang was thus totally lost.

As to the exterior finish of the ang-chui or beak of the ang, we find later examples to be universally curved. In the same section of the *Ying-tsao-fa-shih* we read that the face of the beak should be concaved two fen, and all Ming and Ts'ing ang-chuis are shaped in this fashion. But the ang-chui of the Kuan-yin Ke is a pure, simple bevel, making an angle of approximately 35 degrees with the ang itself, giving an appearance much like those represented in the Tun-huang cave paintings. This style was still used in the Sung period as is found in one of the small notes in the same section, that "there is also the method of cutting diagonally from the bottom of the tou to the end (of the ang), so that the face of the ang will be a straight even surface, called the p'ei-chu-ang." This is precisely the method employed in making the ang-chui of the Kuan-yin Ke. The ang-chui of the wooden pagoda of Ying Hsien, Shansi Province is also shaped in the same manner, and it is undoubtedly usual during the T'ang and Liao periods. The gradual softening of the straight, vigorous p'ei-chu-ang of the Liao to the dainty, delicate curvature of the ang-chui of later times is merely a natural evolution so inevitable that it seems that no mature art can escape from this beaten track.

ⓢ **Chuan-chiao-p'u-cho** This again may be analyzed as the intersection of chu-t'ou-p'u-cho from two sides (Figure 38). On the lu-tou, there are four hua-kungs intersecting each other, forming a figure in plan. The second t'iao consists of hua-kungs extended from the lowest chu-t'ou-fang, a corner kung and a diagonal kung. The third and fourth t'iaos on the center-line consist of the two angs, while on the corresponding level, the ends of the corner kung and the diagonal kung are each accentuated by two more t'iaos of hua-kungs. The two that intersect at the end of the corner kungs are the extension of the double-kungs at the end of the second t'iao of the front and side hua-kungs, while those on the diagonal kungs are extended from the interior p'ing-ch'i-fang.

昂之后尾，实为上层柱头铺作最有趣部分。上下二昂，伸过柱头枋后，斜上直达草栿（清称“三架梁”）之下。昂之外端，受檐部重量下压，其尾端因之上升，而赖草栿重量之下压而保持其均衡。利用杠杆作用，使出跳远出，以补平出华拱之不逮。《法式》卷四《造昂之制》有“如当柱头，即以草栿或丁栿压之”之句，盖即指此。宋代建筑用昂之制，尚以结构为前提。明清以后，斗拱虽尚有昂，而徒具其形而失其用，只平置华拱（翘）而将其外端斫成昂嘴状，非如辽宋昂之具“有机性”矣。

昂嘴部分，宋以后多为曲线的。《法式》卷四谓：

“……昂面中顱二分，令顱势圜和。”

清式亦如此。然观音阁昂嘴，则为与昂底成三十五度之斜直线，其所呈现象，颇似敦煌壁画所见。此式宋代殆尚有之，见于《造昂之制》文内小注中：

“……亦有自斗外斜杀至尖者，其昂面平直，谓之‘批竹昂’。”

适与此处所见符合。应县佛宫寺塔亦如此，其为唐辽盛行之式无疑。其后刚强之直线，受年代磋磨，日渐曲柔，至明仲之世，已成“亦有”之一种，退居小注之中；此固所有艺术蜕变之途径，希腊之成罗马，乔托之成拉斐尔，[62] 顾虎头之成仇十洲，其起伏之势，如出一辙，非独唐宋建筑之独循此道也。

50 Interior tou-kungs of the upper story, Kuan-yin Ke. 观音阁上层内檐斗拱

But on the mitre-line, there are three angs on the corner kungs, the lower two stretching out to receive the intersection of the t'i-mu and liao-yen-ch'uan or eave-purlin, while the third is extended further, with the "cushioning" of the pao-p'ing, to support the two corner rafters. It is to be noticed that these three corner angs or chiao-angs are so placed that their horizontal projection makes the same angle with the ground as that of the front and side angs, while the true angle is considerably smaller. Consequently the slope of these corner members is gentler than that of the front and side, and, with the further raise of the chiao-liangs or corner beams, the gentle upward curve at the corners is the natural result.

It is interesting to note that the second t'iaos of the hua-kung, corner kung and the diagonal kung, are each, theoretically, provided on their ends with a hua-tze-kung to support the man-kung above. But since they are fitted into each other in such a way that there would not be room enough for each of them to have their separate kua-tze-kung, the latter are combined into one through the carving of three false kungs out of one piece of timber. At the point where they combine, the two kungs are made to share one tou (Figure 50). This is what is called the yuan-yang-chiao-shou-kung in the *Ying-tsao-fa-shih*.

This entire chuan-chiao-p'u-cho is a gigantic motif, decorative and complicated in appearance, but structural, simple and logical in function, designed and constructed to take care of the important corners of this edifice.

ⓣ **Pu-chien-p'u-cho** Used in the inner bays, and ommited in the end bays. Two t'iaos of hua-kung intersecting with the two tower chu-t'ou-fangs are arranged in the t'ou-hsin manner with a ling-kung on the end of the second t'iao to receive the lo-han-fang. The lowest chu-t'ou-fang is carved into a wing-shaped kung. The intersection of the hua-kung and chu-t'ou-fangs is put on a chiao-hu-tou which was supported by a short stud that is now missing. The second and third chu-t'ou-fangs are carved with a double kung in relief. The rear of the p'u-cho is merely a hua-kung with a ling-kung to support the p'ing-ch'i-fang (Figure 51).

51 The rear of chu-t'ou-p'u-cho and pu-chien-p'u-cho, interior and exterior tou-kungs of the upper story. 观音阁上层内外檐柱头及补间铺作后尾

19. 转角铺作 在柱头中线上，正侧二面各层拱昂之结构与程次与柱头铺作者同，所异者唯第二跳跳头重拱与同层他拱相列（图 38）。角线上角拱二跳，角昂二跳，其上更有“由昂”，上置宝瓶，以承角梁。此三重角昂，在正面及侧面之投影，与正昂投影之角度相同，然其与地面所成之真角，度数实较小，而斜度较缓和，宜注意也。第二跳角拱之上，有正侧二面第二跳上之重拱伸出而成华拱二跳，与角昂相交；上跳跳头置散斗以承替木。第二层角昂之上，置令拱两件相交，与由昂相交；令拱上置散斗，以承其上相交之正侧二面替木。此外尚有斜华拱两层，与角拱成正角而与正拱成四十五度角，相交于栌斗口内（图 50）；其上又置拱两跳，与角拱上之两拱夹衬于正昂之两旁。与此拱相交者重拱，其外一端与角拱上之华拱相列，其内一端则慢拱与柱头铺作上相埒之慢拱“连拱交隐”。

此转角铺作之全部，殊为雄大，似繁而实简，结构毕现焉。

20. 补间铺作 正面当心间次间及山面居中两间用之。华拱两跳，偷心造，跳头横施令拱，以承罗汉枋。下层华拱与下层柱头枋交于交互斗内，枋雕作翼形拱。二层枋以上则雕重拱，铺作后尾唯拱一跳，上施令拱，以承平棊枋（图 51）。交互斗下，原有直斗，今已无存。

52 Different exterior kungs on the lu-tou, chuan-chiao-p'u-cho of the upper story, Kuan-yin Ke. 观音阁上层外檐转角铺作栌斗上各拱

With the exception of the central bay to the northern side, all the pu-chien-p'u-cho in the interior of the upper story is similar to those of the exterior. But there is a slight modification in those of the east and the west because of the narrow space accommodating them, thus eaving the ling-kung and the man-kung to be combined with those of the adjacent chuan-chiao-p'u-cho (Figure 51).

6. Interior Tou-kung of the Upper Story

There are four different kinds of tou-kungs in the interior of the upper story.

ⓤ **Chu-t'ou-p'u-cho** The front of the p'u-cho, facing the inside of the building, is identical to the exterior chu-t'ou-p'u-cho of the lower story, being composed of four t'iaos of hua-kung, double-kung and t'ou-hsin (Figure 52). The rear of the chu-t'ou-p'u-cho is identical to those of the exterior chu-t'ou-p'u-cho with the exception of the angs (Figure 51). The distribution of kung, the extension of hua-kungs into beams or fangs are all identical.

ⓥ **Chu-t'ou-p'u-cho on the Two Columns that Form the Central Bays** On account of the position of Eleven-headed Kuan-yin which is towards the rear of the hall, the octagonal pyramidal "baldachin," which is really a part of the ceiling, is forced slightly northward. This throws the "baldachin"

53 Chu-t'ou-p'u-cho of the central bays, interior tou-kung of the upper story, Kuan-yin Ke. 观音阁上层内檐北面柱头及当心间补间铺作

off the longitudinal center-line so that it rests on the p'ing-ch'i-fang on the southern side and on lo-han-fang on the northern side where the p'ing-ch'i-fang is interrupted. This causes the ling-kung on the fourth t'iao, the outer end of which is supporting the lo-han-fang, to have its inner end cut off at the angle of 45 degrees to support the side of the octagon above (Figure 53).

上层内檐补间铺作，除当心间北面一朵结构特殊外，其余皆与外檐补间铺作相同。其中略异之一朵，乃内檐山面补间铺作，因地位狭窄，其令拱、慢拱皆与两旁铺作连拱交隐（图51）。

上层内檐斗拱四种：

21. 柱头铺作 正面与下层外檐柱头铺作完全相同，为华拱四跳，重拱，偷心造（图52）。后尾则与上层外檐柱头铺作完全相同（图51）。上层内檐柱头铺作之特殊者为当心间北面柱头铺作。

22. 当心间北面柱头铺作 因观音像之位置不在阁之正中，而略偏北，故像顶上之斗八藻井亦随之北偏；因是之故，藻井之南面承于平棊枋上。而北面乃承于罗汉枋上，而平棊枋至当心间而中断。于是华拱第四跳跳头之令拱，在次间内之一端承平棊枋，而在当心间内之一端则斫作四十五度角，以承藻井下之抹角枋。而罗汉枋遂为抹角枋与藻井下北面枋相交点之承支者，遂在其相交点之下，承之以斗，而斗下雕作拱形（图53）。

ⓦ **Chuan-chiao-p'u-cho** On the mitre-line bisecting the right-angle formed by the interior chu-t'ou-fangs of its adjacent sides are four t'iaos of chiao-kungs in the t'ou-hsin manner. On account of the very narrow space which renders the application of the double-kung impossible, the end of the second t'iao is treated with two short intersecting wing-shaped kungs, and the end of the fourth t'iao has two short intersecting ling-kungs to support the p'ing-ch'i-fang (Figure 52).

The rear of this chuan-chiao-p'u-cho is similar to that of the one on the lower story. The second t'iao is extended in the form of beams, supported at the outer ends by the p'u-chos of the exterior. The fourth t'iao is extended as the su-fang described in article r.

ⓧ **Pu-chien-p'u-cho of the Northern Central Bay** It is different from the other pu-chien-p'u-chos because the ling-kung of the second hua-kung is raised into a carved relief on the lo-han-fang, and replaced by a short wing-shaped kung (Figure 53).

In the structure of the Kuan-yin Ke, we find a grand exhibition of tou-kungs, in all 24 varieties, each designed to fulfill a particular function. In seeming complication, the underlying principals are logical and simple. To permeate a structure with such a sense of logic and organic being could only have been achieved by artists of the highest order.

Ⓕ Ceiling Construction

The ceilings of both stories of the Kuan-yin Ke are built in caisson, known in the *Ying-tsao-fa-shih* as the p'ing-ch'i. The p'ing-ch'i is supported on the side parallel to the facade by the p'ing-ch'i-fang, and perpendicular to it, by the shuan-ch'eng-fang which runs parallel and above the ming-fu or exposed beam. The p'ing-an-ch'uans which form the check square of the caisson are arranged rather close to each other, forming very small caissons of about 28 cm. square, much smaller than and therefore totally different in appearance from those more commonly seen today (about 70 cm. square) (Figures 45, 51). The *Ying-tsao-fa-shih* specifies only that the p'ing-ch'i should be evenly and squarely distributed, without reference to its actual size. Japanese structures of the Kamakura period, which were undoubtedly the result of direct Sung influence, have caissons of precisely the same proportion as those of the Kuan-yin Ke, still with the original paintings preserved. The ceiling of the Kuan-yin Ke shows sufficient similarities for us to draw the conclusion that the present caisson ceiling was built on the model of the original if it is not the original itself.

23. 转角铺作 角拱四跳，偷心造，因地位狭小，其势不能容重拱之交列，故第二跳跳头之上，唯短小之翼形拱与第三跳相交。翼形拱与切几头相列，交于柱头枋上。其上则施短令拱与第四跳相交，而在山面，则短令拱与补间铺作上之令拱连拱交隐。第四跳上则短令拱二件相交，以承平棊枋（图 52）。

正侧二面，则泥道拱相交，其上慢拱之后尾及第二层华拱之后尾皆为梁，第三层柱头枋之后尾则为枋，皆三面分达角柱及其旁二柱，于结构上至为重要焉。

24. 当心间北面补间铺作 与他间略同，所异者乃华拱跳头只置翼形小拱，更上则于罗汉枋上雕令拱形，上置三散斗，以承藻井下枋（图53）。

全阁斗拱共计二十四种，各以功用而异其结构，条理井然，种类虽多而不杂，构造似繁而实简，以建筑物而如此充满理智及机能，艺术之极品也。

❻ 天花

观音阁上下二层项部皆施天花。天花宋称“平棊”[63]，其主要干架即斗拱上之素枋名“平棊枋”者，及与之成正角而施于明栿（梁）上之“算桯枋”（？）也。支条（宋称平闇椽）纵横交置枋上，其分布颇密，而井口亦甚小。约0.28米见方，与今所见约二尺（0.70米）见方之天花，其现象迥异（图45，51）。《法式》于平棊之大小，并无规定，只曰“分布方正”，其是否如此，尚待考。今天花板泰半已供年前驻军炊焚，油饰亦非旧观，然日本镰仓时代之兴福寺北圆堂及三重塔内天花，皆与此处所见大致同一权衡，且彩画尚存，与《营造法式》彩画极相类似，可相鉴较也。

Most of the sheathing of the ceilings of the Kuan-yin Ke has been destroyed, leaving only the squares formed by the p'ing-an-ch'uan. The octagonal "baldachin" in the central bay is formed by a number of triangles. It is totally different in scale to the other parts of the ceiling, and whether it is a part of the original design or not is subject to dispute.

The spaces between the p'ing-ch'i-fang and the lo-han-fang, and between the latter and the chu-t'ou-fang are all covered by a "cove," formed by putting p'ing-an-ch'uans over the fangs, and covered with sheathing from above. Such examples are still to be seen in many Japanese buildings of the Kamakura period or earlier.

Ⓖ The Liangs and Fangs

In the Shan-men, all structural framing members are exposed and visible from below. But in the Kuan-yin Ke, there is the p'ing-ch'i or caisson ceiling, all structural members hidden above which are invisible to the spectator below, and therefore, left undressed. In Chapter II of the *Ying-tsao-fa-shih,* under the general definition of p'ing-ch'i, there is a note as follows:

"In palaces of today, the members above the ceiling, such as the beam and purlins that are loaded with the weight of the roof, or members for tying and bracing in all directions, are all left undressed..."

The ts'ao-fu mentioned in previous paragraphs is the general term for all these hidden beams, in contrast to the ming-fu or exposed beams.

On the chu-t'ou-p'u-chos of the Kuan-yin Ke, the rear ends of the second or third t'iaos are all extended to become the ming-fu, above and parallel to which is the shuan-ch'eng-fang (Figure 51), as has already been discussed in previous paragraphs. But the function of the ming-fu and the shuan-ch'eng-fang is to tie and brace the interior and exterior p'u-chos, and receive the p'ing-ch'i, while the load of the roof is supported entirely by the liangs and fangs which are undressed and hidden above the p'ing-ch'i.

The general principle in the construction and arrangement of the liang-chia or "truss" here is similar to that of the Ts'ing Dynasty. It is not a "truss" in the real sense that exerts a thrust among its different members, but a series of posts and lintels superposed one on top of the other. The aisle around the entire building is spanned by beams supported by the inner and exterior columns, called the ju-fu, (or shuang-pu-liang in the Ts'ing style). The distance between the front and rear inner peristylar columns, which is equivalent to two bays' width, is spanned by the yen-fu (or wu-chia-liang in the Ts'ing style). On this yen-fu, at points half a bay's distance from either end are placed t'o-tuns or beam-blocks, which supported the p'ing-liang (or san-chia-liang in the Ts'ing style). On the p'ing-liang stands the chu-ju-chu, the dwarf column (or chi-kua-chu in the Ts'ing style). The difference between the liang-chia of the Kuan-yin Ke and that of today lies, therefore, not in the methods of ensemble of the different members, but in the size and proportion of the beams.

天花与柱头枋间，亦用平闇椽斜置，上遮以板，日本遗物，尚多如此。

当心间像顶之上，作“斗八藻井”，其“椽”尤小，交作三角小格，与他部颇不调谐。是否原形尚待考。

❼ 梁枋

山门屋内上部，用“彻上露明造”之制，一切梁枋椽桁，自下皆见。观音阁则上施平棊。平棊以上之梁枋等等，自下不见，故其做法，亦较粗糙。《法式》卷二《总释》平棊下小注云：

“今宫殿中，其上悉用草架梁栿承屋盖之重，如攀额……方槫之类，及纵横固济之物，皆不施斤斧。……”

其后常用之“草栿”，即指此不施斤斧之梁枋而言；而与之对称者，即“明栿”是也。

观音阁各柱头斗拱上，第二或第三跳华拱之后尾，皆伸引为“明栿”，明栿背上架“算桯枋”（图51），已于斗拱题下论及。然明栿及算桯枋之功用在拘前后铺作，及承平棊；屋盖之重，及纵横固济之责，悉在平棊以上不施斤斧之梁栿之上焉。

此处用梁之制，与清式大同小异。檐柱与内柱之上施“双步梁”（宋称“乳栿”），内柱与内柱之上施“五架梁”（“檐栿”），五架梁之上置柁橔，上施“三架梁”（“平梁”），三架梁上立“脊瓜柱”（“侏儒柱”），其上承脊槫。其与今日习见所不同者，厥为其大小比例及其与柱之关系。

According to the Ts'ing regulations, the liang (beam) is invariably two ch'un (Chinese inch) wider than the diameter of the column, and the depth of the beam is set at either five-quarters or six-fifths of its width, regardless of the length of the span or the load it has to carry. The proportion of the width to the depth of the beam is, therefore, either 8:10 or 10:12, evidently ignoring the fact that the strength of the beam lies more in the depth than in the width. The Sung builders seemed to have a better understanding of the mechanics of the material they employed and specified that the ratio of width to depth should be 2:3. This is clearly showed in the *Ying-tsao-fa-shih.*

The following calculation of the two principal yen-fu of the Kuan-yin Ke will bring out an interesting fact in the comparison of the sizes of the beams of the Liao and Ts'ing styles:

清式造梁之制，其大梁不论长短及荷重如何，悉较柱宽二寸，而梁高则为宽之四分之五或五分之六。就此即有二问题须加注意者：一，梁对荷重之比例；二，梁宽与梁高之比例。关于第一问题，当于下文另述。横梁载重之力，在其高度而不在其宽度；宋人有见于此，故其高与宽为三与二之比。载于《法式》，奉为定例。清人亦知此原则，故高亦较大于宽，然其比例已近方形。岂七八百载之经验，反使其对力学之了解退而无进耶？

至于梁之大小，兹亦加以分析，并与清式比较：

<table>
<tr><th colspan="4">Sizes of the beams 梁之尺寸</th></tr>
<tr><td>Length of beam</td><td>梁长</td><td colspan="2">7.43 m.</td></tr>
<tr><td>Length of each chia</td><td>每架长</td><td colspan="2">1.86 m.</td></tr>
<tr><td>Width of central bay</td><td>当心间面阔</td><td colspan="2">4.73 m.</td></tr>
<tr><td>Raise of ridge from beam</td><td>举高</td><td colspan="2">2.51 m.</td></tr>
<tr><td>Length of slope</td><td>斜项长</td><td colspan="2">4.40 m.</td></tr>
<tr><td>Area of roof over central bay</td><td>当心间项面积</td><td colspan="2">4.40×2×4.73 = 41.7 sq.m.</td></tr>
<tr><td>Cross section of beam</td><td>梁横断面</td><td colspan="2">0.305×0.585 m.</td></tr>
<tr><th colspan="4">Dead load 静荷载</th></tr>
<tr><td colspan="3">Timber (T'o-tun, p'ing-liang, chu-ju-chu, tous, fangs, purlins, rafters, sheathing, etc. included.)</td><td rowspan="2">7.069 cu.m.</td></tr>
<tr><td colspan="3">木料（柁墩，三架梁，侏儒柱，斗座，襻间，槫，椽，望板均在内）体积</td></tr>
<tr><td>Tiles (Tubular and plate tiles)</td><td>瓦（筒瓦板瓦）体积</td><td>3.13 cu.m.</td><td rowspan="2">5.26 cu.m.</td></tr>
<tr><td>Do (Ridge tiles)</td><td>脊体积</td><td>2.13 cu.m.</td></tr>
<tr><td>Earth (ground for tiles)</td><td colspan="2">苫背体积</td><td>3.13 cu.m.</td></tr>
</table>

Weight of timber 木料重量		
per cu.m.	每立方米	720 kg.
Volumn	体积	7.069 cu.m.
Dead load	静荷载	7.069×720=5,100 kg.
Weight of tiles (brick) 砖瓦重量		
per cu.m.	每立方米	2,000 kg.
Volume	体积	5.26 cu.m.
Dead load	静荷载	5.26×2,000=10,520 kg.
Weight of earth 苫背重量		
per cu.m.	每立方米	1,600 kg.
Volume	体积	3.13 cu.m.
Dead load	静荷载	3.13×1,600=5,000 kg.
Total dead load 总静荷载		5,100+10,520+5,000=20,620 kg.

Weight of yen-fu（五架梁自身重）:

$0.585 \times 0.305 \times 7.43 \times 720 = 954$ kg.

From the above dead load（用上得之静荷载，则）:

The maximum bending moment of the yen-fu is（五架梁所受之最大挠曲弯矩为）:

$10{,}310 \times 1.86 + 954 \times \frac{7.43}{8} = 20{,}100$ kg. m.

The maximum vertical shear is（其所受最大之竖切力为）:

$10{,}310 + \frac{954}{2} = 10{,}800$ kg.

And the maxium bending stress on the yen-fu is（则五架梁中之最大挠曲应力为）:

$\frac{6 \times 20{,}100}{0.305 \times 0.585^2} = 1{,}160{,}000$ kg./sq.m.

And the maximum shearing stress is （其最大切应力为）:

$\frac{10{,}800}{0.305 \times 0.585} \times \frac{3}{2} = 91{,}000$ kg./sq.m.

Live load（活荷载）:

The live load on the roof includes both snow and wind pressure, assumed at 195 kg. per sq.m. Being a beam supported at two ends, the total live load is（屋顶之活荷载包括屋顶所受之雪压及风力等数。此项荷载，通常可假定为 195 公斤 / 平方米，然其重量之四分之一，已由梁之两端，直下内柱之上。由梁身转达柱上者，只其余四分之三。故其活荷载总量为）:

$195 \times 41.7 \times \frac{3}{4} = 6{,}100$ kg.

The maximum bending moment is (其最大挠曲弯矩为):

3,050 × 1.86=5,670 kg.m.

The maximum vertical shear is (其最大竖切力为) :

3,050 kg.

And its maximum bending stress is (其最大挠曲应力为) :

$$\frac{6 \times 5{,}670}{0.305 \times 0.585^2} = 326{,}000 \text{ kg./sq.m.}$$

And the maximum shearing stress is (其最大切应力为) :

$$\frac{3{,}050}{0.305 \times 0.585} \times \frac{3}{2} = 25{,}600 \text{ kg./sq.m.}$$

Since the strength of timber varies greatly according to its age and the climatic conditions to which it is subject, it is difficult to decide with any accuracy the strength of the wood of the Kuan-yin Ke without testing it. But as the maximum bending strength of timber varies between 3,000,000 kg. to 4,600,000 kg., and the maximum shearing strength between 120,000 kg. to 230,000 kg., it is fairly safe to assume the medium, i.e., 3,800,000 kg. for its bending strength and 180,000 kg. for shear. The factors of safety of the yen-fu are:

木料之强度，至不一律，且因年龄与气候而异。观音阁梁枋木料之最大强度果为若干，未经试验，殊难臆断，但木料之最大挠曲强度约在3,000,000—4,600,000公斤/平方米间；而其最大切强度约在120,000—230,000公斤/平方米。若以上述之平均数为此阁木料之最大强度，则其挠曲强度为3,800,000公斤/平方米，而切强度为180,000公斤/平方米，则此五架梁之安全率约如下表：

	Bending 挠曲		Shear 切	
	Stress 应力 (kg./sq.m.)	安全率 f.s.	Stress 应力 (kg./sq.m.)	安全率 f.s.
Dead load 静荷载独计	1,160,000	3.23	91,000	1.98
Dead & live load 静活荷载并计	1,486,000	2.56	116,600	1.54

The above figures show that the factor of safety was slightly smaller than the most desirable, but still within the allowable limit of good practice, and the existence of the building for a thousand years is surely a sufficient test of its stability.

The same beam, when designed in accordance to Ts'ing regulations, is 74 by 59 cm., as large as two Liao beams. The Ts'ing builders were apparently far behind the Liaos in both knowledge of strength of material and economics! Figure 54 is a comparison of the widths of beams of the Liao, Sung and Ts'ing periods, all the beams being of the same depth.

It should be noted here that the yen-fu and the columns are not joined directly to each other, but interposed by the inner ends of the ju-fu, which unlike the ming-fu of the lower story, are merely placed on top instead of being incorporated into, and becoming an integral part of, the chu-t'ou-p'u-cho.

54 Comparison of the widths of beams of Liao, Sung and Ts'ing. 辽、宋、清梁横断面比较

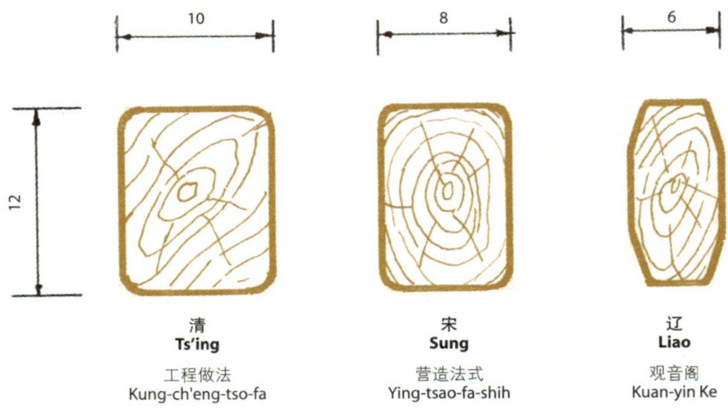

兹安全率，虽微嫌其小，然仍在普通设计许可范围之内，且各部体积，如瓦之厚度，乃按白板瓦底至筒瓦上作实厚许，未除沟陇之体积；脊本空心，亦当实心计算，故静荷载所假定，实远过实在重量。且历时千载，梁犹健直，更足以证其大小至为适当，宛如曾经精密计算而造者。今若按清式定例计算，则其高当为 0.74 米，宽为 0.59 米，辟为二梁，尚绰有余裕，清人于力学与经济学，岂竟皆不如辽宋时代耶？（图 54）。

至于梁与柱安置之关系，则五架梁并非直接置于柱或斗拱之上者。五架梁之下，尚有双步梁，在檐柱及内柱柱头铺作之上；然双架梁亦非如明栿之与铺作合构而成其一部，而只置于其上者。双架梁之内端上，复垫以檄，上置五架梁，结构似嫌松懈。然统和以来，千岁于兹，尚完整不欹，吾侪亦何所责于辽代梓人哉！

Many of the auxiliary parts of the "truss" were made of old materials. The t'o-tun of the yen-fu are of special interest as they are nothing but enormous old kungs, two at each end, one piled on top of the other. They are much larger than the kungs on the Ke, and must have been either parts of the original building which is now substituted by the present Kuan-yin Ke, or of other buildings, and cannot be of a later date than the glorious T'ang period!

Purlins, round in cross section, are placed at regular distances, four on each side of the slope and one at the ridge. At points where they are supported, t'i-mu is invariably used, apparently to reduce the shearing force. Beneath the t'i-mu, and interposed by tous, are the p'an-chien or fang, of which the one on the chu-ju-chu or under the ridge-purlin is specially large and interesting because short struts are used between the t'i-mu and p'an-chien causing the three to act somewhat like a single member.

55 Hsieh-chu in the interior of the mezzanine floor, Kuan-yin Ke. 观音阁中层内部斜柱

From either side of the principal p'an-chien is a hsieh-chu ("slanting column"), like the principal rafters of a truss with the chu-ju-chu as the king post (Figure 55). This is not found in structural systems of later periods. The hsieh-chu is also used in the surrounding aisle of the mezzanine floor as a bracing to the framework. It may or may not be a part of the original construction. Though the use of diagonal bracing is seldom found elsewhere in China, it may be too hasty to conclude that those of the Kuan-yin Ke were put in after the building had begun to show signs of incline. Besides, if the hsieh-chu is applicable to the sides of the purlins, there is no reason to deny the possibility of its being used elsewhere in the building.

The most important discovery in the study of the structural side of the

Liao architecture of the Tu-lo Ssu is the high degree of standardization of structural members. The regulation of the Ts'ing style sets the tou-kou (or mortise on the tou to receive the kung) as the standard unit measure, involving a very complicated process in both designing and execution of the work. But here in the gigantic structure of the Ke, the structural members are of only six different sizes, an amazingly high degree of standardization.

The opening paragraph of Chapter IV of the *Ying-tsao-fa-shih* may be quoted here, on the construction of framing carpentry:

"In constructions of all kinds, the ts'ai is always the first consideration. There are eight different sizes of ts'ai, and they are to be used according to the size of the building.... The depth of the ts'ai is to be divided into 15 fen, and its width will be equal to 10 fen. It is with this fen as a unit that the height and breadth of the building, the length of different parts, the curve of the roof, and everything else governed by the compass, the square and the plumb are determined."

草栿之附属部分，多用旧料，其中如垫五架梁之柁橔，皆由雄大旧拱二件垒成，较今存拱尤大；是必统和重葺以前原建筑物或他处拆下之旧拱，赫然唐木，乃尚得见于兹，惜顶中黑暗，未得摄影为憾耳。

三架梁及五架梁头，并双步梁上柁橔及三架梁上侏儒柱上皆置槫（桁），槫与梁或橔间，皆垫以替木；替木之下，复有襻间（枋），长随间广，与梁相交。侏儒柱上襻间尤大。襻间与替木间，复支以短柱；使槫、替木、襻间三者合成一"复梁"作用焉。

脊襻间之左右，有斜柱支撑于平梁之上。以下每槫之下，皆有斜柱支撑，此为清式所无，而于坚固上，固有绝大之关系也。

斜柱之制，不唯用于梁架之上，于中层暗部亦用之（图 55）。此部或为后世修葺所加；然当初若知用于梁上以支槫，则将此同一原则转用于此处，亦非不可能也。

此次独乐寺辽物研究中，因梁枋斗拱分析而获得之最大结果，则木材尺寸之标准化是也。清式用材，其尺寸以"斗口"为单位，制至繁而计算难。而观音阁全部结构，梁枋千百，其结构用材，则只六种，其标准化可谓已达极点。《营造法式》卷四，大木作制度，辟头第一句即谓：

"凡构屋之制，皆以材为祖。材有八等，度屋之大小，因而用之。……各以其材之广，分为十五分，以十分为其厚。凡屋宇之高深，名物之短长，曲直举折之势，规矩绳墨之宜，皆以所用材之分以为制度焉。"

After giving the dimensions of the eight standard sizes, it continues:

"The ch'i is 6 fen wide and 4 fen thick. When a ch'i is added to the ts'ai, it is called a chu-ts'ai."

These are undoubtedly the standard measures of the Sung style of architecture. But since the ts'ai and ch'i are not properly defined, it is difficult to know their proper mode of application, though the dimensions and proportions are given. It is only after a study of the structural members of the Tu-lo Ssu that we know to what an extent the system is applicable, and how much convenience it brings to the designing and execution of the work as well as saving of material and labor.

Since the ts'ai and ch'i are standard measures for construction, every part of the building is expressed in terms of either the ts'ai or the ch'i, or a multiple of either or both of them. It is necessary therefore to define the ts'ai. Firstly, it may be described as a unit measure, where the depth of a kung is called a ts'ai. Secondly, it is a standard member, the cross section of which is that of the kung, regardless of its length. The ni-tao-kung, man-kung, chu-t'ou-fang, etc., are, for instance, all of the same size in cross section, and are, therefore, each a ts'ai.

在八等材尺寸比例之后，复谓：

"栔广六分，厚四分。材上加栔者谓之足材。"

此乃宋式营造之标准单位，固极明显。然而"材"、"栔"之定义，并未见于书中；虽知其大小比例，而难知其应用法，及其应用之可能度。今见独乐寺，然后知其应用及其对于设计及施工所予之便利及经济。

"材"、"栔"既为营造单位，则全建筑物每部尺寸，皆为"材"、"栔"之倍数或分数；故先考何为一"材"。"材"者：（一）为一种度量单位；以拱之广（高度），谓之"一材"。（二）为一种标准木材之称，指木材之横断面言，长则无限制。例如泥道拱、慢拱、柱头枋等，其长虽异，而横断面则同，皆一材也。

The ch'i is 6 fen in width and 4 fen in thick, where 6 fen is 6/15 of a ts'ai, and its height (thickness) is that of the space or void between two kungs or fangs. It is, therefore, also a term used both for a unit measure as well as a standard member.

Measurements show that the depth of the kungs and fangs of the Kuan-yin Ke vary from 24.1 to 25 cm. The variation may be due to either inaccuracy in workmanship or the climatic effect of nearly a thousand years. However, the average depth is about 24.5 cm., which is the ts'ai of both the Hall and the Shan-men. The average ch'i is about 10 cm., approximately 2/5 of a ts'ai, which is fairly close to 6/15 of it. It is then clear that the use of the ts'ai as a unit measure is a system common to both the Liao and Sung regulations of construction, and consequently indicates a common origin, probably from the T'ang Dynasty or even earlier.

“栔广六分，厚四分”：其“广”即散斗之“平”（升腰）及“欹”（斗底）之总高度，即两层拱间之空隙；六分者，“材”之广之十五分之六也。“栔”为“材”之辅，亦为度量单位名称；用作木材时，则以补拱间之隙，非主要结构木材也。材栔二者，用为度量单位时，皆用其“广”（高度）。栔“厚四分”者，材之广之十五分之四也。“厚”从不用作度量单位，只是标准木材之固定大小而已。

观音阁山门各部拱枋之高，自 0.241 米至 0.25 米不等。工匠斧锯之不准确，及千年气候之影响，皆足为此种差异之原因，其平均尺度则为 0.244 或 0.245 米，此即阁及门“材”之尺寸也。其“栔”则平均合 0.10 米，约合“材”之五分之二强（虽略有出入，合所谓“六分”——十五分之六）。然则以材栔为度量之制，辽宋已符，其为唐代所遗旧制必可无疑。

The solution of the ts'ai and ch'i riddle precedes that of a number of hitherto perplexing problems. The ni-tao-kung, man-kung, kua-tze-kung, ling-kung and all other kungs; chu-t'ou-fang, lo-han-fang, p'ing-ch'i-fang, and most other fangs; the angs, are all ts'ai, or more specifically tan-ts'ai as distinguished from the chu-ts'ai which is the combination of a ts'ai and a ch'i. Chu-ts'ai members of the Ke are the lan-erh, p'u-p'ai-fang, hua-kung, etc. The ming-fu is one ts'ai & one ch'i; ta-ch'ian, about two ts'ai; p'ing-liang, two ts'ai; yen-fu, two ts'ai & one ch'i. There are only these six different dimensions for the thousands of structural pieces in the building. The high degree of standardization is certainly amazing, and the statement in the *Ying-tsao-fa-shih* that "in construction of all kinds, the ts'ai is always the first consideration" is certainly a principle that no student of Liao or Sung architecture can afford to overlook.

Ⓗ Chiao-liang

The chiao-liang or hip-rafter is similar to that of the Shan-men in construction. The yin-chiao-liang or "hidden corner beam" is not used in the Kuan-yin Ke, as neither the top nor the lower roof necessitates the extension of the "corner beam." The upper story hip-rafter terminates where the gable roof starts, and the one of the lower story is not carried beyond the mezzanine corner column. The end of the lao-chiao-liang is shaped into two convexed surfaces for the lower story and three similar curvatures for the upper. The curvature is a simple curve, severe and dignified, rather Greek in feeling, unlike the wriggling pa-wang-ch'uan used for ta-chiao-liang of later periods. The tze-chiao-liang is on the lao-chiao-liang, extending further out but slender in proportion, with a t'ao-shou, a dragon head tile cap on its tip. Copper bells are hung from underneath the chiao-liangs.

Ⓘ Chü-che

The pitch and curve of the roof is worked out exactly according to the same method as described in the *Ying-tsao-fa-shih*. The distance between the front and rear liao-yen-ch'uan is 17.42 m. with an altitude of

4.76 m., measuring from the top of the liao-yen-ch'uan to the top of the ridge-purlin. One-quarter of the distance is 4.36 m., the basic raise, 8% of which is nearly 0.35 m. making 4.71 m. as the total raise according to the method described in the *Fa-shih*. Here the measurement of the Kuan-yin Ke is 4.76 m., about 1% more than the specified proportion which may be due to settlement or the effect of age and weathering. It is, therefore, the best existing example of the raise in the Sung manner.

The curve, it is slightly straighter than that laid down in the *Fa-shih*. The dotted line of figure shows the regulation curve as compared with the existing specimen (in black line); the difference between the two being very slight. The general contour is, however, radically different from that of the Ts'ing buildings.

材栔之义及用既定，若干问题即迎刃而解。例如：泥道、慢、瓜子、令诸拱；柱头、罗汉、平棊等枋；昂，皆“单材”也（其广一材，其厚为广三分之二）。阑额、普拍枋、华拱皆“足材”也（其广一材一栔，其厚为一材之三分之二）。明栿广一材一栔；劄牵（双步梁）[64]广约二材弱；平梁（三架梁）广二材，檐栿（五架梁）[65]广二材一栔。共计凡六种，此外其他部分亦莫不如是，其标准化可谓已达最高点。《法式》谓“构屋之制，以材为祖”信不诬也。

❽ 角梁

下层大角梁卷杀作两瓣，而上层则作三瓣；其卷杀之曲线严厉，颇具希腊风味。下层角梁后尾安于中层角柱之上。而上层后尾与角昂、由昂，皆置上层内角柱之上。仔角梁较大角梁短小，头戴套兽。大小角梁下皆悬铜铎，每当微风，辄吟东坡“东风当断渡”句，不知蓟在山麓，无渡可断也。

❾ 举折

观音阁前后橑檐槫相距 17.42 米，举高为 4.76 米，适为五五举弱。较山门举度（五举）略甚。按《法式》之制，殿阁楼台，三分举一分，而筒瓦厅堂则四分举一分又加百分之八，五五举弱适与此算法相符，是非偶然，盖以厅堂举法而施于殿阁也。

至于其折高，则第一举为三二五举，第二举为五举弱，第三举为六举强，第四举为六五举弱，第五举为七五举，其折法不如《法式》之制，与清制亦异。

Ⓙ The Rafter and the Eave

The rafters, or ch'uan, are made of round posts, about 14 cm. in diameter, and above them are the fei-tze or flying rafters. Like the rafters of the Shan-men, they are tapered slightly at the tips, in exactly the same manner.

As we have noted before, the overhang of the eave buildings is much greater than that of the Ts'ing style. The height from the top of the t'ai-chi (base) to the top of the liao-yen-ch'uan is 6.57 m., and the horizontal distance between the center-line of the columns and the tip of the fei-tze is 3.28 m., just one-half of the height. The overhang of the upper eave is about the same as the lower one, but the height of the top story columns is much shorter. The general impression one gets of these two decks of far overhanging roofs is, therefore, that of vigor and free, quite unlike the timid elaboration of the later styles (Figure 31).

56 The construction of liang-chi, Kuan-yin Ke. 观音阁两际结构

Ⓚ Gables

The roof of the Kuan-yin Ke is in the hsieh-shan manner, a peculiar roof construction characteristic of the Chinese architecture. A gable is made to intersect with the sloping roof of the end of the building, thus geometrically it is just the reverse of the roof, in which the gable is interrupted by the slope. The shan-hua as the gable is called by the Ts'ing builders, is known in the *Sung Book* as liang-chi (Figure 56).

The liang-chi of the Kuan-yin Ke is constructed by extending the purlins about 1.45 m. beyond the "truss" between the intermediate and end bays, to allow an overhang of the roof. The cantilever of the purlin is taken care of by a t'i-mu and a kung, which is shaped out of the end of the p'an-chien underneath each purlin. The three central bays are, therefore, under the front and rear slopes while the two end bays are under the side slopes of the roof. Onto the ends of the purlins is attached the po-feng-pan which may be called a "gable plate."

The hsieh-shan roof that is common in China today is somewhat different both in appearance and construction from the liang-chi of the Sung style. The recess of the vertical triangle of the gable from the end facade in the Ts'ing style is smaller than in the Sung style. It is due to the extraordinarily long cantilever of the purlin-ends which almost reaches the entire width of the end bay. The result is that the triangular space of the gable is much enlarged and the main ridge of the roof lengthened. But, on account of the heavy overhang, the later architects found that the cantilever was not strong enough to support the weight of the roof, so that an extra set of framework was necessary to hold the gable in place. As this addition is illogical and unsightly, a board, the shan-hua-pan, is nailed on to hide the ugliness behind.

❿ 椽及檐

椽皆以径约 0.14 米之杉木造。椽头略加卷杀，飞子亦然，如山门所见。

清式檐出为高三分之一。观音阁下层自橑檐槫背至地高 6.57 米，而自檐柱中至飞头平出檐为 3.28 米，适为高之半。上檐出与下檐出大略相同，因童柱之移入及侧脚之故，故较下檐退入约 0.33 米。然吾侪平日所习见之明清建筑，上檐多造于内柱之上，故似退垒而呈坚稳之状；而观音阁巍然两层远出如翼，其态度至为豪放（图 31）。

橑檐槫及罗汉枋间，罗汉枋及柱头枋间，皆有似平闇椽之斜椽，上安遮椽板。

⓫ 两际

屋顶为歇山式，其两际之结构，与清式颇异。清式收山少，山花几与檐柱上下成一垂直线。收山少则悬出多，其重量非自梁上伸出之桁（槫）所能胜，故须在山花之内，用种种方法——如蹋脚木、草架柱子等——以支撑之；而此种方法，因不甚合理，故不美观，于是用山花板以掩藏之。

The later style is decidedly degeneration as compared with the frank exposure of all structural members in the Sung method. The Kuan-yin Ke is found with shan-hua-pan at both gables. But behind them may still be seen the kung-shaped ends of the p'an-chian with tous and t'i-mu. The end of the large p'an-chien under the ridge-purlin is shaped into a simple cyma, reaching to half the length of the overhang. The two hsieh-chus that hold the ridge in position were originally also exposed, with the spaces inside them filled in with partitions to shut out the heat and cold; but now the little triangular walls have been taken away and their work is undertaken by the shan-hua-pan, which, from both structural and aesthetic points of view, is far inferior to the original construction.

Right underneath the apex of the shan-hua, there must once have been a hsüan-yü, the "hanging fish," with jeh-ts'ao on both sides. Those shown in the side elevation are drawn according to the *Ying-tsao-fa-shih.*

Ⓛ Roof-tiles

The grey tiles of the Kuan-yin Ke, like those of the Shan-men, are not the originals of the Liao period. The cheng-wen (ridge-end ornament), cheng-chi (main ridge), ch'ui-chi (hip), ch'ui-shou (hip beast), tsun-shou (sitting beasts), pin-chia (angel or lady-in-waiting) are probably all of the Ming Dynasty.

宋以前则不然，两际之构造，颇似清式之“悬山”；无山花板，各层梁枋槫头等构材，自下皆见。观音阁两际今则掩以山花，一望而知其非原物；及登顶细察，则原形尚在（图 56），惜为劣匠遮掩，自外不得见。

侏儒柱上大襻间，头卷杀作简洁之曲线，长及出际之半。平槫下襻间与平梁（三架梁）交，伸出长如大襻间，卷杀如拱，上置散斗，以承替木。斜柱与侏儒柱之间，其先必填以壁，以防风寒吹入，今则拆去，而于槫头博风板下，掩以山花。既不合理，又复丑恶，何清代匠人之不假思索耶?

博风板之下，原先必有悬鱼惹草等装饰，今亦无存。谨按《营造法式》所见。

⑫ 瓦

与山门瓦同，青瓦，亦非原物，其正吻、正脊、垂脊、垂兽、仙人等，殆为明代重修时所配者。

57 Ornaments of roof-tiles, Kuan-yin Ke. 观音阁瓦饰

The cheng-wen is similar to that of the Ts'ing style, but with a much larger "tail," and its end does not turn inward in the form of a spiral. The relief of the facial features is more prominent. The top of the "back" is a slope instead of the level shelves of the Ts'ing style. The chien-pa or sword handle is very realistic in modeling, sticking on the "back" at an angle (Figure 57).

The cheng-chi or main ridge has a small pavilion in the middle, which shelters a tablet. Inhabitants of the town told me that prior to the restoration in the Kwang-hsü period, there were inscriptions on the tablet with the date and name of the architect as follows: "Erected under the supervision of Yü-ch'ih ching-teh in the 10th Year of Cheng-kwan."

But a careful scrutiny with a telescope failed to bring out these characters. It was very probable that there were inscriptions on the tablet, but the date of Cheng-kwan and the name Yü-ch'ih Ching-teh are probably not genuine. The name especially is unreliable as it is one that has for ages been legendary to carpenters and builders. A local legend tells that the sacred lamp of the She-li Pagoda in Pan-shan descends the hill and visits the city at midnight on New Year's Eve. It lands on the little tablet first and then goes to other temples in the city. The lamp is known as one of the eight sights of Chi-chou, and is called "Tu-lo-ch'en-teng" (the Sacred Lamp of Tu-lo). The long narrow panels of the ridge are decorated with dragons playing the flaming pearl.

The ch'ui-chi or hip is decorated with floral designs. The ch'ui-shou is entirely different from the Ts'ing ch'ui-shou; it is a sort of unicorn with mouth wide open, and a little human figure riding on its back, holding onto its horns. The sitting beasts, though slightly different from those of later dates, are nothing very unusual. The pin-chia is a husky warrior in helmet and armor, sitting on the end of the hip looking down proudly onto the worshipers below the sacred roof. All these tiles might be several centuries old.

The tubular and plate tiles are similar to those of the Shan-men.

Ⓜ Walls

Except for the three central bays on the southern facade and the one central bay on the north, the spaces between the exterior peristylar columns of the lower floor are filled in with massive masonry walls, about one meter thick. The top of the wall just reaches the bottom of the lan-erh, and is about four times its own thickness. There is a slight decrease in thickness towards the top, and a sharp inward turn near the lan-erh. The ch'ün-chien or base of the wall is only about one-seventh of the height, much lower than the regulation proportion of one-third as specified in the Ts'ing style, and therefore still further from the Ming proportion which is even higher. The base of the wall of the Wooden Pagoda of Fo-kung Ssu is also of a similar proportion. It might have been a Liao characteristic.

正吻颇似清式，然尾翘起甚高，亦不似清式之如螺旋之卷入。须眉口鼻皆较玲珑。吻背之上皮，斜上尾部，不若清式之平。其剑把则似真剑把，斜插于吻背之背。背兽颇瘦小（图57）。

正脊为双龙戏珠纹样。其正中作小亭。相传每届除夕夜午以后，盘山舍利塔神灯，下降蓟城，先独乐而后诸刹。神灯降临则亭中光芒射出，照耀全城，称“独乐晨灯”，为蓟州八景之一云。小亭之神话，尚不止此。蓟人告予，光绪重修以前，亭内有碑，碑刻“贞观十年尉迟敬德监修”云云。吾以望远镜仔细察良久，未见只字。碑上原有文字当无可疑，贞观敬德，颇近无稽；尉迟敬德监修寺庙，亦成匠人神话，未可必信也。

垂脊亦有花纹，但无龙。垂兽为清式所不见。似仙童骑于独角犀牛上，双手攀犀角，颇饶谐趣。走兽虽略异，亦无奇。仙人乃甲胄武士，傲然俯视檐下众生。亦历数百寒暑矣。

筒瓦、板瓦与山门同，详见图五十七，不复赘。

⑬ 墙壁

下层除南面居中三间及北面居中一间外，皆于柱间砌砖墙。墙高至阑额下。厚约一米，计合墙高四分之一。墙收分之度，约为2%。墙顶近阑额处，斜收入为墙肩。下肩甚低，约合墙高七分之一。清式定例，下肩高为墙高三分之一。明物则下肩尤高。而观音阁及山门与应县佛宫寺塔，下肩皆特低，绝非偶然，窃疑其为辽制。

In one of the Emperor Ch'ien-lung's poems on the Tu-lo Ssu there is a line on "the faded paintings of Buddha's twelve origins," and a note attached giving the explanation that "Buddha has twelve origins, a favorite topic for mural paintings in Buddhist Temples." It is certain that the walls were originally decorated with paintings which were already faded in Ch'ien-lung's time.

The interior partitions of the mezzanine floor and the exterior walls of the upper floor are all constructed of plaster on lath. The lath is of small branches tied together, and the plaster is local clay mixed with a small proportion of lime and straw. A diagonal post is built in each of these partitions to act as bracing.

Ⓝ Doors

None of the original doors are preserved. During the Ts'ing restorations, doors with geometrical floral grills were used. Traces of these are still to be seen in a few of the transoms. The movable parts have all been destroyed.

Ⓞ Floor

On the p'u-pan-fang (joists) that rests on the chu-t'ou-p'u-cho of the mezzanine story is placed the floor of the upper story, which is finished with a coat of plaster about 3 cm. thick. The joists are placed more than 2 m. apart, and in some places the floor sags so much under the weight of men walking on it that it actually threatens to give way.

Ⓟ Balustrades

On both the mezzanine and upper floors, around the wall that surrounds the figure, are wooden balustrades. Round posts are placed at points where the railing turns a corner, and short posts called shu-chu are placed at intervals in between. The head of the shu-chu is shaped into a tou, upon which is placed the hsün-chang or rail. Other horizontal members are the p'en-ch'un at the middle and the ti-fu or foot rail below. Between these two is the hua-pan, which is usually treated with different combinations of the swastika, similar to those seen in the mural paintings of Tun-huang. The pattern of the mezzanine floor balustrades is identical to the painting. The six sides of the upper story balustrade are divided into twelve panels with six kinds of designs (Figure 58). The balustrades around the exterior balcony on the upper floor are modern replacements with modified designs.

乾隆御制诗《过独乐寺戏题》有“梵宇久凋零，落色源流画”句，其夹注则曰“佛有十二源流，僧家多画于壁间”，是独乐寺本有画壁，其画题则十二源流，当时已“落色”，必明以前画也。

上层外墙及中层内墙系在柱间先用绳索系枝为篱，然后将草泥敷于篱上，似今通用之板条抹灰墙；然所用绳索枯枝，皆甚粗陋。壁内藏有斜柱，以巩固屋架之结构。

⓮ 门窗

原物无丝毫痕迹。清代修葺，门窗改用菱花槅子。下层横披尚见。其活动部分，已全被年前驻军拆毁。

⓯ 地板

在中层各铺作上铺板枋上，敷设地板，板上敷灰泥约一寸。枋间距离，至短者亦在二米余以上，而板则厚仅一寸。人行板上，板上下弯曲弹动，殊欠安稳。清式于“承重”梁上加“楞本”，无弹动之虞。每年旧历三月中，蓟人举行酬神盛会，登楼者辄同时百数十人，如地板不加坚实，恐惨剧难免发生。

⓰ 栏杆

中层内平坐上，绕像一周；上层内地板上，六角形空井一周，及上层外檐平坐一周，皆绕以栏杆。栏杆于转角处立望柱，其间则立短小之蜀柱。柱下为地栿，中部为盆唇，上为寻杖，蜀柱之间盆唇之下为束腰。其各部名称见于《营造法式》，而形制则较似敦煌壁画所见。中层栏杆束腰花纹，与敦煌者尤相似。上层内栏杆六面十二格，花纹六种（图 58），虽各不同，而精神则一贯。上层外檐栏杆，云拱瘿项改作花瓶形，已失原意矣。

58 Modified designs of balustrades, interior of upper story, Kuan-yin Ke.
观音阁上层内勾栏束腰纹样

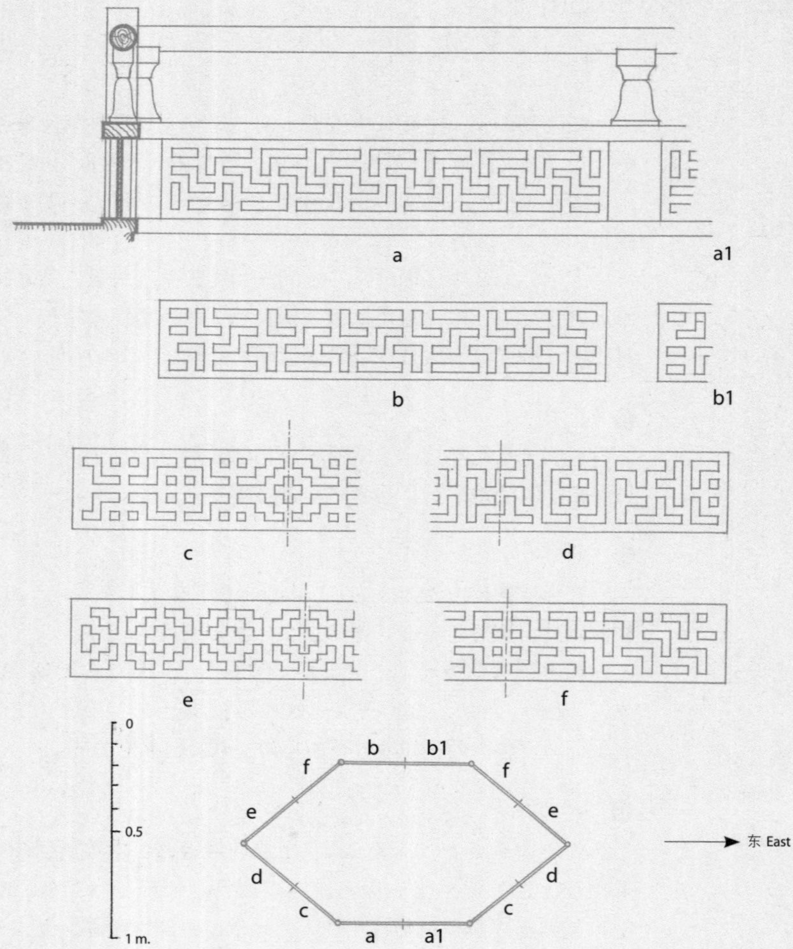

Ⓠ Stairway

The stairway, which is the only access to the upper floors, is located in the western end bay. The mezzanine is reached by one long flight, running upwards from south to north. It then turns back southward leading to the upper floor. The incline of the stair is rather steep, making an angle of almost 45 degrees with the ground. The lower end of the lower flight rests on a low platform. The carriages, which are at the same time strings, are rather large in size. They are terminated at the lower end by a wang-chu or newel, in the form of a simple cylindrical post, and at the upper end by a shu-chu. There are a few more shu-chu, in between the two ends, and on them rests the hsün-chang (hand rail). The carriage acts at the same time as the ti-fu, while the hua-pan is substituted by a long post, square in cross section, and placed cornerwise (Figure 59).

The present stairway consists of one flight of twenty-eight steps and one flight of twenty. An examination of the inner face of the carriage from underneath shows that the present steps are only half as large as the original, mortises of which are still traceable, measuring 38 cm. for the rise and 43 cm. for the thread (Figure 60).

59 Head of stairway on the upper floor of Kuan-yin Ke. 观音阁上层梯口

⑰ 楼梯

位于西梢间居中两间内，自地北向上至中层，复折而南至上层。梯斜度颇峻，约作四十五度角。梯脚下有小方坛，梯立坛上。梯之两框，颇为长大，辅以栏杆，略如上述。其上下两端，立以望柱；望柱之间，立蜀柱数支，其间贯以盆唇寻杖，其不同者，为束腰部分，不用板而代以一方杖。梯之上端，穿地为孔，孔之三面复以小蜀柱及盆唇束腰栏护焉（图59）。

今梯下段分二十八级，上段分二十级。仰察梯底，乃知今每级只原阶之半，原级之大，实倍于今，下段十四而上段十级，每级高0.38米，宽0.43米，卯痕犹在，易复原状也（图60）。

60 Architectural drawings of stairway, Kuan-yin Ke.

观音阁楼梯详样

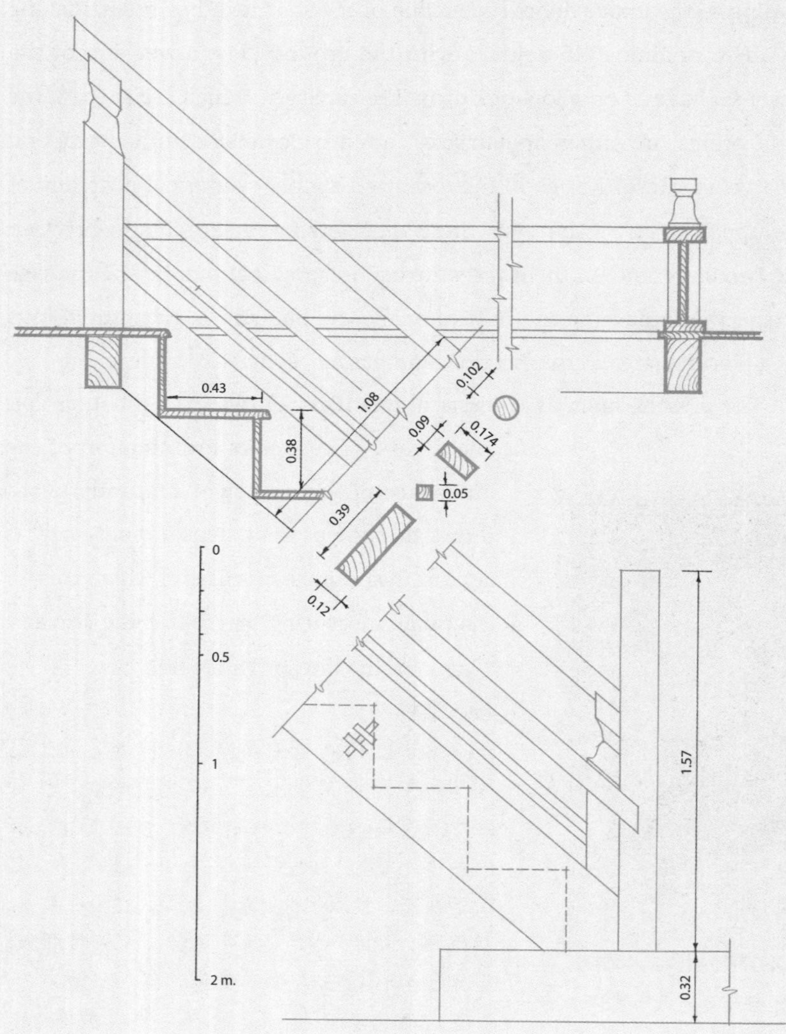

Ⓡ Painted Ornaments

It is customary in China to repaint all the painted ornaments. Therefore an old painted ornament is even rarer than an old building. The paintings of the Tu-lo Ssu buildings are no exceptions, having being repaired during the Kwang-hsü restoration. The basic function of the paint is to protect the wood, and to prolongate its life, the decorative element being merely a by-product. A well applied ornament helps to give expression and proper emphasis to the structural members and thus should change according to the difference in structural systems.

The painted ornaments of the Kuan-yin Ke, like those of the Shan-men, are a forced application of the Ts'ing system onto a Liao building. The exterior paintings are especially bad. Emphasis and accentuation are almost always applied in the wrong place, such as the use of the tangent-circle motif known as the Hsiao-tze with the "panels" put so that they are half-covered by the tous. This is an arrangement so awkward that it should not be employed under any circumstance. The painters have here shown great embarrassment in dealing with this fang which is always hidden above the rows of p'u-cho in later styles, but here is entirely exposed in the Ke in the frankest manner. The paintings are not only unsuitable, but positively comical.

⑱ 彩画

我国建筑，每逢修葺，辄“油饰一新”，故古建筑之幸存者，亦只骨架，其彩画制度，鲜有百岁以上者。独乐寺彩画，亦非例外，盖光绪重修时所作也。彩画之基本功用在保护木料而延其寿命，其装饰之方面，乃其附带之结果。善施彩画，不唯保护木材，且能籍画以表现建筑物之构造精神。而每时代因其结构法之不同，故其彩画制度亦异。

观音阁及山门，皆以辽式构架，施以清式彩画。内部油饰，犹简单稍具古风，尚属可用。外檐彩画，则恶劣不堪，“大点金”也，各种“苏画”或“龙锦枋心”也，橑檐槫、阑额及斗拱上，尚因古今相似，勉强可观。而各层柱头枋及罗汉枋，在清式所占地位极不重要，在平时几不见，故无彩画，但在辽式，则皆各露，拙匠遂不知所措，亦画以“旋子（学子）”、“枋心”等等纹样。有如白发老叟、衣童子衣，又复以裤为衣、以冠为履，错置乱陈，喧哗嘈杂，滑稽莫甚焉（见外檐各图）！

Ⓢ Statues and Their Platform

The colossal statue of the Eleven-headed Kuan-yin is the main subject of the Hall—or the Temple. The statue is about 16 meters in height and is the largest free-standing figure known in China. Legends told that the statue was carved out of a single piece of sandalwood, but in reality it is modeled in clay over a gigantic armature. The figure is characterized by arched brows over long, narrow eyes, wedge shaped nose and a subtle smile. The body inclines slightly forward with a protruding belly. The drapery is fluent, with two long sashes hanging from the arms and straight down to the foot, touching the sides of the lotus-flower-pedestal. All these characteristics show the strong influence of T'ang sculpture, and there is little doubt of the statue having been remodeled in 984. The reparation and restoration of successive ages have undoubtedly caused some change to the figure, but the general characteristics are still those of the late T'ang style. The statue is sadly abused by vulgar painted ornaments of later periods (Figure 62).

To the left and right of the principal figure on the platform are two attending Bodhisattvas. Their posture and drapery are especially "T'angish" in spirit (Figure 61).

61 Figure of the attending Bodhisattva in the east.
东面侍立菩萨像

⑲ 塑像及须弥坛

十一面观音像，实为本阁——或本寺——之主人翁。像高约十六米，立须弥坛上，二菩萨侍立。相传像为檀香整木刻成，实则中空而泥塑者也。像弯眉楔鼻，长目圆颔，微带慈笑；腹部微突，身向前倾；衣褶圜和，两臂上飘带下垂，下端贴莲座上，皆为唐代特征。然历代重修，原形稍改，而近代彩画，尤为可厌（图 62）。

坛上左右侍立菩萨，姿势手法，尤为精妙，疑亦唐代物也（图 61）。坛上尚有像数尊，率皆明清以后供养，兹不赘。

62 Eleven-headed Kuan-yin. 十一面观世音像

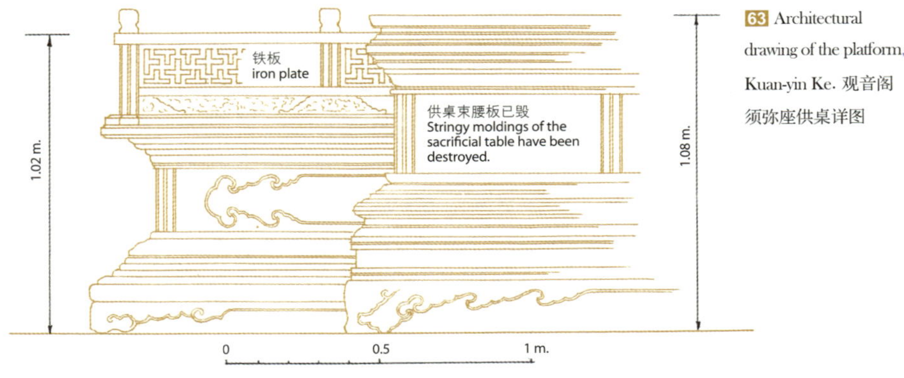

63 Architectural drawing of the platform, Kuan-yin Ke. 观音阁须弥座供桌详图

There are a few other figures on the platform, probably of the Ming and Ts'ing periods, deserving no special attention. The platform, on which all the statues are placed, is of solid masonry and finished with wooden moldings and panels all the way around. A low balustrade of swastika pattern runs all the way round. The sacrificial table in front of the platform is treated with an enormous number of stringy moldings (Figure 63). These woodworks are probably of the Kwang-hsü period.

像所立之须弥坛及坛前供桌，制作亦颇精巧。坛下龟脚、束腰，及上部之栏杆，皆极有趣。供桌叠涩太复杂，与坛似欠调谐（图63）。

⑳ 匾

阁尚有匾额三，下层外额曰“具足圆成”，内曰“普门香界”，乾隆御书。上层外额曰“观音之阁”，匾心宽1.63米，高2.08米，每字径几1米，相传李太白书，笔法古劲而略拙，颇似唐人笔法。阁字之下署“太白”二字，其为后代所加无疑。朱桂辛先生则疑为李东阳书，而后人误为太白也（图64）。

Ⓣ Pien

The principal tablet or pien under the front upper eave, with the characters "Kuan-yin-chih-ke" is also considered a treasure of the city. The calligraphy on it is attributed to Li Po, famous poet of the T'ang Dynasty. Judging from the penmanship, it is of the T'ang school, very vigorous but slightly clumsy. The signature "T'ai-po" appears under the character "ke," but there is very little doubt of its being a forgery. It is more likely that Li Tung-yang of the Ming Dynasty was the calligrapher and was later mistaken for Li Po (Figure 64).

64 Pien of Kuan-yin Ke. 观音阁匾

陆 今后之保护

观音阁及山门，既为我国现存建筑物中已发现之最古者，且保存较佳，实为无上国宝。如在他国，则政府及社会之珍维保护，唯恐不善。而在中国则无人知其价值，虽蓟人对之有一种宗教的及感情的爱护，然实际上，蓟人既无力，亦无专门智识，数十年来，不唯任风雨之侵蚀，且不能阻止军队之毁坏。今门窗已无，顶盖已漏，若不及早修葺，则数十年乃至数年后，阁、门皆将倾圮，此千年国宝，行将与建章、阿房同其运命，而成史上陈迹。故对于阁、门之积极保护，实目前所亟不容缓也。

保护之法，首须引起社会注意，使知建筑在文化上之价值；使知阁、门在中国文化史上及中国建筑史上之价值，是为保护之治本办法。而此种之认识及觉悟，固非朝夕所能奏效，其根本乃在人民教育程度之提高，此是另一问题，非营造师一个所能为力。故目前最重要问题，乃在保持阁、门现状，不使再加毁坏，实一技术问题也。

木架建筑法劲敌有二，水火是也。水使木朽，其破坏率缓；火则无情，一炬即成焦土。今阁及山门顶瓦已多处破裂，浸漏殊甚，椽檩已有多处呈开始腐朽状态。不数年间，则椽檩将折，大厦将颓。故目前第一急务，即在屋瓦之翻盖。他部可以缓修，而瓦则刻不容缓，此保持现状最要之第一步也。

瓦漏问题既解决，始及其他问题；而此部问题，可分为二大类，即修及复原是也。破坏部分，须修补之，如瓦之翻盖及门窗之补制。有失原状者，须恢复之，如内檐斗拱间填塞之土取出，上檐清式外栏杆之恢复辽式，两际山花板之拆去等皆是。二者之中，复原问题较为复杂，必须主其事者对于原物形制有绝对根据，方可施行；否则仍非原形，不如保存现有部分，以志建筑所受每时代影响之为愈。古建筑复原问题，已成建筑考古学中一大争点，在意大利教育部中，至今尚为悬案；而愚见则以保存现状为保存古建筑之最良方法，复原部分，非有绝对把握，不宜轻易施行。

防火问题，亦极重要。水朽犹可补救，火焰不可响尔。日本奈良法隆寺由政府以三十万巨金，特构水道，偶尔失慎，则顷刻之间，全寺可罩于雨幕之内；其设备之周，管理之善，非我国今日所敢希冀。然犹可备太平桶水枪等，以备万一之需。同时脊上装置避雷针，以免落雷。在消防方面，则寺内吸烟及佛前香火，尤须永远禁绝。阁立寺中，周无毗连之建筑物，如是则庶几可免火灾矣。

在社会方面，则政府法律之保护，为绝不可少者。军队之大规模破坏，游人题壁窃砖，皆须同样禁止。而古建筑保护法，尤须从速制定、颁布、施行；每年由国库支出若干，以为古建筑修葺及保护之用，而所用主其事者，尤须有专门智识，在美术、历史、工程各方面皆精通博学，方可胜任。日本古建筑保护法颁布施行已三十余年，支出已五百万。回视我国之尚在大举破坏，能不赧然？唯望社会及学术团体对此速加注意，共同督促政府，从速对于建筑遗物，予以保护，以免数千年文化之结晶，沦亡于大地之外。

1929 年世界工程学会中，关野贞博士提出“日本古建筑物之保护”一文，实研究中国建筑保护问题之绝好参考资料。蒙北大教授吴鲁强先生盛暑中挥汗译就，赐载本期汇刊。籍资借鉴，实所至感。

In Search of Ancient Architecture in North China

华北古建调查报告[1]

[1940]

Extract 节选

With Illustrations from Photographs by the Author

插图照片由作者拍摄[2]

For the last nine years, the Institute for Research in Chinese Architecture, of which I am a member, has been dispatching twice every year, on trips of two or three months' duration, small teams of field-workers, headed by a research fellow, to comb the country for ancient monuments. The ultimate aim is the compilation of a history of Chinese architecture, a subject that has been virtually untouched by scholars in the past. We could find little or no material in books. We have had to hunt for actual specimens.

We have, up till today, covered more than two hundred hsiens or counties in fifteen provinces and have studied more than two thousand monuments. As head of the section of technical studies, I was able to visit most of these places personally. We are very far from our goal yet, but we have found materials of great significance which may be of interest to the general reader.

过去九年间，我参加的中国营造学社经常派出野外考察小分队，由一名资深研究人员带领，在乡间探觅古代遗迹。这种考察每年两次，每次为时两到三个月。我们的最终目标是编撰一部中国建筑的历史，过去的学者们实未涉足这一课题。典籍中的材料寥寥无几，我们必须去搜寻实际遗例。

迄今为止，我们到过十五个省、二百多个县，研究过两千余处遗迹。作为技术研究部门的主管，我得以亲临这些遗迹中的大多数。我们的目标尚遥不可期。但是我们发现了一些极重要的材料，或许普通读者也会对之感兴趣。

I. CHINESE ARCHITECTURE, ESSENTIALLY OF WOOD, IS AT THE DESTRUCTIVE MERCY OF NATURE AND MAN

Unlike European architecture, which uses stone as its principal material, Chinese architecture is essentially of wood, a much more easily perishable material. Even structures in masonry are mere imitations of wooden forms in brick or stone. A student must, therefore, first of all, familiarize himself with the wooden structural system. It is like learning the Vignola, a necessary step before one could proceed with the study of European architecture. In field work too, the student must pay the greatest attention to wooden structures. He is actually racing with time, for these structures are all the while undergoing a steady and uncompromising process of disintegration. Waves of new influences, stirring up the whims of a few men in a conservative town, can innocently deface a masterpiece by their efforts at so-called "modernization" of an "old-fashioned" structure. Delicate window traceries, finely carved door-panels, are always among the first to suffer such heartless outrages. Seldom does one find to one's satisfaction a real gem left in peace and beauty by nature and man alike. A stray spark from an incense stick may also reduce a whole temple to ashes.

壹 任凭自然与人类肆意毁坏的中国木建筑

欧洲建筑主要取材于石料，与此不同，中国建筑是木构的，这种材料极易受损。纵有砖石建筑，亦以砖或石材模仿木建筑的结构形式。因而，学生的首要任务便是熟悉木构体系，就像研习欧洲建筑之前必先研习维诺拉[3]一样。同样，在野外考察时，学生必将主要精力集中于木结构上。他实际上是在与时间赛跑，因为这些建筑无时无刻不在遭受着难以挽回的损害。在较保守的城镇里，新潮激发了少数人的奇思异想，努力对某个“老式的”建筑进行所谓的“现代化”，原先的杰作随之毁于愚妄。最先蒙受如此无情蹂躏的，总是精致的窗牖、雕工俊极的门屏等物件。我们罕有机会心满意足地找到一件真正的珍品，宁静美丽，未经自然和人类的损伤。一炷香上飞溅的火星，也可能会把整座寺宇化为灰烬。

Besides, there was the threat of a Japanese war, such an uncalled-for instance of human cruelty and destructive ability. The love and preservation of antiquity are no business of the Japanese warlords, though their nationals normally should share with us the special love and respect for our old culture from which they derived their own. Even as early as 1931 and 1932, most of my trips were abruptly disrupted by the renewed booms of Japanese guns, each time drawing nearer than the last, meaning business. It was quite evident that the days we could work in North China were limited. Before we were prevented from doing so, we decided to put our entire effort in that part of the country. The once cheerless prescience has been now, for almost three-and-half years, a painful fact. With the Institute physically removed to the far corner of China's southwest, recollections of field work over now enemy-trodden northern lands are the more vivid and dear with our ever increasing nostalgia and concern.

此外还有日本侵略战争的威胁，它是如此突如其来，例证了人类的残忍和毁灭性。日本军阀全然不知珍爱与保存古迹，尽管照理说他们的国民也应该和我们一样，对我们古老的文化特别地热爱与敬重，因为这也是他们自己的文化的源泉。早在 1931、1932 年，日军的炮声一天近似一天，我的旅行就多次被迫蓦然中止。显然，我们还能在华北工作的时日有限了。我们决定，抓紧最后的机会，竭尽全力考察这个地区。近三年半来，当时这令人难过的预感已成惨痛的事实。目前，营造学社的机构迁至中国西南边陲，北方的土地遭受着敌军铁蹄的践踏，我们的怀念和关注与日俱增，曾经在那里进行过的野外考察的记忆愈发鲜活而亲切。

II. OUR TRIPS

Every season's trip was preceded by careful preparations in library research. Books on history, geography and Buddhism yielded a list of places where we hoped to find something. An itinerary was made up from the list for the team to follow in its field trips. Every item on the list must be located, identified, and, if still existing, measured and photographed.

The finds of our trips were numerous and of varied degrees of interest and significance. Often we got from literary sources wonderful visions of certain old monuments, only to find, after hundreds of miles of anticipatory pilgrimage, a heap of ruins, with perhaps a few roof-tiles and stone column-bases for reward.

Our trips themselves were also adventures full of unexpected ups and downs. With physical discomfort taken for granted, we enjoyed frequently unforgettable experiences of rare charm and delight. Generally, the journeys, like odd kinds of picnics prolonged, were either extremely disconcerting or highly entertaining when we encountered comical but disastrous mishaps.

贰 我们的旅行

每季出行之前，我们都要在图书馆里认真进行前期研究。根据史书、地方志和佛教典籍，我们选列地点目录，盼望在那里有所发现。考察分队在野外旅行中就依此目录寻访。必须找到与验明目录上的每一条，并对尚存者进行测绘和拍照。

旅行中的寻获和发现极多，其趣味与意义各有千秋。时常，我们从文学典籍中读到某个古代遗迹的精妙景致，但满怀期望地千里朝拜后只找到一堆荒墟，或许尚余零星瓦片和雕石柱础聊充慰藉。

我们的旅途本身同样是心情沉浮不可期的探险。身体的苦楚被视作当然，我们常在无比迷人而快乐的难忘经历中锐感快意。旅途常像古怪的、拖长了的野餐，遇到滑稽而惨痛的麻烦时，或惶急无比，或乐不可支。

Unlike the highly expensive expeditions of archaeologists, big game hunters, or any tropical or arctic scientific explorers, the equipment for our trips were scanty. Besides instruments for surveying and photographing, our luggage consisted mostly of gadgets of the home-made order, designed and modified by our members as they accumulated experience. Knapsacks like an electrician's, to be carried while working perched precariously on top of any part of a building, were among our favorite treasures which include anything from a spool of string to a telescopic pole that could be extended like a long, rigid fishing-rod. We following the philosophy of the famous white knight in Alice's wonderland, believed that one never knows what will prove to be useful in case of emergency, so were willing to fall off horses' backs for our burdens.

Often we had to make camp, cook, eat and sleep under such very different circumstances each day and night and our means of transportation were so uncertain, ranging from the most ancient and quaint to the more usual and up-to-date, that what we considered essentials could not help being peculiar, resilient tin-cans of one sort or another.

Aside from architecture, we often came across subjects of artistic and ethnological interest—handicrafts of different localities, archaic dramatics of out-of-the-way towns, queer customs, picturesque fairs, etc, but economy of film often prevented me from photographing liberally pictures of them. In most of my trips, I was accompanied by my wife, herself an architect. But being also a writer and lover of dramatic art, she, more often than I, let her attention stray and enthusiastically insisted on some subjects for the camera at any cost. I was always glad after we returned from a trip to have the valuable pictures of scenes and buildings which would otherwise have been neglected. But many interesting subjects and happenings in our trips I shall not be able to relate in detail. For economy of space I can give here only rambling and rather random accounts of some of the high-lights of our searches and researches.

III. THE IMPERIAL PALACES OF PEIPING

My first "field work," very naturally, started with the Imperial Palaces in Peiping, in a courtyard of which the Institute's office was appropriately located. However, the work of surveying the entire Palace group as a complete project was not taken up till some years later. As the Palaces are already well known to Westerners, and our "discoveries" are mostly of a technical nature, I shall not here indulge in the discussion on them.

不比耗费巨资的考古探险队、追踪狮虎的猎人抑或任何热带与极地的科学探险队，我们的旅途装备极少。除了测绘和摄影的仪器以外，我们的行囊里，最常见的装备多由队员们根据经验在家自行设计改装而成。像电工包似的旅行背包，就是我们最心爱的宝贝。登上一座建筑物任何部位的高处工作时都可以背着它，里面什么都可以装，从一团绳子到可以变成一根刚硬的长钓竿状的伸缩竿。我们遵奉《爱丽丝漫游仙境》里著名的白骑士的哲学，深信在急难中万物皆有用，于是不惜离开马背，以便多运些装备。

日复一日，我们扎营、举炊和食宿的条件悬殊，交通方式亦全无定式，从最古旧离奇到比较现代普通的，无所不有，因此我们认为的必需品莫过于形形色色奇特的、颠簸的老式汽车。

除建筑而外，我们常会不期而遇有趣的艺术品或民族用品——各地的手工艺品、偏僻小镇的古戏、奇异的风俗、五光十色的集市，诸如此类——但是，由于胶卷匮乏，我难得随心所欲地拍摄这些东西。我的多数行程都有我的妻子相伴，她也是一名建筑师。此外她更是作家，深爱戏剧艺术。因此，她比我更会转移注意力，热切地、坚持不惜代价地拍摄某些主题。归程之后，我总是庆幸获得了这些珍贵照片，其中的景色与建筑原本可能被忽略。但是，途中遇到的许多趣物趣事无法逐一细述。限于篇幅，在此我只能从我们的探索与研究当中，信手拈来若干最精彩的部分作一说明。

叁 北平的皇宫

很自然，我最早从北平的皇宫开始进行“野外考察”，营造学社的办公室就妥贴地安置在其中一角的院落里。然而，测绘整个宫殿群的完整计划直至若干年后方得施行。由于西方世界已经熟知了故宫，而且我们的“发现”主要是技术性的，在此不作详论。

IV. THE HALL OF KUAN-YIN, CHI HSIEN, A STRUCTURE OF UNFAMILIAR PROPORTIONS

In the spring of 1932, in the walled-city of Chi Hsien, about fifty miles east of Peiping, I set my eyes for the first time on a wooden structure with proportions entirely different from the familiar Manchu Palace buildings which were mostly built according to a set of "Rules" published by an imperial mandate in 1733.

That memorable trip was my first experience of traveling away from main trunklines of communications and departure from a metropolis like Peiping or Shanghai. The old model-T that would have been, were it in America, sold long since as scrap-iron, was still made to run regularly—or rather, irregularly—between Peiping and the little town. When we were a few miles out of the East Gate of Peiping, we came to the Chien-kan River. Its main flow was reduced to less than thirty feet wide in the dry season. But the river-bed of very fine sand measures about a mile-and-half from bank to bank. After crossing the stream by ferry-boat, the bus could not move even an inch in the soft ground. We—the passengers—had to help push the old buggy the entire width of the river-bed, while the engine roared and the rear wheels turned frantically, only to blow the sand right into our eyes and noses. There were other difficult stretches where we had to get off and on the bus many times. It took more than three hours to cover the fifty-mile ride. But it was excitement and fun. I did not know then that for the next few years to come, I was to get used to rides like that and think nothing unusual about them.

The Hall and the Statue

The Kuan-yin Ke, or the Hall of Avalokitesvara, of Tu-lo Ssu, the Temple of Solitary Joy, was the objective of my trip. It stands high above the city-wall and could be seen from a great distance. From afar, one gets an impression of a building of great vigor and suavity. That was the first time I opened my eyes to a building of real archaeological interest.

The Hall was built in 984 AD. That was the beginning of the Sung Dynasty, but the land was then held by the Liao Tartars. The Hall is a two-storied building with a mezzanine floor. The "brackets," a characteristic system of construction of Chinese architecture, composed of a series of super-imposed cantilevers to enable a far overhang of the eave, are large and simple (Figure 1). They are supported by slightly entasised columns and crowned by deep, overhanging eaves. The balcony around the upper floor is likewise supported by such "brackets." Thus they form three decorative bands which are basically structural. These present a marked contrast to the straight columns and small, crowded "brackets" of later periods. To those who are familiar with the T'ang Dynasty paintings of the Tun-huang Caves, it shows a striking resemblance to the architecture therein depicted.

肆 蓟县观音阁

由城墙拱卫着的蓟县去北平东约五十英里[4]。1932 年春，我首次目睹此地的一座木构，其比例迥异于清代宫殿，后者建造时所依据的主要是 1733 年敕令发布的一整套“法式”。

那次难忘的旅程是我第一次体验远离主要交通干线，远离北平和上海这类大都市。如果是在美国，老式的福特 T 型车早就只能卖作废铁了，而在北平和小城之间，它还被用作定期的——毋宁说是不定期的——交通工具。出北平东门数英里以外，我们来到了箭杆河。河水的宽度在旱季萎缩至不足三十英尺。但是，细沙的河床大约宽达一英里半。乘船渡过河流以后，汽车陷入松软的地面寸步难行。我们这些旅客只得帮着把这辆老破车推过整个河床，同时引擎轰鸣，后轮疯转，把细河沙掀得我们满眼满鼻。此后尚有其他崎岖路段，我们不得不反复地从汽车里跳上跳下。五十英里的路程耗时三个小时不止。但那真是刺激有趣。那时我尚懵然不知，今后数年我会习于这样的奔波且安之若素。

观音阁与塑像

我此行的目标是独乐寺的观音阁。它高耸于城墙之上，遐迩可见，远观时益觉其活力与祥和。那是我首次看见一座真正古趣盎然的建筑。

观音阁建于公元 984 年。彼时宋朝初立，而此地尚为辽所踞。观音阁分两层，其间夹有平坐一层。中国建筑用独有的结构体系斗拱支撑出檐，在此为一系列巨大而简洁的双下昂（图 1）。其下支柱中段微凸，顶上是深远的屋檐。环绕上层的平坐同样由这种斗拱支承。于是，它们构成了三条基本上是结构性的饰带。这些与后来的直柱、细小密集的斗拱形成了鲜明对照。凡熟悉敦煌石窟中唐代壁画者，均感觉它与那些壁画中的殿宇惊人地相似。

1 Hall of Kuan-yin, Chi Hsien, second oldest wooden structure in China. Built in 984 AD, the Hall was the oldest wooden structure known in China till July 1937, when a ninth-century building was found. The use of brackets to support the overhanging eaves is a characteristic of all formal Chinese architecture.

蓟县观音阁，中国第二古老木构。观音阁建于公元984年，至1937年7月发现一处9世纪建筑之前，一直是中国已知的最古木构。运用斗拱支承出檐是中国所有正规建筑的一大特征。

The Hall houses a colossal clay statue of an Eleven-headed Kuan-yin, sixty feet in height. The upper two floors had to be built with an opening in the center to form on each a sort of gallery at the levels of the waist and chest of the statue (Figure 2). It is the largest clay figure known to exist in China today.

Incidentally, this Hall, together with the Gate House in front of it, my two very first finds, remained for long the oldest wooden structures in the Institute's record, and were not antedated until I came across a T'ang Dynasty building early in July, 1937, just a few days before the outbreak of the present Sino-Japanese war.

观音阁中有一庞大泥塑，为高达六十英尺的十一面观音。靠上的两层阁板只得在中央留出空腔，在像腰及像胸的高度上形成展廊状空间（图2）。这是迄今中国已知的现存最大泥塑像。

顺便提及，这座观音阁和它前面的山门——我最早的两个发现——在营造学社的记录中长期保持为最古的木构，且其年代记录一直未被打破，直到1937年7月初我偶遇一座唐代建筑。数日后，现正进行的中日战争就爆发了。

V. A SEVENTY-FOOT BRONZE STATUE

At Chengting, on the Peiping-Hankow railway, is the magnificent Buddhist temple of Lung-hsing Ssu. Founded in the sixth century, the temple has undergone in turn a series of destructions and reconstructions during the last thirteen centuries. There are still preserved in the temple-compound several buildings of the Sung Dynasty (960–1127). Alongside these ancient buildings is a catholic Mission and its Gothic-like cathedral which had sprung up sometime in the last century at the place where Emperor Ch'ien-lung's "travel palace" once stood.

伍 一座七十英尺高的铜像

宏伟的隆兴寺位于北平—汉口铁路线上的正定。这处寺宇建于6世纪，在以往十三个世纪里，它曾相继经历过多次的倾圮与重建。群殿之间，几座北宋（公元960—1127年）的建筑至今犹存。一个天主教的传教团住在这群古建筑旁，上世纪时哥特式天主教堂赫然拔地而起，替代了一度坐落于此的乾隆皇帝的行宫。

2 The Eleven-headed Kuan-yin of Chi Hsien, largest clay figure in China. The upper floors of the Hall are opened in the center to form galleries at the waist and chest heights of the figure. Brackets are used to support the galleries as well as the ceiling above.

蓟县十一面观音，中国最大的泥塑像。观音阁上层中央留空，以在像腰及像胸高度处形成展廊。展廊与头顶藻井一样以斗拱支承。

The dominating feature of Lung-hsing Ssu is the colossal bronze statue of a forty-two-armed Kuan-yin, about seventy feet high, standing on a beautifully carved marble platform (Figure 3). It was originally sheltered by a three-storied Hall which was extensively repaired in the eighteenth century, but is now again in such dilapidated condition that the upper portions are all gone, leaving the Bodhisattva standing in the open, with all the forty "extra arms" missing.

A stone tablet in the Temple tells the dramatic story of the casting of the statue. When Emperor T'ai-tsu, founder of the Sung Dynasty, came to Chengting during one of his campaigns, he enquired after the famous bronze statue there which was said to be forty feet high.

Being a devout Buddhist, he was grieved to hear of its destruction a few years before. Then in the garden of the Temple, "the earth shone with rays of light at night that could be seen by priests and laymen alike." Furthermore, torrential rains brought down by way of the Fu-t'o River "thousands of timbers which were clogged by a huge log" at Chengting. "Manjusri, Bodhisattva of Wu-t'ai Shan, has sent down the timber for the construction of Kuan-yin's Palace" was the enthusiastic conclusion.

隆兴寺最醒目处是它巨大的四十二臂青铜观音像，约七十英尺高，立于雕工精美的大理石宝座上（图3）。其上原覆有一座三层阁，曾在18世纪大举修葺过，但目前已复倾颓，阁上部消失得无影无踪，露天而立的菩萨像上四十只“多余的手臂”都不见了。

庙中一座石碑记载了铸造铜像的传奇[5]。宋朝的开国之君太祖皇帝在一次征战中驾临正定，欲拜谒此处著名的铜像，据说该像高达四十英尺。

太祖是一个虔诚的佛教徒，听说铜像已于几年前被毁，他深感痛心。此后，庙后菜园夜间“有祥光出其上”，时人皆见。随后，暴雨大作，沿滹沱河[6]“浮栋梁材千万计，自五台山而下”，直至被一大木拦住，停在了正定。狂热的信徒得出的结论是，“五台山文殊菩萨送下木植与镇府大悲菩萨盖阁也！”

3 At Lung-hsing Ssu, Chengting, is the 10th-century seventy-foot bronze statue of Kuan-yin. Existing buildings in the temple are mostly of the 10th and 11th centuries, extensively repaired in the 18th. The tower to the right was recently constructed to protect the colossal figure which was left standing in the open for nearly 200 years.

正定隆兴寺的10世纪七十英尺观音铜像。寺内现存遗构多为10世纪与11世纪之物，曾于18世纪广为修葺。右侧高塔新建不久，以蔽露天站立近二百年的巨像。

The Emperor was much pleased with the miracles and ordered a new statue to be cast. An imperial architect and the chief of the Imperial Mint were dispatched to take charge of the building of the Hall and the casting of the statue. Three thousand workmen and soldiers were detailed to the task.

The stele also tells of a foundation of seven cast-iron piles, "supporting a cast-iron platform forty feet square and six feet thick, the top of which is flush with the ground." The design of the Bodhisattva "had to be drawn three times before it met the great Emperor's approval." The casting was done in seven sections. When completed, the statue "measured seventy-three feet high." It was commenced on "the twentieth day of the seventh month of the fourth year of K'ai-pao," (971 AD) but the date of completion was not mentioned on the stele.

When I visited the Temple last time, we still saw some original portions of the three-storied Hall mixed with later repairs. The Kuan-yin was subsequently "renovated" by the devout but ignorant abbot. The beautiful patina I so loved was covered by coats of paint in bright primal colours, giving the Bodhisattva the appearance of an ugly giant doll. I had to comfort myself by thinking that the paint will not last very long, perhaps not more than a century! A niche as high as the Niche of the Pine Cone in the Vatican was built to shelter the newly dolled-up deity. The new structure, a happy accident, looking like a slender, graceful tower, crowned by a Chinese roof, could be seen miles away.

In the fall of 1937, Chengting was subjected to heavy bombardments by the Japanese who later occupied the city. The fate of the Statue is yet to be ascertained.

VI. A SIXTH-CENTURY OPEN-SPANDREL BRIDGE

The most astonishing piece of bridge engineering among China's relics is the "Great Stone Bridge" of Chao Hsien, about forty miles southeast of Chengting where the colossal bronze statue stands. I found this magnificent bridge not through studious research in books, but was led to it by a popular folk-song. I thought it was going to be merely another of those arched bridges so common in China. But when I came confronting the single arch of nearly 120-foot-span, with two smaller arches resting on it at each end, I could hardly believe my eyes (Figure 4). It was nothing short of what is today called in engineering an "open-spandrel bridge"!

皇帝见此奇迹龙颜大悦，敕令新铸铜像。宣派八作司十将及铸钱监内差负责建阁铸像。下军三千工役于阁下。

碑上记载亦提及，“留六尺深海子自方四十尺，海子内栽七条熟铁柱，……海子内生铁水铸满六尺”。菩萨像的设计“三度画相仪进呈方得圆满”。铸造分七段而成。完工后的塑像“举高七十三尺”。工程至开宝四年七月二十日下手修铸（公元971年），但是完工的日期在石碑上未见提及。

我们上次探访此地时，犹见三层阁的零星遗构，混于后世修葺部分之间。后来，虔诚而愚妄的住持“翻新”了观音像。我所心爱的铜绿被覆以一层艳丽的原色油漆，菩萨像变成了丑陋不堪的巨偶。见此唯有自我开解，油漆不耐光阴，也许熬不过一个世纪！为遮蔽这座装点一新的神像，建造了一座佛龛，高度类于梵蒂冈的大松球龛。新建的这一佛龛可谓意外之喜，它看上去像个细高而优雅的高塔，而又给添了个中国式的屋顶，数里远之外都清晰可辨。

1937年秋，正定遭日军猛烈炮轰，随即沦陷。塑像的命运存疑。

陆 6世纪的开拱桥

青铜巨像所在的正定县城外，去城西南四十英里许，是中国古迹中最惊人的桥梁工程作品——赵县的“大石桥”[7]。我不是通过精研典籍，而是由一首妇孺皆知的民歌指引，发现了这座精妙绝伦的桥梁。我以为它只是又一座在中国俯拾皆是的普通拱桥。但是，它的单拱跨度将近一百二十英尺，两端各有两个比较小的空撞券[8]。面对此桥，我几乎不敢相信自己的眼睛（图4）。它完全相仿于当代工程里所谓的“开拱桥”！

In the West, such methods of construction did not come into general use until the present century, though it once made its appearance in France in the 14th. But this Chinese bridge was built in the beginning of the Sui Dynasty, sometime between 591 AD and 599 AD. According to an old book on archaeology, one of the abutments once bore the signature of the builder, Li Ch'un, which had since weathered off. But we still could see numerous names of admiring passers-by from the T'ang Dynasty (619–906 AD) till today. A citation, by a prime minister of the T'ang Dynasty, specially mentioned the unusual small arches at the two ends and also the name of the builder. Since it is unusual to give credit to an architect or engineer in ancient China, such special mention may be taken as a proof that the bridge is not a product following the general mode of construction of the time, but the creation of an ingenious and great mind.

4 This modern looking open-spandrel bridge was not built in America today but in China during the sixth century. Built sometime between 591 AD and 599 AD by Li Ch'un, the master builder, the main arch has a span of 116 feet, with two smaller arches resting on it at each end. Such construction did not come into general practice in the West until the beginning of the present century. 这座现代外观的开拱桥并非建于今日之美国，而是6世纪的中国。由建筑大师李春建于公元591年至599年间，主拱跨度116英尺，两侧各有两个小空撞券。如此建造方法直至本世纪方才普遍运用于西方。

如此建造方法直至本世纪方才普遍运用于西方，尽管法国曾在14世纪出现过一个例子。但是，这座中国桥建于隋代之初，即公元591年至599年之间。据一本考古典籍记载，其中一个桥墩上一度镌刻着建桥者李春的签名，后为时光剥蚀。但我们依旧可以看见自唐（公元619—906年）[9]以降心怀崇敬的无数过客的名号。有一段铭文引用了唐时一位中书令的话，特地提及了两端非凡的小券和建桥者的名字。中国古代很少会有建筑师或工匠得获荣名，因此这样特地的提及多少可以证实，这座桥的造法与式样不是沿袭当时的定式，而是天才的独创。

In spite of its thirteen-and-half centuries, the noble structure has the streamlined appearance of an ultra-modern bridge. Had it not been for the inscriptions of different ages, it would be difficult to believe its very early date. So far as I know, it is the oldest bridge existing in China.

In the same city is another bridge of identical design but much smaller dimensions, called the "Little Stone Bridge." Built during the Chin Tartar Dynasty (late 12th century) by a Tartar builder, Pao ch'ien, it was evidently an imitation of the "Great" one. Even then, it is older than the French bridge by more than a hundred years.

VII. HONAN PROVINCE, THE ANCIENT "CENTRAL LAND"

The Province of Honan has been known in China as the "Central Land" and has been the heart of Chinese civilization and culture for thousands of years. It is the key to the domination of China, a trophy that a champion must necessarily acquire. It has been a favourite arena for most of the important battles in Chinese history. It was at Loyang, many times capital of the Empire and one of the principal cities of the province, that the first Buddhist temple in China was built a century before the Christian era began. Along the rivers and up on the mountains of Honan we have some of the most noble monuments of Buddhism.

An Ancient Observatory

At Kao-ch'eng, not far from Sung Shan, is one of the few old observatories in China (Figure 5). It is the Chou-kung's Tower for the Measurement of the Shadow of the Sun, one of the several built by Kuo Shou-ching of the Yuan Dynasty (1280–1376).

By setting up a vertical at the end of a horizontal to measure the shadow of the sun, the exact duration of the solar year was calculated. The purpose of the Tower, with a "slit" on the northern side, is to erect the vertical which was 40 Yuan feet high. The horizontal, 128 Yuan feet long, is a long stone bench or platform with a channel on the top-side over the entire length, so that a perfect level could be obtained by filling it with water. With the exception of the small house on top of the tower, which is a later addition that has nothing to do with the original purpose, this structure answers exactly to the descriptions in the chapter on Astronomy, the *History of the Yuan Dynasty*.

This curious monument that looks like a city-gate, standing on a wide, flat plain, was restored in 1936 by order of Generalissimo Chiang Kai-shek and under the technical supervision of the Institute.

虽已历时十三个半世纪，这高贵的建筑物看去犹如最新型的超级摩登桥梁。若非上面那些不同年代的铭记，它极其古老的年代简直令人难以置信。据我所知，它是中国尚存最古老的桥梁。

同一县城里尚有另外一座桥，设计相仿而尺寸远逊，名为“小石桥”，由一位名为褒钱的女真人建于女真族的金朝（12世纪末）。它显然是“大石桥”的摹本。即以那时论，它也比法国的单拱桥提早百年不止。

柒 古老的“中原”河南省

河南省在中国向以“中原”闻名，几千年来，它是中国文明与文化的中心。得天下关键处即在中原，乃兵家必争之地。中国历史上，大多数重要战役都在这个著名的舞台上演。早在公元纪年开始之前一个世纪，河南的重镇、历朝故都洛阳，就建起了中国的第一座寺庙。溯河上行至河南群山间，我们发现了一些最恢弘的佛教遗迹。

古观星台[10]

去嵩山不远的告成镇有中国少数占观星台之一（图5）。这处周公测景台为元代（公元1280—1376年）[11]郭守敬所建。

在水平面上立起一根垂直的立表，通过测量日影可以算出太阳年的确切时间。建此台的目的是立起高达40元尺[12]的立表。此台北侧，有一直漕。圭面长128元尺，为一长条石或石台，上有通长水渠，注水其中则可获完美的水平面。台顶有一小屋，为后世加建，与其原本用途毫无关系。除此而外，这座观星台完全符合《元史・天文志》中的描述。

这座珍贵的遗迹形似城门，立于广阔平坦的原野上。1936年，蒋介石总司令下令修复，营造学社担任了技术监理。

5 Chou-kung's Tower for the Measurement of the Shadow of the Sun. Built in the 13th century, the slit on the side of the tower is for holding up a vertical which makes a right angle with the long horizontal bench at its foot. By the shadow of the vertical the exact duration of the solar year was calculated. 周公测景台。建于13世纪。台边直漕用于立表，垂直于足下水平长石条。据立表投影可以计算太阳年的确切时间。

VIII. SIAN, TWO-THOUSAND-YEAR CAPITAL OF THE CHINESE EMPIRE

Sian, the provincial capital of Shansi, and "Ch'ang-an" of ancient times, was the capital of the Chinese Empire from 1132 BC to 906 AD almost continually. The province, especially in the neighborhood of Sian, is immensely rich in historic remains. Being the capital, it became the objective of every dynasty founder and was seldom spared from wars; its destruction at every dynastic change became almost a matter of course. Consequently, no wooden structure of any appreciable date has been left to posterity. Other remains of historical significance—ruined sites of Han palaces, tombs of even earlier dates—of interest to the student of architectural history are, however, numerous.

A 1500-square-mile Graveyard

Among the profusion of historical sites may be mentioned the tombs of the Chou, Han and T'ang Dynasties. To the west of Sian, in the counties of Hsien-yang, Hsing-p'ing and Wu-kung, over an area measuring about thirty to fifty miles in length and width, are innumerable immense earthen mounds. They are tombs of emperors, princes, ministers and generals during the two thousand years. Mostly square in plan, they have a trapezoid elevation, resembling huge mastabas. Some are attributed to a certain historical figures, but most of them are yet to be identified.

One of the most interesting is the tomb of the great general Huo Ch'ü-ping, conqueror of the Huns in the Han Dynasty (2nd century BC). After his death, Emperor Wu-ti ordered his tomb be made to resemble the Ch'i-lien Mountains, where he had one of his greatest victories. This is the only tomb that is decorated with rocks. At this tomb were found several stone sculptural pieces in granite, portraying the warrior's career. "A Horse Treading on a Hun" is the best known and has already been introduced to the West. Recent excavations revealed a few more. The sculptors seemed to have taken good advantage of the natural shaped of the big rocks and turned them into human figures of great vigour, strangely resembling to the Menhirs (Figure 6). But with the beasts, the artist seemed to have a totally different, and more intimate, understanding, such as is shown in the bull with big, round eyes (Figure 7).

About fifteen miles from Huo Ch'ü-ping's tomb is the pretentious tomb of the father of Empress Wu of the T'ang Dynasty. The approach to the tomb is an avenue flanked on both sides by chimeras, lions, horses, as well as civil and military attendants (Figures 8,9). Such arrangements are to be found in imperial tombs of later ages. In grandeur and workmanship the T'ang Dynasty is unequalled. But in these figures, one feels the lack of the deep understanding of animals found in the animal sculpture of the Han Dynasty.

捌 中国的两千年皇城西安

西安是陕西省的省会，古代的“长安”。从公元前1132年至公元906年，中国的皇都几乎毫无间断地设在此地。尤其毗邻西安一带，该省的历史遗迹极其丰富。每个朝代的开国君主都视此都城为必得之物，因此它罕有机会逃脱战祸；每逢改朝换代，它似乎理所当然地要遭受灭顶之灾。因而，后人已经见不到任何有年代可考的木构建筑。然而尚存无数有历史意义的残迹，如更早期的汉代宫殿与陵墓的废墟等，当令研习建筑历史的学生深感兴趣。

方圆一千五百英里的陵墓区

在丰富的历史遗址当中，周、汉、唐诸代的陵墓值得一提。它们位于西安的西侧，咸阳、兴平和武功县境内，在方圆达三四十英里的区域，隆起无数庞然土堆。这些帝王、国君、文臣武将的陵墓陆续建于这两千年间。其平面多为方形，立面多为梯形，像似巨型石室坟墓。可以确知有些墓主是历史上某个人物，但是大多数陵墓的主人尚待考证。

最有趣的一座陵墓属于汉代远征匈奴的征服者——大将军霍去病（公元前2世纪）。在他身后，汉武帝敕令建陵如祁连山形，他曾在那里赢得最伟大的胜利。这是唯一饰以岩石的陵墓。在此发现的几件花岗岩石雕，描摹着这位武士的征战生涯。最著名的一件是“马踏匈奴”，已经介绍给了西方世界。最近的挖掘又有新的发现。看来雕刻家善于利用大石材的天然形状，以此雕作栩栩如生的人像，出奇地相似于史前巨石阵（图6）。而对动物，艺术家的认识似乎更加深刻且有所不同，例如大环眼的牛像所示（图7）。

距霍去病墓约十五英里外，是唐代的武后之父顾盼自雄的陵墓。神道两侧俱为麒麟、狮子、马和军民侍役（图8，9）。此类布置亦见于后世皇家陵墓。唐代的雄浑和工艺无与伦比。但是此地的雕像似觉对动物缺乏深刻认识，逊于汉代的动物雕刻。

6 "The Giant Devouting a Hog" at Huo Ch'ü-ping's tomb is strangely like the Menhirs. The ancient Chinese seemed to have less understanding of the human form than the animal. This Giant was carved out from the natural shape of the stone and has an appealing sense of humor. 霍去病墓的"野人抱熊"与史前巨石阵出奇地相似。古代中国人对人的认识似乎不及对动物的认识深刻。巨人形得之于石材的天然形状，颇为风趣。

7 The bull at Huo Ch'ü-ping's tomb reveals the perfect understanding of the animal by the Han sculptor. Up till the discovery by the Academia Sinica of some Shang Dynasty stone figures at Anyang a few years ago, this and a few other stone sculpture at the tomb of the great conqueror of the 2nd century BC were the oldest stone sculpture known in China. 霍去病墓的牛像显示了汉代雕刻家对动物的深刻理解。直到几年前中央研究院在安阳发现商朝石刻，出土于这位公元前2世纪伟大征服者陵墓的此件石刻及另外几件是中国已知最古的石刻。

8 **9** The tomb of Empress Wu's father has an avenue flanked by colossal stone animals and men. These monolithic giants measure about 13 feet in height. Compared with the animal sculpture of the Han Dynasty, the perfected craftsmanship is of little significance when the basic understanding of the animal is lost. 武后之父的陵墓，神道两侧皆为巨大的石人石兽。这些整石巨像高十三英尺许。形诸汉代动物刻像，由于缺乏对动物的基本理解，此处精良的雕工甚无意义。

IX. THE HOLY LAND OF CHINA

The Province of Shantung was in the Chou Dynasty the principalities of Ch'i and Lu, the latter being the native land of Confucius. In the city of Ch'ü-fu today is the temple of the Sage. Perhaps no other building-project in the world can boast of a longer history. Immediately after the death of Confucius in 479 BC, a few of his disciples kept the Master's house as in his living days and paid regular homage there. The simple abode of three rooms gradually became the symbol of reverence in later ages. From the Han Dynasty downward it became the affair of the State not only to have the sacred place kept in proper order, but also to raise the Sage's descendants to a hereditary peerage with the title of duke. During the last two thousand years the Temple continued to grow in size and complexity, till today it covers one-third of the entire area of the walled-city of Ch'ü-fu.

玖 中国的圣地

山东省在周朝时是齐国和鲁国的封地，后者是孔夫子的故乡。今曲阜城内有孔庙。也许举世再无另一建筑工程能够夸口其历史更为久远。孔夫子逝于公元前 479 年，一些门生在他身后维持乃师的居处如其生前状况，在此定时拜祭。三间屋的简朴住处在后世逐渐演变为尊严的象征。自汉代以降，有序地维护圣地，并封圣人后裔为世袭贵族“公”，则成为国事之一。两千年来，孔庙日益扩大，日渐复杂，直至今日，它覆盖了曲阜城内三分之一的区域。

10 The library building of the Temple of Confucius. On the site of an older building which was destroyed by fire, the present structure was built at the end of the 15th century when an extensive restoration was carried out on the Temple. 孔庙书楼。15世纪末大举修缮孔庙时建于旧楼遗址，原楼被大火烧毁。

11 The carved marble columns of the Temple of Confucius at Ch'ü-fu are familiar to many Westerners. From a simple abode of three rooms, the Sage's home "grew" in 24 centuries' time into this magnificent hall, with surrounding buildings and courtyards covering a third of the city of Ch'ü-fu. In the side buildings are also enshrined Confucius' 72 disciples and other deserving scholars of later ages. 曲阜孔庙的大理石雕石柱为许多西方人熟知。24个世纪里，圣人的住处由陋室三间"长"成这个堂皇大殿，周遭殿宇群及天井覆盖了曲阜城的三分之一。偏殿内配享孔子的七十二门徒及后世硕儒。

In the Temple compound are numerous stele from the Han Dynasty downward, recording the more important happenings in the House of K'ung and in the Temple ground. However, of the existing structures, the oldest is a stele-pavilion dating only from the Tartar Dynasty of Chin, 1195. Most of the buildings were built in the reign of Emperor Hung-chih (about 1500) of the Ming Dynasty, the K'uei-wen Ke or Library being the most important representative (Figure 10). The Ta-ch'eng Tien, or Hall of Supreme Perfection where a large statue of Confucius is enshrined, may not be unfamiliar to Westerners for its beautifully carved marble columns (Figure 11). However, to the student of Chinese architectural history, this 1730 building is of no special significance, except as a good example of the execution of the "Rules" of 1733.

在孔庙建筑群中有无数汉代以降的石碑，记录了孔府和孔庙发生的大事。然现存建筑物中，最古老的碑亭，其纪年亦只及女真族的金朝（公元1195年）。楼宇多建于明弘治年间（约公元1500年），最重要的代表是奎文阁，或称"书楼"（图10）。祭祀孔夫子巨像处为大成殿，它的大理石雕刻石柱美丽精致，西方人因此对它很熟悉（图11）。而在研习中国建筑历史的学生目中，这座建于公元1730年的大殿并没有独到的意义，只是实施1733年"法式"的一个佳例。

In this Temple is worshipped not Confucius alone. He is "attended" by his 72 disciples. In the side buildings on both sides of the courtyard in front of the Ta-ch'eng Tien are a great number of "spirit-tablets," each bearing the name of a distinguished scholar or a deserving official of the last two thousand years. The chosen ones were solemnly admitted by imperial decrees dynasty after dynasty. It is the highest possible posthumous honour that could be conferred upon a Confucian scholar.

In the courtyards to the left are halls to house Confucius' ancestors of five generations back while to the right are his parents' quarters. His wife is enshrined in a special hall behind the Hall of Supreme Perfection. There are also in the Temple compound halls for different ceremonial purpose. The entire compound is preceded in front by a series of courtyards and gateways which make the entrance to the temple ground most impressive.

As a whole, the Temple of Confucius is a magnificent example of Chinese planning, and historically there is perhaps no other building in the world comparable to it in its continuity of development.

In 1935, the Chinese Government planned another grand-scale repair of the sacred Temple, and I was honoured to be chosen as the architect for its restoration. But the plan was frustrated when the Japanese started to press their way into North China. Today the city of Ch'ü-fu, with the Temple in it, has fallen under Japanese control. "Duke" K'ung Te-ch'eng, 77th-generation-grandson of the Sage, whose present republican title is "High Commissioner in Charge of the Worship of the Sage, " has fled to Chungking so that he, true to his ancestor's teachings on Loyalty, would not be taken by the Japanese and made a political tool.

X. THE PROVINCE OF SHANSI, RICH CONSERVATORY OF OLD WOODEN STRUCTURES

The Province of Shansi, shielded on the east by the T'ai-hang Mountains, bounded on the west and south by the majestic Yellow River, and protected on the north by the Great Wall and Mongolian deserts beyond, has been spared the destruction of wars when other provinces have had to build up new cities on top of ruins over and over again since the beginning of the Sung Dynasty (960 AD). Until the Japanese came in the autumn of 1937, Shansi had enjoyed an uninterrupted peace for almost a thousand years. Consequently it became the rich conservatory of a great number of old wooden structures. Between 1931 and 1937, I took altogether six trips to that province, three to the northern part, and another three to the middle and south.

殿内享祀者除孔夫子外，尚有七十二门徒“配享”在侧。大成殿前，于天井两侧厢房供奉大量灵位，其上神主均为两千年间的硕儒或良臣。历年历代，由皇帝敕令庄严地批准这些人选。一位儒者身后的哀荣莫过于此。

左跨院内大殿祭祀孔夫子上五代先祖，右跨院内祭祀夫子考妣。大成殿后设一殿专供其妻。孔庙建筑群另有其他多种仪式功能。整个建筑群前面，层层天井与重门使得孔庙的入口无比庄严。

作为一个整体，孔庙出色地例证了中国规划思想，而且，在世界历史上，可能亦无他处能与它的持续发展相提并论。

1935 年，中国政府计划再次大规模修缮孔庙，我有幸入选为负责修缮的建筑师。但是，日军开始入侵华北，计划被迫搁置。如今，曲阜城和孔庙一起落入了日军掌中。现由民国政府授职“大成至圣先师奉祀官”的圣人七十七世孙、衍圣公孔德成飞去了重庆，他恪守先祖尽忠国家的教诲，不愿落入日本人手中，成为政治工具。

拾 木质古构的富饶温床山西省

山西省东倚太行山，西、南临壮丽的黄河，北有长城和蒙古沙漠拱卫，因此有宋（公元960年）以来一直远离战祸，而其他省份却于改朝换代之际反复地在层层焦土之上重建新城。直至1937年秋日军入侵，山西安享太平几近千年。于是这富饶的温床孕育了大量的木质古构。在1931年至1937年之间，我六度赴晋，三次访晋北，其余三次访晋中与晋南。

In almost every town or walled-city, or in the mountains, one could hardly fail to come across some ancient looking buildings, Buddhist or Taoist temples of the 12th and 13th centuries, or even earlier dates. It was in Shansi Province, totally unexpectedly, that we found, on our way to T'ai-yuan, near Yü-tz'u, dangerously missing the railway track by only 20 yards, a small structure, most neatly constructed, bearing the date corresponding to 1008, the third oldest wooden building so far known; at T'ai-ku, three temples of the Sung and Chin periods in perfect state of preservation; at Tsin-tz'u, the Garden-temple to the Goddess of the Spring, built sometime between 1023 and 1031, a most beautiful grouping of landscape and architecture; and such odd little subjects as the residence with a 100-foot retaining-wall as foundation, overlooking the Fen River at Ling-shih; or the cast iron Buddhist seated among the ruins of the huge temple of Ling-yen Ssu off the highway near Fen-yang (Figure 12); etc. It would be impossible for me to go over all the important finds in Shansi one by one. I can only choose a few of the most outstanding.

An Early 11th-century Library Building

Ta-t'ung is famous not only for the great Wei caves at Yun-kang but also for the Liao (937–1125) and Chin (1125–1234) temples within the city itself. The Upper and Lower Hua-yen Ssu were originally one temple, covering a large area with a grouping of a hundred buildings. But in nearly a thousand years, much of the temple ground was encroached upon by the profane. The library was thus separated from the Temple proper and became known as the Lower Temple; it is a structure of particular interest (Figure 13). The purpose of the building was housing the Buddhist scriptures which were kept in wall cabinets built along the three sides of the Hall. The cabinets, rare examples of their kind, are surmounted with miniature temple buildings symbolizing the Heavenly Palaces (Figure 14). In the center of the Hall and arranged on a large platform, is one of the finest groups of clay figures in China. Three Buddhas are seated on their thrones, attended by Arhats and Bodhisattvas and guarded by Lokapalas.

Unlike most of the ancient figures in China, this group graceful and with mellowed, tarnished tint is not spoiled by later "renovations." Under one of the beams, written in black Chinese ink, is the date corresponding to 1038, giving the time of the construction of the Library building. This is an age-old custom in China, but this is one of the very few of the early dates that have been thus preserved.

几乎在每座小城镇里，或在群山之间，总会遇到一些外观古旧的楼宇、佛寺或道观，其年代早至 12、13 世纪或更久远。正是在山西省，在我们赴太原中途，位于榆次附近离火车铁轨不到二十码处，一座小建筑与我们不期而遇。它极为匀称，纪年为公元 1008 年，是迄今已知的第三古老的木构建筑[13]；在太谷，三座宋、金时期的庙宇保存完好；祭祀清泉圣母的花园寺庙晋祠，建于公元 1023 年至 1031 年间，是最美丽的并垣名胜；奇特的小建筑如俯瞰汾河的灵石民房，地基为高达一百英尺的挡土墙；汾阳附近大路边，铸铁佛像趺坐于灵岩寺堂皇残址的瓦砾间（图 12）；如此等等不一而足。我不可能逐一讲述在山西省的所有重要发现，只能挑选一些最出色的例子。

11 世纪早期的薄伽教藏

大同之盛名不仅得之于云冈伟大的北魏石窟，亦得之于城中辽（公元 937—1125 年）[14]、金（公元 1125—1234 年）时期的寺宇。上下华严寺原为一体，占地辽阔，楼阁有上百之数。然近千年内，大多庙产逐渐为世俗用途所蚕食。从此薄伽教藏彻底脱离上寺，开始以下寺而知名；它是一座特别有趣的建筑（图 13）。建殿意在收藏佛经，沿大殿三面墙上置壁柜式经橱藏之。这些经橱极罕见，橱顶有微缩楼阁以象征天宫（图 14）。殿心大坛上为中国最精美的泥塑佛像群之一。三本尊趺坐于宝座，胁侍尊者、菩萨、金刚护卫。这组群像外形秀丽，色泽柔美黯淡，所幸没像中国众多古老造像那样遭后世“翻新”之厄。在一根梁下用墨汁写有建殿年代，为公元 1038 年。这种做法在中国虽然由来以久，但这一年代是以这种方式保存下来的极少数早期年代之一。

12 How the divine bears a human wound. Among the ruins of Ling-yen Ssu near Fen-yang are three seated iron Buddhas of the 15th century. One, bearing a wound on the neck, bends slightly in an unusually benevolent repose. 神佛蒙受人间伤痛。汾阳附近的灵岩寺荒墟上，三座15世纪的铁佛趺坐。其一颈上带伤，以非凡的仁静微微倾欹。

13 The oldest library building existing in China, built in 1038 to house Buddhist scriptures. This was once part of Hua-yen Ssu, a large temple of a hundred buildings in Ta-t'ung. In 900 years, the temple lost much of its ground and the Library, thus separated from the main-group, is now known as the Lower Temple. 中国最古老的藏书楼薄迦教藏，为藏佛经建于公元1038年。它原为大同殿宇过百的华严大寺的一部分。九百年间，大寺失去了许多地界，而薄迦教藏则脱离了主寺，现以下寺知名。

14 Heavenly Palaces decorate the cabinets in the library of Hua-yen Ssu. Arranged along walls of the three sides of the Library, the cabinets, rare examples of their kind, are surmounted by miniature temple buildings symbolizing the Heavenly Palaces. 华严寺薄迦教藏经橱上的装饰天宫。沿薄迦教藏三面墙布置的经橱顶有微缩楼阁象征天宫，为类中罕例。

The discovery, in 1933, of a complete set of Chin (1149) edition *Tripitaka* at Kuang-sheng Ssu was a great event to students of Chinese Buddhist bibliography. It was the discovery of the scriptures that led to our visit to the Temple.

About fifteen miles east of Chao-ch'eng, at the southern spur of the Huo Mountains, are the Upper and Lower Temples of Kuang-sheng Ssu. There we found two groups of buildings, probably all of the Yuan Dynasty (1280–1376) of most unusual construction. The external appearance of the buildings conforms well with that of the usual Chinese structure. But the framing of beams for the support of the roof is anything but orthodox. Slanting members with long cantilevers are freely employed, showing a good deal of originality and ingenuity on the part of the designer (Figure 15). Such organic use of the wooden frame has not been found in other places in our trips.

15 The free use of slanting members and cantilevers is uncommon. The 14th-century buildings of Kuang-sheng Ssu, Chao-ch'eng, have peculiar, unorthodox constructions. The beams and purlins are organically held in equilibrium by the slanting cantilevers. 斜昂的自由运用不同凡响。14世纪遗构赵城广胜寺的建造方法独出心裁。梁、檩俱由斜昂灵活有机地平稳支撑。

拾壹 霍山广胜寺，非凡的建筑与非凡的壁画

1933年，在广胜寺发现一整套金代版（公元1149年）《三藏经》，这是中国佛教典籍研究界的一件大事。正是经书的发现把我们引向了这里。

上下广胜寺位于赵城以东约十五英里的霍山南脉山头。我们在那里发现了两组建筑，可能俱为元代的罕贵遗构（公元1280—1376年）。建筑外形与常见的中国建筑很吻合，但支撑屋顶的梁枋体系却绝非正统，而是自由运用了出挑深远的斜昂，展示出设计师的极大原创力和才智（图15）。对木结构如此灵活有机的运用在我们的旅途中尚属初见。

Alongside the Lower Temple is the Temple of the Dragon King, god of the great spring that gushes from under the hill (Figure 16). The temple itself, rebuilt in 1319, is nothing extraordinary. It is some of the mural paintings on its walls that attracted our attention. In our past trips, we have only come across mural paintings of religious subjects, and it was here that we, for the first time, saw secular scenes thus depicted. Most interesting among these is a scene of a theatrical performance. The actors are seen with either Sung (Chinese) or Mongolian costumes. The conventionalized facial make-up shows a prototype of the elaborate designs used on the stage in later periods. This painting is most important for the study of both Chinese painting and drama of the Yuan Dynasty. It is the more valuable for its inscription and date, corresponding to 1326.[15]

16 Temple of the Dragon King at Kuang-sheng Ssu. Rebuilt in 1319, wooden structures like this is nothing unusual in Shansi Province. It is the mural paintings in this building that are of particular interest. 广胜寺龙王庙。此木构重建于公元1319年，在山西省不足为奇。此寺特别有趣处在其壁画。

下寺旁边是拜祭山麓泉水的龙王庙（图16）。龙王庙重建于公元1319年，本身并无特别之处。但其壁上有一些壁画吸引了我们的注意。在以往的旅途中，我们所遇壁画均取宗教题材，而在这里，我们首次目睹了如此描绘的世俗场面。其中最有趣的是一个演戏的场景。演员们的服饰宋（汉）、蒙互见。程式化的面部化妆显为后世精研的舞台化妆的原型。这幅壁画对研究中国绘画和元剧都至为重要。更珍贵的是，它的铭文纪年为公元1326年。

（林鹤 译 李道增 校）

Buddhist Cave Sculpture

[1940]

佛教石窟造像[1]

Buddhist cave sculpture on cliffs in China is a most important phase of Chinese art that has been sadly overlooked by the Chinese during the past. Such monuments were often given brief mention in old books on geography and in travelers' diaries, sometimes even with contempt by Confucianists. Buddhist sculpture, or rather sculpture of any kind, has never been regarded by the Chinese as an art, or anything worth a gentleman's attention. It is only in recent years that the Chinese began to realize the greatness of these monuments and give the art of the sculptor its due recognition.

I. THE YUN-KANG CAVES

Perhaps no name is more inspiring than Yun-kang to one who is interested in Chinese sculpture. Located on the band of the Wu-chou River about ten miles from Ta-t'ung, once capital of the Northern Wei Dynasty (386–534 AD), the place was made, in 1935, easily accessible to tourists from Peiping by bus connections provided by the Railway. But my first few visits were still made during those mule-cart days. When nearing Yun-kang, the springless vehicle had to bump over miles of saw-toothed, slanting rock strata. It is an experience to remember a lifetime.

The vertical sandstone cliff, about 150 feet high and a mile long, is hollowed by numerous caves and niches which are covered with thousands of images of the Buddhist pantheon. Among them, the five colossal figures, about 70 feet high, are well known to many travelers who have been to Peiping and Yun-kang. The village at the foot of the cliff has a present day population of about two hundred. Some of the caves are even occupied by villagers as convenient, ready-made homes. But from old records we could easily visualize the grandeur and pop of the temples at the height of their glory.

We stayed in the Temple for several days during our first visit there. To our great dismay, we found that we could not get even the simplest kind of food. A lieutenant of the small army detachment stationed there finally helped us with a few ounces of sesame oil and two cabbages in exchange for half-a-dozen thumb-tacks!

The creation of the Yun-kang caves was started in the reign of Emperor Hsiao-wu-ti of the Wei Dynasty, 454 AD. The group of rock-out images is the most important example of early Buddhist art in China. The caves and niches were placed at random on the face of the cliff. Emperors and commoners alike, to seek blessings for their beloved, could have images caved according to whatever size and position they wished. The iconograhic activities at Yun-kang lasted exactly half a century, and ended abruptly when the Wei capital was moved south to Loyang in 494 AD.

中国崖壁间的佛教石窟造像是中国艺术里最重要的一章，惜乎曩日为国人所忽视。古人的方志和游记对此类遗迹常一笔带过，儒者有时竟至于轻藐以对。佛教造像，或毋宁说任何种类的雕塑，从未被国人目为艺术，士大夫辈不齿为此花费心思。直到近年，国人才开始发现这些遗迹之伟大，并且还雕塑艺术以应有的重视。

壹 云冈石窟

关心中国雕塑艺术的人，或以云冈为最令人激动之地。它位于武周河岸，去大同十英里许。1935年，铁路局由北平通汽车至大同，旅行者辄易于抵此北魏国都（公元386—534年）。但是，我的头几次探访尚在此前的骡车年代里。接近云冈的时候，艰涩的车行不得不颠簸于一里又一里犬牙交错的倾斜石面上。这种经历终生难忘。

垂直的砂石质崖壁高约一百五十英尺，一英里长，被无数石窟和佛龛镂空，里面有数以千计的佛教诸神之像。其中，五座巨型塑像高约七十英尺，为履及北平和云冈的旅客所熟知。崖壁脚下的村落目前约有人口二百。一些石窟竟至于被村民占据，成为方便现成的居家。但是，依据旧时记载，我们很容易想见当日寺宇鼎盛时何其宏伟壮丽。

我们第一次探访期间，在庙里住了几天。我们极其沮丧地发现，连最简单的食物亦无处可觅。最终，我们用了半打大头钉，从派驻此地的一支小部队的排长手里换得几盎司芝麻油和两棵卷心菜！

云冈石窟始建于北魏文成帝时期（公元454年）[2]。石刻群像是中国早期佛教艺术最重要的遗例。石崖表面随机散布石窟与佛龛。上自帝王下至庶民，均可随意各择尺寸位置，凿龛造像为至爱祝祷。云冈的造像活动持续了半个世纪，至公元494年魏室南迁定都洛阳时，方兀然中止。

1 Niches of some caves at Yun-kang are architecturally treated, complete with columns, brackets and roof. In decorative motifs, there is an unmistakable "Greco-Buddhist" influence. The "egg-and-dart" is Greek. But most interesting is the translation of the Persian "double-bull" capital into the Chinese bracket. 云冈石窟某些佛龛得到了艺术处理，配以柱、斗拱及屋顶。装饰母题无疑表现出"希腊—佛教"的影响。"卵箭饰"为希腊式。但最有趣的是波斯"双牛"柱头被移植为中国的斗拱。

2 The Yun-kang caves are melting pots of Chinese, Greek and Indian decorative elements. In niches like this, the "Greco-Indian" influence dominates. The "angels" may be a mixture of Han and Indian prototypes. The trapezoidal arch is not Chinese. The Ionic-esque scrolls on capitals deserve special attention of the student. 云冈石窟融汇了中国、希腊与印度的装饰元素。在这类佛龛中，明显有"希腊—印度"的影响，"飞天"或许混杂了汉与印度的原型。五边拱并非中国式样。柱头爱奥尼克式的涡卷特别值得注意。

A number of the caves in Yun-kang are large and spacious. Some are preceded by an antechamber. The sanctuary has usually a core in the center in the form of a pagoda, a Chinese version of the Indian chaitya, after which the Chinese caves were modeled. Here we find a jumble of "Greco-Buddhist" elements. Some columns even have capitals like Ionic scrolls, and the original Chinese "bracket" was ingeniously translated into the Persian "double-bull" capital motif (Figures 1, 2). But, in spite of all that, the architecture remains fundamentally Chinese. From these caves we gathered a good deal of information about the wooden architecture of the Wei Dynasty of which we have, so far, found no actual specimen. Of the large number of caves of later periods in different parts of China, with the exception of the T'ien-lung Shan caves near T'ai-yuan, none is quite as rich in architectural treatment as these early ones.

云冈的石窟有若干庞大卓异者。有些带有前廊。窟殿中心通常有一中央塔柱，是印度"支提"的中式翻版，为中国石窟模仿的蓝本。我们在此发现了"希腊—佛教"的元素相互掺杂。有些柱上坐斗甚至如同爱奥尼克式卷纹的柱头，而中国本土的斗拱灵活地变形为波斯"双牛"的兽形柱头母题（图1，2）。然建筑物大体仍为中式。我们从这些石窟里采得北魏木构建筑的大量资料，这段时期迄今尚无实际遗例。中国各地后世出现了大量石窟，除了太原附近的天龙山石窟以外，无一如这些早期石窟般具有如此丰富的建筑处理细节。

II. THE LUNG-MEN CAVES

To students of Chinese sculpture, the caves of Lung-men, about ten miles south of Loyang, are equally as important as the caves of Yun-kang. When the Wei Tartars moved their capital here from Ta-t'ung, the iconographic artists came with them. The miles of limestone cliffs on both bands of the Yi River offered an excellent base for sculptural work. The activity started there in 495 AD, and lasted over a period of more than 250 years.

The earlier caves have figures executed with an archaic feeling similar to the Yun-kang carvings—the cylindrical form dominates. The facial expressions of the figures are singularly tranquil and enchanting. In recent years, these figures became victims of the vandalism of curio-dealers and several of the best examples found their way in museums in Europe and America.

The most monumental group of statues at Lung-men did not appear until Empress Wu had the colossal vairochana hewn in 676 AD. An inscription tells how her Imperial Majesty ordered all the court ladies to donate their "powder-and-rouge-allowance" towards the fund for the carving of the eighty-foot seated statue, complete with attendants: Arhats, Bodhisattvas and Lokapalas. The entire group was originally sheltered by a wooden hall of nine bays that has disappeared long since. But holes and grooves on the cliff still indicate clearly the position and curvature of the roof as well as the location of many beams.

The walls of the hundreds of grottoes of Yun-kang bear innumerable inscriptions, giving the names of donors and dates of their donations, making the dating of most of the images easy. From the point of view of an architectural archaeologist, however, the Lung-men caves are of far less importance than the Yun-kang caves.

Besides Lung-men, there are a number of other places in Honan Province where are cave images of early date, notably at Tz'u Hsien, Chun Hsien and Kung Hsien. As groups they are all smaller and of less importance than the Yun-kang and Lung-men caves.

In 676 AD Empress Wu ordered all her court ladies to donate their cosmetic allowance for the caving of this colossal vairochana group at Lung-men. The entire group was sheltered by a wooden hall that has disappeared. Holes and grooves on the cliff still indicate clearly the position and curvature of the roof and the location of many beams. 公元676年，武后颁旨所有宫娥捐献脂粉钱在龙门开凿这组卢舍那巨型群像。群像原覆有木构寺阁，现已不存，崖上龛壁处仍有卯孔与凹槽清楚指示屋顶刻槽位置及梁柱位置。

贰 龙门石窟

在研习中国雕塑者目中，洛阳南面十英里的龙门石窟当与云冈石窟同等重要。当北魏鲜卑族从大同迁都至此时，造像艺术家亦随之而来。伊河两岸连绵的石灰石崖壁为雕刻作品之上佳基址。造像活动始于公元 495 年，持续时间逾二百五十年而不止。

早期石窟造像具有和云冈相似的古雅感觉——主要形式为圆雕。雕像的表情异常静谧而迷人。近年来，这些雕像遭到古董商的恶意毁坏，最杰出的作品流落到了欧美的博物馆中。

龙门最不朽的雕像群成于武后时，即公元 676 年开凿卢舍那龛。据一处铭文记载，皇后陛下颁旨所有宫人捐献“脂粉钱”为基金，雕刻八十英尺高的坐佛、胁侍尊者、菩萨及金刚神王。群像原覆以面阔九楹的木构寺阁，惜早已不存。但崖上龛壁处尚有卯孔和凹槽历历在目，明确指示出屋顶刻槽的位置和许多梁楣的位置。

与云冈不同，逾百龛壁上铭文无数，记录了功德主的名字与捐献日期，便于确认大多数雕像的年代。然而，从建筑考古的角度来看，龙门石窟的重要性远逊于云冈石窟。

除龙门石窟以外，河南境内尚有其他早期石窟，较大者有磁县、浚县及巩县各处。作为组群，其规模与重要性都不如龙门石窟和云冈石窟。

Statues of Buddha and Lotus in Lung-men Caves 龙门石窟中的佛像及莲花洞

III. THE T'IEN-LUNG SHAN CAVES

For studying the architecture of the Ch'i and Sui Dynasties, the caves at T'ien-lung Shan, some forty miles southwest of T'ai-yuan, in the Province of Shansi, offer some most valuable material. Unlike Yun-kang and Lung-men, where the caves are carved out of rock-cliffs on river banks, the T'ien-lung Shan caves are high and dry up on the mountain. The group here is comparatively small, only about twenty caves in all. The largest figure, about thirty feet high, is a dwarf compared with the giants of either Yun-kang or Lung-men. The other caves have mostly figures about life-size. They represent a period of high accomplishment in Chinese sculpture. Unfortunately, almost every one of them, except the largest, were ruthlessly cut down and removed by curio-dealers. The stolen pieces are now scattered in museums all over the world. Some of them are objects of admiration in the Winthrop Collection in New York. Some others, characteristically, found their way to a certain private collection in Japan.

Architecturally, these caves are of the greatest importance. Some of them are preceded by a porch, executed in most faithful imitation of the wooden construction of the time. Though merely facades, we could get from them not only a general idea of the parti, but even the exact proportions and the delicate shades of refinement.

叁 天龙山石窟

山西省会太原西北四十英里许，有天龙山石窟，它为研究北齐与隋朝的建筑提供了许多珍贵资料。云冈石窟和龙门石窟开凿于岸边崖壁，而天龙山石窟则高踞于群山之上的旱地。这里的组群相对较小，统共仅约二十窟。最大的佛像高约三十英尺，与云冈或龙门的巨像相比，简直像是侏儒。其他诸窟的塑像多为真人尺寸。它们代表着中国雕塑史上造诣高超的一段时期。不幸的是，除最大的一尊外，几乎所有塑像都被无情地凿下，流落于古董商手中。失窃的残片现在散见于世界各地的博物馆里。其中一些在纽约的温思罗普藏品中为人称羡，另外若干照例落入了某些日本私人收藏家之手。

这些石窟在建筑意义上极其重要。其中一些前有柱廊，极为忠实地模仿当时的木构建筑。尽管只有立面，我们从中不仅大致认识到了总体组合的思路，甚至于还认识到了具体的比例和细部的阴影。

（林鹤 译 李道增 校）

The thirty-foot Buddha of T'ien-lung Shan is a dwarf compared with the giants of Yun-kang and Lung-men. This statue, though started at the later part of the 6th century, was not completed until the 7th. With its attending Bodhisattvas, it is the only group at T'ien-lung Shan that had escaped the vandalism of curio-dealers. 天龙山的三十英尺高的佛像与云冈及龙门的巨佛相比简直为侏儒。此像始造于6世纪末期，但直至7世纪方得完成，旁立胁侍菩萨。这是天龙山逃脱古董商掠毁之厄的唯一群像。

The T'ien-lung Shan caves are the most architecturally treated. Some of them are preceded by a porch, executed in most faithful imitation of the wooden construction of the time, even the exact proportions and the delicate shades of refinement. 天龙山石窟最富建筑处理之功。类似的一些石窟前有柱廊，精工细做，忠实模仿木构，连细部的微妙光影也不放过。

Five Early Chinese Pagodas

五座中国古塔[1]

[1941]

In Sung Shan, the Central Holy Mountain, in Teng-feng Hsien, Honan Province, is the ancient Buddhist temple, Sung-yueh Ssu. Within its compound stands a most unusual pagoda, one of five early pagodas of North China visited by me and my fellow workers of the Institute for Research in Chinese Architecture in the process of collecting material for a history of Chinese architecture from study of actual specimens. Built in 523 AD, this is the oldest brick pagoda existing in China today.

The temple was originally the summer villa of Emperor Hsiao-ming of the Eastern Wei Dynasty. The pagoda was built for the salvation of the Emperor's deceased mother, the Empress Dowager. It has brought her blessing through fourteen hundred years. The pagoda, entasised to give a silhouette like that of a modern artillery shell, has both grace and grandeur. Its twelve-sided plan is unique. Pagoda contemporary with this one are usually square in plan, whereas those of later periods are octagonal.

在河南省登丰县的中岳嵩山，有一座古代佛寺——嵩岳寺，寺内矗立着一座非同寻常的古塔，它是我和我在中国建筑营造学社的同仁们从实例研究开始进行中国建筑史史料收集过程中所造访的中国北方五座古塔之一。该塔建于公元 523 年，是中国现存最古老的一座砖塔。

嵩岳寺最初是北魏孝明帝[2]的夏宫，嵩岳寺塔则是为其母灵太后禳病所建，此后该塔带着太后的恩泽一直延存了 1400 年。嵩岳寺塔的整体轮廓向上逐渐收分，像是一个现代的炮弹壳，优美而秀丽。塔的十二边形平面形式也很独特，因同时期的塔常为四边形平面，而此后塔的平面又多为八角形。

1 The oldest brick pagoda in China is in the compound of the ancient Buddhist temple of Sung-yueh Ssu at Sung shan, Honan. The pagoda, built in 523 AD, is very unusual in style having, as it does, twelve sides and fifteen stories. 这座中国现存最早的砖塔位于河南嵩山嵩岳寺院内。该塔建于公元523年，其十二边形和十五层的形制极为罕见。

The fifteen stories of the pagoda also constitute an uncommon feature. On a very high base is the tall first-story, above which are fifteen decks of cornices of roof-eaves. Though regarded as fifteen-stories, a pagoda with such arrangement may perhaps be more appropriately described as one-storied, fifteen-deck-roofed. The first story is embellished at the corners with polygonal engaged columns with lotus-blossom capitals. Each of the doorways on the four sides facing the cardinal points is arched, the extrados of the arch being shaped like a lotus petal and ending in volutes at the spring-line. The other eight sides each has a niche in the form of a Ssu-men T'a or one-storied, four-doored, square pagoda. Undoubtedly these niches were once occupied by statues which were lost long ago. The architectural motifs show unmistakable Indian influences. The general parti of the edifice is the primogenitor of a pagoda-form that later became very popular in China. (Figure 1)

Such a Ssu-men T'a as I have mentioned is to be found at Shen-t'ung Ssu in the mountains thirty miles south of Tsinan, in Shantung Province. These thirty miles we covered on our visit to the pagoda in a whole day's pleasant travel along rocky paths, in the date-flower-scented breeze of early summer, watching the ever-changing silhouette of rugged mountains against the sky, until we reached the seldom visited region lying at the back of T'ai Shan, the Eastern Holy Mountain, which was our destination.

The small, one-storied stone pagoda bearing the date corresponding to 544 AD on one of the marble statues it shelters, is the oldest of its kind in China. Short and stubby on first observation, the structure may be described as a pavilion square in plan, with a core in the center and an arched doorway on each facade. The roof is a stepped pyramid, surmounted by a "pinnacle" which in essence is a miniature Indianesque stupa. (Figure 2)

该塔的外观亦不同一般。在高大的第一层塔身上，叠涩出 15 层的密檐。虽然被视为 15 层，但像这种类型的塔也许称其为一层塔身、15 层密檐顶更为恰当。一层塔身各隅砌有角柱，柱头呈莲花样式。塔身东西南北四个主面上设有拱门，拱背形如莲瓣并在起拱线处呈涡卷饰。塔身其余八面各设佛龛一座，状似四门塔样式，即一层四门的方形塔。

2 China's oldest stone pagoda, erected at the back of T'ai Shan, probably in 544 AD, is a simple structure, a single-storied pavilion unlike what is generally known as a pagoda. Its doorways are arched; its roof is a stepped pyramid with a stupa.
神通寺四门塔——中国现存最早的石塔，大约建于公元544年，位于泰山之阴。它是一个与一般概念的塔不同的单层简单结构。塔门呈拱状，塔顶为窣堵坡样式的金字塔。

无疑，龛内原曾有佛像，但早已佚失。塔的建筑风格显然深受印度影响，其整体设计样式成为后来盛行于中国的一种塔的形式的始祖。（图 1）

在山东济南城南 30 英里的群山之中的神通寺，就有一座上文提及的四门塔。我们花了一整天的时间才走完 30 英里的路途，找到该塔。这是一段愉快的旅途：行走在山岩间的小径上，我们一边呼吸着早夏时节风中的花香，一边浏览着蓝天下步移景异的山峦起伏，最后来到了旅途的终点——位于东岳泰山之阴的一处人迹罕见之地。

这座单层的小石塔内的石像上有公元 544 年的题刻[3]，它是国内该类型塔中最古老的一座。这个初看短粗的结构实际上是一个方形平面的亭子，亭中心为塔心柱，四面设拱门。屋顶是一个阶梯形的金字塔，上覆以一个缩小的印度窣堵坡样式的尖顶。（图 2）

My study of a large number of pagodas in China led me to the conclusion that the Chinese pagoda is an interesting combination of an original multiple-storied Chinese structure and an Indian stupa which crowns the former. The Ssu-men T'a of Shen-tung Ssu is one of the earliest and simplest examples of this combination and should be given a most prominent position in the evolution of the Chinese pagoda.

The two pagodas described above date from the period of the Six Dynasties. When we come to the T'ang period, it is no surprise to find two important pagodas among the innumerable Buddhist remains of this period in the Sian area, in Shensi. These are the Ta-yen T'a and Hsiao-yen T'a, the Great and Little Gander Pagodas. Rising high above the vast plain, they stand about two miles to the south of the Celestial City and are themselves about two miles apart. The "great" one, a little earlier in date, is the more important. It stands in the temple grounds of Tz'u-en Ssu, where it was built to house the Buddhist scriptures.

The present structure represents a rebuilding of an even earlier pagoda. The original was only five stories high, and was founded by the great monk Hsüan-tsang, in 652 AD. It was said that the Master, after his return from his nineteen-year pilgrimage to India, obtained the Emperor's permission to build this pagoda to house the scriptures he brought back. On the day when the ground was broken at the building site, he carried on his own shoulder the first shovels of earth and encircled the site three times in prayer. Unfortunately this original pagoda was badly damaged in war shortly after completion. It was completely rebuilt between 701 AD and 705 AD and made seven stories high. (Figure 3)

The plan of the pagoda is square, the construction entirely of brick. The exterior of each story is treated with pilasters and architraves in delicate relief, and a corbelled "cornice." The general silhouette of the Ta-yen is not often seen elsewhere in China. Instead of the usual graceful entasis, its upper stories diminish in an uncompromising incline. Sturdy and dignified, it stands as a most fitting monument to the great Buddhist pilgrim and scholar who was its founder.

3 The "Great Gander" Pagoda, Sian, is one of the most sacred monuments of Buddhist China. The present pagoda replaced in the 8th century one erected by the great 7th-century monk Hsüan-tsang but soon war-damaged.
西安大雁塔是中国最重要的佛教纪念性建筑物之一。现存的大雁塔是公元 8 世纪重建的，原塔由 7 世纪的名僧玄奘所建，但不久便毁于战火。

西安慈恩寺大雁塔平面图

The plan of the "Great Gander" Pagoda of Sian

公尺 5 0 10M.

对大量中国古塔的研究使我得出了这样一个结论：中国古塔是在其传统多层结构之上覆以印度窣堵坡样式的有趣结合。神通寺四门塔是这种融合样式最早和最简洁的实例之一，它在中国古塔的演进过程中具有极其重要的地位。

上述两塔都建于六朝时期。当我们转向研究唐朝时，在陕西西安地区众多的佛教建筑遗迹中发现的两座佛塔无疑是最重要的，这就是大雁塔和小雁塔。这两座塔高高耸立于西安古城以南约两英里的开阔平原地带，两塔间相距也约两英里。相较之下，稍早建成的大雁塔更为重要，它立于慈恩寺内，为存放佛经而建。

现存的大雁塔是由一座更早的古塔重建而成。最初它只有五层高，是由著名的唐僧玄奘于公元 652 年所建。据说玄奘西行印度 17 年 [4] 朝圣归来后，经皇帝恩准建造此塔以珍藏其带回的佛经。在该塔破土动工之日，玄奘曾亲自执锹铲土并绕行场址三周行祷告礼。遗憾的是，最初的佛塔建成不久就因战乱而遭严重毁坏。它于公元 701 至 705 年间彻底重建并加高到七层。（图 3）

大雁塔平面呈方形，全部由砖建造。外部各层设有壁柱，带有精美浮雕的柱顶过梁和出挑的"檐口"。其外廓在中国其他地方实属罕见，它并非通常的逐渐收分，而是每上一层都有明显的向内收退。坚定而庄严的性格，使大雁塔成为最恰当地纪念其缔造者——那位伟大的佛教学者和朝圣者——所矗立的一座丰碑。

The only wooden pagoda existing in China today dates from the Sung period. It stands about fifty miles south of Ta-t'ung, Shansi, not far outside the inner stretch of the great wall in the town of Ying Hsien.

This miserable town, on alkaline soil, poverty-stricken, with only a few hundred mud houses and barely a dozen trees within the city enclosure, is about twenty-five miles away from the nearest highway bus station. This distance I traveled by mule-cart on my trip to the pagoda, suffering six hours of bumpy ride. It was sunset time when I reached a point about five miles west of the town. Most unexpectedly I saw ahead of me, at the far end of the almost straight trail, a sparking jewel on a dark purplish background: the red and white pagoda, reflecting the golden setting sun, against the mountain beyond. Rising about two hundred feet above the surrounding plain, the five-storied tower is visible, in good weather, from places nearly twenty miles away. (Figure 4)

It was dark when I reached the walled city. The bulk of the pagoda towered over the whole town like a black giant. But on the southern side of the top story was visible a light, a spark that penetrated the enveloping darkness. That, I found out later, was the "ten-thousand-year lamp" that had been burning there day and night for nearly nine hundred years.

中国现存的唯一一座木塔建于宋代[5]，它位于山西大同以南约 50 英里处的应县城内。

在我们考察时，应县是一个建在盐碱地上的贫困小镇。它距离最近的公路汽车站约 25 英里，城内只有百来栋土坯房，树木稀少。我坐在骡车上，经过六个小时的颠簸后才从车站来到木塔前。当我到达镇西约 5 英里处时，正是日落时分，出乎意料之外，我看见在几乎笔直的小路尽端暗紫色的天空背景下一个熠熠闪光的宝石：红白相间的古塔，在其后群山的衬托下，披上了金黄色的落日余辉。木塔在平原上耸起约 200 英尺高，在晴朗的天气下，大约 20 英里以外都能看到这座古塔。（图 4）

当我抵达小镇时，夜色已深。古塔像个怪物般耸立在小镇的上空。不过在塔的顶部南侧可以看到一丝闪亮，它穿透了漆黑的夜空。我后来才知道，那是一盏"万年灯"，它已经历了近九百年的日日夜夜而长明不熄。

4 A poverty-stricken Shansi town, Ying Hsien, boasts the only wooden pagoda known to exist in China, built in 1056 AD. Its eaves and stories are supported by a system of brackets.

山西穷镇应县以中国目前现存唯一木塔而自豪。木塔建于公元 1056 年。各层出檐及平坐各有斗拱支撑。

The pagoda was built in 1056 AD. Octagonal in plan and constructed entirely of wood, its structure is essentially the super imposition, in five tiers, of single-storied Chinese buildings. The first story has double-decked eaves, supported by huge brackets, stylistically identical with those of the Kuan-yin Ke in Chi Hsien, Hopeh. Each of the four upper stories has a surrounding balcony and an overhanging eave, supported by its own system of brackets. On each story, doors are opened on the four sides facing the cardinal points, the other four sides being walled-in with plaster on lath, decorated with paintings of Arhats and Bodhisattvas.

On the ground floor, seated in the center of the octagonal sanctuary, is a colossal clay statue of Sakyamuni, while on the upper floors are different Buddhas, usually attended by Arhats and Bodhisattvas.

The top of the pagoda is finished with an elaborate spire of wrought iron, secured to the corners of the uppermost roof by eight iron chains. I was up on that spire one sunny, clear afternoon, absorbed in measuring and photographing, when the clouds closed in rapidly but unnoticed. Suddenly a terrific thunderbolt struck nearby. Taken by surprise, I nearly lost my hold on the icy-cold chain two hundred feet above the ground. My only other experience at all similar to this was when, without the usual alarm, some Japanese planes dropped several 250-pound bombs around my house, the nearest one only twenty feet away.

This pagoda, generously spared by nature, is entering its last century of a thousand-year cycle. We wonder, here in the Southwest, whether it has survived the fortunes of war. The Japanese besieged and took the town of Ying Hsien in the fall of 1937.

The last and latest of these five pagodas is the Hua T'a, or "Flowery Pagoda" of Chengting, on the Peiping-Hankow Railway, in Hopeh Province. It is a brick structure of the Chin Dynasty, twelfth century AD. Its name is a tribute to its very complicated shape. Though it is octagonal in plan, with doors on the four sides facing the cardinal points of the compass, the other four sides each have a hexagonal chamber attached on the outside. The exterior finish in stucco is modeled to represent columns, beam and brackets of wood. The "pinnacle" is profusely decorated with high reliefs of elephants, lions and small, one-storied stupas. It is a chaotic but not too unhappy mixture of the Indian stupa and the Chinese pagoda, a compact presentation of the "five-pagoda" composition. In all my later trips I never came across another similar structure. (Figure 5)

应县木塔建于公元1056年。其平面为八角形，是一个全部为木构的五层结构[6]。首层由巨型的斗拱托起重檐，风格与河北蓟县（独乐寺）观音阁相类似。上部四层各有回廊平坐与挑檐，由自身的斗拱系统支撑。塔各层东西南北向设门，其他四面由壁柱和板墙围合，木板隔墙上饰有阿罗汉和菩萨像。

底层八角形圣坛中央，设有巨大的泥塑释迦牟尼像，上部每层均有各种佛像，多为阿罗汉与菩萨像。

塔顶为一精美的铁制塔刹，固定在屋顶八角尽端的铁件上。在一个阳光明媚的下午，我攀上塔刹去测量和拍照，由于全神贯注，我竟然没有注意到浮云的迅速掩近。突然，不远处炸起一个闪电，惊吓之中，我险些在离地200英尺的高空中松开握住冰冷铁链的双手。我唯一与此类似的一次经历，是在没有任何警报下，日军的飞机在我住所周围投下了几枚250磅的炸弹，其中最近的一颗距我只有20英尺。

大自然宽厚赦免的这座木塔，行将步入它千年周期的最后一个世纪。在日军于1937年秋季攻占了应县后，我们不知道这座位于城西南的古塔，是否在战火中幸免于难。

五座古塔中的最后一座、也是年代最近的，是位于河北省北平—汉口铁路线上的正定花塔（亦称华塔）。这座砖塔是公元12世纪的金代遗物。花塔的名称源于其繁复的造型。虽然其塔身平面为八角形，在东西南北四面设有塔门，但在其他四个面上又有附建的六角形小塔。塔的外部用灰泥仿制出木构的柱、梁和斗拱样式。塔刹大量地饰以象、狮和小的一层窣堵坡高浮雕。它是印度的窣堵坡和中国佛塔混杂但并不太令人厌烦的结合，是一种集中而小巧的“五塔样式”[7]。在我此后的考察途中，再未遇见过另一个类似的塔的实例。（图 5）

（单军 译 高亦兰 校）

5 The "Flowery Pagoda" of Chengting was so named for its complicated shape: to four sides of the octagonal plan are attached hexagonal chambers. The brick structure is finished in stucco; its upper part is profusely embellished with stupas, elephants and lions in high relief. 正定花塔（华塔）因其繁复的形状而得名：在其八角形主塔的四面又有四个六角形小塔依附其上。砖结构的表面装饰以灰泥。塔的顶部有高浮雕的窣堵坡、大象和狮子等装饰。

China's Oldest Wooden Structure

中国最古老的木构建筑[1]

[1941]

Panorama of Fo-kuang Ssu, Wu-t'ai Shan, Shansi

山西五台山佛光寺全景

Wu-t'ai Shan, the sacred mountain of the Bodhisattva Manjusri, whom the Chinese call Wen-shu P'u-sa, has been holy to Chinese Buddhists since even before the T'ang Dynasty. For over a thousand years its wealthy temples have been constantly being rebuilt and kept in shining gilt and glaring paints for the pilgrims. But around the outskirts of the Mountain, where the fashionable did not care to go, and the poverty-stricken monks could not afford to undertake large building measures, here, if anywhere, ancient buildings might remain for centuries intact.

The Institute for Research in Chinese Architecture, of which I am a member, has for the past nine years been combing the country for ancient monuments. Our ultimate aim is the compilation of a history on Chinese architecture, a subject which has been virtually untouched by scholars in the past. Since little or no material existed in books, we have to hunt out the actual specimens. This search has, to date, taken us to fifteen provinces, where we have studied more than two thousand monuments. But from 1932 the earliest structure we had found of wood , that highly perishable material, dated from the early Sung Dynasty, 984 AD. In June of 1937, our search for a wooden building of the still earlier T'ang Dynasty led us to the Wu-t'ai Shan, where it was at last rewarded.

I set off from Peiping with my architect-wife, Lin Hui-yin, and a small group of field workers, for Tai-yuan and thence, by automobile, eighty miles to Tung-yeh. At Tung-yeh we changed to mule-litters to enter the Wu-t'ai Shan by the uncustomary route, along which, unknown to us, lay the temple we sought. Outside the South T'ai, about three miles beyond the town of Tou-ts'un, we entered the gateway of Fo-kuang Ssu, the Temple of Buddha's Light.

The temple stands on a high terrace on the mountain-side, facing a large courtyard in front, framed by twenty or thirty very old pines. It is a majestic building. Only one story in height, it has large, strong, simple brackets and a far overhanging eave which, at a casual glance, at once tell its very old date. But could it be older than the oldest wooden structure we had yet found?

山西省五台山，是中国称为文殊菩萨的文殊师利菩提萨埵的神山，该处对中国佛教徒而言，在唐代甚至以前就已经成为圣地了。千余年来，其中大量寺庙曾不断重修，并为朝拜者保持着灿烂的外观和耀眼的彩画。但是在山岭的周边外围则讲时髦的人不爱去，贫穷的僧人也无力从事大规模的修建工程。如果有什么地方的古代建筑经过若干世纪仍然保持原状，可能就在这里。

我作为成员之一的研究中国建筑的营造学社，在过去九年里，已经在全国到处搜寻古代建筑遗迹。我们的最终目标是编纂一部中国建筑历史，它是过去学者们从没有真正接触过的一个课题。由于在文献中极少或者缺乏材料，我们不得不寻找实例。迄今为止，这项调查已经使我们走遍了十五个省，研究了两千多处建筑遗迹。不过自 1932 年以后，我们发现年代最早的极易腐朽的木构建筑是宋代早期的（公元 984 年）。1937 年 6 月，为了寻找年代更早的唐代木构建筑，我们去了五台山，在那里最终得偿所愿。

我和我的妻子林徽因建筑师以及几位工作人员，从北平去了太原，再坐汽车到 80 英里外的东冶。从东冶我们改乘骡车走很少有人走的土路进五台山，当时并不知道沿路就有我们要寻找的庙宇。在南台外围，大约过豆村三英里，我们走进了佛光寺大门。

这座庙宇位于山坡的一处高台上，面对一座大院，周围有二三十棵古松环绕。它是一个雄伟的建筑物，仅一层高的大殿，有着巨大、宏伟、简洁的斗拱和深远的出檐，一眼望去，立即表明了它远古的年代。但是，它能比我们以前发现的最古老的木结构更古老吗？

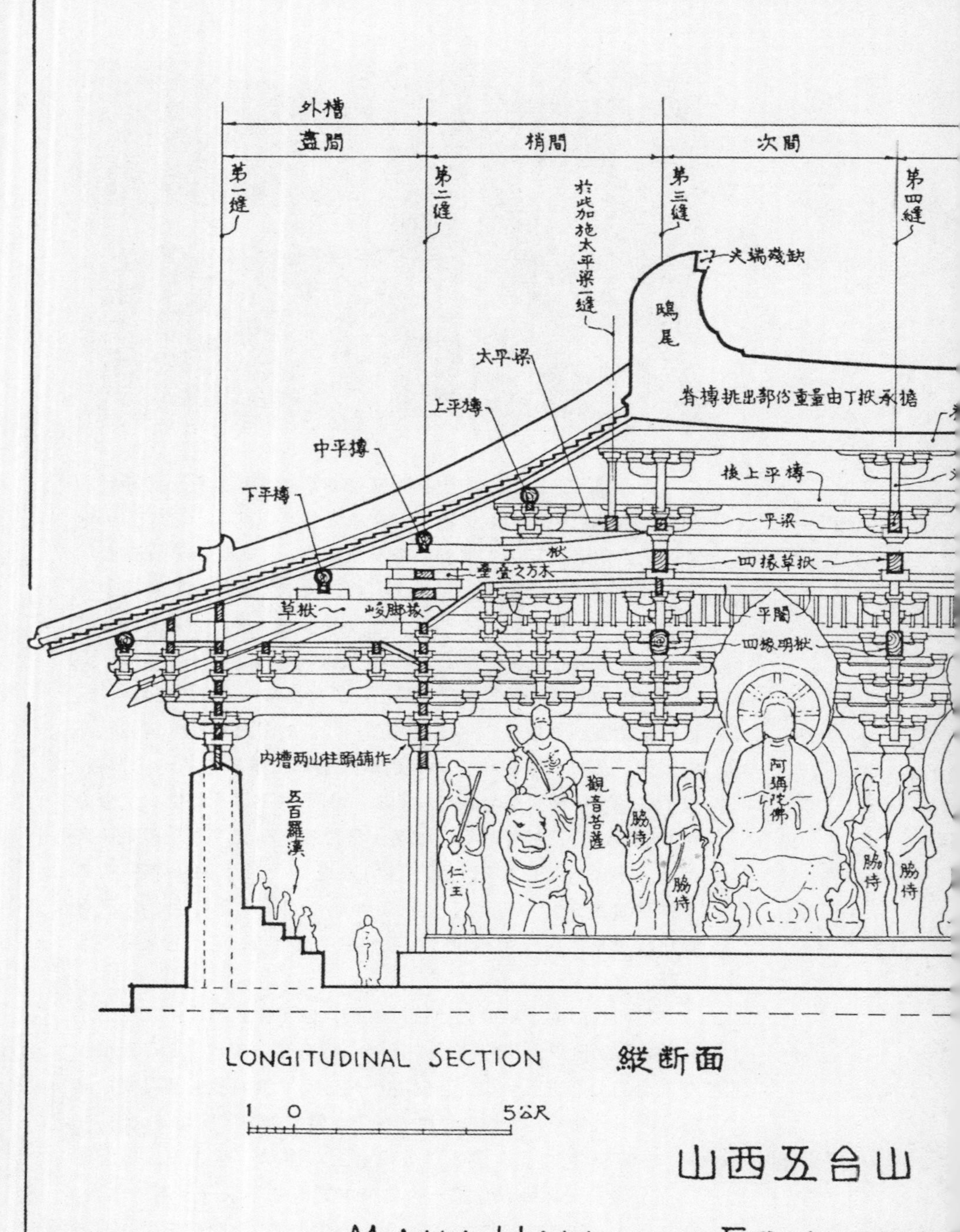

外槽
盡間
梢間
次間
第一縫
第二縫
第三縫
第四縫
於此加施太平梁一縫
尖端殘缺
鴟尾
太平梁
上平槫
中平槫
下平槫
脊槫挑出部份重量由丁栿承擔
平梁
丁栿
壘疊之方木
四椽草栿
草栿
峻脚椽
平闇
四椽明栿
內槽兩山柱頭鋪作
五百羅漢
觀音菩薩
仁王
脇侍
阿彌陀佛
LONGITUDINAL SECTION 縱斷面
1 0 5公尺
山西五台山
MAIN HALL OF FO-KUAN

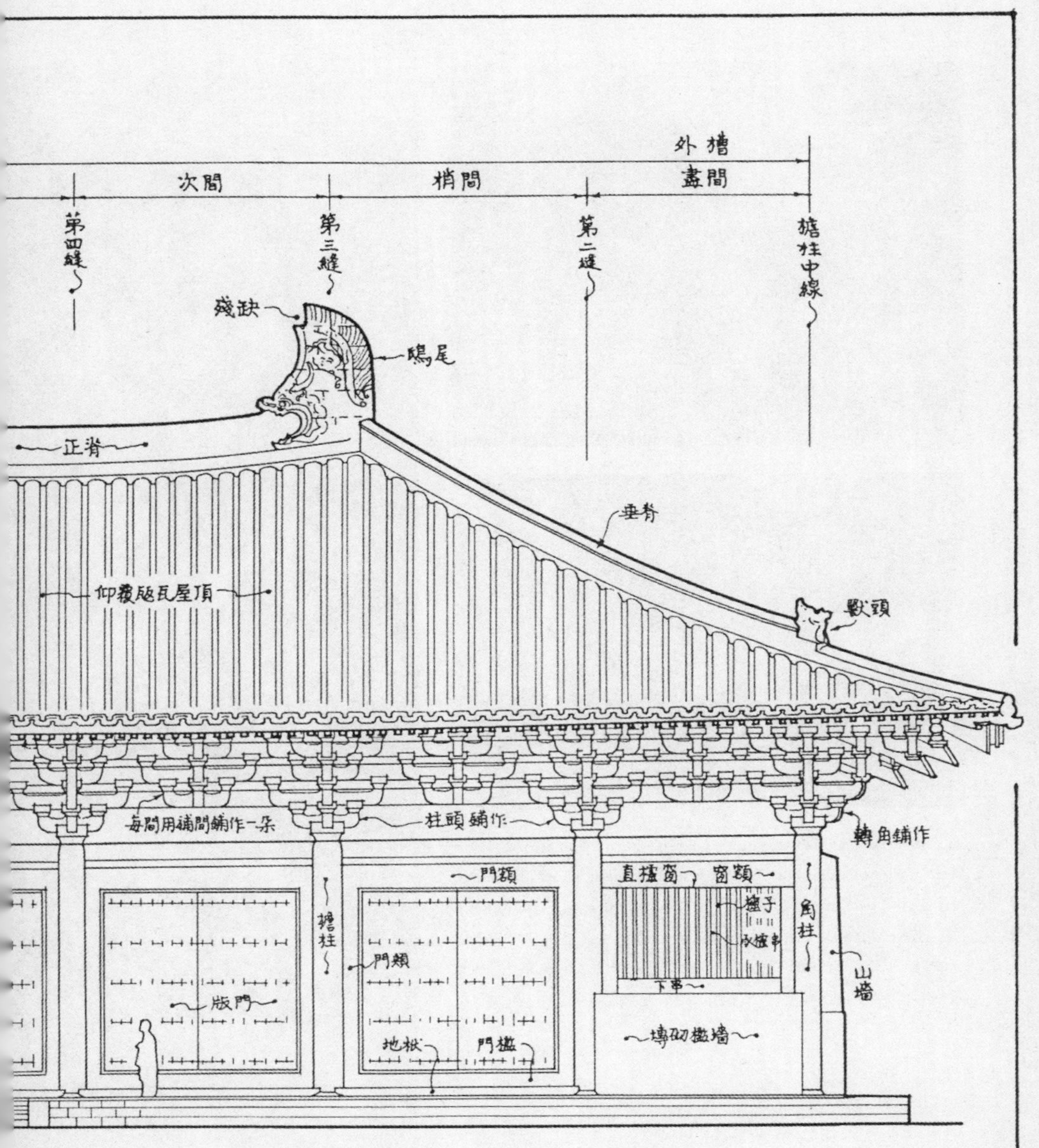

西立面 WEST ELEVATION

寺大殿 唐大中十一年建 857 A.D.

·WU-T'AI SHAN·SHANSI

The Main Hall of Fo-kuang Ssu—a T'ang temple, built in 857 AD—near Wu-t'ai Shan, is the oldest wooden structure now known in China. Associated with it are examples of T'ang sculpture, painting and calligraphy, a unique combination. 佛光寺大殿——唐代庙宇，建于公元857年，位于五台山附近，是现知中国最古老的木构建筑。同一大殿中尚有唐代的雕塑、绘画及书法，汇成无双的组合。

大明萬曆四十二年二月日奉
佛光真
容禪寺
旨重修御馬監太監立

The huge doors were at once thrown open for us. The interior, seven bays in width, was more than impressive in the twilight. On a large platform, seated statues of Buddha, a P'u-hsien and a Wen-shu and numerous attending Arhats, Bodhisattvas and Lokapalas rose before us like an enchanted deified forest. At the extreme left end of the platform was a seated figure of a woman in secular dress, a life-size statue, but very small and humble amidst the group of deities (Figure 1). She was, the monks told us, the wicked Empress Wu. The entire group, though glaring with fresh color from a recent renovation, was without doubt of the late T'ang period. But, if these were the original T'ang clay figures unharmed, the building that covered them could not but be the original T'ang structure. Obviously any rebuilding would have damaged everything under it.

1 At the very end of the platform bearing the great clay figures of deities is the life-size figure of a woman, obscure, in secular dress. Named "Empress Wu" by the monks, she proved instead to be Lady Ning Kung-yü, donor of the temple. 承载着巨型塑像的坛台的最边上，是一座真人大小的妇女像，她姿态谦恭，身着世俗服装。僧人称之为“武后”，她实际却是佛殿的捐献者宁公遇夫人。

巨大的殿门立即被我们用力地推开了。面宽七开间的室内，在昏暗之中非常动人。在太平坛上，坐着佛陀像，两边是普贤和文殊以及众多随侍的罗汉、胁侍菩萨及金刚神王等，像迷人的众神之林出现在我们面前。在坛上最左边是一个真人尺度的、穿着世俗服装的妇女坐像，在诸神之间显得十分渺小和谦恭（图 1）。僧人告诉我们，她是邪恶的“武后”。整个塑像群虽然经过近来的重修显得色彩光鲜，但毫无疑问是晚唐时期的作品。但是，如果这些是未经破坏的原来唐代泥塑，那么覆盖它们的建筑物也只可能是原来唐代的结构。显而易见，任何房屋重建都会破坏下面的所有东西。

In Fo-kuang Ssu is a magnificent group of T'ang Dynasty clay figures, perhaps the only remaining group in China proper, aside from those found at Tun-huang. In spite of the recent "renovation," the figures reveal unmistakable late T'ang characteristics. 佛光寺中精妙的泥塑群像。除敦煌雕塑以外，此处或许是中国境内迄今所存唯一唐代泥塑群像。虽经新近“翻修”，塑像特点无疑为晚唐风格。

Next day we started a careful investigation. The brackets, the beams, the checkered ceiling, the carved stone bases of the columns were all anxiously examined. One and all yielded to us their unmistakable late T'ang characteristics. But my greatest surprise came when we climbed into the dark space above the ceiling; there I found roof trusses (Figure 2) built in a way I knew only from T'ang paintings. The use of two "main-rafters" (to borrow the terms of a modern truss) without the "king-post," just the reverse of later methods of Chinese construction, was overwhelmingly unexpected.

This "attic" was inhabited by thousands of bats which clustered around the ridge-purlin like a thick spread of caviar, thus preventing me from

2 The truss without the king post was used in T'ang architecture—this is the only known specimen. The underside of the ridge-purlin was covered with the innumerable bats that inhabited the attic and made its study difficult. 应用在唐代建筑的没有中腹杆的桁架——这是唯一已知的实例。脊檩下面布满无数蝙蝠，它们栖息在阁楼里，造成研究上的困难。

次日，我们开始细心的调研。对于斗拱、梁枋、棋盘式天花板、石刻的柱础，我们全部急切地加以考察，每项都告诉我们其明确的晚唐时代特征。而当我们爬到天花板上的黑暗空间时，则令我大感惊奇；我发现屋顶桁架的构造方式（图2）以前只是在唐代绘画中见过。它使用两根“主椽”（借用现代桁架用语）而没有“中腹杆”，这与中国较后的结构正好相反，令人感到莫大的意外。

finding a possible date written thereon. In addition, the timbers were infested with millions of bed-bugs that live on the bats. The upper side of ceiling, on which we stood, was covered with a thick layer of fine dust, deposited there perhaps during the last few centuries and strewn with little corpses of dead bats here and there. In complete darkness and amid the vile odor, hardly breathing with a thick mask over our noses and mouths, we measured, drew and photographed with flashlights for several hours. When at last we came out from under the eaves to take a breath of fresh air, we found hundreds of bed-bugs in our knapsack. We ourselves had been badly bitten. Yet the importance and unexpectedness of our find made those the happiest hours of my years of hunting for ancient architecture.

这个“阁楼”里住着成千上万只蝙蝠，它们群集在脊檩周围，像是涂了一层厚厚的鱼子酱，因而我难以发现可能写在梁上的年代。另外，木料上布满了靠蝙蝠为生的千百万只臭虫。我们所站的天花板上面，是一层厚厚的尘土，大概是过去若干世纪所沉积的，并且到处散布着蝙蝠的尸体。在完全黑暗和恶臭之中，在戴着遮住口鼻的厚口罩而令人难以呼吸的情况下，我们一连测量、绘图和用闪光灯拍照了数个小时。当我们最后从屋檐下出来，呼吸到新鲜空气的时候，发现背包里竟有数百只臭虫。我们自己也已经被咬得伤痕累累了。然而，我们这次发现的重要和意外收获，却成了我搜寻古代建筑时期中最愉快的时光。

Frescoes must originally have decorated the walls of the Hall. But the only frescoes parts preserved today are the "frieze," the plastered portions above the lintel and between the brackets. Different sections of the frieze have paintings of very different standards of draftsmanship and evidently of different dates. There is a section, painted with Buddhas in medallions, which bears the date corresponding to 1122 AD. Alongside it is a section painted with Buddha and attending Bodhisattvas, definitely older in date and superior in artistic merit. The analogy of this section of mural painting to those of the Tun-huang caves is most striking. It can be of no other date than the T'ang Dynasty. Though merely a "strip" of wall occupying a position of minor importance, it is the only T'ang mural painting I know of in China proper besides those of the Tun-huang caves.

大殿的墙壁一定曾经饰以壁画。但仅存至今的壁画部分只有“檐壁”，即梁上面和斗拱之间的抹灰部位。檐壁的不同部分具有极为不同的绘画标准，并且显然是不同时期的。有一处绘有团花中的佛陀像，标明的日期相当于公元 1122 年。旁边一处画有佛陀和胁侍的菩萨像，肯定时期要更早并且艺术价值更高。将这部分壁画与敦煌石窟的壁画加以对比，结果极为明显。它不可能不是唐代的。虽然只是墙上一条，又非重要位置，而据我所知，却是中国在敦煌石窟以外唯一的真正唐代壁画。

On the third day of our work in the Main Hall, my wife noticed on the bottom of one of the beams very faint indications of calligraphy in Chinese ink. The effect of the discovery on our party was electrifying. There is nothing we like better than the dates of a building actually written on its beams or carved in stone beside it. Here was this glorious T'ang structure, the first we had found—but how was I to report its date? The T'ang Dynasty had lasted from 618 AD to 906 AD. Now the timbers that bore the faint traces of calligraphy would soon give me the much desired answer. While the rest of us were busy with the problem of arranging for a scaffolding to be erected between the valuable statues for the purpose of cleaning the beams and studying the inscription close at hand, my wife went directly to work. Straining her head back, she tried her eager eyes on the beams from various angles below. After some time of such strenuous efforts she was able to read a number of dubious names with long, official titles of the T'ang Dynasty. Of these the most important was on the beam to the extreme right, only partly readable then: "Donor of the Hall of Buddha, Sung-kung of Shang-tu, Woman Disciple of Buddha, Ning Kung-yü."

我们在大殿工作的第三天，我的妻子觉察到在一根梁底上有非常模糊的毛笔字迹象。这个发现使我们大家极为兴奋，没有比将建筑的年代实际写在其梁下或刻在旁边的石头上更令我们高兴的。这里是我们第一次发现的极好的唐代建筑，但是我将如何报告其年代呢？唐朝从公元 618 年延续到 906 年。现在这块带有模糊字迹的木材，不久将给我极为渴望的答案。当我们为了清洗木梁和研究近在手边的题词正忙于在有价值的塑像之间搭脚手架时，我的妻子直接投入了这一工作。她仰起头，努力从梁下不同的角度，用热切的目光观察。经过一段时间的这种紧张的努力以后，她已经能够读出许多带有冗长唐代官衔的、不清楚的人名。其中最重要的是在大梁最右边的、部分清晰的文字，即“佛殿主上都送供女弟子宁公遇”。

3 A "dhanari" column in front of the Main Hall confirmed the inscription on a beam naming Lady Ning Kung-yü as donor. The inscription on the column, erected contemporaneously with the Hall or soon afterward, established a date. 大殿前面的"经幢"柱上确认了写在一根梁上的捐献者宁公遇夫人的名字。柱子是与大殿同时或稍后建立的（上面文字中有年代记载）。根据这个可以证实大殿的年代。

Donated by a woman! That this young architect, a woman, should be the first to discover the donor of China's rarest old temple to have been a woman, seemed too unlikely a coincidence. She feared she might have misread some of the less decipherable characters by too lively an imagination. But she remembered having seen similar names with official titles on the stone dhanari column (Figure 3) which stood on the terrace outside. She left the Hall in the hope of verifying her reading from the column inscription. There, to her great delight, she found, apart from the long list of imposing officials' names, the same phrase clear and distinct: "Donor of the Hall of Buddha, Woman Disciple Ning Kung-yü." The column bore the date "The 11th year of Ta-chung, T'ang Dynasty," which corresponds to 857 AD.

佛殿是由一位妇女捐献的！而我们这个年轻建筑师，一位妇女，却是第一个发现这座中国最难得古庙的捐献者也曾是一位妇女，这似乎未必是巧合吧。她怕自己由于想象力太活跃而误读了些难辨认的字，但她记起在外面平台上的石经幢（图 3）上面好像见过有类似官衔的一些名字。她离开大殿，希望从石柱的刻字上去核实自己的解读。这回，她大为高兴，因为发现除去一连串显赫官员的名单外，同样的词句赫然在目，即"佛殿主女弟子宁公遇"。这颗石经幢带有纪年为"唐大中十一年"，相当于公元 857 年。

Then it dawned upon us that the small figure of a woman in secular dress, sitting humbly at the end of the platform, whom the monks called "Empress Wu," was none other than the donor Lady Ning Kung-yü herself.

Assuming that the dhanari column was erected soon after the completion of the Hall, the date of the building can be closely ascertained. It is earlier by 127 years than the oldest wooden structure previously found. It is the only wooden building of T'ang date we have yet encountered in these years of search. Moreover, in that one Hall, we have T'ang painting, T'ang calligraphy, T'ang sculpture and T'ang architecture. Individually they are extremely rare but, collectively, unique.

Our investigations were cut short by the news, already a week old, that the war had begun. We left our T'ang temple for the devious journey back to Peiping and thence, with the other educational institutions, to the Southwest. In the ensuing years Shansi has been an important battleground, and the site of the temple, Tou-ts'un, from its previous obscurity has appeared again and again in the papers, sometimes as the base used by the Japanese for an offensive into the Wu-t'ai Shan, sometimes as the objective of Chinese counter-attacks. Whether there will be anything left of the T'ang building after the war is highly questionable. Already my photographs and drawings may be—I hope not—the only records of it now left.

于是它使我们理解到：那位身着世俗服装、在坛末谦恭地坐着的妇女塑像，僧侣们称之为"武后"的，原来就是宁公遇夫人本人。

假定石经幢是大殿完成后不久所立，建筑物的年代也就可以大致肯定。它比过去发现的最古老的木构建筑还早127年。它是我们在这些年的寻访中所遇到的唯一唐代木结构。而且在一座殿堂中，我们拥有唐代绘画、唐代书法、唐代雕塑和唐代建筑。从每项来说，它们已属难得，何况集中一起，则更是罕见。

"战争已经开始"这个迟到一周的消息，立即打断了我们的调查。我们离开了我们的唐代庙宇，迂回地回到北平，以后又随其他教育机构到了西南。在以后的几年中，山西已成为重要的战场，而唐宇所在的豆村，则从原先的默默无闻转而一次又一次地出现在报纸上，有时成为日本人进攻五台山的基地，有时成为中国人反攻的目标。战后该唐代建筑还能剩下什么是很成问题的。我不希望我的照片与图纸竟为它唯一现存的记录。

（英若聪 译 程慕胜 校）

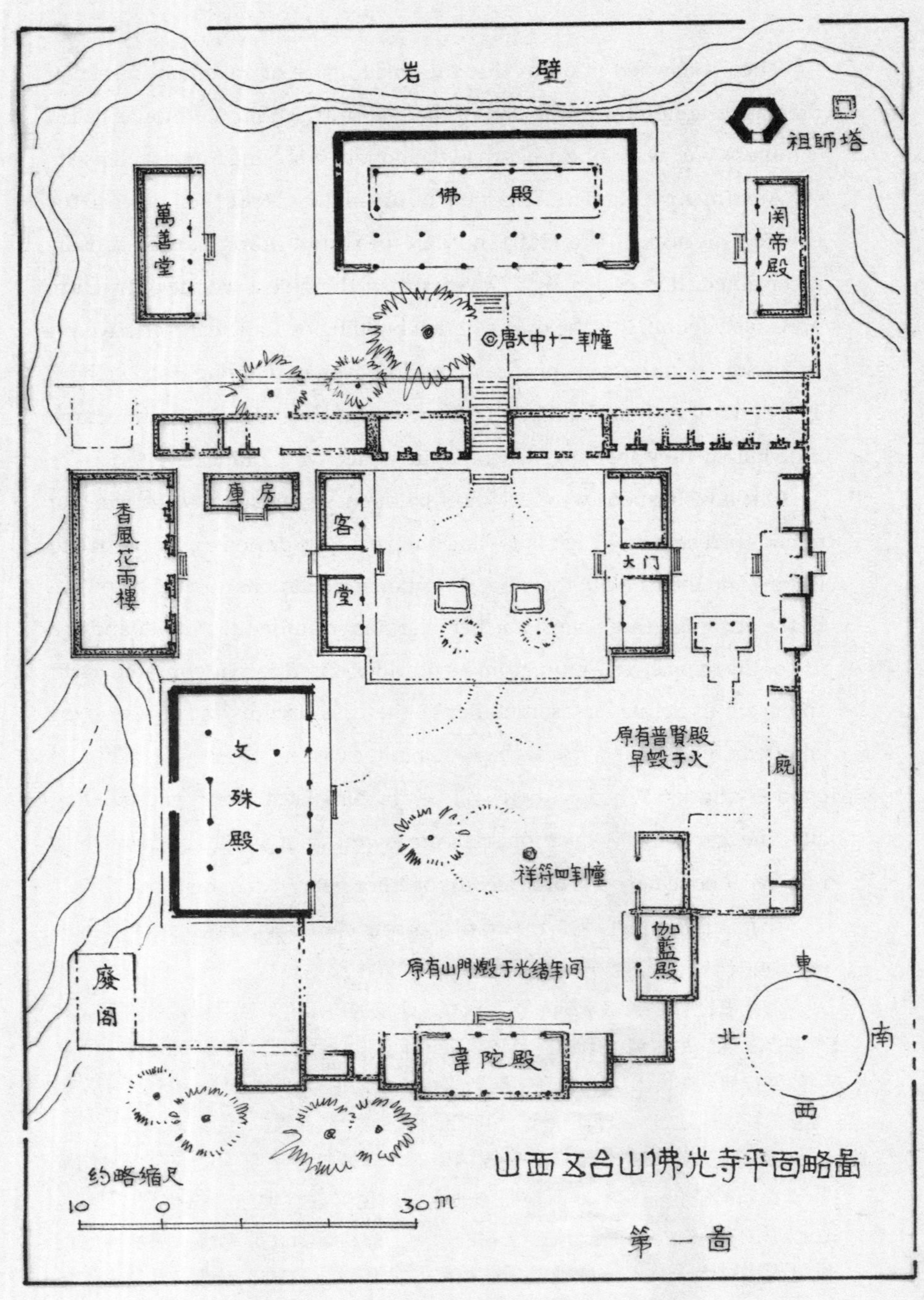

山西五台山佛光寺平面略图

第一图

山西五台山佛光寺大殿 ·南側立面圖樣·

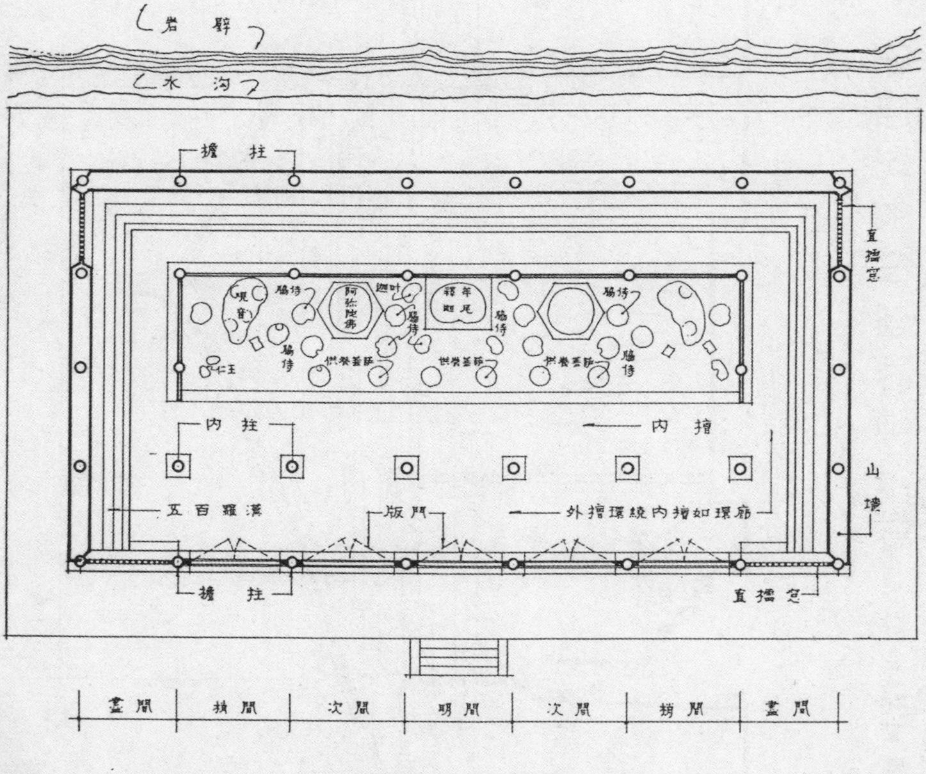

岩壁

水沟

檐柱

直欞窗

内柱

内槽

山墙

五百羅漢

版門

外槽環繞内槽如環廊

檐柱

直欞窗

盡間	梢間	次間	明間	次間	梢間	盡間

山西五台山佛光寺大殿 ·平面圖樣·

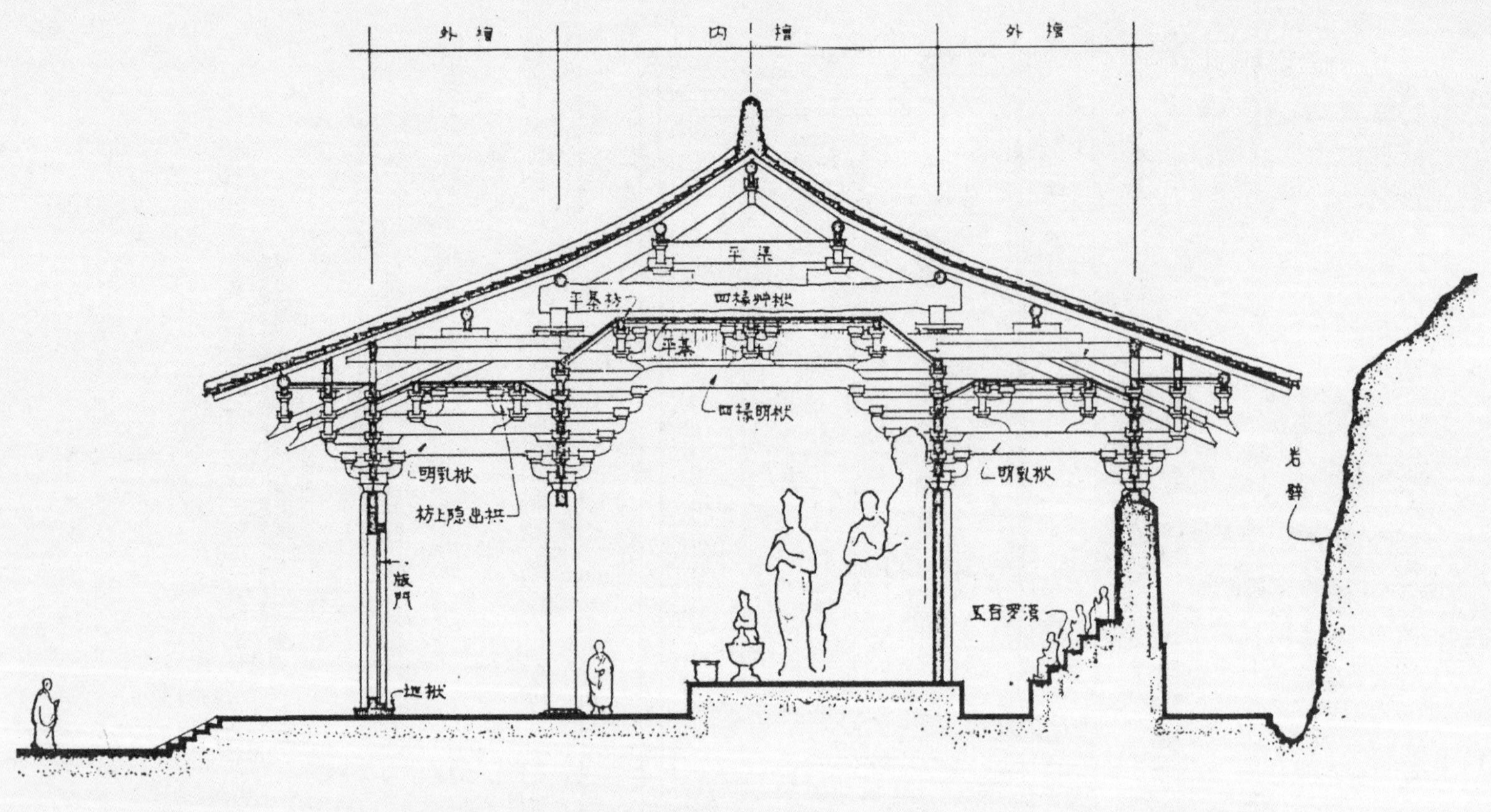

山西五台山佛光寺大殿　當心間横断面

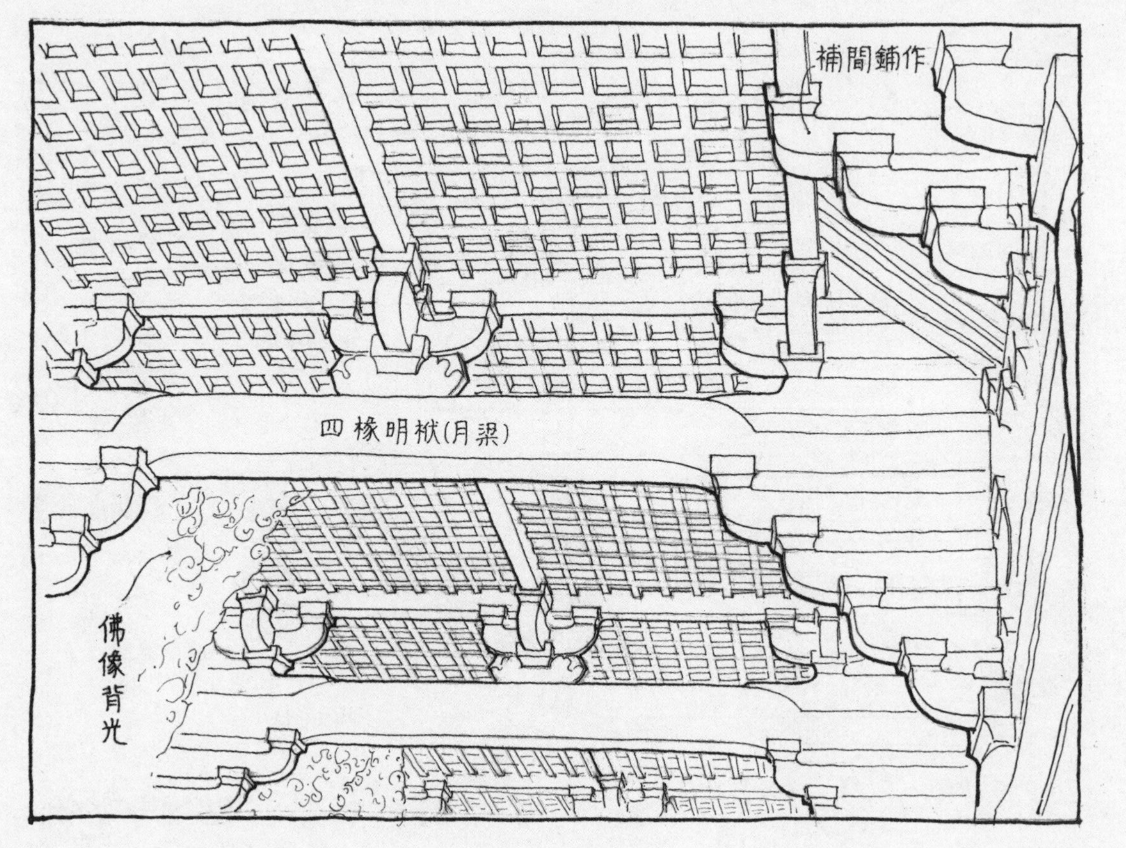

唐山西五台佛光寺大殿

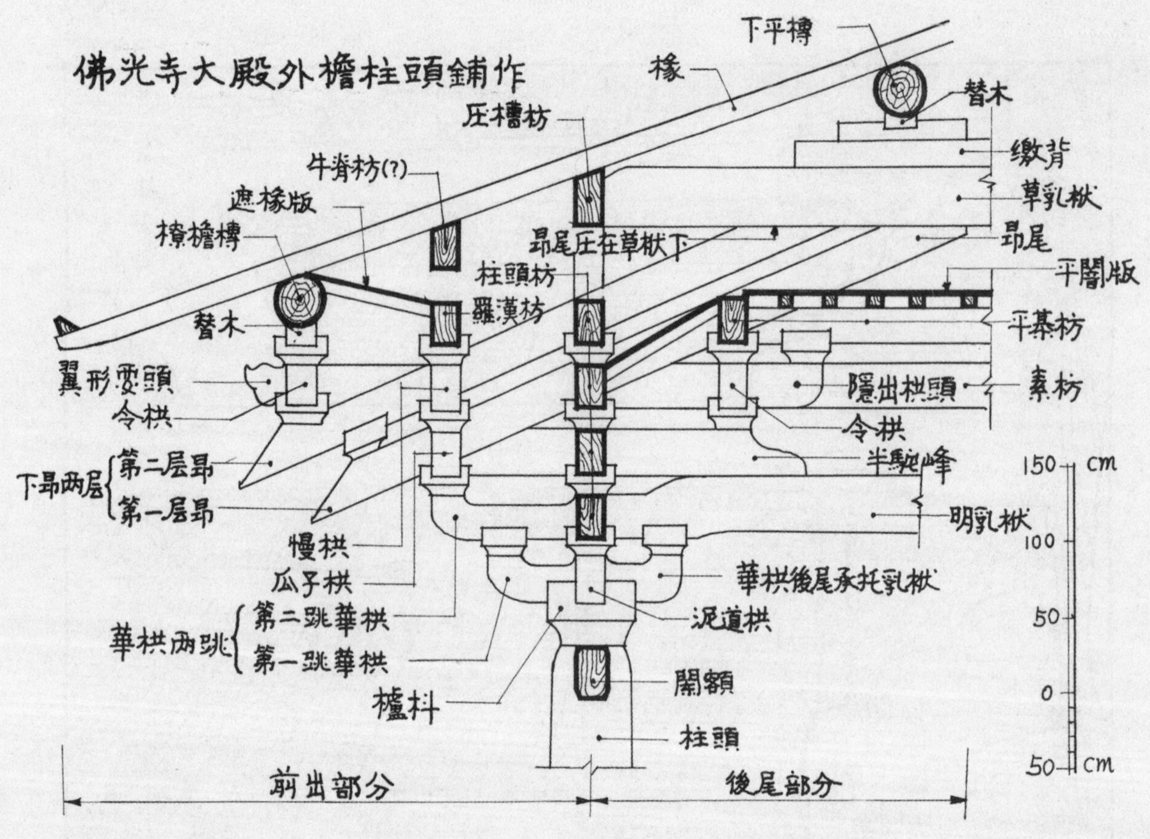
佛光寺大殿外檐柱頭鋪作
下平槫
椽
替木
压槽枋
縩背
牛脊枋(?)
草乳栿
遮椽版
橑檐槫
昂尾压在草栿下
昂尾
柱頭枋
平闇版
替木
羅漢枋
平棊枋
翼形耍頭
隱出栱頭
素枋
令栱
令栱
半駝峰
第二层昂
下昂两层
第一层昂
明乳栿
慢栱
瓜子栱
華栱後尾承托乳栿
第二跳華栱
泥道栱
華栱两跳
第一跳華栱
闌額
櫨枓
柱頭
前出部分
後尾部分
150 cm
100
50
0
50 cm

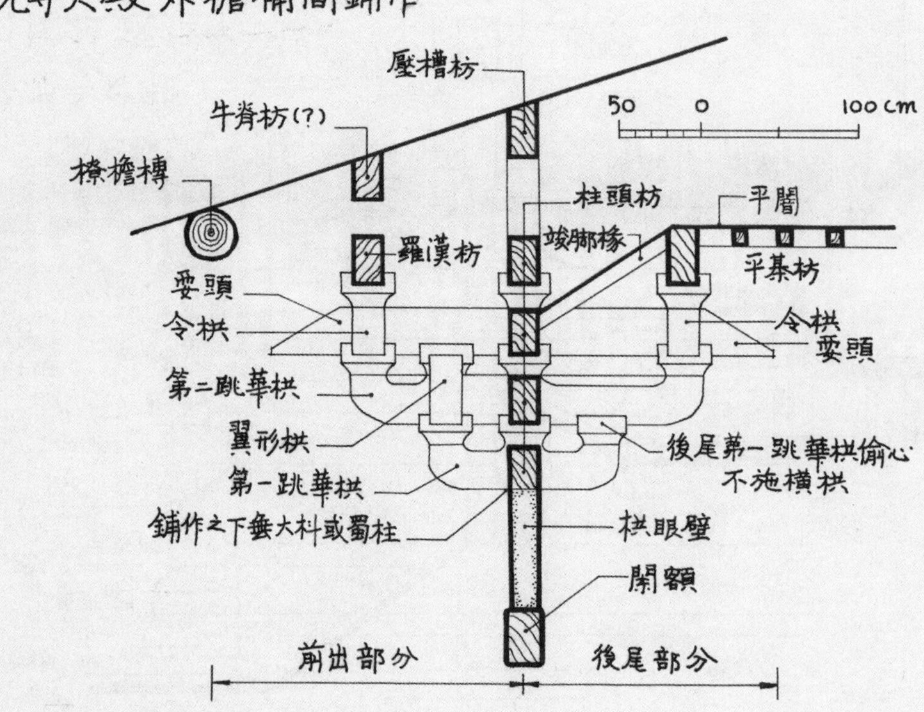
佛光寺大殿外檐補間鋪作
壓槽枋
牛脊枋(?)
橑檐榑
50
0
100 cm
柱頭枋
平闇
峻脚椽
羅漢枋
平棊枋
耍頭
令栱
令栱
耍頭
第二跳華栱
翼形栱
後尾第一跳華栱偷心
不施橫栱
第一跳華栱
鋪作之下垂大枓或蜀柱
栱眼壁
闌額
前出部分
後尾部分

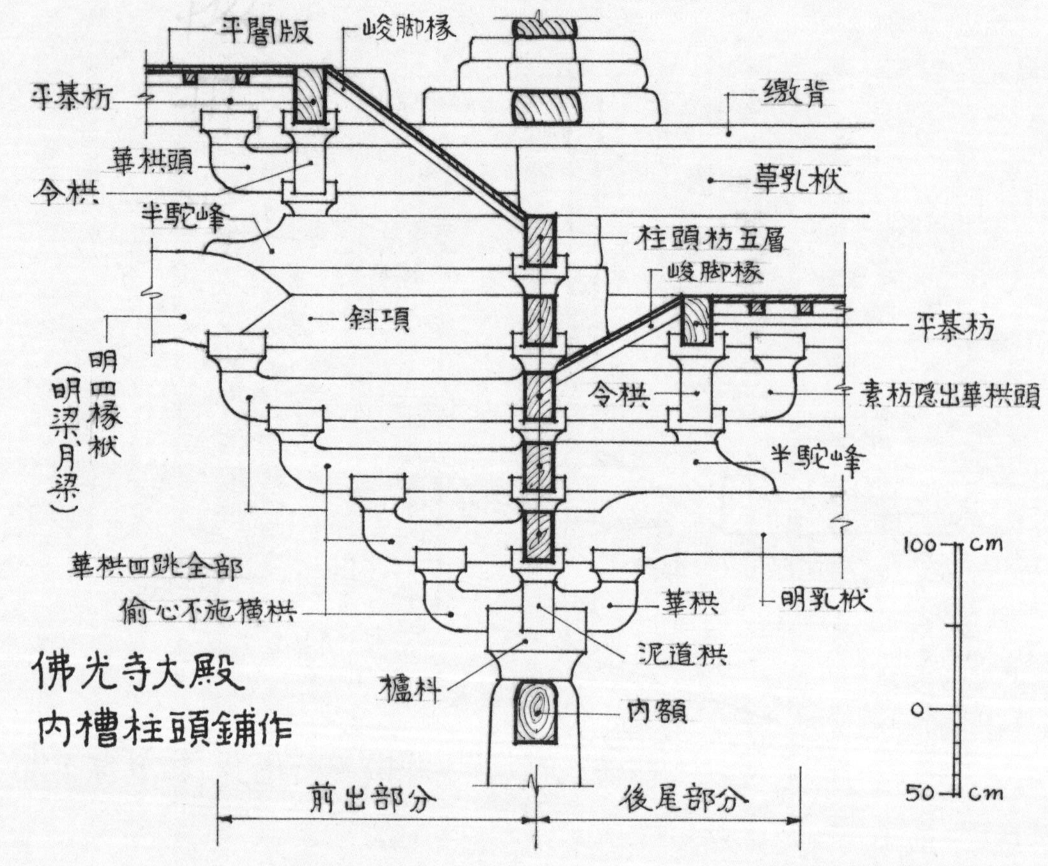

佛光寺大殿
內槽柱頭鋪作

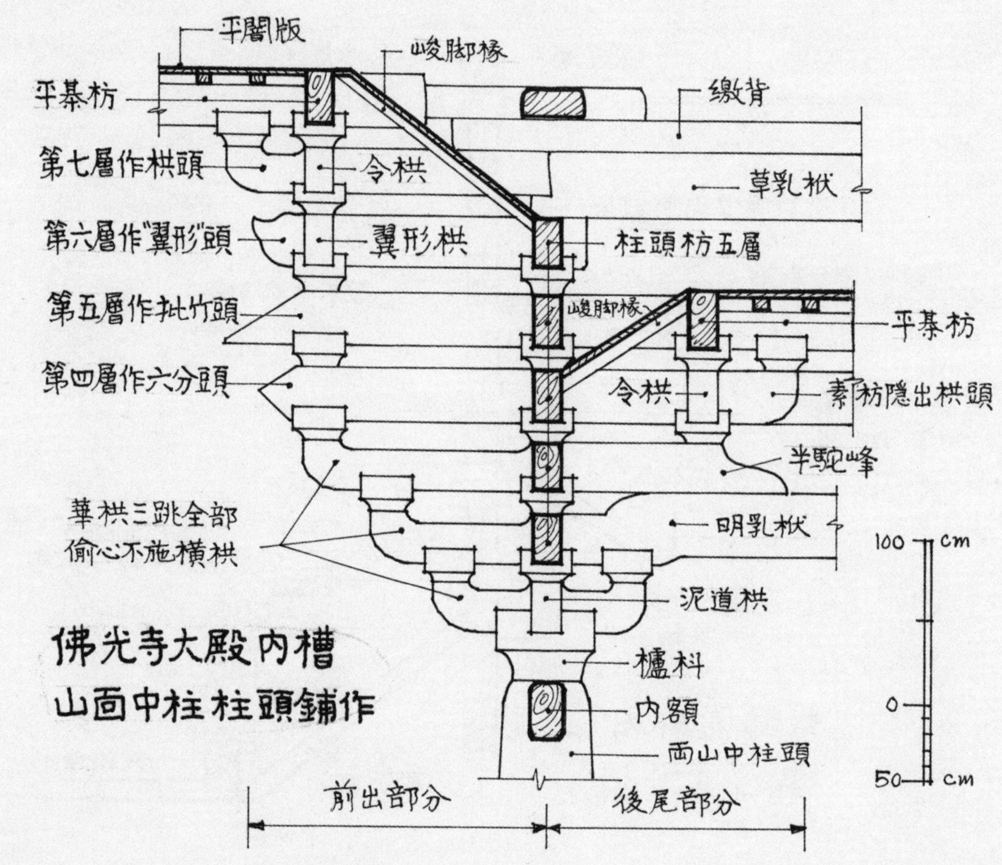
平闇版
峻脚椽
平棊枋
繳背
第七層作栱頭
令栱
草乳栿
第六層作"翼形"頭
翼形栱
柱頭枋五層
第五層作批竹頭
峻脚椽
平棊枋
第四層作六分頭
令栱
素枋隱出栱頭
半駝峰
華栱三跳全部
偷心不施横栱
明乳栿
泥道栱
櫨枓
内額
兩山中柱頭
前出部分
後尾部分
100 cm
0
50 cm
佛光寺大殿内槽
山面中柱柱頭鋪作

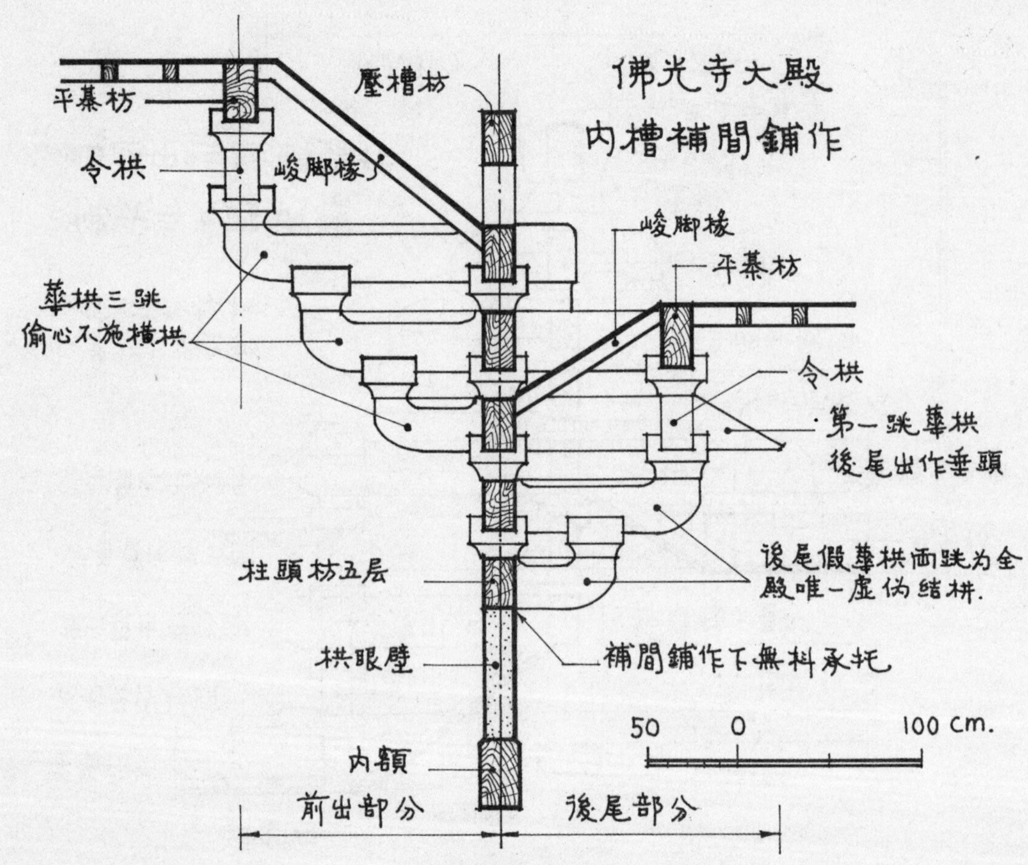
佛光寺大殿
内槽補間鋪作
平棊枋
令栱
峻脚椽
壓槽枋
峻脚椽
平棊枋
華栱三跳
偷心不施横栱
令栱
第一跳華栱
後尾出作垂頭
柱頭枋五层
後尾假華栱而跳为全
殿唯一虚伪結构.
栱眼壁
補間鋪作下無枓承托
50
0
100 cm.
内額
前出部分
後尾部分

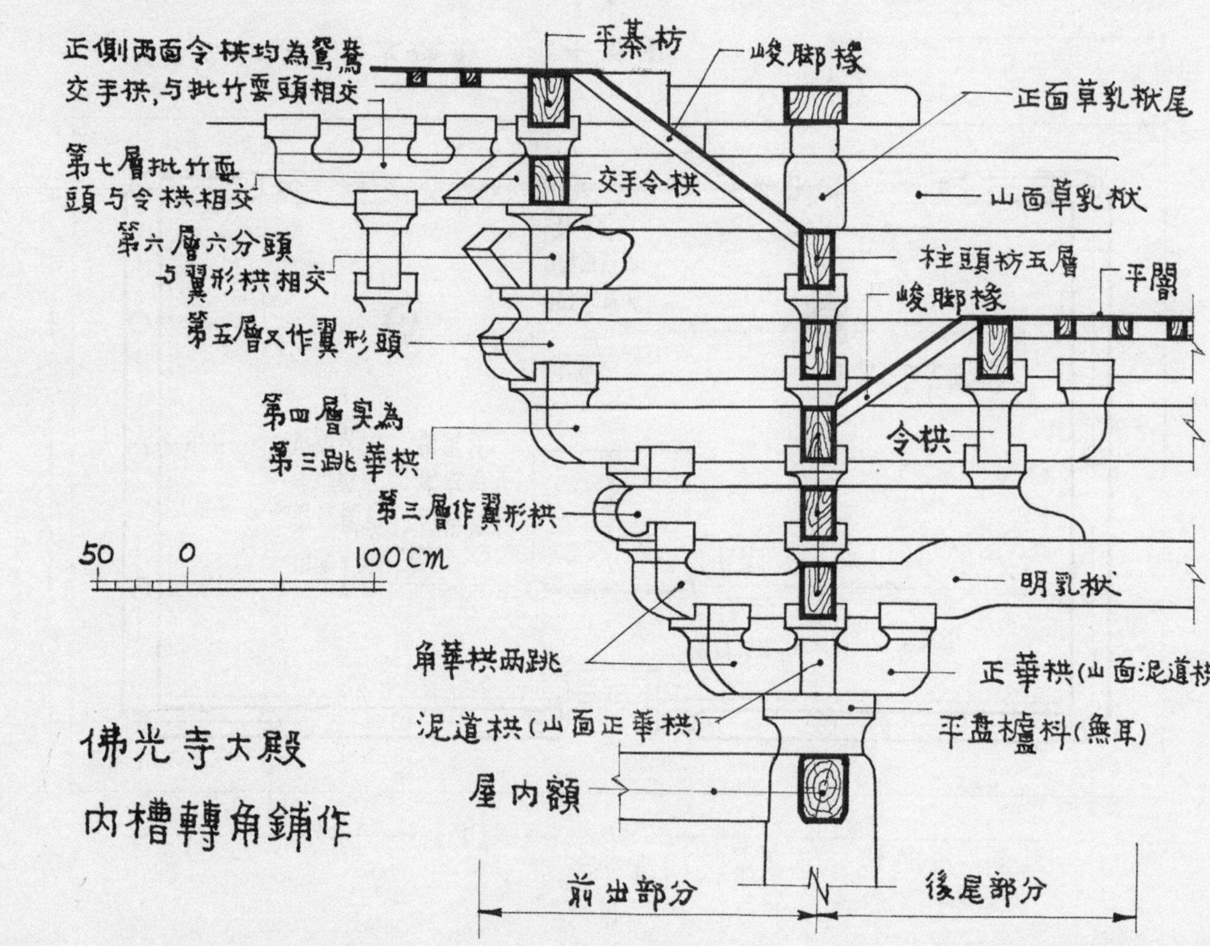

佛光寺大殿
内槽轉角鋪作

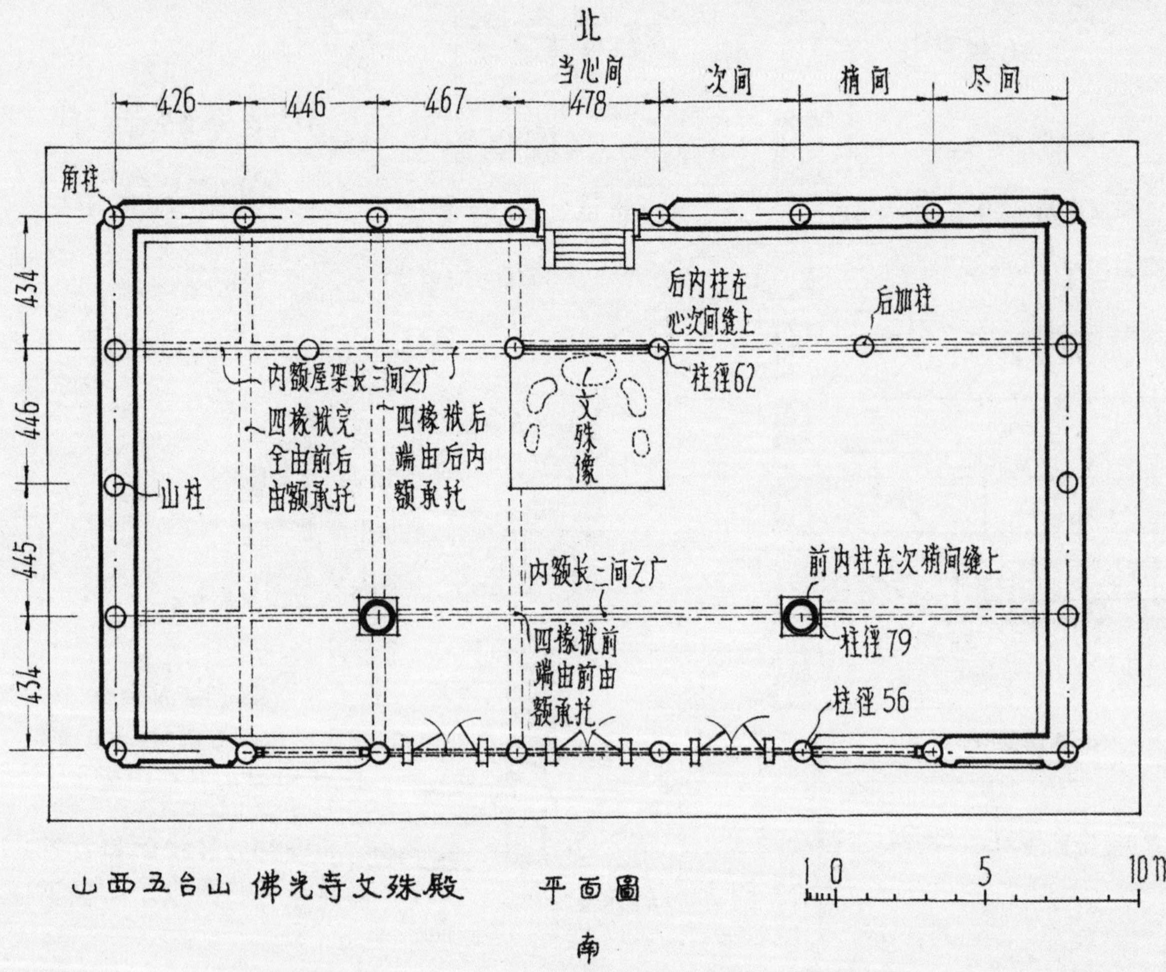

山西五台山 佛光寺文殊殿　平面圖

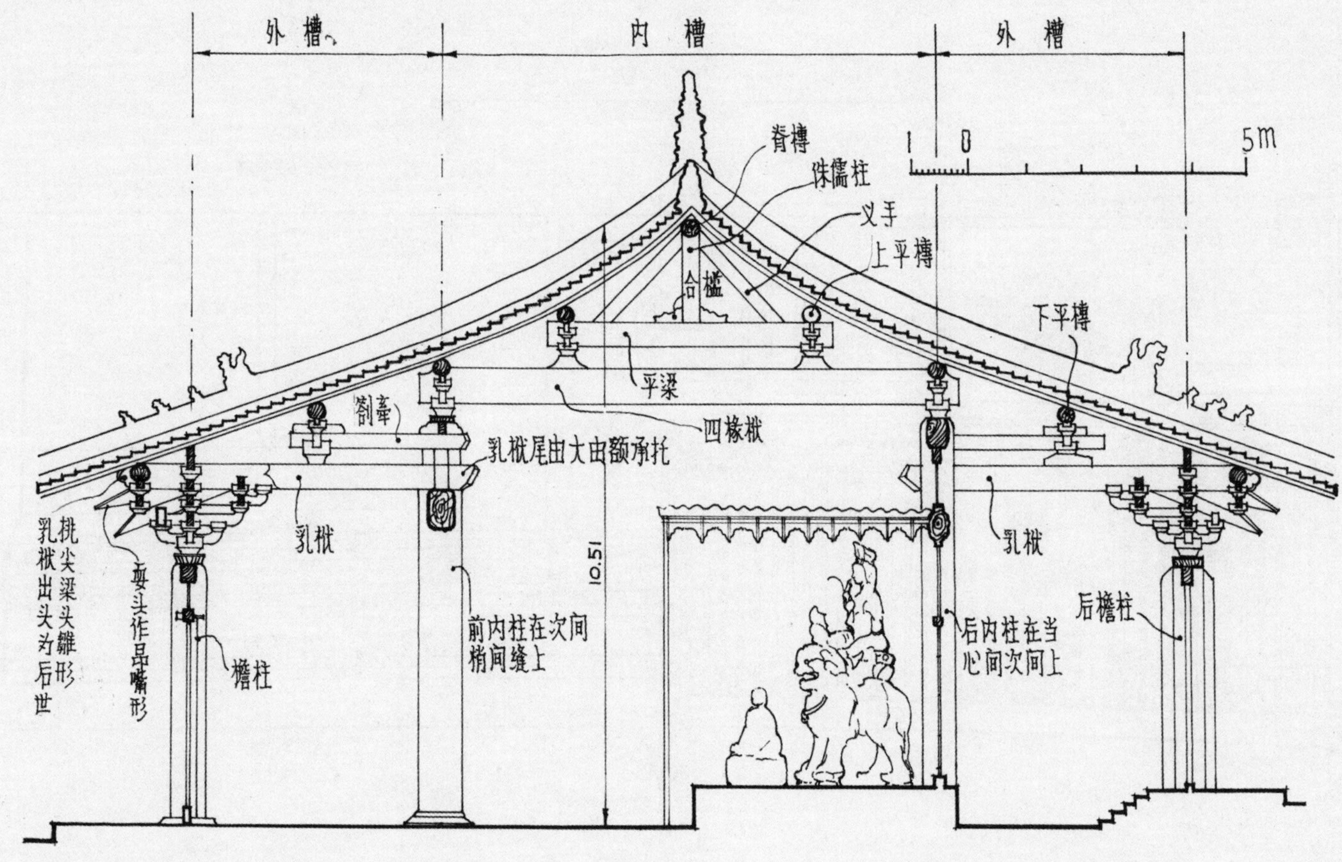
外槽
内槽
外槽
1 0 5m
脊槫
侏儒柱
叉手
上平槫
合楷
下平槫
平梁
四椽栿
劄牵
乳栿尾出大由额承托
乳栿
乳栿
挑尖梁头雏形
乳栿出头为后世
耍头作昂嘴形
檐柱
前内柱在次间
梢间缝上
10.51
后内柱在当
心间次间上
后檐柱

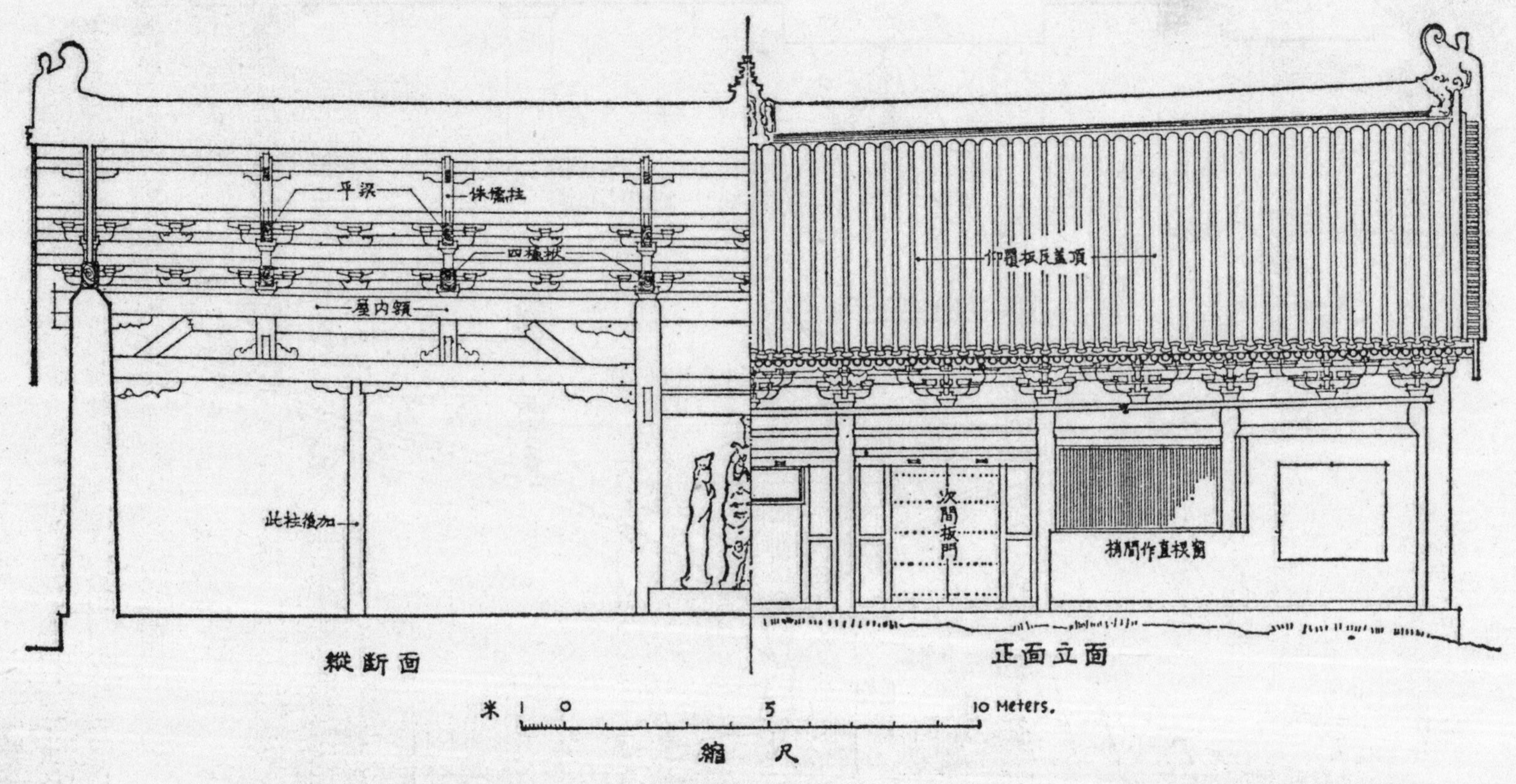
平梁
侏儒柱
四椽栿
屋内額
仰覆板瓦蓋頂
此柱後加
次間板門
梢間作直棂窗
縱斷面
正面立面
米 1 0 5 10 Meters.
縮尺

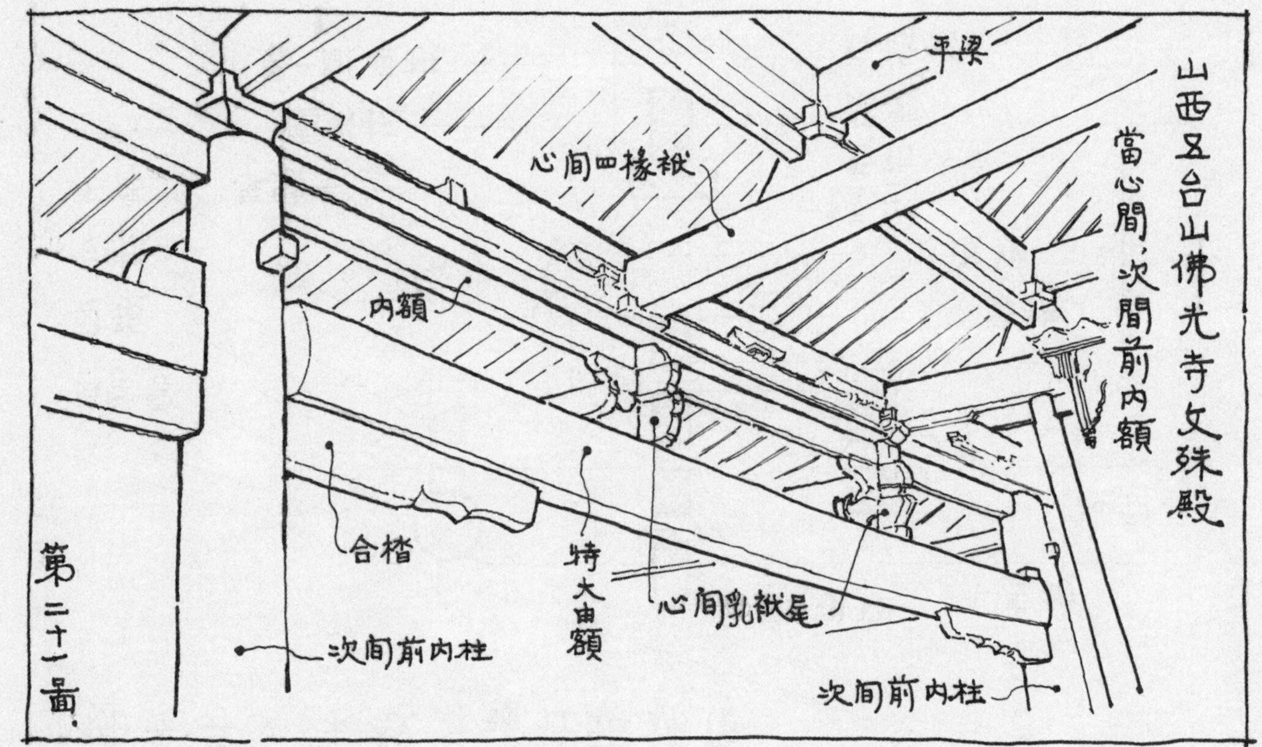

山西五台山佛光寺文殊殿
當心間，次間前內額
平梁
心间四椽栿
內額
合楷
特大由額
心间乳栿尾
次间前内柱
次间前内柱
第二十一圖

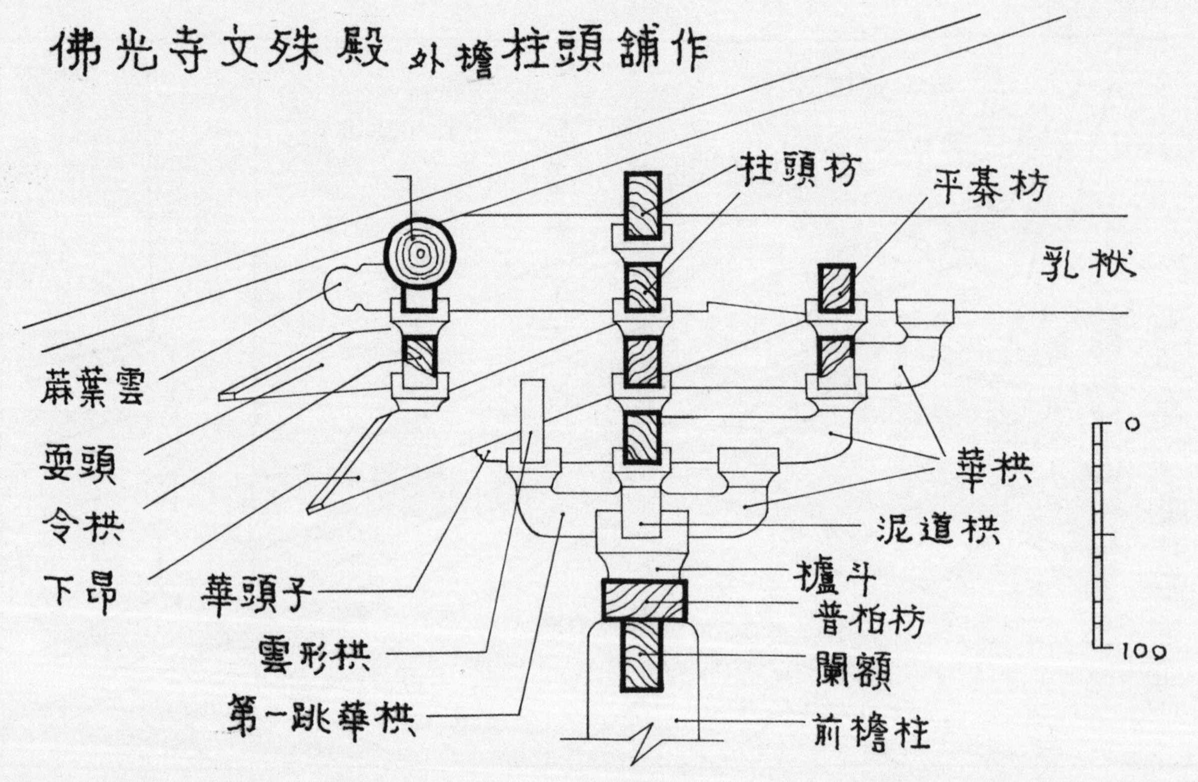
佛光寺文殊殿外檐柱頭鋪作
柱頭枋
平棊枋
乳栿
麻葉雲
耍頭
令栱
下昂
華栱
泥道栱
華頭子
櫨斗
普柏枋
雲形栱
闌額
第一跳華栱
前檐柱
0
100

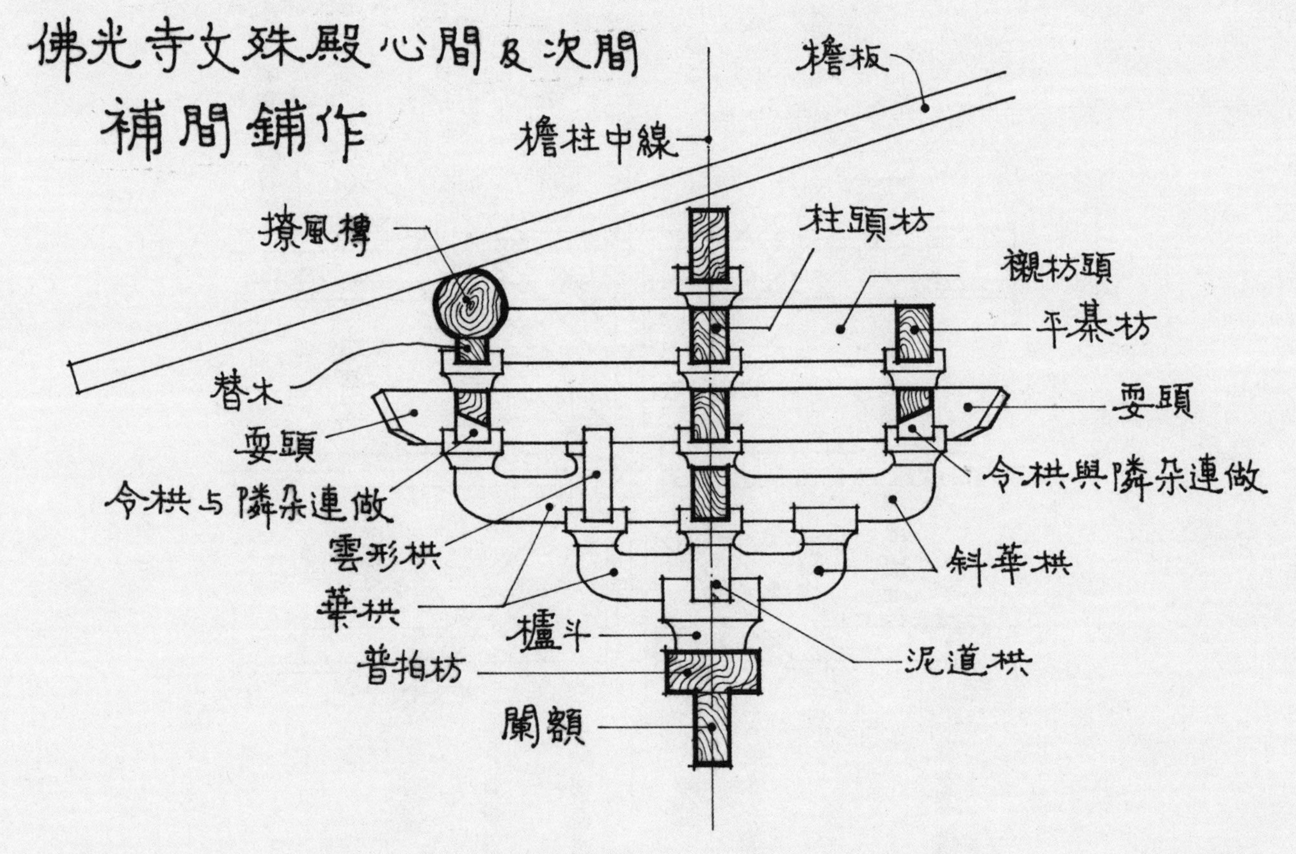
佛光寺文殊殿心間及次間
補間鋪作
檐板
檐柱中線
撩風槫
柱頭枋
襯枋頭
平棊枋
替木
耍頭
耍頭
令栱与隣朵連做
令栱與隣朵連做
雲形栱
斜華栱
華栱
櫨斗
泥道栱
普拍枋
闌額

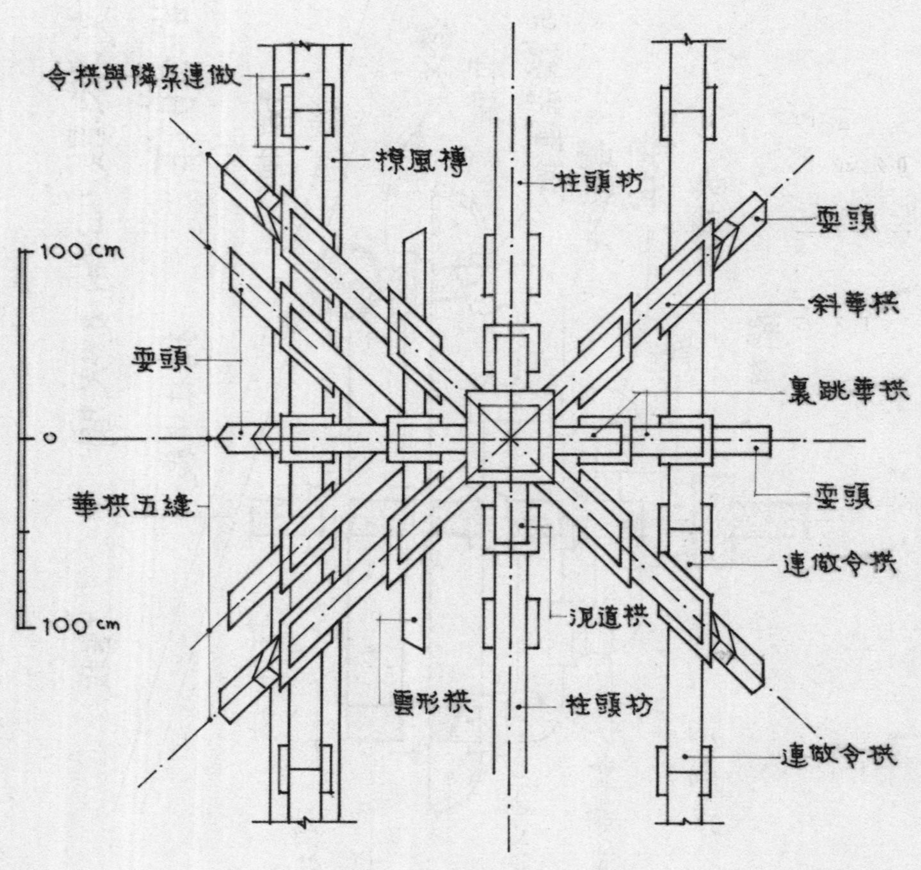

令栱與隣朵連做
橑風槫
柱頭枋
耍頭
斜華栱
100 cm
耍頭
裏跳華栱
0
耍頭
華栱五縫
連做令栱
泥道栱
100 cm
雲形栱
柱頭枋
連做令栱

佛光寺文殊殿前檐梢間及盡間 補間鋪作

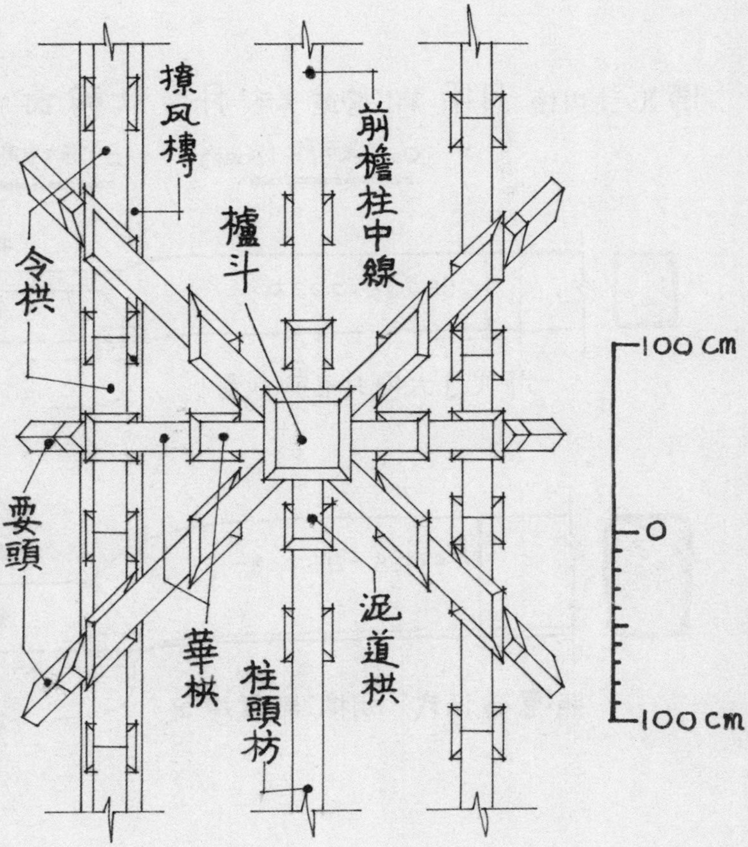

撩风槫
前檐柱中線
令拱
櫨斗
要頭
華栱
柱頭枋
泥道栱
100 cm
0
100 cm

佛光寺内檐月梁與"營造法式"月梁比較圖 假定用同等材

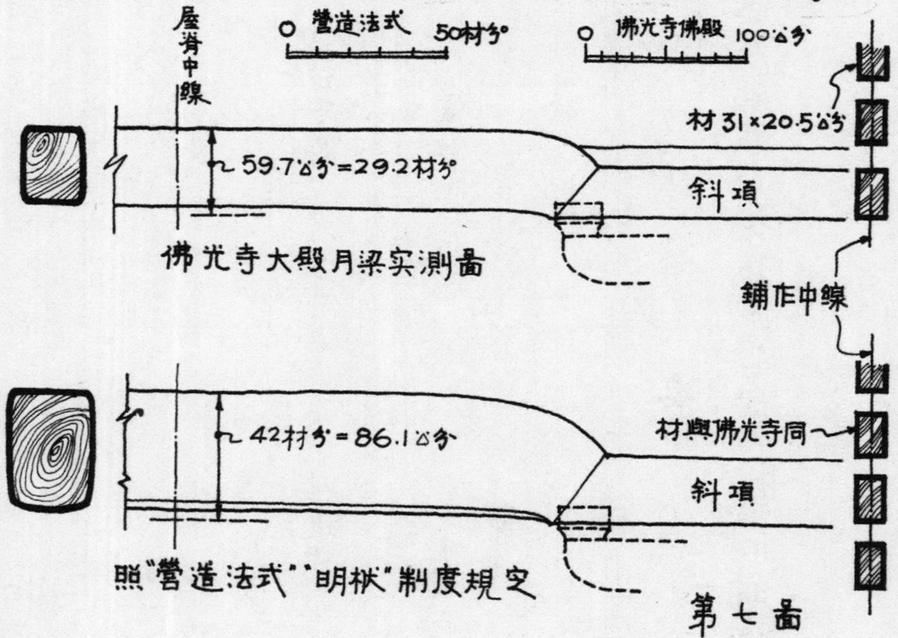

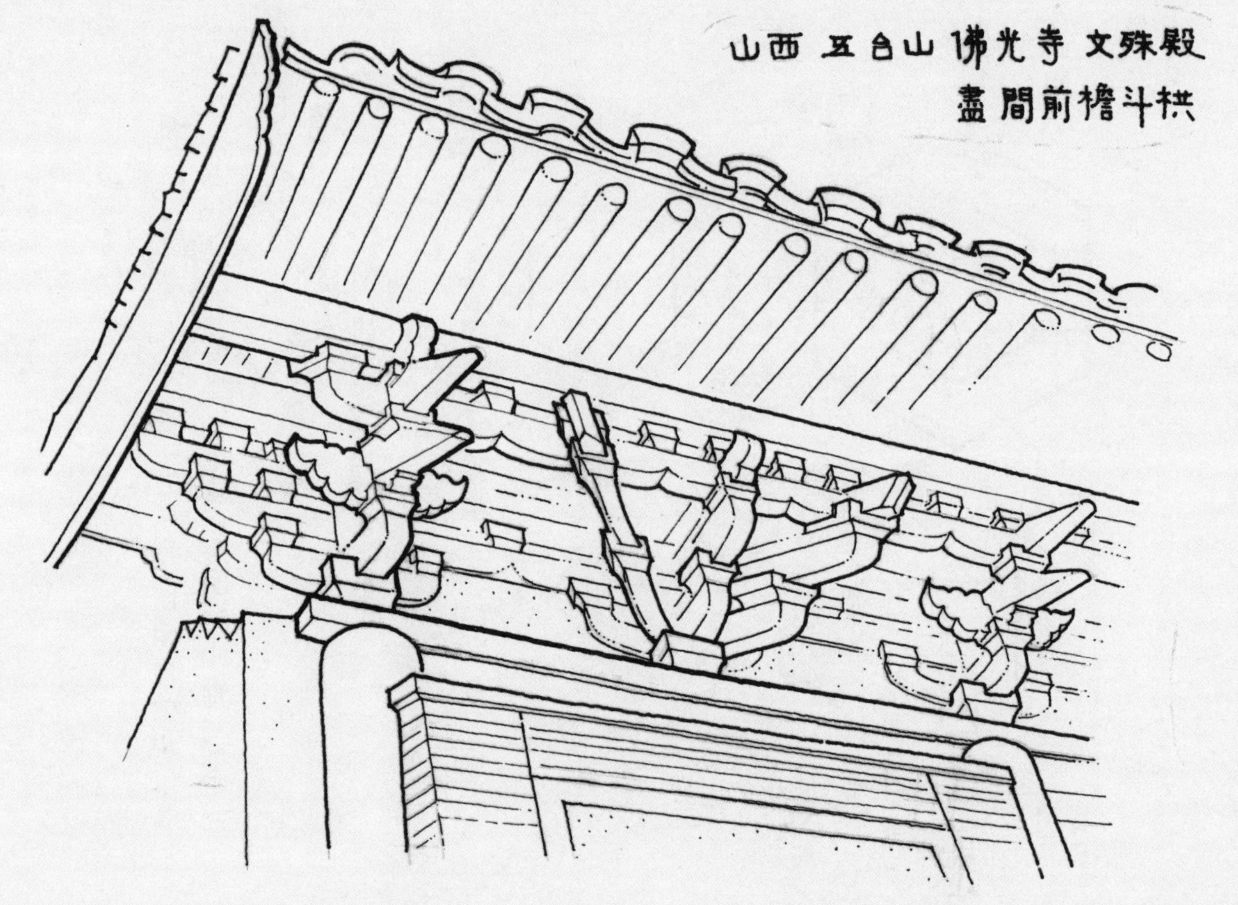

山西 五台山 佛光寺 文殊殿
盡間前檐斗拱

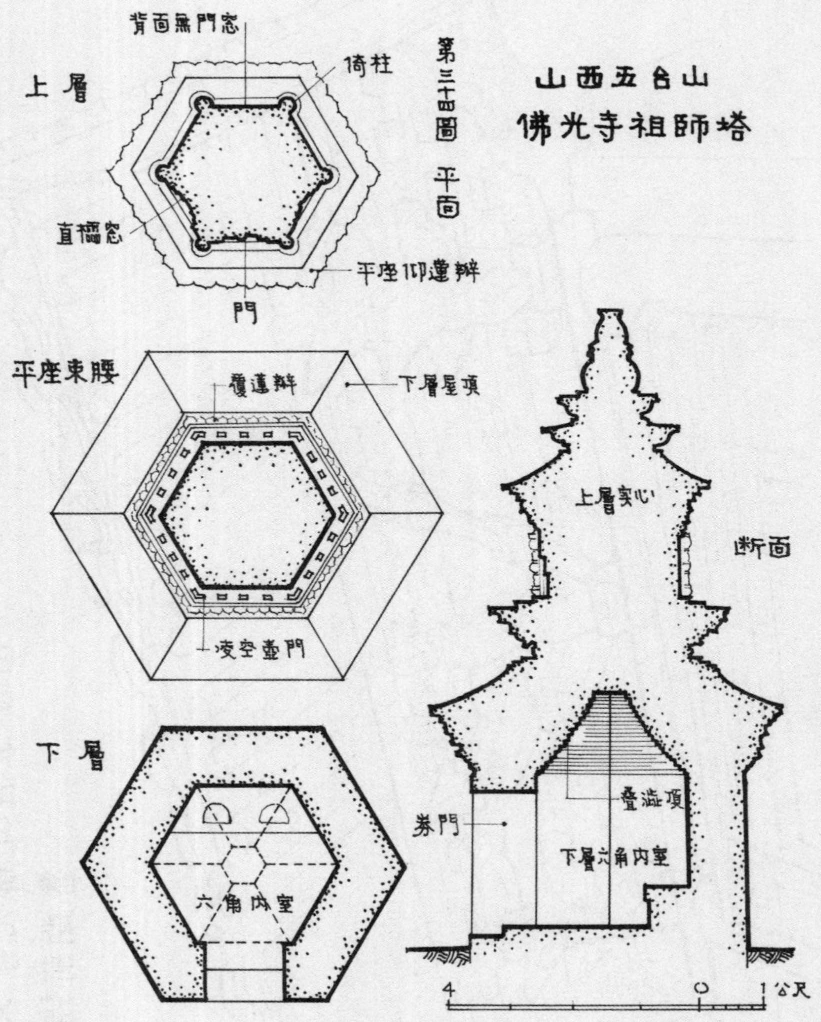

第三十四圖 平面

山西五台山
佛光寺祖師塔

Art and Architecture

[1947]

中国的艺术与建筑[1]

I. ARCHITECTURE

Although the ancient Chinese never considered architecture a fine art, in China as in the West it has been the mother of the fine arts. It was through the medium of architectural decoration that painting and sculpture matured and gained recognition as independent arts.

Ⓐ Technique and Forms

The architecture of China is an indigenous system of construction which was conceived in the dawn of Chinese civilization and has been developing ever since. Its characteristic form is a timber skeleton or framework standing on a masonry platform and covered by a pitched roof with overhanging eaves. The spaces between the posts and lintels of the framework may be filled in with curtain walls whose sole function is to separate one portion of the building from another, or the interior from the exterior. The walls of the Chinese building, unlike those of the conventional European building, are free from the weight of the upper floors and the roof, and may be installed or omitted as required. By adjusting the proportion of the open and walled-in spaces, the architect may admit or exclude just the amount of light and air appropriate to any purpose and to any climate. This high degree of adaptability has enabled Chinese architecture to follow Chinese civilization wherever it has spread.

As the Chinese system of construction evolved and matured, rules like the orders of classical European architecture were developed to govern the proportion of the different members of the building. In buildings of a monumental character the order is enriched by tou-kung, sets of brackets on top of the columns supporting the beams within and roof eaves without. Each set consists of tiers of outstretching arms called kung, cushioned with trapezoidal blocks called tou. The tou-kung are functional members of the structure, carrying the beams and permitting the deep overhang of the eaves. As they evolved, they assumed different shapes and proportions. In earlier periods they were simple and large in proportion to the size of the building; later they became smaller and smaller and more complicated. Hence they serve as a convenient index to the date of construction.

The planning problem of the Chinese architect is not that of partitioning a single building, since the framing system makes the interior partition mere screens, but of placing the various buildings of which a Chinese house is composed.

壹 建筑

中国古人从未把建筑当成一种艺术，但像在西方一样，建筑一直是艺术之母。正是通过作为建筑装饰，绘画与雕塑走向成熟，并被认作是独立的艺术。

❶ 技术与形式

中国建筑是一种土生土长的构筑系统，它在中国文明萌生时期即已出现，其后不断得到发展。它的特征性形式是立在砖石基座上的木骨架即木框架，上面有带挑檐的坡屋顶。木框架的梁与柱之间，可以筑幕墙，幕墙的唯一功能是划分内部空间及区别内外。中国建筑的墙与欧洲传统房屋中的墙不同，它不承受屋顶或上面楼层的重量，因而可随需要而设或不设。建筑设计者通过调节开敞与封闭的比例，控制光线和空气的流入量，一切全看需要及气候而定。高度的适应性使中国建筑随着中国文明的传播而扩散。

当中国的构筑系统演进和成熟后，像欧洲古典建筑柱式那样的规则产生出来，它们控制建筑物各部分的比例。在纪念性的建筑上，建筑规范由于采用斗拱而得到丰富。斗拱由一系列置于柱顶的托木组成，在内部它承托木梁，在外部它支承屋檐。一攒斗拱中包括几层横向伸出的臂，叫“拱”，梯形的垫木叫“斗”。斗拱本是结构中有功能作用的部件，它承托木梁又使屋檐伸出得远一些。在演进过程中，斗拱有多种多样的形式和比例。早期的斗拱形式简单，在房屋尺寸中占的比例较大；后来斗拱变得小而复杂。因此，斗拱可作为房屋建造时代的方便的指示物。

由于框架结构使内墙变为隔断，所以中国建筑的平面布置不在于单幢房屋之内部划分，而在于多座不同房屋的布局安排，中国的住宅是由这些房屋组成的。

These are usually grouped around courtyards, and a house may consist of an indefinite number of such courtyards. The principal buildings are usually oriented toward the south, so that a maximum amount of sunlight can be admitted in winter, while the summer sun is cut off by the overhanging eaves. Apart from the variations required by special topographical conditions, the same general principles apply to all domestic, official, and religious architecture.

Ⓑ Historical Development

The oldest architectural remains in China are some tombs of the Han Dynasty. Both the burial chamber and the ch'üeh, or gate piers, include translations into stone of timber construction, showing a highly accomplished carpenter's art rendered by an equally masterful touch of the sculptor's chisel. The important role played by the tou-kung is seen even in that early period.

No timber structure built during the long interval up to the middle of the 8th century AD has as yet been found standing in China. Yet glimpses of the outward appearance of such structures may be gathered from the details of construction in some of the cave temples and from the paintings on their walls. In the caves of Yun-kang, near Ta-t'ung, Shansi, constructed about 452–494 AD, and in those of Hsiangtang Shan, on the border of Honan and Hopeh Provinces, and T'ien-lung Shan, near Yanku (Tai-yuan), Shansi, which were built about 550–618 AD, the facades and interiors are treated architecturally, carved from the rock cliffs to emulate the contemporary timber structures. On the tympanum of the west portal of the Tz'u-en Ssu pagoda (701–704 AD), in Sian (Chang'an), Shensi, is an engraving showing in accurate detail a Buddhist temple hall. The frescoes on the walls of the 6th to 11th centuries caves at Tun-huang, Kansu, are paradise scenes with elaborate architectural backgrounds. These relics are graphic records of the architecture of a period that has left us no standing specimens. Here, too, we notice the importance of the tou-kung, whose evolution may be clearly traced.

Such indirect evidence of the character of early Chinese architecture is well supported by groups of buildings still standing in Japan. They were erected in the Suiko (Asuka), Hakuho, Tempyo, and Konin (Jogan) periods, corresponding to the Sui and T'ang Dynasties in China. In fact, until the middle of the 19th century the architecture of Japan reflected as in a mirror the changing styles of continental builders. The early Japanese structures may justifiably be called colonial Chinese, and some are actually known to have been erected by continental architects.

房屋通常围绕院子安排。一所住宅可以包含数量不定的多个院子。主房大都朝南，冬季可射入最多的太阳光，在夏天阳光为挑檐所阻挡。除了因地形导致的变体，这个原则适用于所有的住宅、官府和宗教建筑物。

❷ 历史的演变

中国最古的建筑遗存是一些汉代的坟墓。墓室及墓前的门墩——阙，虽是石造的，形式却是仿木结构，高起的石雕显现着同样高超的木匠技艺。斗拱在如此早期的建筑中已具有重要作用。

在中国至今没有发现存在公元 8 世纪中叶以前漫长时期里所造的木构建筑。但从一些石窟寺的构造细部和它们墙上的壁画我们可以大略知晓 8 世纪中期以前木构建筑的外貌。山西大同附近的云冈石窟建于公元 452 年至 494 年；河南、河北交界处的响堂山石窟和山西太原的天龙山石窟建于公元 550 年至 618 年间，它们是在石崖上凿成的佛国净土，外观和内部都当作建筑物来处理，模仿当时的木构建筑。陕西西安慈恩寺大雁塔西门门楣石刻（公元 701 年至 704 年）准确地显示出一座佛寺大殿。甘肃敦煌公元 6 世纪到 11 世纪的洞窟的壁画中画的佛国净土，建筑背景极其精致。这些遗迹是未留下实物的时代的建筑状况的图像记录。在这样的图像中，我们也看到斗拱的重要性，并且可以从中追踪到斗拱的演变轨迹。

这些中国早期建筑特点的间接证据可从日本现存的建筑群得到支持。它们造于推古（飞鸟）、白凤、天平和弘仁（贞观）时期，[2] 相当于中国隋朝和唐朝。事实上，到 19 世纪中期为止，日本的建筑像镜子一样映射着中国建筑不断变化着的风格。早先的日本建筑可以被称之为中国殖民式建筑，而且那里有一些建筑物还真是出于中国匠人之手。

Earliest of these is the Horyuji group, near Nara, which was constructed by Korean builders and completed in 607 AD. Another is the Kondo of the Todaiji, Nara, built by the Chinese monk Ganjin (Chien-chen, died 763 AD) in 759 AD.

The oldest extant wooden structure in China itself is the main hall of the Buddhist temple Fo-kuang Ssu, Wu-t'ai Shan, Shansi. It is a one-story building of seven bays, with tou-kung of gigantic size, showing an unparalleled vigor and dignity in proportion and design. The temple was built in 857 AD, shortly after the nationwide Buddhist persecution of 845 AD. It is the only wooden structure known to date from the T'ang Dynasty, the golden age of Chinese art. The hall houses specimens of sculpture and calligraphy and a fresco frieze, all of the same period. The congregation in one spot of all the major arts of T'ang date makes this temple and its contents a unique treasure in China.

Wooden structures of later periods are found in increasing numbers. A few of the more outstanding monuments may be chosen to represent the Sung Dynasty, together with the contemporaneous Liao and Chin Dynasties.

The Hall of Kuan-yin (Goddess of Mercy) of the Tu-lo Ssu, Chi Hsien, Hopeh, was built in 984 AD. It is a two-story structure containing an eleven-headed Kuan-yin, standing upright. A mezzanine story is inserted between the two main stories, so that the structure is actually built of three superposed "orders." Here the function of the tou-kung is shown to best advantage.

The group of buildings at Tsin-tz'u, near Yanku, was built about 1025. The two principal buildings are each one story in height, but the main hall has double-decked eaves. The main hall of the Hua-yen Ssu, Ta-t'ung, is a huge single-story structure with single-decked eaves. Built about 1090, it is one of the largest Buddhist structures in China. Of considerably later date (1260) is the main hall of the Pei-yueh Miao, Chuyang, Hopeh. The inner structural members supporting the upper part of the roof have been extensively rebuilt, but the lower part and the outward appearance of the building as a whole are essentially unaltered.

A comparative study of these few examples reveals that the tou-kung tends to become smaller and smaller in proportion to the building. Another common characteristic is an increase in the height of the columns toward the corners of the building. This latter refinement brings about a gentle curvature of the eave line (with the exception of the Hua-yen Ssu hall), and of the roof ridge, giving an appearance of elegance.

最早的是奈良附近的法隆寺建筑群，由朝鲜工匠建造，公元 607 年建成。奈良唐招提寺金堂是中国鉴真和尚（公元 763 年去世）于公元 759 年建造的[3]。

中国现存最早的木构建筑是山西省五台山佛光寺大殿。它单层七间，斗拱雄大，比例和设计无比地雄健庄严。大殿建于公元 857 年，在公元 845 年全国性灭法后数年。佛光寺大殿是唯一留存下来的唐代建筑，而唐代是中国艺术史上的黄金时代。寺内的雕塑、壁画饰带和书法都是当时的作品，这些唐代艺术品聚集在一起，使这座建筑物成为中国独一无二的艺术珍品。

唐朝以后的木构建筑保留的数量逐渐增多。一些很杰出的建筑物可以作为宋代和同时期的辽代与金代的代表。

河北省蓟县独乐寺观音阁建于公元 984 年。这是一座两层建筑，当中立着一座十一面观音像。两个楼层之间又有一个暗层，实际是三层。在观音阁上，斗拱的作用发挥到极致。

太原附近晋祠的建筑群建于公元 1025 年，两座主要建筑物都是单层，但主殿为重檐。大同华严寺大殿是一座巨大的单层单檐建筑，建于公元 1090 年，是中国最大的佛教建筑物之一。许多年后的公元 1260 年，河北曲阳的北岳庙建成，它的屋顶上部构件经过大量改建，但其下部及外观整体基本未变。

对上述这些建筑物的比较研究表明，斗拱与建筑物整体的比例越来越小。另一共同特点是越往建筑物的两边柱子越高。这一细致的处理使檐口呈现为轻缓的曲线（华严寺大殿是个例外），屋脊也如此，于是建筑物外观变得柔和了。

With the coming of the Ming Dynasty, the subtle refinements disappeared. This trend is especially noticeable in the monuments built under imperial patronage, and is best exemplified in the sacrificial hall at the tomb of Emperor Yung Lo, built in 1425 at Changping, Hopeh, 25 miles (40 km) north of Peking. Here the tou-kung has shrunk to insignificance; its presence can be detected only at close view.

Despite the retrogressive features of individual building of the Ming and Ts'ing Dynasties, we have in the imperial palaces of Peking a superb example of planning on the grandest scale, showing the aptitude of the Chinese for conceiving and executing a design of colossal proportions. The hundreds of audience halls and apartments within the Forbidden City, a walled enclosure measuring about 3350 feet (1020 meters) by 2490 feet (760 meters), are mainly structures of the late Ming and the Ts'ing Dynasties. The entire area was conceived as a single architectural unit, with one main axis dominating the Forbidden City and the entire Imperial City surrounding it. The halls, pavilions, verandas, and gates are grouped in innumerable courtyards connected by colonnades. The buildings themselves are raised on white marble terraces. Columns and walls are generally painted red, while the tou-kung are decorated with intricate designs in blue, green, and gold, forming a cool belt which accentuates the deep shady overhang of the eaves. The whole structure is crowned by a roof of glazed yellow or green tiles. The ingenuity of the Chinese in applying color to architecture on an all-inclusive scale has never been equaled.

C Multi-storied Timber Structures

Because of the limitations of the material, high structures in timber are rare. The best known is the Ch'i-nien Tien of the Temple of Heaven, Peking. It is a building of circular plan, standing on three tiers of white marble terraces and crowned by three tiers of blue glazed tile roofs, the uppermost of which converges into a cone whose apex is about 108 feet (33 meters) above the ground.

The finest example of multi-storied timber construction in China is the little-known wooden pagoda of Ying Hsien, Shansi. Erected in 1056, it is a five-story structure with four additional mezzanine stories, built on an octagonal plan. Each of its main and mezzanine stories is a complete "order" in itself. The pagoda as a whole therefore comprises nine superposed "orders." Scarcely any of its members is idle: every timber has its part in supporting the building. The top roof, which is an octagonal cone, is surmounted by a wrought iron spire whose tip is 215 feet (65 meters) above the ground. Although most of the early pagodas were of wood, this is the only one of its kind still standing in China.

到了明朝，精巧的处理消失。这个趋势在皇家的纪念性建筑中尤其明显。建于公元 1425 年、北平以北 40 公里的河北省昌平县明朝永乐皇帝陵墓的大殿是突出的例子。它的斗拱退缩到无足轻重的地步，非近观无法看见。

虽然明、清两代的个体建筑退步，但北平故宫是宏伟的大尺度布局的佳例，显示了中国人构想和实现大范围规划的才能。紫禁城用大墙包围，面积为 3350 英尺 × 2490 英尺（1020 米 × 760 米），其中有数百座殿堂和居住房屋。它们主要是明、清两代的建筑。紫禁城是一个整体。一条中轴线贯穿紫禁城和围绕它的都城。殿堂、亭、轩和门围着数不清的院子布置，并用廊子连接起来。建筑物立在数层白色大理石台基上。柱子和墙面一般是刷成红色的。斗拱用蓝、绿和金色的复杂图案装饰起来，由此形成冷色的圈带，使檐下更为幽暗，显得檐部挑出益加深远。整个房屋覆在黄色或绿色的琉璃瓦顶之下。中国人对房屋整体所作的颜色处理，其精致与独创性举世无双。

❸ 多层木构建筑

因为材料的限制，高层木构建筑很少。北京天坛祈年殿是著名的高大木构建筑。这是一座圆形建筑，立在三层白色大理石基座上，上部为三层蓝色琉璃瓦顶，最高层束成圆锥形。顶尖高于地面 108 英尺（33 米）。

最好的一个多层木构建筑是山西应县木塔，但不那么有名。它建于公元 1056 年，有五个明层和四个暗层，平面为八角形。木塔的每一层，不论明暗，都有完整的木构架。因此全塔由九个构架累积而成。其中每一构件都起支承作用，没有多余之物。塔顶屋面为八角锥体。最上为铁铸塔刹，最高点距地面 215 英尺（65 米）。虽然早期大多数塔为木塔，但应县木塔是该类型的塔的唯一留存者。

Ⓓ Masonry Pagodas

The early wooden pagodas have disappeared, but many of their counterparts in brick—or, in rare cases, stone—have survived the destructive forces of man and nature. Contrary to the general assumption, the design of the Chinese pagoda was not imported from India; rather, it is a cross between the architectural ideas of the two civilizations. The body is entirely Chinese, the Indian element finding expression only in the spire, which is derived, often in much modified form, from the stupa. Many of the pagodas are brick and stone translations of wooden prototypes embodying the traditional Chinese architectural conceptions.

Chinese masonry pagodas may be divided into five principal types:

1. One-story Pagodas

A stupa is a monument marking the site where some Buddhist relic is buried; the tomb stupa of a deceased monk may properly be called a pagoda. Most of the bomb stupas of the 6th to the 12th centuries are small, square pavilion-like structures, one story high, with one or two strings of cornices. The earliest examples of the one-story form is the Ssu-men T'a (which is not a tomb), built in 544 AD near Tsinan, Shantung. More typical is the tomb of Hui-ch'ung at Ling-yen Ssu (mid-7th century), Changching, Shantung.

2. Multi-storied Pagodas

The multi-storied pagoda retains most of the characteristics of the indigenous multi-storied building. Counterparts in wood are still extant in Japan, but only brick structures of this type remain in China. One of the earliest and best examples is the Hsiangchi Ssu pagoda, built in 681 AD, near Sian. It is a square pagoda of 13 stories, 11 of which are intact. The stories are marked by strings of corbelled cornices; and the exterior walls of each story, in addition to their doorways and windows, have delicate reliefs of simple pilasters and architraves supporting tou.

In the Sung Dynasty the octagonal plan became general. Representation of columns or pilasters on the walls is often omitted, but the cornices are in most cases supported by numerous tou-kung. In some instances, such as the twin pagodas of Tso Hsieh, Hopeh (about 1090), the outward appearance of the wooden pagoda has been faithfully reproduced in brick.

3. Multi-eaved Pagodas

The multi-eaved type seems to be a mutation of the single-story pagoda, produced through increasing the number of cornices. In appearance, it presents a high main story crowned by a great number of closely decked eaves. The earliest example is the 12-sided, 15-story pagoda of Sung-yueh Ssu, built about 520 AD, on Sung Shan, a sacred mountain in Honan. During the T'ang Dynasty the square plan was the only one chosen for this type of pagoda. The pagoda of Fa-wang Ssu (about 750 AD), also on Sung Shan, is an excellent example.

❹ 砖石塔

早期木塔大都消失了，留存下来的多是砖塔，也有少数石塔，它们经受了人为的和自然的损害。与一般人的看法相反，中国塔的设计并不是从印度传入的，它们是中国与印度两种文明交会的产物。塔身完全是中国的，印度因素只在塔刹部分可以见到，它来自窣堵坡（stupa），但已大大改变。许多的砖塔或石塔演绎着木塔原型，木塔才是中国传统建筑观念的体现。

中国砖石塔有五大类型：

1. 单层塔 印度的窣堵坡是浮屠遗骸埋葬地的标志，而死去的僧人坟墓窣堵坡就叫“巴高大”(pagoda)[4]。6世纪到12世纪的坟墓窣堵坡大都做成单层小亭子似的建筑，上面有单檐或重檐。山东济南附近的四门塔建于公元544年，是最早的单层塔的例子（它不是坟墓）。更典型的例子是山东长清灵岩寺的慧崇禅师塔墓。

2. 多层塔 多层塔保持中国土生土长多层建筑的许多特点。日本尚有多层木塔屹立至今，中国只保存了此种类型的砖塔。西安附近的香积寺塔，建于公元681年，是最早和最好的例子。那是十三层的方塔，其中十一层保存完好。楼层用叠涩砖檐分划，各层外墙上用浅浮雕显示门洞、窗子之外，尚有简单而精细的浮雕壁柱和额枋，上承大斗。

宋代多八角形塔。墙上的壁柱常被省去。砖檐常由许多斗拱支承。有些例子，如河北涿县的双塔（约公元1090年），是在砖塔上忠实地复制出木塔的外貌。

3. 密檐塔 密檐塔似乎是单层塔而上面有多重檐口所形成的变体。外观上看，它有一个很高的主层，其上为密密的多重檐口。公元520年建的河南佛教圣地嵩山嵩岳寺塔，十二边形，十五层，是最早的实例。在唐代，这种塔全采用四方形。最杰出的一例是法王寺塔（约公元750年），也在河南嵩山。

The octagonal plan was introduced about the middle of the 9th century and after the 11th century became accepted as the standard shape for a pagoda. A great number of pagodas of this type, enriched by tou-kung under the eaves, were built in North China from the 10th to the 12th centuries. The best-known example is the pagoda of the T'ien-ning Ssu, Peking, a structure of the 11th century which has been much repaired.

4. Stupas

The stupa in its original Indian form, though known in China through the early Buddhist missionaries, was never transplanted there. When the stupa finally did become established in China, in much modified form, it arrived through Tibet in conjunction with the spread of Lamaism. The Tibetan stupa is generally bottle-shaped and raised on a high base. The best example is the stupa of Miao-ying Ssu, Peking, which was built in 1260 by Kublai Khan. Later the bottle became more slender, particularly the neck. This part, which originally resembled a truncated cone, came to resemble a smokestack. Typical of the later stupas of the Tibetan type is the one in North Sea Park, Peking, built in 1651.

5. Diamond-based Pagodas

The chin-kang pao-tso t'a, or diamond-based pagoda, consists of a group of pagodas on a common base. Its development was foreshadowed as early as the 8th century in the pagoda group of Yun-chu Ssu, Fangshan, Hopeh, which is composed of a large pagoda and four small ones on a single, very low platform. The form did not reach full architectural maturity until the Ming Dynasty. An excellent example is the Wu-t'a Ssu (Five Pagoda Temple), built in 1473 outside one of the west gates of Peking. This structure reminds the observer in various ways of the 8th-century Borobudur in Java.

Ⓔ P'ai-lou

In most of the towns and on many of the country roads of China are found monumental archways called p'ai-lou. Although the p'ai-lou is considered a purely Chinese architectural concept, one cannot fail to notice an analogy between this form and the gateways of the railings surrounding certain Indian stupas, such as those of Sanchi. In South China stone p'ai-lou are common; in northern cities the street scene is often enlivened by gaily painted timber ones.

9 世纪中有了八角塔，到 11 世纪以后，这已经成了塔的标准型式。从 10 世纪到 12 世纪，在中国北方建造了大量的这种塔，檐下用斗拱装饰。最出名的一个例子是北平的天宁寺塔，建于 11 世纪，经过多次重修。

4. 喇嘛塔（窣堵坡） 印度窣堵坡的原貌，通过早期的佛教传布者，在中国早已为人所知，但其长期未移植于此。后来，随着喇嘛教的传播，终于通过西藏植根于中原，其形貌发生了较大的改变。西藏喇嘛塔一般做成壶形，立在高高的基座上面。公元 1260 年由忽必烈下令建造的北平妙应寺窣堵坡是最好一例。后来它的壶状身躯变得细巧了，塔的颈部尤其如此。这个颈部原先像截了一段的锥形，后来渐渐像烟筒。这种后出的西藏式窣堵坡的一个典型例子是北平北海公园里的白塔，建于公元 1651 年。

5. 金刚宝座塔 在一个基座上耸立数个塔，称金刚宝座塔。早在 8 世纪建造的河北省房山县云居寺塔是这种塔型的先兆。云居寺塔有一个宽阔的低台，上面立着一座大塔和四座小塔。到明代此种形制始臻于成熟。公元 1473 年建的北平西郊的五塔寺是一个绝好的作品，它在很多方面使人联想起公元 8 世纪爪哇的婆罗浮屠。

❺ 牌楼

在中国大多数城镇和不少乡村道路上，都可见到称为牌楼的纪念性的大门。虽然牌楼纯粹是中国的建筑，但可以看到与印度桑契的窣堵坡围栏上的门有某种相似之处。中国南方多石牌楼，北方城镇的街道常有华丽的木牌楼。

Ⓕ Bridges

The building of bridges is an ancient art in China. Early examples were either simple timber structures or pontoon bridges, and it was not until the middle of the 4th century AD that the arch was used to span a water barrier. The most notable example of Chinese bridge building is the Great Stone Bridge, Chao Hsien, Hopeh. This is an open-spandrel bridge (one with small arches piercing the triangular space between the roadway and the ends of the main arch) whose principal arch has a span of 123 feet (37 meters). Built in the Sui Dynasty, it is a feat of engineering to amaze even a modern engineer. The more common type of bridge, exemplified by the celebrated Marco Polo Bridge near Peking, uses intermediate piers. Suspension bridges are often employed in the mountainous regions of Southwestern China, and bridges with huge stone lintels, sometimes measuring 70 feet (20 meters) or more, are not uncommon in Fukien.

❻ 桥梁

造桥在中国是一种古老的技艺。早期的例子是简单的木桥或是浮桥。直到 4 世纪中期以后开始用拱券跨过水流。中国桥梁建造最有名的一个例子是河北赵县的大石桥。它是一座敞肩拱桥（在主拱两头桥面以下的三角形部位，又开着小拱洞）。赵州桥的主拱跨度为 123 英尺（37 米）。赵州桥建于中国隋代，是使现代工程师感到惊讶的工程奇迹。较常见的一种拱桥可以北平著名的马可波罗桥[5]为例，有许多桥墩。中国西南部的山区常用悬索桥。福建有许多用长长的石梁和石墩造的桥，有的总长度[6]可达70英尺（20米）。

II. PAINTING

Painting as an art first appeared in China in the form of decorations on banners, dresses, gates, walls, and other surfaces. The aesthetic appeal and suggestive power of this medium were utilized by kings and emperors of the earliest days as a convenient means of teaching and governing the people.

Ⓐ Pre-T'ang Painting

In the Han Dynasty the art of painting reached technical maturity, and murals were used to decorate the interiors of halls and palaces. In 51 BC, Emperor Hsuan-ti (reigned 73 BC–49 BC) ordered portraits of 11 of his ablest generals and ministers, who had brought about the surrender of the shan-yu (king) of the barbarian Hsiung-nu, painted on the walls of Ch'i-lin Ke—an indication that portrait painting had already become a recognized art. Paintings were executed on walls and on silk. A considerable number of paintings on silk are reported to have been included in the imperial collections of the T'ang Dynasty, but these have disappeared.

贰 绘画

作为艺术的绘画，在中国首先作为装饰出现在旗帜、服装、门、墙及其他东西的表面上。早先的帝王们利用这种媒介的审美感染力和权势暗示力得心应手地教化和统治人民。

❶ 唐以前的绘画

在汉代，绘画技术已趋成熟，壁画被用来装饰宫殿内部。公元前 51 年，汉宣帝（公元前 73—公元前 49 年在位）命令为十一名在降服匈奴首领单于过程中立功的大臣和将军画像于麒麟阁内墙上。这件事表明画像在当时已被承认为一种艺术。当时的绘画不是画在墙壁上便是画在绢上。据记载，唐朝宫廷收藏了大批绢画，但实物没有留下来。

A painted brick discovered in a tomb at Naknang (Lolang), Korea, which was the capital of a Chinese province from 108 BC to 313 AD, is in the Museum of Fine Arts, Boston. It affords a glimpse of painting in a frontier province of the great Han Empire. Numerous stone slabs with designs engraved or in relief also provide indirect but valuable evidence of the character of Han mural painting.

The oldest existing Chinese scroll painting, attributed to Ku K'ai-chih (344 ?–406 ? AD), is treasured in the British Museum in London. Ku K'ai-chih was a celebrated painter of the Chin (Tsin) Dynasty. The scroll, probably a T'ang copy, is labeled *Admonitions of the Instructress to the Court Ladies* and depicts scenes illustrating a series of proverbs or morals. The figures are painted with a brush on silk, in lines of great accuracy and dexterity, but no attempt was made to set them against a background. The painting shows conceptions of the human form and of space which still adhere to some extent to the archaic methods of presentation on the Han relief stone slabs. Yet it also contains the essential characteristics of the 5th- and 6th-century Buddhist sculpture.

Ⓑ Painting of the T'ang Dynasty

Painting, like other branches of art, blossomed into its full glory during the T'ang Dynasty. Yen Li-teh and his brother Yen Li-pen (about 600–673 AD) are the first of a long list of great T'ang painters. Li-teh was also an architect, while Li-pen was the greater painter. Attributed to the latter is the scroll *Portrait of Emperors and Kings*, in the Museum of Fine Arts, Boston, in which many of the characteristics of the Ku K'ai-chih scroll are traceable.

Wu Tao-tzu (about 700–760 AD) became the most celebrated Chinese painter. The first to make full use of the flexible of the brush, he employed undulating lines varying in thickness, with third-dimensional effects. This was a radical departure from the wirelike lines of the earlier painters and gave him greater freedom of expression. "Wu's wind-blown draperies" became a phrase familiar to every student of Chinese painting, and succeeding painters depicted movement ever more vividly. Wu, with his free and masterly brush, excelled in painting subjects of all kinds, sacred and secular—figures, animals and plants, landscape, and architecture. The number of his murals recorded in the *Li-tai Ming-hua Chi* (*Famous Paintings of All Ages*) by Chang Yen-yuan (late T'ang) totals more than 300. Most have been destroyed.

朝鲜的乐浪在公元前 108 年至公元 313 年是中国的一个郡，[7] 那里的一处坟墓中出土一块有绘画的砖，现藏于美国波士顿美术馆。它让我们看到了当时汉帝国边疆省份的绘画作品。大批带有线刻和平浮雕的石板是汉朝壁画的特点的间接然而有价值的证物。

现存最早的中国画卷被认为是顾恺之（公元 344—406 年）的作品，现在珍藏于伦敦大英博物馆。顾恺之是东晋时的著名画家。那卷画可能是唐代的摹本，题名《女史箴》，画的内容是图解一系列道德箴言。人物用毛笔在绢上画成，线条精确流畅，但不画背景。人物形象和空间的表现在相当程度上保持汉朝画像石的古拙风格，但同时显露出 5 世纪至 6 世纪佛教雕塑的主要特征。

❷ 唐代的绘画

绘画和别的艺术门类一样，在唐代进入繁盛期。阎立德和阎立本（约公元 600—673 年）兄弟二人名列一大串唐代大画家名单之首。立德兼作建筑家，立本是更大的画家。阎立本的《历代帝王图卷》现藏波士顿美术馆，其中许多笔意可追溯到顾恺之的画卷中去。

吴道子（约公元 700—760 年）是最有名的中国画家，他第一个把毛笔的灵活性发挥至极致。他运用深浅不同的波动的线条表现三度空间的效果。摆脱早期线条的僵硬性，表现极为自由。每一个学中国画的学生都知道“吴带当风”之说，后继的画家因而更鲜活地表现运动。吴道子以他自由而纯熟的笔，在画中精妙地画出各式各样的题材——神和人，动物和植物，风景和建筑。据晚唐张彦远《历代名画记》记载，吴道子的壁画作品有三百件之多，多已损毁。

By the T'ang Dynasty, decorating temple walls with paintings had become almost a universal practice. Several hundred items are recorded in the *Li-tai Ming-hua Chi*: scenes of paradise and hell, images of Buddha, Bodhisattvas, Lokapalas, demons, and other legendary beings. And these were from collections in the two capitals only—from Sian and Loyang (Honan). There were also many paintings by lesser artists in other cities and on the sacred mountains. Almost no works of this kind have been preserved in the central provinces, but the caves of Tun-huang on the Silk Road are a rich source of information on Buddhist mural painting in a frontier province.

By the beginning of the 8th-century landscape, which was to become the noblest form of Chinese painting, had freed itself from its role as a mere background to figure painting. Li Ssu-hsun, who was born about 651 AD and died in 716 AD, and his son, Li Chao-tao, are generally recognized as the liberators of landscape painting. Known as the Two Li Generals, they founded the Li or northern school of painting. The work of this school is characterized by careful, wirelike drawings colored with bright blue and green and accented with specks of gold and vermilion. It is highly decorative but somewhat stiff, with every detail minutely and laboriously depicted. While the Two Li Generals were perfecting this style, Wu Tao-tzu painted on the walls of the Ta-t'ung palace, in one day, in ink and only faintly tinted with colors, the panoramic *Three Hundred Li on the Chialing River*—a work widely different in technique and style from the products of the Li school.

About a half century later, the poet-painter Wang Wei (699–759 AD) was to be hailed as the master of ink landscape. His work, in contrast to the rigid draftsmanship of the Li school, is characterized by boldness and freedom. Wang Wei excelled in depicting mist and water and was the first to succeed in capturing atmosphere in nature. It is said of him that there are pictures in his poetry and poetry in his pictures. He, too, had his followers, and was hailed by Ming critics as the founder of the southern school of landscape painting, just as the Li Generals were called the founders of the northern school.

Among other great T'ang painters were Ts'ao Pa and Han Kan (about 750 AD), both celebrated for their pictures of horses, and Chou Fang and Chang Hsuan (late 8th century), who depicted domestic and feminine scenes. A copy of one of Chang's scrolls, made by Emperor Hui-tsung (reigned 1101–1125 AD) of the Sung Dynasty, is in the Museum of Fine Arts, Boston.

在唐代，用壁画装饰寺庙墙壁蔚然成风。《历代名画记》记载了数百幅，其中有佛国净土和地狱，佛陀、菩萨、护世天王、恶魔及其他神话人物。而这只是对长安和洛阳两个首都的寺庙壁画的记录。在其他城镇和名山圣地还有众多二流画家的作品。在中原省份这些壁画几乎早消失了。但是在丝绸古道上的敦煌石窟是有关边陲佛教壁画信息的富源。

到 8 世纪初左右，山水从人物画的背景独立出来，将要成为中国画中最高尚的一个品类。李思训约生于公元 651 年，殁于公元 716 年，他和他的儿子李昭道被普遍认为是山水画的解放者。他们被称为“大小李将军”，创立了“北派”或称“李派”山水画。其特点是采用精致而挺拔的线条、鲜艳的青色和绿色，重点的地方加上金或朱红色点。这种画极富装饰性，笔触细致入微，不免流于匠气。当大小李将军在完善他们的风格时，吴道子在大同宫的墙壁上用墨和淡色作画，一天就完成了《嘉陵江三百里山水》，其技法与风格与“二李”作品迥异。

又过了大约半个世纪，诗人画家王维（公元 699—759 年）被认为是水墨山水画大家。他的作品的特点是自由而大胆，也与“二李”僵化的匠气风格成鲜明对照。王维善于表现雾和水，是成功地描绘大自然神韵的第一人。他被认为是“画中有诗，诗中有画”。他也有追随者。明代的评论家指出，王维是“南派”山水画的始祖，正如“二李”是“北派”的创立者。

唐代大画家还有曹霸与韩干（约公元 750 年），两人以画马著称。周昉和张萱（8 世纪晚期）擅长画家庭生活及妇女。宋朝皇帝徽宗（公元 1101—1125 年在位）临摹张萱的一个画卷的摹本现藏波士顿美术馆。

🅒 Five Dynasties and Sung

During the chaotic Five Dynasties period there flourished a number of artists who heralded the great Sung painters. Ching Hao, who lived at the end of T'ang and the beginning of this period, was the master of the great landscapist Kuan T'ung who exerted a tremendous influence on the landscape painting of the Sung Dynasty. The monk Kuan-hsiu, who was active about 920 AD, was famous for his figures, particularly lohans. Hsü Hsi and Huang Ch'üan were painters of birds and flowers.

Mural painting, though less popular than it had been in the T'ang period, was still common during the Northern Sung Dynasty, and a few Sung murals have escaped destruction and survived for posterity. In the Tun-huang caves are examples of the work done in a frontier province.

Working at the court academy under imperial patronage were such great painters as Kuo Hsi (1020–1090), the landscapist, and Huang Chü-ts'ai, son of Huang Ch'üan, who like his father painted birds and flowers but was a finer artist.

Among the scholar painters of the early Sung period, Li Ch'eng and Tung Yüan (late 10th century) are generally recognized as the greatest landscapists. Another painter, Fan K'uan, often covered his hilltops with heavy vegetation, and placed high, rugged cliffs along riverbanks. Mi Fei (1051–1107) filled his scenes with heavy mists and clouds, and rendered his protruding hilltops with the horizontal, broad, short "egg-plant" strokes so much imitated by later painters. Li Lung-mien (Li Kung-lin, 1040–1106) is well known to the Western world. His line drawings of figures and horses, executed with extreme facility and dexterity, are examples of the highest achievement in draftsmanship.

Toward the end of the Northern Sung Dynasty, Emperor Hui-tsung, himself an accomplished artist who aimed at extreme naturalism, became a great patron of art. Nevertheless, though he devoted far more attention to the academy than had earlier emperors, it did not produce any outstanding artist.

While painting in general flourished in the Southern Sung Dynasty,

Buddhist painting receded into almost complete obscurity. By this time Buddhism had died out in the land of its origin. Confucian scholars launched merciless attacks on it, and the Buddhists themselves, now dominated by the Ch'an (Zen) sect, while not entirely iconoclastic, substituted meditation for image worship. Buddhist painters of this period preferred such themes as "Kuan-yin in White Dress by the Moonlit Pool," "Meditating Sages," or "Sixteen Lohans"—themes which were not bound by rigid rules calling for dignity and symmetry, as were the religious paintings of earlier periods.

❸ 五代和宋朝的绘画

在混乱的五代，有一批艺术家风华正茂，他们是宋朝画家的先驱者。荆浩生活于唐末和五代之初，是大山水画家关仝的老师，他对宋代山水画有重大影响。贯休和尚活跃于公元 920 年前后 [8]，擅长人物，尤善画罗汉。徐熙和黄筌是花鸟画家。

这一时期壁画虽不若唐代兴盛，但在北宋仍是常见。少数宋代壁画逃过劫难，留至后世，敦煌石窟有宋代壁画，是边陲的作品。

宋代宫廷画院中聚集了许多著名画家。如山水画家郭熙（约公元 1020—1090 年），黄筌的儿子、同为花鸟画家但略胜一筹的黄居寀。

宋代初年的文人画家有李成和董源（10 世纪末），是山水画大家。范宽画山覆有厚厚的植被，河流两旁岩峰峥嵘。米芾（公元 1051—1107 年）的山水画云雾缭绕，高耸的山顶散落着短、平、宽的墨点，后世画者多有仿效。李龙眠（李公麟，公元 1040—1106 年）的作品现在西方很著名。他用线条画人和马，极其娴熟流畅，为笔墨技法的最高成就。

北宋末期，徽宗皇帝本人在艺术上有很高的造诣，他追求极端的自然主义。徽宗醉心于书画，对宋代画院的兴盛起到推动作用。不过尽管他比先前的君王更重视画院，画院却没有再出现伟大的画家。

南宋的画风仍盛，但佛教绘画却由盛转衰，日渐湮没。其时佛教在其发源地印度近于消失。中国儒家学者无情地攻击佛教。佛教徒中禅宗成为主流，他们虽然不是彻底的偶像破坏者，但注重冥想而不重偶像崇拜。这时佛教画家偏爱的题材多是“月下湖畔的白衣观音”、“沉思中的贤者”或“十六罗汉”之类。这一类作品脱出了早期佛教绘画要求庄严、对称的严格规矩的束缚。

In a world dominated by neo-Confucianism and Ch'an Buddhism, painters turned to landscape as their preferred medium of expression. In the late 12th and early 13th centuries the academy numbered a host of great landscape painters, including Liu Sung-nien, Liang K'ai (about 1203), Hsia Kuei (about 1195–1224), and Ma Yüan (about 1190–1225). Liu Sung-nien excelled in landscape of the blue-and-green (Li) style, and Liang K'ai was a master of the technique of line drawing of human figures against a landscape background, also in line. But the two great figures in ink landscape of the Southern Sung Dynasty were Hsia Kuei and Ma Yüan. Hsia Kuei's strength and boldness are best seen in his famous *Ten Thousand Li of the Yangtze River*. Ma Yüan, who placed his horizons rather low, is more readily appreciated by Westerners. His landscapes, in contrast to those of Hsia Kuei, are marked by tranquility and delicate atmosphere, best illustrated by a pine tree silhouetted against a misty background, a motif familiar to every student of Chinese painting. Up to his time, Chinese landscape painters had tried to include all they saw. Ma Yüan's compositions show merely a few rocks and one or two trees. This pattern—simple in construction and sparse in detail—is perhaps closer to the Western conception of landscape painting than the all-inclusive of the Yüan Dynasty.

Ⓓ Yüan Painting

The comparatively short Yüan period had a number of great painters. Chao Meng-fu (1254–1322), best known as a painter of human figures and horses, was equally at home with landscape. He was also calligrapher of the first rank. His best-known work is the *Horse with Groom*. Among the scholars who avoided Mongol officialdom was Ch'ien Hsüan (1235–about 1290), renowned as a painter of flowers, birds and insects.

Wu Chen (1280–1354), Huang Kung-wang (1261–1354), Ni Tsan (1301–1374), and Wang Meng (died 1385) are honored as the Four Great Masters of Yüan. They were all landscape painters. Wu Chen treats his material somewhat heavily, but he has a keen sense of space. He is also well known for his bamboos. In striking contrast are the airy scenes of Huang Kung-wang and Ni Tsan, who used washes very sparingly, obtaining their effects with lines consisting mainly of dry brush strokes. This is particularly true of Ni Tsan, who emphasized this style through his choice of extremely simple subjects. Wang Meng painted his scenes heavily, building them up laboriously with individual strokes.

在新理学和禅宗佛教统治之下，山水画成了画家们最喜爱的表现媒介。12 世纪末到 13 世纪初，画院又产生一批著名的山水画家，其中有刘松年、梁楷（约公元 1203 年）、夏珪（约公元 1195—1224 年）和马远（约公元 1190—1225 年）。刘松年的青绿山水超过“二李”。梁楷善用线条画人物，背景中的山水也用线条画。但是南宋时期水墨山水画大家首推夏珪和马远二人。夏珪的《长江万里图》充分表现出他的大胆和力度。马远画作中地平线安排得靠下，更受西方人的赏爱。马远的山水画与夏珪不同，他表现一种静寂精致的情调，如云雾背景中的松树。每个学中国画的学生对此题材都极谙熟。在马远以前，画家总是把看见的东西都收入画内。马远的画只有几处山石和一二株树。构图简洁，细部略省，比元代包罗万象的作品更接近西方人对于风景画的观念。

❹ 元代绘画

年代较短的元朝有很多大画家。赵孟頫（公元 1254—1322 年）以画人物和马著称，但亦擅长山水，同时又是第一流的书法家。他的最著名的画是《鞍马图》。在元朝避官不仕的知识分子中，钱选（公元 1235—约 1290 年）[9] 是著名的花鸟画家。

吴镇（公元 1280—1354 年）、黄公望（公元 1261—1354 年）[10]、倪瓒（公元 1301—1374 年）和王蒙（公元 1385 年卒）被推崇为元代四大家。他们都是山水画家。吴镇下笔厚重，但富有空间感，他也擅长画竹。与吴镇鲜明对照的是黄公望及倪瓒，此二人很少用渲染，多用枯笔。倪瓒尤其如此，他常画简单的对象以突出他的风格。王蒙风景画浓墨重笔，一笔一画极为工整。

Ⓔ Ming and Ts'ing Dynasties

The Ming Dynasty, relatively recent, has left us many paintings. Mural painting became rare, but some examples which have come down to us, such as those in the Fa-hai Ssu, near Peking, show superlative craftsmanship. Yet connoisseurs and critics do not classify these murals as art, looking to the scrolls alone for the work of the great masters. Early Ming academicians strove to emulate T'ang and Sung paintings, but the spirit of their work is entirely different. Wu Wei, the landscape painter, who modeled himself on Ma Yüan, became the founder of the so-called Che (Chekiang) school. Pien Wen-chin (Pien Ching-chao, about 1430) and Lü Chi (about 1500) were well known for their flowers and birds in the manner of Huang Ch'üan and Huang Chü-ts'ai; Lin Liang founded a school in which the same subjects were treated in an extremely facile and sketchy manner. The leading exponent of the Che school is Tai Chin (Tai Wen-chin, about 1430–1450), originally an academician, but expelled from the academy through the intrigues of jealous colleagues. Like all painters of the period, he modeled himself upon Sung masters—specifically, on Ma Yüan—but created a style of his own, simple and articulate in stroke, light in rendering.

❺ 明清绘画

明代离我们不远，留下较多的画作。壁画很少了，但有些留传至今，如北平附近的法海寺就有明代壁画，技艺相当不错。可是鉴赏家和评论者不把那些壁画看作艺术品，他们只把卷轴画看作艺术大家的作品。明代初期士人们努力仿效唐宋的绘画，但他们的作品的气质与唐宋大不相同。山水画家吴伟追学马远，却创立了“浙派”。边文进（边景昭，约公元 1430 年）和吕纪（约公元 1500 年）以花鸟画著称，风格接近黄筌和黄居寀。林良创立一个画派，作花鸟画特别流畅，类似速写。“浙派”的最重要的诠释者是戴进（字文进，约公元 1430—1450 年）[11]，本是画院画家，后受人嫉害被逐出画院。像当时所有的人那样，他追从宋代大师，尤重马远，结果却创立了自已的画派，画风简洁清新。

Both the academic and the Che schools gradually died out, the latter being reincarnated in the "literary man's style," best represented by the Four Masters of Ming: Shen Chou (1427–1509), T'ang Yin (1470–1523), Wen Cheng-ming (1470–1559), and Tung Ch'i-ch'ang (1554–1636). Ch'iu Ying (about 1522–1560), who learned his craft as a lacquer painter, was a master of detail. In his paintings we see the pleasures of everyday life exquisitely and faithfully recorded. A salient characteristic of Ming painters is their masterly manipulation of the brush. It does not merely make a line or a wash; it conveys tone, strength, and spirit. In this dynasty the technique of the brush attained perfection.

Ts'ing Dynasty art is a continuation of the Ming tradition. Early in this period the southern school of landscape painting, best represented by the four Wangs—Wang shih-min (1592–1680), Wang Chien (1598–1677), Wang Hui (1632–1717), and Wang Yüan-ch'i (1642–1715)—came into prominence.

学院派和“浙派”都渐渐消失了。后者演变成所谓的“文人画”风格。明代“文人画”的四大代表者是沈周（公元1427—1509年）、唐寅（公元1470—1523年）、文征明（公元1470—1559年）和董其昌（公元1554—1636年）。仇英（约公元1522—1560年）[12]原来学习漆画，是工笔画大师，他的作品细致忠实地记录下当时日常生活的乐趣。明代画家有一个突出的共同点，即毛笔的运用极为熟练，笔画出不止是一根线或一小片洇墨，还表达出风格、力度和气韵。明代毛笔的运用达到完美的程度。

清代艺术承继了明代的传统。清初“南派”山水画的代表是“四王”，他们是王时敏（公元1592—1680年），王鉴（公元1598—1677年），王翚（公元1632—1717年），王原祁（公元1642—1715年）。

Wang Shih-min and Wang Chien, who took Tung Yüan and Huang Kung-wang as their masters, formed the vanguard of Ts'ing painting. The former is known for his bold brush strokes. Wang Hui was a disciple of Wang Shih-min, and excelled him in control of the medium. He is said to have combined the northern and southern schools, and was proclaimed by his masters the Sage of Painting. Wang Yüan-ch'i, grandson of Wang Shih-min and the most learned of the four, best caught the spirit of Huang Kung-wang. He is known for his landscapes with light tinges of color.

Ch'en Hung-shou (1599–1652) originated a style in which, despite an appearance of carelessness, each stroke is skillfully conceived and precisely executed. He had many imitators. Shih T'ao was another "careless" painter of landscapes and bamboos. Both men reached maturity in the Ming Dynasty, but they lived into the early years of Ts'ing and their influence on later painters places them as artists of the later rather than of the earlier dynasty.

王时敏和王鉴师法董源和黄公望，是清代画家的先驱。王时敏以粗大笔触闻名。王翚是王时敏的弟子，在运笔上超越乃师。据认为他把“南派”和“北派”风格加以融合，他的老师称他为“画圣”。王原祁是王时敏的孙子，是“四王”中学问最大者，他最得黄公望的意境。王原祁以淡彩山水画著称。

陈洪绶（公元 1599—1652 年）创立一种绘画风格，看似无意，实则每笔均精心考虑、精心落墨。仿效陈洪绶的人颇多。石涛善画山水及竹，也是一位看似“随意”的画家。这两人的画技在明代末年已经纯熟，他们活到清初。由于他们对后人的影响大，陈洪绶与石涛被视作清代画家。

III. SCULPTURE

Sculpture, like architecture, was not accorded due recognition by the Chinese. While we know the great painters, the sculptors are anonymous.

Ⓐ Early Sculpture

The oldest specimens of Chinese sculpture were found in the Shang Dynasty tombs at Anyang. The owl, tiger, and turtle are favorite motifs, and the human figure also appears occasionally. These marble pieces are in the round, some of them being architectural elements. Their surfaces are decorated with patterns like those found on the contemporary bronzes. In decorative pattern, in basic concepts of form and mass, and in spirit, the sculpture and the bronzes are one. Bronze masks have also been found, some of the t'ao-t'ieh, some of human beings. They are often well modeled.

Human figures and animals in the round began to be used as decorative motifs on the bronzes around 500 BC. The human figures were first carved in the kneeling position molded in strict conformity with the law of frontality, but the art soon freed itself to portray action. In general, the human figures are short and stubby, rendered with little feeling for modeling, but the animal forms show keen and subtle touches of the chisel, based on careful observation of nature.

叁 雕塑

像建筑一样，雕塑在中国也未获得应有的承认。我们知道大画家的名字，但雕塑家都默默无闻。

❶ 早期的雕塑

最早的雕塑是在安阳商朝的墓葬中发现的。猫头鹰、老虎和乌龟是常见的雕刻母题，也偶有人的形象。那些大理石作品都是圆雕，有些就是建筑部件。表面装饰同那个时代的青铜器的纹样相同。石雕和青铜器在装饰纹样、基本形体和气质方面是一致的。出土的铜面具有的是饕餮，有的是人形。它们都铸造得很好。

公元前500年前后，青铜器开始以人和动物形体的圆雕做装饰题材。初时人像是正画跪姿，严格按照“正面律”制作。不久，艺术摆脱束缚去表现动作。总的来看，人物造型矮而且呆板，而动物造型显现出刀凿的运作精准有致，这是基于对自然的准确观察。

Ⓑ Han, Three Kingdoms, Six Dynasties

In the Han Dynasty sculpture gained importance in conjunction with architecture. Reliefs decorate interior wall surfaces, such as those found in a number of tomb shrines, notably the tombs of the Wu family at Chiahsiang, Shantung. Human figures and animals (lions, lambs, and chimeras) in the round stand in pairs flanking the avenues leading to tombs, temples, and palaces. At Ch'üfu, Shantung, the human figures are typically rigid, lumpy, and ill-modeled, bearing only a vague resemblance to the human form. Yet the animals are in general well modeled, robust, vigorous, and animated. The lions and chimeras are usually winged. (Since figure sculpture, animal or human, had never been employed by the Chinese of earlier times as guardian monuments to an architectural approach, it is possible that the idea was imported from the Occident through contact with the barbarian tribes of the west and north.) On some of the contemporary ch'üeh in Szechwan are found reliefs of birds, dragons, and tigers that rank with the best decorative sculpture.

With the spread of Buddhism during the period of the Northern and Southern Dynasties, an anthropomorphic sculpture assumed an important role. A few small images of the early 5th century have come down to us. The first important monuments are in the caves of Yun-kang, near Ta-t'ung, first capital of the Northern Wei Dynasty (386–535 AD). These are undoubtedly Chinese versions of Buddhist caves in India. Yet, aside from decorative motifs (the acanthus leaf, the frets, the beads, and even the Ionic and Corinthian capitals) and the basic conception of the caves themselves, there seems to be no traceable Indian influence to give the sculpture an Indian or otherwise un-Chinese character. There are a few characteristically Indian figures, but the group remains essentially Chinese.

The work on the caves near Ta-t'ung was begun by imperial order in 452 AD and stopped abruptly in 494 AD, when the capital was moved south to Loyang. The plan of some of the caves is fairly similar to the chaitya caves of India, with the chaitya, or stupa, in the center. The architecture and sculpture, however, are basically Chinese.

The earliest, and larger, figures, some measuring over 70 feet (21 meters) in height, are heavy and sturdy. The pleated draperies cling to the body. Later the figures grew more slender, and the head and neck became almost tubular. The eyebrows are arched and join with the bridge of the nose. The wide forehead is almost flat, turning sharply back at the temples. The eyes are mere slits; the lips, thin, forever smiling. The chin is often sharply pointed—a feature especially noticeable in some bronze statuettes of the period.

❷ 汉、三国、六朝

到汉代，雕塑在建筑上的重要性增加了。室内墙壁上有浮雕装饰，这可以从许多汉墓祭室中得到印证。尤如山东嘉祥武氏墓群，人和动物（狮、羊、吐火兽）的圆雕成对地排列在通往墓室、宫庙的大路两旁。山东曲阜的人像非常呆拙、粗糙、模糊一团，只大致有点像人形。面兽像则造型优美、雄壮，栩栩如生。狮子和吐火兽常常有翼（考虑到中国早期建筑不用人像和兽雕保卫大门，这一做法很可能是在与北方和西方蛮族接触中从西亚传入的）。四川发现的汉阙常有鸟、龙、虎的浮雕，它们是装饰雕刻的上品。

南北朝时，佛教盛行，人像雕刻多起来。有一些5世纪早期的小佛像留传下来。第一批重要的纪念性雕像见于大同云冈，大同（时称平城）是北魏（公元386—535年）第一个首都。云冈石窟是印度石窟的中国翻版。除了一些装饰题材（叶饰、回文饰、念珠，甚至爱奥尼克或科林斯柱头）和洞窟的基本形制外，看不出在雕刻上有什么印度或其他非中国的特点。固然有少数典型的印度式佛像，但群体还是中国的。

云冈石窟由皇帝下令于公元452年开始建造，但因首都南迁洛阳，而于公元494年突然停止。云冈的一部分石窟与印度的“支提”十分相似。中间是圣坛或窣堵坡。建筑与雕塑则基本是中国式的。

早期的较大的雕像有的高度超过70英尺（21米），粗壮结实，身上紧裹着有褶的服装。后来佛像变得苗条些，而头及颈部却几乎是圆柱形的。眉毛弯弯，与鼻梁相接。前额宽而平，在太阳穴处突然后折。眼是细长缝，薄唇，永远微笑。下巴尖尖的，这一特征多在同时期的小型铜佛像上见到。

The draperies no longer cling to the body, but hang from it, often flaring out at ankle level, and are arranged symmetrically on the right and left, with the pointed, almost knife-like, ends of the folds spread out like a bird's wings. (It is not by accident that pointed ends are also characteristic of the strokes of the calligraphy of the period.) The Bodhisattvas of these statuary groups, whose Indian counterparts wear princely attire, are stripped of most of their ornaments. They wear a simple tiara and a heart-shaped necklace, and from the shoulder of each figure hangs a long sash, the ends crossing through a ring hung in front of the thighs.

A project similar to that at Ta-t'ung was begun by the Wei emperors about 495 AD at Lung-men, near Loyang, on the cliffs of the I (Yi) River. Here the heads are less tubular and more rounded, and the draperies less pointed and more fluent, though still symmetrically arranged, achieving a superb decorative effect. The walls of some of the caves are decorated with reliefs representing the emperor on one wall and the empress on the opposite one, each attended by an entourage, forming compositions of the highest order. The activity of the cliff sculptors at Lung-men continued until the latter part of the 9th century.

The Northern Ch'i (550–577 AD) rulers were devout but extravagant Buddhists, yet it was not until nearly the end of their brief dynasty that they began the caves at T' ien-lung Shan. Most of the figures of these caves assume a standing posture. Their heads are almost round. The forehead is markedly lower; the eyes, though still very narrow, are wider. The nose and lips are fuller, with the enchanting smile of earlier periods almost completely suppressed. The draperies are simpler, hanging vertically.

Ⓒ Sculpture of the Sui and T'ang Dynasties

In the Sui Dynasty the standing figures begin to show a peculiar protrusion of the abdomen. The head has become smaller in proportion to the body, and the jaws and nose are fuller. The eyes, though still narrow, show some convexity in the upper lids, emphasizing the presence of the eyeballs. The slightly convex surface intersects the curved plane under the brow in a gentle "valley." The line of intersection appears as a wide arc, repeating the rhythm of the brow and the eye. The subdued smile is produced by more fully modeled lips, and the mouth is smaller. The neck has assumed the peculiar shape of a truncated cone, protruding sharply from the chest and joining the head with similar abruptness. The cone is circumscribed about halfway up by a groove-like fold. The drapery is shown in more natural folds, and the hem rarely flares. In contrast to the costume of Buddha, which is austerely draped in all periods, that of the Bodhisattvas has become more gaudy. The tiara and the necklace are now bedecked with jewel-like ornaments. Strings of beads, hanging from the shoulders and interrupted at intervals with pendants, reach far below the knees.

衣服不再紧贴，而是披挂在身上，在脚踝处张开，左右对称，衣褶尖挺如刀，像鸟翼似地张开（这并非偶然，这时期中国书法常有尖锋）。佛像组群中有菩萨像，在印度菩萨作公主般打扮，在中国则几乎取消全部装饰，只戴简单的头巾和一个心形项圈，有长长的肩带，穿过在大腿前的环。

公元495年，在洛阳附近的龙门，在伊川河的山岩上开始开凿龙门石窟，情形与大同云冈近似。这里的佛像头部更圆润而较少圆柱形，衣褶不那么尖了，仍然对称，但更流畅，富有高雅的装饰性。有些洞窟的墙面上有浮雕，一面是皇帝像，对面是皇后像，各有随从侍候，表现着最高级的构图。龙门的雕凿工作持续到9世纪后期。

北齐（公元550—577年）统治者笃信佛教而奢靡。但在其统治的末期，方才开始开凿天龙山石窟，这些石窟里的大部分佛像站立着，头部是浑圆的，额头明显较低，眼睛虽然仍细但比较长，鼻与唇比较饱满。先前时期那种迷人的微笑几乎不见了，衣褶简单，直上直下。

❸ 隋与唐的雕塑

隋代立像的腹部独特地挺出。头占全身的比例变小，鼻子和下颚较以前丰满。眼睛仍细，但上眼皮凸出一些，显出其下的眼珠。这微微凸出的眼皮与眉毛下面的弧形平面相交形成柔和的凹沟。这交线像一张弓，重复了眉和眼睛的韵律。嘴变小了，造型精致的双唇使雕像微带笑意。颈子如截去尖端的圆锥体，从胸部突然伸出，与头部生硬相接。颈部中段横一道深深的皱褶。衣服上的衣褶自然，卷边精致，很少展开，如来佛的服饰永远保持朴素，与之相反，菩萨的服饰变得华丽。头巾和项链上嵌着宝石般的装饰。珠链从肩上垂下，间隔地挂着饰物，抵至膝部以下。

Sculpture, especially Buddhist sculpture, reached its zenith in China in the T'ang Dynasty. The work begun at Lung-men by the Wei Tatars attained new heights, and the creation of Buddhist images was advanced with similar zeal throughout the empire. About the end of the 9th century, however, cave sculpture seemed to lose the interest of the worshipers of central China. It was continued at Tun-huang, but the center for China proper shifted to Szechwan, which contains many late T'ang caves. The activity in that province continued through the Sung and Yüan periods into the Ming Dynasty.

It is difficult to differentiate sharply between the Sui and early T'ang styles, but toward the middle of the 7th-century T'ang characteristics definitely emerged. The figures have become more naturalistic. The S-curve appears in most of the standing figures, which are balanced on one leg, with the hip of the relaxed leg and the shoulder on the same side slightly lowered. To maintain equilibrium, the head is tilted slightly toward the side of the supporting leg. The body is more fleshy, although the waist remains slim. The face, especially that of the Bodhisattva, is pleasingly plump. The gracefully arched eyebrow is not carried quite so far as in the previous periods, but curves naturally, clearly defining the temple. The ridge of the eyebrow is now seldom incised with a groove. The area of the upper eyelid extends farther up, and the curved plane below the brow is narrower. The nose is shorter and less sharply ridged. The lips are definitely sensuous, and the distance of the upper lip from the nose is markedly shortened. The hair is now carried very low, reducing the height of the forehead. The Bodhisattvas of this period are less garishly ornamented. The tiara is often simplified, but the hair is drawn into an enormous knot on top of the head. The garments are modeled to conform closely to the body, and the beads, though still often worn, are bare of most of their former pendants.

About the beginning of the 8th century a very earthly type of Buddha was introduced. He is represented as a complacent, fat creature of this world, with a flabby chin, scarcely any neck, and a full, protruding abdomen—a most unusual conception of the ascetic who wandered the woods of Buddha Gaya. Not many figures of this type have been found, but all are evidence of superlative achievement in the plastic representation of the human form.

Toward the end of the T'ang Dynasty, in the caves of the seclude Szechwan area, there appeared a type of sculpture characterized by the iconographic tributes and fantastic physiology of the newly popular mi-tsung or mi-chiao (secret sect or religion). In its treatment of the human form and of the draperies, however, it shows no perceptible break with T'ang tradition. An entire wall area is often used for a single subject. The paradise scene, which is pictured over and over again in the contemporary mural painting at Tun-huang, is here executed in relief, forming a single composition—a plastic conception never found in cave sculpture of earlier periods.

中国的雕塑，尤其是佛教雕塑，在唐代直抵顶峰。北魏开始的龙门石窟达到新的高度。在唐帝国版图之内，到处都热情地雕凿佛像。大约在 9 世纪末，中原的信徒们对石窟失去了兴趣。敦煌石窟仍在继续，而在中国中部，石窟开凿转移到四川，那儿有一些晚唐的石窟。这一活动在四川历经宋、元，延续到明代。

唐初与隋代的风格接近，很难明确区分。到 7 世纪中期，唐代自己的风格出现了。雕像更加自然主义了。大多数立像呈 S 形姿势，由一条腿平衡，放松的那条腿的臀部和同侧的肩部略向前倾。头部稍稍偏向另一边。躯体丰满，腰部仍细。菩萨的脸部饱满，眉毛优雅地弯曲，不像前一时期那样过分，很自然地呈弧形勾画出天庭。眉弓下也不再有凹沟。眼睛上皮更宽，眉下的曲面减窄。鼻子稍短，鼻梁稍短也稍低。鼻端与嘴稍近，嘴唇更有表情。发际下移，额头高度稍减。这时期的菩萨像的装饰不那么华丽了。头巾简化，头发在头顶上堆成高髻。服装更合身；仍然戴着珠串，但挂着的饰物减少了。

到 8 世纪初，出现一种非常人性化的如来佛像。他被雕凿成一个自我满足的、心宽体胖的俗世之人，下巴松弛，看不见颈子，大腹便便。这是一种关于在菩提伽耶森林中漫步的苦行者的极不寻常的观念。这样的佛像不多见，但就人体形象的雕凿而言是十分高超的。

唐末，在四川人迹罕至的地区的石窟中出现由新传播的密宗（或密教，意为秘密教派）搞的反映奇幻心理的偶像。不过人和服饰的处理与唐代传统相似。那里，一整片墙只描绘一个题材。同时期在敦煌一再出现的描绘净土的壁画，此处则用堆塑来表现，形成单一的构图。这在先前的石窟雕塑从未见过。

T'ang sculptors were extremely skillful in portraying animal forms, many examples of which have been preserved in the grounds of the T'ang imperial tombs. Some smaller pieces are on view in museums of the United States and European countries.

Ⓓ Sung Sculpture

With the fall of the T'ang Dynasty the creation of Buddhist images in stone almost ceased. Statues in Sung temples were carved in wood, modeled in clay, or, rarely, cast in bronze. The only exceptions are found in the caves of Szechwan. Few of the bronze images escaped melting down in later periods. One notable exception is the 70-foot statue of Kuan-yin in Chengting, Hopeh, cast by order of the first Sung emperor, T'ai-tsu (reigned 960–976 AD). Clay figures are numerous. A superb example of this work is the altar group in the Hua-yen Ssu, Ta-t'ung. The eleven-headed Kuan-yin of the Tu-lo Ssu, Chi Hsien, closely follows the T'ang tradition; it measures about 60 feet (18 meters) in height and is the largest clay figure in China. Many wooden statues of the Sung period have found their way to the museums of the West.

The most noticeable characteristic of Sung statues is the rounding of the face. The forehead is broader than in previous periods. The nose is short and almost bulbous. The eyebrows are less arched, and the convex surface above the upper lid is ever wider, reducing to a narrow strip the concave plane under the eyebrow. The lips are thicker, and the mouth is very small. The smile has almost vanished. The neck is rendered naturally, emerging above the chest and supporting the head without any demarcation.

The S-curve of the T'ang Bodhisattvas seems to have been forgotten. Even when the figures are not completely rigid, the ease with which T'ang figures carry their weight, and the consequent lowering the relaxed side of the body, seem beyond the grasp of the Sung sculptors. The Ch'an Buddhists introduced a new pose for the Kuan-yin, showing the goddess seated on a rock with one leg hanging down and the other foot resting on the rock. This complicated pose presented the sculptor with new problems of arrangement of the body and the draperies.

Szechwan cave sculptured of the Southern Sung period shows evidence of a decline in the sculptor's art. This is especially noticeable in some of the Bodhisattvas. By this time they have taken on an unmistakably feminine appearance. They are gaudily dressed and overburdened with jewelry and ornaments. The pose is rigid, almost frigid; the expression is blank. The best example of this work is the group of young, matron-like Bodhisattvas in Tatsu.

唐代雕刻家雕刻动物的技艺特别高超，许多作品藏在唐代帝王陵墓中的地下。欧洲和美国博物馆展出了小件作品。

❹ 宋代雕塑

唐朝之后，石造佛像几乎停止了。宋代庙宇中供奉的佛像是木刻的或泥塑的，偶尔也有用铜铸的。只有四川地区的石窟例外。几乎没有铜佛像能逃避被熔化之祸。最有名的例外是河北正定的 70 英尺高的铜观音，它由宋太祖（公元 960—976 年在位）下令铸造。泥塑佛像不计其数。极精美的一组在大同华严寺祭台上。河北蓟县独乐寺十一面泥塑观音像高 60 英尺（18 米），风格十分接近唐代传统，是中国最高大的泥塑佛像。许多宋代木雕佛像流入西方博物馆。

宋代雕塑最突出之点是脸部浑圆，额头比以前宽，短鼻，几乎圆鼓；眉毛孤形不显，眼上皮更宽，而致与眉下方凹进处间距缩窄；嘴唇较厚，口小，笑容几乎消失；颈部处理自然，自胸部伸出，支持头颅，与头胸之间没有分明的界线。

唐朝菩萨那种 S 形曲线姿势不见了。宋代雕塑虽然并不僵硬，但唐代那种轻松地支持体重并降低放松的身体一侧的安闲相不是宋代雕刻者所能掌握的。禅宗搞出另一种观音像，她坐在石头上，一脚踏石，一脚垂下。这种复杂的姿势向雕刻家提出了处理身躯和衣褶的新问题。

南宋时期，四川石窟雕刻艺术衰落，尤其是菩萨像，此时日益显现为女身。服装过分华丽，珠宝、装饰太多。姿势僵硬拘谨，表情空漠。四川最好的作品是大足石刻中少女般的菩萨群像。

Ⓔ Yüan, Ming, and Ts'ing Sculpture

During the Yüan Dynasty, Lamaist Buddhism was introduced from Tibet. With it came sculptors whose influence was to last through the Ming and Ts'ing periods. Most of their figures are shown sitting cross-legged. The waist is almost wasp-like, the chest is broad, and the shoulders are square. The head has become more squat, but the rhythm of the torso is repeated in the broadening of the forehead. The top of the head is flattened and surmounted by a grossly elongated ushnisha, the hump characteristic of the sculptured heads of Buddha.

The Ming and Ts'ing Dynasties were a sad period for sculpture in China. The statuary of these periods shows neither the robust vigor of Han, nor the archaic charm of the Six Dynasties, nor the mature self-assurance of T'ang, nor even the rococo elegance of Sung. The sculptor's art had degenerated into uninspired manual labor.

❺ 元、明、清雕塑

元代，喇嘛教从西藏传入中原，该教派的雕塑匠人也来了，他们影响了明、清的雕塑。他们的塑像大都交腿而坐，胸宽，腰细如蜂，肩方。头部短胖，而宽宽的前额重现全身的韵律。头顶是平的，上面有浓密的螺髻，是如来佛头顶上特有的疙瘩形发式。

明、清两代是中国雕塑史上可悲的时期。这个时期的雕像一没有汉代的粗犷；二没有六朝的古典妩媚；三没有唐代的成熟自信；四没有宋代的洛可可式优雅。雕塑者的技艺蜕变为没有灵气的手工劳动。

（吴焕加 译 陈志华 校）

Appendix

附录

LETTER TO ALFRED BENDINER (CV INCLUDED)

1037 Yale Station

April 26, 1947

Dear Al:

Thank you for the note. You & Betty must think me the most ungrateful animal in the world not to have written a word after the wonderful & warm reception given me. However, I know you both will understand and forgive me since I am living the life of slave that is perpetually driven by an invisible whip.

Recently there had been frequent enquiries about my work since I left America last. Once I made a list in answer to an exhaustive questionnaire. I am enclosing a copy for your reference.

My best to you & Betty,

Yours

Ssu-ch'eng

致阿尔弗雷德·班迪纳的信（内附履历）[1]

亲爱的阿尔：

谢谢你的信。你和佩蒂一定觉得我是世界上最忘恩负义的动物——我受到了你们美好热情的招待，之后却没有给你们寄去只言片语。不管怎样，我知道你们一定会理解我、原谅我，因为我正过着奴隶般的生活，总是被无形的鞭子所驱使。

最近，经常有人问到我上次离开美国后的工作情况。我曾列了一张简历表来回答一份详尽的问卷，随信寄给你一份，供参考。[2]

向你和佩蒂致以最良好的问候。

你的

思成

耶鲁车站1037号

一九四七年四月二十六日

LIANG SSU-CH'ENG

Scholarship in Colleges

Graduate, Tsinghua College, Peiping, 1923;

B. Arch., University of Pennsylvania, 1927 (February);

M. Arch., University of Pennsylvania, 1927 (June);

Harvard Grad. School (Fine Arts), 1927–28;

Spayd Brook Gold Medal for merit in architectural design, 1927;

Litt. D. (Hon.) Princeton, 1947;

Honorary fraternities: Sigma Associate, Tau Sigma Delta, Architectural Association of the University of Pennsylvania.

Research & Teaching

Research Fellow & Director of Research, Institute for Research in Chinese Architecture, 1931– (reorganized and introduced scientific approach to its studies);

Assistant Professor in Charge, Department of Architecture Northeastern University, 1928–30 (founded this department);

Professor in Charge, Department of Architecture, North-eastern University, 1930–31;

Lecturer of History of Architecture, National Peking University, Peiping, 1932-33;

Lecturer of History of Architecture, National Tsinghua University, Peiping, 1932-34;

Professor & Chairman, Department of Architecture, National Tsinghua University, Peiping, 1946– (founded this department);

Director, Institute of Architectural Research, National Tsinghua University, 1946– (founder);

Visiting Professor of Fine Arts, Yale University, 1946–47.

梁思成

学校教育

清华学校毕业，北平，1923；

宾夕法尼亚大学，建筑学学士，1927（2月）；

宾夕法尼亚大学，建筑学硕士，1927（6月）；

哈佛研究生院（艺术学院），1927—1928；

因建筑设计成绩获得斯拜德·布鲁克金奖，1927；

普林斯顿文学荣誉博士，1947；

西格玛协会荣誉会员，宾夕法尼亚大学建筑协会。

研究与教学

中国营造学社研究员及研究主任，1931— （对研究工作用科学的方法进行重组和阐释）；

东北大学建筑系助理教授，1928—1930（建立该系）；

东北大学建筑系教授，1930—1931；

建筑历史讲师，国立北京大学，北平，1932—1933；

建筑学讲师，国立清华大学，北平，1932—1934；

教授及系主任，国立清华大学建筑系，北平，1946— （建立该系）；

主任，建筑研究所，国立清华大学，北平，1946— （创立者）；

艺术学院访问教授，耶鲁大学，1946—1947。

Membership and Services to Cultural and Professional Institutions

Fellow Member, Academia Sinica, 1933– ;

Member, National Academy of Peiping, 1934– ;

Member, Association of Chinese Architects, 1928– ;

Member & Specialist on Architecture, Central Commission for the Conservation of Antiquities, 1934– ;

Member, Provincial Commission for the Conservation of Antiquities of Szechwan, 1939– ;

Member & Technical Expert, National Commission for the Restoration of Historical Monuments of the Ancient Capital (Peiping), 1934– ;

Architectural Advisor, National Central Museum, 1936– ;

Architectural Advisor, National Central Library, 1937– ;

Chairman, Committee for Compilation of Historical Materials On Chinese Architecture, National Central Museum, 1939– (founder);

Vice-Chairman, Chinese Commission for the Preservation of Cultural Objects in War Areas (counter-part of the "Robert Commission" of U.S.A.O., 1945–46);

Technical advisor, National Palace Museum, Peiping, 1934;

Correspondence Member, Ostasiatische Kunstgeschichte Something (I forget) 1936 (?)– , Frankfurt or Berlin (I also forget);

Chinese Architect to Board of Design Consultants, UN Planning Board, 1947.

Publications

Official Regulations for Architectural Design in Ts'ing Dynasty Style, 1933;

The Liao Dynasty 984, Structure of the Hall of Avalokitesvara at Tu-le Ssu (Chi Hsien), 1932;

The Architecture of the Temple of Confucius, Ch'üfu, and Plans for Its Restoration, 1935;

Wen-yuan Ke (a report on the architecture of the famous library of Emperor Ch'ien-lung and plans for its restoration) 1932, (in collaboration with Cai Fang-yin & Liu Tun-tseng);

A Report on the Ancient Architecture of Ta-t'ung, 1933 (in collaboration with Liu Tun-tseng);

文化与专业研究机构成员或工作经历

通讯研究员，中央研究院，1933—；

研究员，北平国立研究院，1934—；

会员，中国建筑师协会，1928—；

委员及建筑专家，中央古物保存委员会，1934—；

委员，四川省古物保存委员会，1939—；

委员、技术专家，国家古都历史建筑保护委员会（北平），1934—；

建筑顾问，国立中央博物院，1936—；

建筑顾问，国立中央图书馆，1937—；

主任，国立中央博物院中国建筑史料编纂委员会，1939—（创立者）；

副主任，战区文物保护中国委员会（美国罗伯特委员会的国家分委员会，1945—1946）；

技术顾问，故宫博物院，北平，1934—；

通讯成员，东亚艺术史的什么机构（我记不清了），1936（?），在法兰克福或柏林（我也记不清了）；

联合国总部设计顾问团中国建筑师，1947。

出版物

《清式营造则例》，1933；

《蓟县独乐寺观音阁山门考》，1932；

《曲阜孔庙之建筑及其修葺计划》，1935；

《故宫文渊阁楼面修理计划》（关于清代乾隆皇帝的这一著名藏书建筑的报告和修复方案），1932（与蔡方荫、刘敦桢合著）；

《大同古建筑调查报告》，1933（与刘敦桢合著）；

A Pictorial History of Chinese Architecture (text in both English and Chinese), to be published, possibly in U.S.A.;

A Modern Interpretation of Ying-tsao-fa-shih (a treatise on architecture by Li Chieh, architect to Emperor Hui-tsung, Sung Dynasty, first published in 1100), to be published;

A Grammar of Chinese Architecture, English & Chinese editions, in preparation.

Articles:

What We Know of the Buddhist Temples and Palaces of the T'ang Dynasty, 1932;

The Hall of Three Bodhisattvas of Kuang-tsi Ssu, Pao-ti, 1932;

Plans for the Restoration of the Liu-ho Pagoda, Hang-chou, 1935;

Preliminary Report on the Ancient Architecture, Fen River Valley, Shansi, 1935 (in collaboration with Lin Hui-yin / Mrs. Liang);

The Architecture of the Northern Wei Dynasty found Represented in Yun-kang Caves, 1933 (in collaboration with Liu Tung-tseng & Lin Hui-yin);

The Architecture of the Han Dynasty, 1934 (in collaboration with Liu Tun-tseng & Pao Ting);

Preliminary Report on the Ancient Architecture of Chengting, 1933;

An-chi Ch'iao, the "Great Stone Bridge" of Chao Hsien, 1934;

Open-spandrel Bridges of Ancient China (I. The An-chi Ch'iao at Chao-chou, Hopei; II. The Yung-t'ung Ch'iao at Chao-chou, Hopei) (a condensed English version of the above article), *Pencil Points* Magazine, January & March, 1938;

Five Early Chinese Pagodas, *Asia Magazine*, 1941;

A Report on the T'ang Dynasty Hall, 857, of Fo-kuang Ssu, Wu-t'ai Mountains, Shansi, 1945;

The Oldest Wooden Structure in China (a condensed English version of the above article), *Asia Magazine*, 1941;

Chinese Architecture, for the next edition of *The Encyclopedia Britannica*;

Chinese Architecture and Art, for the next edition of *The Encyclopedia Americana*;

etc., etc., etc.

《图像中国建筑史》(文字为英文和中文)，可能将在美国出版；

《宋营造法式注释》(《营造法式》为宋徽宗的皇家建筑师李诫关于建筑的专著，出版于1100年)，即将出版。

《中国建筑的文法》(英文稿和中文稿)，写作中。

文章

《我们所知道的唐代佛寺与宫殿》，1932；

《宝坻县广济寺三大士殿》，1932；

《杭州六和塔复原状计划》，1935；

《晋汾古建筑预查纪略》，山西，1935(与林徽因合著)；

《云冈石窟中表现的北魏建筑》，1933(与刘敦桢、林徽因合著)；

《汉代的建筑式样与装饰》，1934(与刘敦桢、鲍鼎合著)；

《正定调查纪略》，1933；

《赵县大石桥》，1934；

《两座中国古代的拱券桥》(即上文的英文简写稿)，发表于《铅笔尖》杂志，1938年1月号和3月号；

《中国的五座古塔》，发表于《亚洲杂志》，1941；

《记五台山佛光寺的唐代建筑(857)》，1945；

《中国最古老的木结构建筑》(即上文的英文简写稿)，发表于《亚洲杂志》，1941；

“中国建筑”条目，为新版《大英百科全书》所写；

“中国的建筑与艺术”条目，为新版《大美百科全书》所写；

等等，等等，等等。

Field Trips

In search of architecture in this virgin field of study, field trips were taken by members of the Institute for Research in Chinese Architecture regularly twice every year from 1932 to 1937. Less regularly from 1935 to 1945. Covering more than 200 hsiens (counties) in 15 provinces in China. More than 2200 "units" studies (photographed & measured). Mostly conducted personally by L. S. C. Less than one-tenths of materials thus collected were able to be published.

Creative Work in Architecture

The University of Chi-lin Group, Chi-lin Province, 1930 (in collaboration with Ch'en Chih and T'ung Chun, and Cai Fang-yin);

The University of Communication Group, Chin-chou, 1930 (destroyed in war) (in collaboration with Phyllis Lin);

The Geology Building, National Peking University, Peiping, 1934 (in collaboration with Phyllis Lin);

Women's Dormitory, National Peking University, Peiping, 1935 (in collaboration with Phyllis Lin);

National Central Museum, Nanking (as consulting architect), 1937 (work interrupted by war, resumed in 1946);

And a number of residences and shops, etc., with Phyllis Lin.

Restoration Work

The Temples, Pagodas & Palaces of Peiping, as technical expert to the Ancient Capital Commission (work started in 1934, still going on);

The Temple of Confucius Group, Ch'üfu (interrupted by war);

The Pagoda of Liu-ho T'a, Hang-chou (prevented by war);

The Great Stone Bridge, Chao Hsien (interrupted by war);

The "Little Geese Pagoda," Sian (did not start on account of war);

The Main Hall of Yen-fu Ssu, Hsuan-p'ing (did not start on account of war);

The Yun-kang Caves, Ta-t'ung (plan did not realize on account of prohibitively high expense).

实地考察

在这块研究的处女地中，为找寻建筑，从 1932 年到 1937 年中国营造学社的成员每年固定进行两次调查，从 1935 年到 1945 年则不十分规律，旅行地区覆盖了中国 15 个省的 200 多个县。进行了 2200 多个实例的研究（摄影和测量）。大部分由梁思成指导，将近十分之一已收集到的资料将能出版。

建筑创作

吉林大学，吉林省，1930，与陈植、童寯和蔡方荫合作；

交通大学，锦州，1930（战争中被毁），与林徽因合作；

地质馆，国立北京大学，北平，1934，与林徽因合作；

女生宿舍，国立北京大学，北平，1935，与林徽因合作；

国立中央博物院，南京（顾问建筑师），1937（工作因战争中断，1946 年恢复）；

其他一些住宅和商店等，与林徽因合作。

复原保护工作

作为故都文物整理委员会技术专家，参与北平的寺庙、塔和宫殿的保护（工作开始于 1935 年，现仍在进行）；

曲阜孔庙（因战争而中断）；

六和塔，杭州（因战争而停止）；

大石桥，赵县（因战争而中断）；

小雁塔，西安（因战争而未能开始）；

延福寺大殿，宣平（因战争而未能开始）；

云冈石窟，大同（由于造价限制，计划未能实现）。

（吕舟 译 高亦兰 校）

LETTER TO WILMA FAIRBANK

Tsing Hua, Peking

December 30, 1956

Dear Wilma:

It is a pleasant surprise to hear from you again after all these long years. I was away in Poland and Germany when T. S. came back with your warm letter which reached me only after my return to Peking a few days ago.

Yes, Wilma, I know that you will share with me my grief over P.'s death and I am deeply touched by your sympathy and condolescence. It is more than a year and a half now. She fought most courageously against her poor health and was undaunted till the last moment. It may console you a little to know that she was never so happy over life and work as in her last 6½ years. Like all the intelligentsia in China today, she had already seen with unshakable conviction and absolute self-confidence a picture of the great and bright future for her country and her people. In spite of her very poor health, she proudly shares with other architects the responsibility and burden of reconstructing the country and the training of future generations of architects. She was appointed a top-rank architect of the Municipality of Peking and a member of the City Planning Commission, concurrently teaching in Tsing Hua, and was elected a representative of the People's Representatives' Congress of Peking. She even found opportunities in improving the designs of cloisonné (remember how ugly they could be?!) and "soaked" herself in the workshops for days on a stretch, working together with the artisans and created articles of exquisite beauty.

She was still bending over her drawing board, sitting in bed, against the advice of doctors and disregarding the protests of the family and friends, till a few days before she was taken to the hospital on Feb. 12, '55. She was 50, and ill, but her enthusiasm was as high as ever, as you knew her years ago. She was confident that she would recover soon and be back to work again. But in spite of

致费慰梅的信

亲爱的威尔玛：

多年以后再次收到你的来信，真令我感到惊喜。（钱）端升带回来你热情洋溢的信件的时候，我正在波兰和德国。几天前，我刚结束访问回到北京，就收到了你的来信。

是的，威尔玛，我对徽因的病逝痛不欲生，我想你也会和我一样悲伤。你的同情和慰问让我非常感动。徽因的离去已经超过一年半时间了。她非常勇敢地同病魔战斗，直到最后一刻也没有畏缩。她从来没有像生命中最后六年半时间里那样，为生活和工作而如此幸福——我想这会使你感到稍许宽慰。像今天中国的知识精英一样，徽因对她的祖国和人民伟大光明的前途有着坚定不移的自信。她拖着病体，与其他建筑师一起非常自豪地承担重建国家和培养下一代建筑师的责任和重担。她被任命为北京市高级建筑师和北京市都市计划委员会委员，被推选为北京市人大代表；同时，她一边还在清华教课。她甚至觅得良机去改进景泰蓝的设计（你还记得它们是多么地不堪入目么？！），整天绷紧了弦泡在车间里，与工匠们一起工作，创造精美的款式。

她不听从医生的忠告和家人朋友的反对，即使卧病在床仍然离不开画板，直到1955年2月12日被送往医院的前几天。她当时已经有50岁了，病魔缠身，但是她的激情与你多年前认识她的时候一样高昂。她相信自己将会很快康复，并重新投入工作。尽管医生们竭尽全力，

all the efforts of the doctors, she lost her last battle on April 1st. Perhaps her only regret is that she did not live to see the radiant future for which she contributed every ounce of strength of her last few years' life.

Ever since 1949, she was given the best medical care by the Government (all free of charge, of course) and, after her death, in recognition of her service to the people, was buried in the People's Revolutionary Cemetery near 八宝山. Only if she had such case a few years earlier, she would have a much better chance to recover, and would be able to do much much more.

Yes, Wilma, P.'s death is a terrible blow to me and an irretrievable loss to many of our friends, Lao Chin, Hsi-jo and T. S. especially, and to many younger members of the teaching staff in Tsing Hua. I found work difficult without her cooperation to which I was so accustomed for nearly 30 years. It took me considerable length of time to pull myself together again and proceed with work. But, you can well imagine, how limped I am without her guiding wisdom and never failing encouragement on which I was almost completely dependent.

As to myself, I can only tell you that, like every architect, no, like almost everybody in China today, I have been very, very busy for the last eight years. In 1949, architects were transformed overnight from a mere social ornament to the post of vanguard of the country's reconstruction. Ever since 1949, I have been working on the planning of Peking, but did comparatively little in the designing of individual buildings. If you come today, you will find Peking very much changed. Hundreds of new buildings have sprung up, most of them in the suburbs—enormous cotton mills with their workers' dormitories in the East suburbs where you used to go riding with P.; the North and N.W. suburbs covered with numerous new buildings of new institutions of higher education. All these connected by miles and miles of new roads. And by the way, talking about roads, the road from 西直门 to the Summer Palace is now a double driveway, and on Sundays and holidays, when the Summer Palace (usually) gets as crowded as the Tung-an Shih-chang (unimaginable?), the traffic flow on the driveway presents

她还是在4月1日结束了人生的这场战斗。她在最后几年光阴里耗尽精力为之奋斗的事业，其未来是如何地光辉，这个她没有亲眼见到，也许是她唯一的遗憾。

1949年以来，她一直受到政府最好的医疗护理（当然一切都是免费的）；在她去世以后，为肯定徽因对人民的贡献，她被葬在八宝山附近的人民革命公墓。哪怕更早几年是这种情况，她将会有更好的机会康复，也将会做更多的事情。

是的，威尔玛，徽因的死对我是一个重大的打击，对我们的许多朋友以及清华大学的许多年轻教师而言也意味着不可挽回的损失，特别是老金（金岳霖）、（张）奚若和（钱）端升。近30年来，我早已习惯了她的协作，失之犹感寸步难行。我过了很长时间才使自己恢复平静、重新振作起来投入工作。但是，你能想象得到，她的睿智引导和从未间断的鼓励，是我所完全依赖的；缺少了这个，我就如同跛行夜路一般。

至于我自己，我只能告诉你，像每一个建筑师，不，像今天的大多数中国人一样，我在这八年里非常繁忙。1949年，建筑师从仅仅是社会的装饰品，一夜之间转变为国家重建的急先锋。1949年以来，我一直在忙于北京城市的规划，在单体建筑的设计上所作相对甚少。如果你今天来到北京，会发现北京发生了翻天覆地的变化。成百上千的新建筑如雨后春笋般出现，它们大部分在郊区。在你从前经常和徽因一起骑马的东郊建起了大片的棉纺厂和工人的宿舍。北郊和西北郊满是新建高校的新建筑。穿连其中的则是一条条长长的新公路。说到公路，从西直门到颐和园的公路现在是双向车道。在周日和节日，颐和园（常）像东安市场一般拥挤（不能想象吧？），车流之繁忙为几年前

a sight unthinkable a few years ago, and of course the parking problem in front of the entrance to the Summer Palace duely becomes a headache for the city planner. The area around the former race-course and 八宝山 is now almost completely urbanized. In short, you will find Peking very much different from what you know of it from your memories.

It may also interest you to know that the architectural department in Tsing Hua has grown to more than ten times its original size and by 1958, it will be expanded to about 600 undergraduate (plus about 50-60 graduate students). These boys and girls are all so eager to learn and so confident and aware of their responsibilities in the future that it is a joy to teach them. In spite of these vast expansions, but still, how they clamour for more and more architects.

Engaged principally in planning and teaching, I did comparatively little field work in Chinese architecture since 1949. But many of my former colleagues, who are now working in the Ministry of Culture, had done a great, great deal. Besides many important discoveries, they also did much in repair and restorations of ancient edifices, including the Sui Dynasty bridge at Chao-chou. Batches of archaeological workers from all over the country were given courses in Chinese architecture in successive summer training classes in which I gave series of lectures almost every summer. But recently, the Government decided to establish an Institute of Research in the History and Theory of Architecture, starting with a staff much bigger than that of the Ying-tsao Hsüeh-shê and I expect to devote at least half of my time to it. Perhaps you've already read about it in the *Kuang-ming Jih-pao*.

Perhaps it will be a surprise (or no surprise?) to you if I tell you that P. was already a grandma before she died, and that now I have already three grandchildren!! Tsai-ping (Bao-bao) has a son and a daughter and Chung-chieh (Hsiao-ti), a son. Chung-chieh's wife is Chou Ru-mei (May), Pei-yuan's daughter. Enclosed are a few snap-shots introducing the new members of the family.

所无法想象；当然，颐和园入口处停车的问题令城市的规划者颇为头疼。过去的赛马场和八宝山附近的区域现在已经几乎完全城市化了。简而言之，北京与你记忆中的印象大为不同了。

还有一个消息也许会令你感兴趣：清华大学建筑系的规模已相当于初建之时的十多倍，到1958年它将扩展到拥有600名本科生（以及五六十名研究生）。这些孩子们都非常好学，非常清楚他们未来的责任，并且信心十足；所以，给他们教课是一件令人愉快的事。尽管建筑系扩展得很快，但我们仍然需要越来越多的建筑师。

1949年以后，我主要精力放在城市规划和教学工作上，对中国建筑的实地调查所作相较而言极少。但是我之前的很多同事现在在文化部工作，他们在这方面做了很多很多。除了一些重大的发现，他们在修复包括隋代赵州桥在内的古建筑方面也贡献颇多。连续几个暑期的训练班上，全国各地的考古工作者分批接受中国建筑方面的课程培训，几乎每个暑期我都为此作了一系列讲座。而就在最近，政府决定重新建立建筑历史与理论研究室，人员的数量要比营造学社大很多。我希望能把至少一半的时间投入其中。也许你已经在《光明日报》上看到了这一消息。

如果我告诉你徽因在去世之前已经成为祖母，而且我现在也已经有了三个孙辈孩子了，你也许会感到惊讶（或者不惊讶？）。再冰（宝宝）生了一儿一女，从诫（小弟）有了一个儿子。从诫的妻子是周如枚，是（周）培源的女儿。信里附上几张我家新成员的照片。

About your old friends, all I need to tell you is that they are all well and happy. They are happy in their work and very busy. I hope you and John will come and pay us a visit. (The door of New China is always wide open and many Americans have already been here.) You'll find great changes here. They are worthwhile seeing. And of your old friends, with the single exception of myself, the most noticeable change in their appearance is perhaps in their hair, especially Lao Chin and Hsi-jo, who are now almost completely white, but in spirit, as young as ever. In health, the only one who should be ashamed of himself is myself. I had a rather bad relapse of T.B. last year and was in the hospital for six months and later in the Summer Palace rest-curing for five months. But I have only myself to blame because I still insisted on working with such gusto as I did in the young days, a little too disproportionate to my age and present state of health. Now I have learnt to be wiser and promise to go slow and to apply my brake more diligently. I am determined to keep on going, moderate but conspirito, for at least another 25 years, because New China needs every architect—every single person's strength, no matter how meager his contribution.

In closing—One request and three wishes:

Request:—Will it be too much trouble for you to mail the drawings and photographs of Chinese architecture which I left with you back in '47 to "Miss Chen Lau 刘蕙真, Methodist International House, 76, Osborne Rd., Newcastle-on-Tyne, 2, England"? I wish to make many revisions and additions to those drawings.

Wishes:—(1) that you will write again; (2) that you and J. will come and pay us a visit soon; (3) [much belated] A very Merry X'mas and a Happy New Year!

Yours,

Ssu-ch'eng

关于你的老朋友们，我要告诉你的是，他们都身体很好，也都非常幸福。他们非常开心地投入工作，也非常繁忙。我希望你和约翰（译者注：即费正清）能来看看我们。（新中国的大门永远是打开的，很多美国人已经来过这里。）你将会发现这里发生了巨大的变化。这些都值得看看。除了我以外，你的老朋友们在外貌上最显著的变化就是他们的头发，特别是老金和奚若，头发几乎全白了，但是精气神儿仍旧跟年轻时一样。在健康上，只有我自惭不已。去年，我因为肺结核复发住院六个月，尔后在颐和园疗养了五个月。这只能怨我自己，因为我仍然坚持像年轻时候一样干劲十足地去工作，这与我现在的年纪和健康状况有点不太相称。现在我学聪明了，答应会放慢脚步，勤踩刹车。我决定平和而精神饱满地至少再工作 25 年，因为新中国需要每一个建筑师、每一个人贡献力量，无论他的力量是多么微薄。

最后，一个请求和三个心愿：

请求——可否麻烦你将我 1947 年留在你那儿的中国建筑的绘图和照片邮寄给刘蕙真小姐？她的地址是 Methodist International House, 76, Osborne Rd., Newcastle-on-Tyne, 2, England。我想对那些绘图作多处修订和补充。

心愿——（一）你将会再写信过来；（二）你和约翰很快会来看望我们；（三）迟到的祝福：圣诞快乐！新年快乐！

思成

一九五六年十二月三十日

于北京清华大学

（吴子桐 译）

注释

Chinese Architecture 中国建筑

[1] 半坡遗址分为居住、制陶、墓葬三个区，涉及的房屋遗迹、圈栏、窖穴、陶窑、墓葬等，均在英文术语“pit”的覆盖范围之内——任小玫注。

[2] 阙是从防卫性的“观”演变而来的一种表示威仪和等级名分的建筑，由于双阙孤植而“中间阙然为道”，因而称“阙”——任小玫注。

[3] “如跂斯翼，如矢斯棘，如鸟斯革，如翚斯飞，君子攸跻。”这是《诗经》中对宫室建筑的描述，详见《小雅·斯干》。由此可知西周大屋顶已引人注目，但不知有无翼角——李革胜注。

[4] 根据“匠人营国”的制度，除皇城以外，居住区分为国宅与闾里两部分。“国宅”指王公贵族和朝廷重臣居住的地方，一般都环绕在王城左右或前后。“闾里”则是一般平民居住的地方，但也是分等级的，较上层的从地理位置上看也是对称分布于皇城的东西两侧不远的地方——任小玫注。

[5] 木材加工远比石料快，加上唐宋以后使用了类似今天的建筑模数制的方法（宋代用“材”，清代用“斗口”），各种木构件的式样也已定型，因此可同时加工，制成后再组合拼装——任小玫注。

[6] 欧洲人用来表示中国的“塔”所用的“pagoda”一词来源存疑。很有可能 pa-go-da 只是三个中文字母的摹仿标音：ba（八）、go（角）和 ta（塔）。因此，pagoda 音为 bagota，即“八角塔”——作者注。

[7] The li is a Chinese lineal measure equivalent to 500 meters. The li of the Zhou Dynasty is estimated to be about 440 meters long. 里是中国的长度计量单位，每里相当于 500 米，周朝时则约为 440 米——作者注。

[8] 意思是说，帝王都城的规制是城市平面应当见方九里，各边城门大小三个。城内街道划分成九纵九横。纵向街道宽度应为能同时行驶九辆马车。宫殿的左边是祖庙，右边是社稷。宫殿前面是群臣朝拜的地方，后面则是市场——任小玫注。

[9] 《周礼·天官》中就有此规定：“唯王建国，辨方正位”——任小玫注。

[10] 从战国到北宋初年，都城实行的是坊市制；北宋中期以后，采用的则是街巷制。至于文中所提的“集市区”，即隋代的“都会市”和“利人市”，各用两坊地的面积，因此作者形容其“面积宽敞”。都会市在朱雀街东侧，唐代称为“东市”；利人市在朱雀街西，唐代称为“西市”。东、西两市是商肆集中的商业区——任小玫注。

[11] 明朝初期，曾建都应天（今江苏南京）。1927 年，南京国民政府成立。此后直至 1949 年，除 1932 年“一·二八事变”后短期迁都洛阳和全面抗战爆发后迁都重庆之外，南京一直作为国都——任小玫注。

[12] 在色彩应用上，故宫完全反映了“五行”思想：宫墙、殿柱用红色，红属火，属光明正大；屋顶用黄色，黄属土、属中央，皇帝必居中；皇宫东部屋顶用绿色，属东方木绿，属春，用于皇子居住——曾俊伟注。

A Han Terracotta Model of a Three-story House
一个汉代的三层楼陶制明器

[1] 本文为打字稿，现存清华大学建筑学院档案，估计作于梁思成先生第一次赴美留学期间——英若聪注。

Two Liao Structures of Tu-lo Ssu, Chi Hsien 蓟县独乐寺观音阁山门考

[1] 本文原载于 1932 年《中国营造学社汇刊》第三卷第二期——莫宗江注。中英文均为梁思成先生所作——编者注。

[2] 《周礼·考工记》, *The Book of Works of the Chow Dynasty*——作者注。

[3] 《阿房宫赋》, *An Ode on the Famous Palaces of Chin Shih-huang-ti, Emperor of China, 221 BC–210 BC*——作者注。

[4] 《两都赋》 and 《两京赋》, *Odes on the East and West Capitals of the Han Emperors*——作者注。

[5] 《洛阳伽蓝记》, *Buddhist Temples of Loyang* by Yang Hsien-chih (杨衒之) of the Wei Dynasty——作者注。

[6] 《元故宫遗录》, *Recollections of the Old Yuan Palaces* by Hsiao Hsun (萧洵) of the Ming Dynasty——作者注。

[7] 此是 20 世纪 30 年代日本学界的说法。近年日本学界已公认法隆寺虽为公元 607 年圣德太子创建，但在公元 670 年焚毁。公元 680 年以后在原址西北重建，约在公元 710 年建成，即现存的法隆寺西院中门、塔、堂、回廊等筑。但再建的法隆寺西院仍保持飞鸟时代的风格特点，也仍是现存世界上最古的木构建筑——傅熹年注。

[8] 山西大同华严寺教藏，建于辽兴宗重熙七年（公元 1038 年）——作者注。当时中国营造学社刚开始进行调查古建筑，尚未积累足够的史料，故多参考日本学者的调查资料。如日本常盘大定、关野贞等的著作《支那佛教史迹》等，薄伽教藏是其中有确切纪年之例，故引用之。以后随着营造学社工作的开展，发现了一些更古老的建筑，最后形成一个有纪年的木建筑的排序目录。薄伽教藏现在的年代排序是第 15 名——傅熹年注。

[9] 施嘉炀，1902 年出生，早年赴美留学，回国后在清华大学土木系任教，是清华大学土木系第一任系主任，20 世纪 40 年代任清华工学院院长，现为清华水利系一级教授，已退休。曾长期任水利学会、水利工程学会理事长——傅熹年注。

[10] 蔡方荫，详《故宫文渊阁楼面修理计划》一文——傅熹年注。

[11] 朱启钤，（1872—1964）字桂辛，贵州紫江人，曾任清京师大学堂译学馆监督，辛亥革命后历任交通总长、内务总长、代理国务总理。退休后，于 1929 年发起组织中国营造学社，1930 年正式成立，自任社长，聘梁思成、刘敦桢分任法式部、文献部主任，从事中国古代建筑的调查研究，影响深远。1949 年后历任中央文史馆馆员，第二、三届全国政协委员——傅熹年注。

[12] First published in 1103, reprinted in 1925 by the Commercial Press, Shanghai. 初刊于 1103 年，1925 年上海商务印书馆再版——作者注。

[13] 参阅拙著《我们所知道的唐代佛寺与宫殿》——作者注。

[14] 楼阁外周之露台，古称“平座”。斗拱之在屋角者为“转角铺作”，在柱与柱之间者为“补间铺作”——作者注。

[15] 斗拱大斗安拱之口为“斗口”——作者注。

[16] 日本古代历史时代，起自公元 1185 年，止于公元 1333 年。当中国南宋孝宗淳熙十二年至元顺帝元统元年，镰仓时代建筑受同期中国南方建筑影响较大——傅熹年注。

[17] 梁思成先生在述及中国古代与辽、金、蒙古等少数民族政权并立的汉族政权时，常使用“中国”一词。“中国”的这一用法在古代汉语中十分常见，指“我国中原地区或在中原地区华夏族建立的政权”之义。例如，《史记 · 孝武本纪》：“天下名山八，而三在蛮夷，五在中国。”又如，《汉书 · 匈奴传下》：“[伊黑居次] 云常欲与中国和亲。”——吴子桐注。

[18] 即夏历，1927 年以后推行公历，故称夏历为废历——傅熹年注。

[19] This passage not found in the 1872 edition of the *P'an-shan Chih*. 同治十一年李氏刻本《盘山志》方无此段——作者注。

[20] 查辽史，统和四年碑上提到的“故尚父秦王”应是韩匡嗣，而不是开泰初（公元 1012—1021 年）始加尚父的耶律奴瓜——莫宗江注。

[21]《营造法式》初刊于宋崇宗二年（公元 1103 年）——莫宗江注。

[22] 胡国佐（Hu Kuo-tso），疑为作者笔误，见注 [24]——编者注。

[23]《蓟州志》（官秩 · 户部分司题名）柯维蓁，万历中任是职，王于陛之前任——作者注。

[24] 《蓟州志》（官秩 · 知州题名）胡国佐、三韩人、荫生。修学宫西庑戟门，有记。陞湖广德安府同知，去任之日，民攀辕号泣，送不忍舍，盖德政有以及人也——作者注。

[25] 清东陵，在蓟东遵化县境——作者注。

[26] 建筑物之长度为面阔，深度为进深——作者注。

[27] 如屋五间，居中者为明间或当心间，其次曰次间，两端为梢间——作者注。

[28] 斜坡不作阶级，由一高度达另一高度之道为礓磜——作者注。

[29] 屋顶各面斜坡相交成脊，如屋顶四面皆坡，则除顶上正脊外，四隅尚有四垂脊，即“四阿”是——作者注。

[30] 在建筑物纵中线之上之柱，在明间次间之间，或次间梢间之间者为“中柱”。在最外两端者为“山柱”。在建筑物前后面之柱为“檐柱”，在角者为“角柱”——作者注。

[31] The ch’ih is the Chinese foot, and is equal to about 32 cm. A ch’ih is divided into ten ch’un (inch), a ch’un into ten fen, a fen into ten li. 尺为中国市制长度单位，约相当于32 厘米。一尺等于十寸，一寸等于十分，一分等于十厘——作者注。

[32] 由檐柱中线至台基外边为前后“台出”，由山柱中线至两旁台基外边为两山“台出”——作者注。

[33] 长方形建筑物之两狭面为“两山”——作者注。

[34] 罗马建筑五式之一（爱奥尼克柱式），其柱之长为径之九倍——作者注。

[35] 柱间安窗，先将窗框安于柱旁，谓之“抱框”——作者注。

[36] 柱下大上小，谓之“收分”——作者注。

[37] 将木材方正之端，斫造使圆，谓之“卷杀”——作者注。

[38] 柱下之石，谓名“柱顶石”。其上雕起作盘形部分，宋称“覆盆”，清称“古镜”，宋式繁多，而清式简单——作者注。

[39] 清称“斗拱”，宋称“铺作”——作者注。

[40] 用拱之制，原则上为上层材较下层伸出，层层叠出，即挑檐或悬臂之法是也。《营造法式》拱每伸出一层，谓之一“跳”，拱端谓之“跳头”——作者注。

[41] 敦煌壁画大部为唐代遗物，初祖庵建于宋徽宗宣和七年——作者注。

[42] 见《营造学社汇刊》三卷一期刘敦桢译《法隆寺建筑》补注，补图第十六、第十七——作者注。

[43] 斗拱之全部称“朵”，清称“攒”——作者注。

[44] 栌斗耳、平、欹的高应为 0.11、0.08、0.13 米——莫宗江注。

[45] 1932 年明用陶本《营造法式》缺慢拱条全文——莫宗江注。

[46] 据《营造法式》卷五栋条，应称“橑风榑”，后同——傅熹年注。

[47] 清代已无营造法式中襻间的做法——莫宗江注。

[48] 宋代举屋之法仍应按以上所引《法式》原文，非清式之五举——莫宗江注。

[49]《营造法式》规定檐出按椽径定，而椽径是按殿阁或厅堂而定。如殿阁椽径九分至十分，厅堂椽径七分至八分等——莫宗江注。

[50] 中国屋顶之结构，可分三大类：前后左右皆为斜坡者为“庑殿”，古称“四阿”；前后有斜坡而左右山墙直上者为“悬山”；四周有斜坡而左右两坡之上半截改为直上，如悬山与庑殿相合者为“歇山”——作者注。

[51] 歇山直立部分之三角形为山花，宋式称“两际”——作者注。

[52] 清代在外檐平坐栏杆的四角加支柱，造成类似一周檐廊的错觉，实际是平坐（下同）——莫宗江注。

[53] 文中只有各柱脚间尺寸，无各柱头间尺寸，因此不能看出柱侧脚之度——莫宗江注。

[54] transitional member——作者注。

[55] 表中将上层檐柱、角柱、内柱、中柱的柱高都作 2.75 米，这是当时还不了解古代建筑的柱高有生起之误——莫宗江注。

[56] 欧洲建筑有所谓 superposed order 者，此其真正之实例也——作者注。

[57] shearing force——作者注。

[58] 独乐寺的阁与门柱础上都没有覆盆——莫宗江注。

[59] 罗汉枋长通建筑物之全长宽度或全长度，清式谓之“拽枋”；其在外者为“外拽枋”，在内者为“内拽枋”。柱头枋清式称“正心枋”——作者注。

[60] 角拱仍是 45 度——莫宗江注。

[61]“重杪重昂”清式称“重翘重昂”——作者注。

[62] 乔托（Giotto），文艺复兴初期意大利画家，画纯朴有蕴力。拉斐尔（Raphael），文艺复兴后期画家，写实妙肖——作者注。

[63] 这里所指的是“平阁”，下同——莫宗江注。

[64] 观音阁无劄牵，应是指前后乳栿——莫宗江注。

[65] 内槽柱上的五架梁，不应是檐栿——莫宗江注。

In Search of Ancient Architecture in North China (Extract)
华北古建调查报告（节选）

[1] 本文是梁思成为北京大学和清华大学所作关于建筑历史的英文演讲稿，未曾发表，打字稿现存清华大学建筑学院档案。根据文章内容推断，应写于 1940 年，当时梁家随中央研究院正住在昆明。另据费正清夫人费慰梅女士所著《梁思成与林徽因》一书第 11 章的注释，费慰梅亦保存有本文打字稿，并注明该文 1940 年写于昆明（Wilma Fairbank: *Liang and Lin*, University of Pennsylvania Press, Philadelphia, 1994, P. 199）。本文的部分内容后来整理成《中国最古老的木构建筑》及《五座中国古塔》两篇文章，分别发表于英文《亚洲杂志》1941 年 7 月号和 8 月号——林鹤、李道增注。本篇节选内容未包括《中国最古老的木构建筑》与《五座中国古塔》（单篇见后），另《佛教石窟造像》一节因内容相对独立，亦在本书单独成篇（见后）——编者补注。

[2] 本文全部图片经中国营造学社允许发表——作者注。

[3] 维诺拉（Vignola），意大利建筑师，五柱式建筑的创造者——林鹤、李道增注。

[4] 本文中“英里”、“英尺”等度量单位据原文均为英制，但根据梁思成中文著作比较，应为中国度量单位“里”、“尺”，下同——林鹤、李道增注。

[5] 清王昶辑，《金石萃编》，卷一百二十二，宋一，“正定府龙兴寺铸铜像记，乾德元年五月”——林鹤、李道增注。

[6] 据《金石萃编》记载碑文为叛龙河——林鹤、李道增注。

[7] 作者的一篇文章《中国古代的开拱桥》于 1938 年 2 月与 3 月发表于《铅笔尖》(*Pencil Point*) 上——作者注。

[8] 梁著《中国建筑史》中称“空撞券”，现通称“敞肩拱”——林鹤、李道增注。

[9] 唐代起始年代现通常作公元 618—907 年——编者注。

[10] 梁著《中国建筑史》中称“观星台”，即今之“观象台”——林鹤、李道增注。

[11] 元代起始年代现通常作公元 1271—1368 年——编者注。

[12] 一元尺约合 23.9 厘米或 9 又 7/16 英寸——作者注。

[13] 即永寿寺雨华宫——林鹤、李道增注。

[14] 辽代起始年代现通常作公元916—1125年——编者注。

[15] Cf. L. Sickman, "Wall Paintings of the Yuan Period in Kuang-Sheng-Ssu, Shansi," *Revue des Arts Asiatique*, X1, 2, 1937.——作者注。

Buddhist Cave Sculpture 佛教石窟造像

[1] 节选自《华北古建调查报告》——编者注。

[2] 此处原文"孝武帝"(Hsiao-wu-ti),然梁著《中国建筑史》等各处均为"文成帝"(Wen-ch'eng-ti),疑为当年笔误,据诸本改——林鹤、李道增注。

Five Early Chinese Pagodas 五座中国古塔

[1] 本文原载《亚洲杂志》(*Asia Magazine*)1941年8月号——单军、高亦兰注。

[2] 孝明帝为北魏时期的帝王,在梁思成其他文稿中亦为"北魏"(见《梁思成文集》(三)P. 51),故原文称Eastern Wei Dynasty(东魏),应为英文稿笔误——单军、高亦兰注。

[3] 此塔建于隋炀帝大业七年,即公元611年;年代更早的题刻可能是后来搬入塔内的——单军、高亦兰注。

[4] 玄奘西行印度朝觐,按史书记载共历时17年,即贞观二年至贞观十九年(公元629—645年),所以原文称其为19年(nineteen-year pilgrimage),在时间上有误——单军、高亦兰注。

[5] 应县木塔一般文献多称其建于辽清宁二年,年代上即宋仁宗嘉祐元年,梁思成在其所著的《中国建筑史》中也如是说,见《梁思成文集》(三)P. 135——单军、高亦兰注。

[6] 应县木塔实际为五个明层和四个平坐暗层——单军、高亦兰注。

[7] 五塔式形制源于印度,如佛陀伽耶的大菩提塔(Mahabodhi Stupa),在中国称为金刚宝座塔。正定花塔因为有四个小的扁平六角形佛塔依附主塔上,所以与五塔式类似——单军、高亦兰注。

China's Oldest Wooden Structure 中国最古老的木构建筑

[1] 本文原载《亚洲杂志》(*Asia Magazine*)1941年7月号——英若聪、程慕胜注。

Art and Architecture China: Arts, Language, and Mass Media 中国的艺术与建筑

[1] 本文根据1982年出版的《大美百科全书》(*The Encyclopedia Americana*, Grolier Educational Corp. Danbury, Conn.),为"中国的艺术、语言与大众性媒体"章内之第十一节翻译。英文文字与清华大学建筑学院档案存打字稿(1947)完全相同——左川注。

[2] 推古时期：指传说中的日本天皇谱系中第30代天皇“推古天皇”（女皇）在位时期，一般认定为公元592—628年；飞鸟文化：指的是公元6世纪中期到7世纪上半期，当时的古日本以今日“飞鸟”（地名）为都城的时代，其统治力量在于日本奈良盆地的中部（亦即藤原京时代）。近代研究者把以“飞鸟”为统治中心时期的文化，称为“飞鸟文化”。“白凤文化”与“飞鸟文化”是重叠的学术概念，指传说中天皇谱系第36代的孝德天皇时期的文化。天平时期：一般指称传说中天皇谱系的第45代天皇即日本圣武天皇第6年（公元729年）改元“天平”年号开始，共计四代天皇相继五个“天平”年号的时间段（公元729—766年）。弘仁时期：公元810—823年。贞观时期：公元859—876年——编者注。

[3] 原文Kondo of the Todaiji, Nara，指奈良东大寺。鉴真所建为Toshodaiji，唐招提寺。疑梁先生笔误——吴焕加注。

[4] 今以“塔”对应“巴高大”——陈志华注。

[5] 即卢沟桥——陈志华注。

[6] 总长度，原文如此——陈志华注。

[7] 乐浪郡为西汉汉武帝在朝鲜半岛设置的汉四郡之一，治所在朝鲜县——编者注。

[8] 据《中国大百科全书·美术卷》，贯休生卒年为832—913年——陈志华注。

[9] 据《辞海》（1999年版），钱选生卒年为约1239—约1300年——编者注。

[10] 据《辞海》（1999年版），黄公望生卒年为1269—1354年——编者注。

[11] 据《辞海》（1999年版），戴进生卒年为1388—1462年——编者注。

[12] 据《辞海》（1999年版），仇英生卒年为约1501—约1551年——编者注。

Letter to Alfred Bendiner (CV Included)
致阿尔弗雷德·班迪纳的信（内附履历）

[1] 阿尔弗雷德·班迪纳（Alfred Bendiner），已故美国建筑师，宾夕法尼亚大学建筑学院校友。1947年时是费城房地产信托公司的建筑师。梁思成在耶鲁大学艺术学院访问讲学期间，他邀请梁思成到费城出席校友会和晚餐会并发表演说。这封信件即为梁思成与班迪纳在此期间的通信。原信由班迪纳夫人保存，1982年费慰梅女士写作《梁思成与林徽因》期间，应费慰梅要求，斑迪纳夫人把丈夫和梁思成当时来往的信件提供给宾夕法尼亚大学建筑学院，并转费慰梅。出版使用的复印件得之于宾夕法尼亚大学建筑学院档案室——左川注。

[2] 已对原文及译文中个别与实际有出入的年代等信息校改——编者注。